Connecting Democracy

Connecting Democracy
Online Consultation and the Flow of Political Communication

Edited by Stephen Coleman and Peter M. Shane

The MIT Press
Cambridge, Massachusetts
London, England

For information about special quantity discounts, please email special_sales@mitpress.mit.edu.

This book was set in Sabon by Toppan Best-set Premedia Limited. Printed on recycled paper and bound in the United States of America.

Library of Congress Cataloging-in-Publication Data

Connecting democracy : online consultation and the flow of political communication / edited by Stephen Coleman and Peter M. Shane.
  p. cm.
Includes bibliographical references and index.
ISBN 978-0-262-01656-8 (hardcover : alk. paper)—ISBN 978-0-262-51646-4 (pbk. : alk. paper)
1. Communication in politics—Technological innovations. 2. Internet in public administration. 3. Internet—Political aspects. 4. Communication in public administration—Technological innovations. 5. Political participation—Technological innovations. 6. Political planning—Citizen participation. I. Coleman, Stephen, 1957– II. Shane, Peter M.
JA85.C68   2012
352.3'802854678—dc22
2011016647

10 9 8 7 6 5 4 3 2 1

Contents

Preface

The volume you are reading is neither a proceedings nor a traditional anthology. It is the collective product of a group of nineteen researchers, most of whom have been meeting for three years—exchanging perspectives, hammering out ideas, and critiquing each other's draft chapters of what we have envisioned as an integrated, albeit multiauthored work.

We formed the International Working Group (IWG) on Online Consultation and Public Policy Making in response to a 2006 call for proposals from Sharon Dawes, director of the Center for Technology in Government at the State University of New York (SUNY) Albany, and the late Valerie Gregg, then with the Information Sciences Institute at the University of Southern California. The U.S. National Science Foundation had awarded them a large grant to explore the viability of collaborative international and interdisciplinary research on topics related to digital government, and they decided to use a significant portion of that grant to support up to three test projects. Proposals had to include both a U.S.-based and non-U.S.-based cochair and at least three graduate students. Funded groups were required to meet face to face at least five times over a period of three years. We used the occasion of this request for proposals to recruit what was originally a team of eighteen researchers in law, communication, political science, public policy, and information science to assess the democratic effects of the online-consultation phenomenon. Our original group was based in the United States, the United Kingdom, Australia, France, Israel, Italy, and Slovenia but had personal and professional ties to many other countries, as well. Over time, as competing commitments left a couple of us by the wayside and we began to look for additional colleagues to shore up our collective expertise, we lost Australia but added Sweden to the mix. The result was the roster of contributors to this volume.

Beginning in March 2007, the IWG held five business meetings, usually with some additional public outreach activity attached. We met in March 2007 at Harvard University's Kennedy School, in November 2007 at the University of Leeds, in March 2008 at The Ohio State University, in November 2008 at the Aspen Institute in Washington, D.C., and in April 2009 at SciPo in Paris, France. We decided early to write this joint book and spent a significant portion of our first three meetings refining its structure. The third meeting, at Ohio State, marked something of a pivot point, as we also began to share preliminary drafts with one another. Although the two of us have borne the chief final editing duties, every chapter of this book reflects the insights and suggestions of the entire group. Much of our transatlantic work has also occurred online, although we confess that our experiences have probably made us more, not less, persuaded of the significance of face-to-face interaction for the formulation of any real intellectual consensus.

In relation to much of the work that has gone before us and to which we owe a great debt, we hope this book is distinctive in three ways. The first is its international and interdisciplinary character. Seeing the online consultation phenomenon through the prisms of different disciplines and national perspectives has been an eye-opening experience for all of us, and we hope that the book conveys the intellectual importance of this expansiveness. Second, we have tried to avoid unduly minimizing the online consultation phenomenon, which can happen when observers insist that noteworthy democracy-building public discourse should always take a particular deliberative form. By situating online consultation within a larger universe of political communications, we suggest that it can result in a variety of democratic outcomes and can deepen the deliberative character of collective decision making. Finally, we have tried to avoid the naïve optimism for online consultation that sometimes results from emphasizing technological potential without reference to the inevitable political contestation that surrounds the construction of democratic citizenship. Politics is about power, and power does not give way easily just because new technologies threaten to destabilize existing relations.

It is customary for a preface to include statements of acknowledgment. Stephen Coleman is grateful to Peter M. Shane for inviting him to cochair the IWG and taking the laboring oar in most organizational matters. Peter is grateful to Stephen for helping to recruit a distinguished international network and bringing to bear on this project his wealth of experience as both researcher and e-democracy practitioner. We are also grateful to each other and to our IWG colleagues for the insight, candor, and good will generously displayed over our three-year collaboration. (In addition to the authors included in this volume, we extend these particular thanks to three other researchers who contributed to our group discussions—Beth Noveck, Kerrie Oakes, and Alicia Schatteman.) We thank Sharon Dawes for helping to instigate this collaboration, and we mourn the passing of Valerie Gregg, whose untimely death deprived us and digital government researchers around the globe of a dear colleague. Finally, we are grateful to Ashley Carter, Yasmine Harik, and Benjamin Wilhelm, all students at The Ohio State University's Moritz College of Law, for helping us navigate the final rounds of proofreading and formatting.

1

Online Consultation and Political Communication in the Era of Obama: An Introduction

Peter M. Shane

A Utopian Scenario

Picture, if you will, the imaginary nation of Agora. All permanent residents have affordable access to high-speed Internet connections whenever and wherever they need them. High levels of text and visual literacy are universal. Agorans are skilled producers of online communications and discerning interpreters of the messages they receive. They use email lists and community networks to deepen their personal connections to family, friends, neighbors, colleagues, and fellow Agorans who share their interests and concerns.

The government of Agora posts virtually all public records online. It makes available a large volume of social data about Agora that local governments, businesses, journalists, and the citizenry in general can put to whatever legal uses they see fit. The government posts for online public comment all draft legislation, as well as proposed regulations for the implementation of enacted law. It is easy for Agorans to track their representatives' platforms and voting records, as well as the government's budget and record of expenditures. They can watch legislative sessions, administrative meetings, and judicial hearings online.

In Agora, a large volume of accurate, relevant, and timely national, local, and even hyperlocal news and analysis is produced by networks of semiprofessional citizen journalists. Their work is edited and organized by small but highly skilled and productive teams of full-timers. The reporters' work is amplified by the analyses of a thriving blogosphere. Both government and nongovernment agencies sponsor various forms of online "deliberative polling,"[1] which helps leaders understand how representative groups of Agorans might decide public issues after they become educated about them. From time to time, parliament convenes online videoconferences that allow randomly chosen groups of Agorans, dispersed throughout the country, to come together online and deliberate on issues of common concern.

Not surprisingly, in this environment, the Internet is a powerful tool of political mobilization. (Whether the political culture has produced the social commitment to digital innovation or vice versa is an open issue.) Civil society groups are adept at using the Internet to raise funds, coordinate messages, and organize their members in support of various causes. If no group exists to support an Agoran's personal cause, establishing a new group is a relatively straightforward proposition. As a consequence of all this activity, few pastimes are as widely enjoyed in Agora as talk and debate. In schools, cafés, houses of worship, and public parks—typically furnished with civic information kiosks or digital walls displaying news headlines, art, and community announcements of all kinds—a sort of general will of the community messily but recognizably percolates up out of the seemingly endless web of inclusive discussion and deliberation.

All of the technology that Agora would need to achieve this picture is available now. Digital networks around the world are daily fostering innovative social practices and powerful new technologies of human connection that could sustain a democratic renaissance. Used in tandem with the many enduring legacy tools of personal and mass communication, the information and communication technologies (ICTs) of the digital age can promote knowledge and the exchange of ideas to a degree never before imagined. The ordinary citizen of postindustrial society, equipped with the right tools and a good broadband connection, can access more information through a desktop computer or a mobile device than has inhabited most national libraries from time immemorial. If technology were the key to democratic success, then we would now be living in an age in which we all, without regard to class or social status, would have unprecedented opportunities to achieve our personal aspirations and to shape the collective lives of the communities in which we live.

The Ambiguous Reality of Online Consultations

Even though the global explosion of online activity is steadily transforming the relationship of governments to their publics, no one yet lives in Agora. In the first wave of online government change—*e-government*—the Internet was used to improve management and service delivery. Suddenly, you could register your car, pay your parking tickets, or license your pet online. In short order, e-government was accompanied by some degree of *e-democracy*. E-democracy (sometimes called *digital democracy* or *cyberdemocracy*) involves the design and use of digital information and communication technologies to enhance democratic practice. Governments and civic activists began to innovate in the hope that the Internet might foster a new and inclusive form of many-to-many public dialog. As in the fictional land of Agora, the virtual public sphere would link government officials anew to the citizens they serve. The Internet might provide a technological basis for "a more deliberative view of active citizenship," in which "[n]ew forms of governance" could emerge that would be "increasingly consultative and alive to experiential evidence" (Blumler and Coleman 2001, 6–7). New technologies would step in to facilitate the robust public deliberation that was conspicuously lacking in twentieth-century representative democracies.

One intriguing development on the road to e-democracy is the focus of this book. We use the term *online consultations* to refer to Internet-based discussion forums that represent government-run or at least government-endorsed solicitations of public input with regard to policy making. Such solicitations (like the 2009 U.S. consultation on declassification policy involving the Public Interest Declassification Board) may focus public attention on a specific policy question (Public Interest Declassification Board, 2009). On other occasions, governments may post a consultation document that raises a range of issues within a broad subject on which public input would be welcome (such as a municipal solicitation of reaction to an action plan for revamping important sites throughout the city) (Konga and Proudlock 2010). Although not yet a routine feature of all Western democracies, online consultations are no longer an exotic experience either. They are a relatively routine feature of governance at the level of the European Union and appear episodically in connection with government policy making, both local and national, throughout the developed world.

After more than fifteen years of such consultations, there are at least two reasons to suspect that their democratic potential is nowhere near to being realized. One is that despite the widespread availability of online forums for political expression, few are tied in any ascertainable, accountable way to actual governmental policy making. That is, a citizen participating in most online forums has no assurance that his or her effort will have any effect on the government's decision making process or on the actual policy that emanates from that process.

The second reason—related to the first—is that most exercises in online deliberation attract relatively small numbers of participants. It is not obvious how significant new numbers of citizens could be attracted to the political process by ICT-enabled forums that cannot be shown to affect the lives of those who participate. In short, if the quality of democracy is to be measured by the inclusiveness and deliberativeness of the interactions between government and citizen, the incremental effect of online consultations so far appears to be minimal.

There is a third reason that, so far, the real world and Agora differ. Our imaginary Agora enjoys a substantial level of equality in citizens' access to digital tools and in their capacity to use them, as both producers and consumers of information—a level of equality that cannot be taken for granted in most societies.

In part for these reasons, it is unsurprising that utopian projections like those of Agora now contend in both scholarly and popular literature with a more dystopian view. Although many people today have virtually infinite access to communication tools to serve their every desire, individuals without those advantages risk finding themselves relegated to a new kind of second-class citizenship on the other side of an ever-growing informational chasm. Networks of empowerment stand potentially to become networks of surveillance. For many citizens, the Internet's information riches are more overwhelming than enabling, and they struggle to sort out what is credible, accurate, and well motivated from what is distorted, propagandistic, and malicious. It is so easy to launch online niche information services that society is allegedly in danger of being less, not more unified as we all repair to our respective virtual echo chambers (Sunstein 2007). Members of any geographically defined community might find themselves deriving daily information through such different channels and different media that any common understanding could become all but impossible with regard to the problems and possibilities that confront them as fellow citizens. In such a polarized, information-drenched, but dialogue-deprived world, the authentic distance between the general public and its government institutions might actually seem greater, not smaller.

On the other hand, there is a case to be made for viewing online consultations—and, indeed, the entire turn to e-democracy—in a broader, at least tentatively more hopeful frame. A polity at any level, from the local to the national, lives within a communication ecology, including a set of information flows, that identifies and helps frame the polity as a political community. That communication ecology circulates information that members of the polity, both individually and collectively, engage with in a variety of ways. A measure of optimism for the democratic potential of the Internet seems warranted not only because of the availability of new tools but also because large numbers of people are adopting new media habits that are genuinely participatory and thus engaging in the public sphere in a way that could breed a more deeply democratic culture. The American University Center for Social Media has catalogued five of these habits:

Choice Citizens are actively seeking out and comparing media on important issues through search engines, recommendations, video on demand, interactive program guides, news feeds, and niche sites.

Conversation Comment and discussion boards have become common across a range of sites and platforms, with varying levels of civility in evidence. Users are leveraging conversation tools to share interests and mobilize around issues. Distributed conversations across online services . . . are managed via shared tags. Tools for ranking and banning comments give site hosts and audiences some leverage for controlling the tenor of exchanges.

Curation Users are aggregating, sharing, ranking, tagging, reposting, juxtaposing, and critiquing content on a variety of platforms—from personal blogs to open video-sharing sites to social network profile pages. Reviews and media critique are popular genres for online contributors, displacing or augmenting genres, such as consumer reports and travel writing, and feeding a widespread culture of critical assessment.

Creation Users are creating a range of multimedia content (audio, video, text, photos, animation, etc.) from scratch and remixing existing content for purposes of satire, commentary, or self-expression—breaking through the stalemate of mass media talking points. Professional media makers are now tapping user-generated content as raw material for their own productions, and outlets are navigating various fair use issues as they wrestle with promoting and protecting their brands.

Collaboration Users are adopting a variety of new roles along the chain of media creation and distribution—from providing targeted funds for production or investigation, to posting widgets that showcase content on their own sites, to organizing online and offline events related to media projects, to mobilizing around related issues through online tools, such as petitions and letters to policymakers. "Crowdsourced" journalism projects now invite audience participation as investigators, tipsters, and editors—so far, a trial-and-error process. (Clark and Aufderheide 2009, 21)

These behaviors are really happening, and taken together, these habits suggest that the prospects for a more engaged and inclusive public sphere—routine participation in the creation of cultural products, at least among the information-savvy avant-garde—could make people more interested, more critical, and less passive.

Even so, a cyberrealist must acknowledge that serious gaps persist, at least in the United States, and limit the representativeness of the avant-garde (Knight Commission on the Information Needs of Communities in a Democracy 2009, 42-44). The first is a broadband gap. As of mid-2009, roughly one third of rural communities in the United States could not subscribe to broadband Internet services at any price. Three quarters of U.S. households with annual incomes below $20,000 lack a broadband connection (Peha 2008; Horrigan 2008).

The second is a literacy gap. This is not just a gap in digital literacy (that is, a gap in the skills relevant to the successful use of digital media) but a gap in simple prose competence. One 2003 survey estimated that 43 percent of U.S. adults fell short of an intermediate standard for literacy and that over four in ten adults would have trouble "consulting reference materials to determine which foods contain a particular vitamin" (National Center for Education Statistics 2005, 3–4). Only 13 percent of adults in that study were deemed sufficiently competent to compare accurately the competing viewpoints in two different editorials (ibid.). With high school graduation rates of barely 50 percent in many U.S. cities (Swanson 2009), these facts also point to a substantial hurdle in realizing the democratizing potential of the Internet.

The third is what media scholar Henry Jenkins has labeled the "participation gap"—that is, a gap "in social experiences between [young people] who have a high degree of access to new media technologies at home and those who do not" (Jenkins 2006). As Jenkins argues:

There's a huge gap between what you can do when you've got unlimited access to broadband in your home and what you can do when your only access is through the public library, where there are often time limits on how long you can work, when there are already federally mandated filters blocking access to certain sites, when there are limits on your ability to store and upload material, and so forth. (Ibid.)

If you are on the wrong side of this gap, new technologies empower you less than they do your more connected peers.

The democratic potential of the Internet also confronts an institutional crisis in the world of information intermediaries. For all the anticipation of online disintermediation, the digital age has witnessed less the disappearance of intermediaries than a proliferation of new types of intermediation—some embedded in opaque technologies (Mayer-Schönberger and Lazer 2007, 290). The need for intermediaries currently is greater than ever because of the unprecedented deluge of information confronting all Internet users. People cannot amass from their personal experiences or firsthand investigations all of the information they need to accomplish their individual objectives. No one can generate, in his or her own head, all of the analysis, debate, context, and interpretation necessary to turn raw information into useful knowledge. We all rely on credible intermediaries, both formal and informal, to enable us to engage with information effectively (Knight Commission on the Information Needs of Communities in a Democracy 2009, 13).

But these are challenging times for many well-established intermediaries. In the United States, for example, traditional news organizations are under tremendous stress. Local newspapers—which provide the bulk of original, verified reporting in most communities—are under economic strain and shrinking their newsrooms accordingly (Downie and Schudson 2009; Starr 2009). Overexpansion (and the burden of debt) from the 1990s, plus creative destruction in the traditional advertising model that supported newspapers, have left many metropolitan dailies in serious straits (Free Press 2009). At the same time, universities and libraries are underfunded, even as demands on their capacities are growing. Although new technologies make exciting forms of collaborative news and information production feasible, it is also possible (as a journalist friend wrote to me) that "we are entering a digital Dark Age in which those who shout the loudest, who make the most damning accusations, who appeal to the basest instincts, will command ever-larger audiences and, perforce, larger cultural and political influence."

Democratic Prospects: An Early View of the Obama Administration

These competing considerations might lead people to question whether online consultations hold genuine potential to deepen the legitimacy of representative democracy. The term *legitimacy* is used here to signify the moral relationship of a government to its citizens—in particular, the features of that relationship that morally entitle a relatively few persons to make laws and issue commands that bind others. The legitimacy of any government rests in significant part on its respect for and protection of fundamental human rights. In Western societies, however, such legitimacy rests also on the dedication of the government to the meaningful realization of two fundamental ideals—political freedom and political equality. People are politically free if they are able to share in acts of collective self-determination and experience themselves as meaningful actors in public life to the extent they choose to participate. People enjoy political equality to the extent that government decision making takes into serious account the interests of everyone affected by those decisions. This is not to say that all decisions are made by consensus or that anyone is guaranteed equal happiness with the outcome of every community decision. Western democracy, however, is founded on the premise of the moral equality of all human beings. The moral equality of all human beings implies a community obligation to take seriously the interests and concerns of all (Shane 2004, 67).

Genuinely inclusive, deliberative, and efficacious online consultations can buttress legitimacy in both these ways. Such consultations can add to the store of government information about the ways in which proposed actions might affect different segments of the community and render decision making more transparent. Participation can become a meaningful form of political agency, assisting in the evolution of a democratic citizenship identity within the community that is oriented toward the public interest. Consultation thus can serve the ends of both freedom and equality, especially if conjoined with other, less formal, less demanding, but nonetheless helpful ways of acquiring collective knowledge and including citizens in a genuinely inclusive and effective public sphere.

Whether such potential is likely to be realized, however, depends very much on conditions of power. To amplify voices that are currently underrepresented means reducing the influence of others in deciding on collective outcomes. Deepening the experience of self-determination for members of the public who are subject to some form of domination means undermining some of the forces that constrain these citizens' life prospects. Whether online consultations can help destabilize power relations that currently limit the reach of democracy is a question that can be answered only historically by looking at the social, political, and economic forces in a society as they are arrayed at particular moments.

As this book is being written, the United States is in an intriguing democratic moment. President Barack Obama swept into office in November 2008 in large part on the promise of a dramatic turn toward increased government openness and transparency. On his first full day in office, a presidential memorandum to all executive branch agencies declared a commitment "to creating an unprecedented level of openness in Government." President Obama promised that his administration would "work together to ensure the public trust and establish a system of transparency, public participation, and collaboration."[2] A look at the Obama campaign and the Obama administration's early moves toward online consultation and related citizen-engagement initiatives reveals some of the potential but also some of the challenges entailed in this vision.

The Obama campaign was famously successful in its online creativity. It used the Web to raise money, mobilize local campaign activities, fight attacks by opponents, get out the vote, and measure voter attitudes. Online video also played a major role in the campaign. By one count, 104,454 videos about Obama were uploaded during the campaign, and these were viewed about 889 million times. This record compares with 64,092 videos about McCain that were viewed 554 million times (Aun 2008). There seems little doubt that the superior Obama video presence was a significant help with younger voters.

The Obama team continued to innovate in the deployment of online engagement opportunities after the election. Between the November 2008 election and the inauguration on January 20, 2009, the Obama-Biden Transition Project created a Web site, http://change.gov, as a portal to elicit public dialogue. Participants were offered a number of consultation options. A special form was provided for public input on health care policy. An "Open for Questions" feature allowed people to pose and vote on potential questions to be answered online by the transition (later White House) press secretary, Robert Gibbs. A feature called "Your Seat at the Table" allowed the public to track meetings between the transition team and interest groups and to view and comment on documents provided to the transition team by such groups. Perhaps most prominently, anyone could contribute proposals or vote on the proposals suggested by others for inclusion in a "Citizens Briefing Book" which contained ideas and recommendations for the new administration. According to Michael Strautmanis, director of public liaison and intergovernmental affairs for the transition, "over 70,000 people participated," and the project elicited "half a million votes, and tens of thousands of wonderful ideas" (McSwain 2009).

As early indicators of the Obama administration's potential online engagement initiatives, these projects seemed something of a mixed blessing. On one hand, they offered some degree of openness, affording a window of at least indirect access to the President's thinking on policy issues and some transparency with regard to the Transition Project's contacts with interest groups. Furthermore, the consultation options seemed well calculated to help cement supporters' sense of personal involvement with and connection to the new President.

It was far less clear, however, whether any of this activity was calculated to affect actual policy making or even agenda setting. The incoming administration seemed well positioned to control the shape of whatever discursive spaces it was opening. A summary of the public suggestions on health care was fed back to the public through a video summary, but there was no way to test the representativeness of the summary—which seemed to track pretty closely the incoming administration's campaign platform on health care. Likewise, "Open for Questions" was not calculated to be a significantly revealing interrogation of the new government. The "Citizens Briefing Book" proved to be an interesting exercise, leading to a thirty-three-page summary of some of the "top ideas"— "unvarnished and unedited"—that were identified from among the 44,000 ideas that had been contributed and voted on by roughly 125,000 users (Obama-Biden Transition Project 2009). It is to the administration's credit that it was willing to acknowledge, among the most popular ideas, the legalization of marijuana. Far less clear was what the presence of that proposal in the briefing book meant either for the scope of actual popular support for the idea or for the effect its inclusion might have on the new administration's thinking. As a result, it could be asked whether the transition initiatives were harbingers of a newly participative public sphere in the United States or simply the launch of a more intense form of politics of personality around a newly elected, highly charismatic president.

In its first year, however, the Obama administration ratcheted up its commitment to e-democracy on a variety of fronts. On the transparency front, a USASpending.gov Web site was created to allow the public to track government spending with unprecedented ease. Its most innovative tool, as of mid-2009, was a new "IT Dashboard," at http://it .usaspending.gov, which provided the public "with details of Federal information technology investments and . . . the ability to track the progress of investments over time." The Obama administration also announced that it would promote democratic information flow by expanding public access to government data of all sorts. Data.Gov was launched in May 2009 to provide citizens with easy access to a wide array of government data sets, both in raw, machine-readable form and through a series of applications that allowed the data to be mined fairly easily. The site began by offering access to a limited catalogue of data sets that were apparently easy to link to a central portal, but it also allows users to make suggestions for other data sets to be added.

In terms of public collaboration, the administration's most ambitious effort involved an online consultation with the public for developing administration policy on openness and transparency in government. Fol-

lowing President Obama's first-day openness and transparency memorandum, his newly configured White House Office of Public Engagement
launched a three-phase public dialogue to generate ideas for carrying the
memorandum's openness and transparency principles into practice
(Noveck 2009). Phase I called for the public to "brainstorm" by suggesting and voting on ideas for developing and implementing open government policy. Phase II was a discussion phase. The administration provided
a summary of what it took to be the most compelling ideas from the
brainstorming phase, as well as an independent analysis from the National
Academy of Public Administration of all the Phase I input. Perhaps
most impressive, the process of narrowing the options was relatively
transparent. Beth Noveck, the deputy chief of the Technology Office for
Open Government, provided a clear explanation of the criteria used to
determine those Phase I proposals that were selected for further consideration. Phase III then allowed participants to use a collaborative
authoring tool called MixedInk to help draft recommendations on
sixteen topics.

Less celebrated but arguably even more remarkable given the sensitivity of the topic, the administration supported an effort by the congres-
sionally created Public Interest Declassification Board to gather public
ideas for the reform of federal information classification policy. The
Office of Science and Technology Policy in the Executive Office of the
President used its blog to host a "declassification policy forum" which
aimed, in part, at reforming a presidential executive order on classification and declassification (Faga 2009). The blog, although eliciting a far
smaller volume of participation than the general call for suggestions
on transparency and openness in government, was designed to be a
genuinely deliberative space, including a set of protocols for participation plainly aimed at sustaining a civil, transparent, and inclusive
discussion.

Whether these initiatives reliably point the way to a genuinely rein-
vigorated public sphere is uncertain. After all, it appears from http://
www.mixedink.com/opengov that the final collaborative drafting phase
of the Obama openness and transparency dialogue drew contributions
from only 375 contributors and a total of 2,256 ratings for the various
recommendations—a dramatic dropoff from the earlier, less labor-
intensive stages of the public consultation. Doubters might further
suggest that even the earlier phases, which did elicit significant input,
were chiefly calculated to align the public with the administration's starting points in terms of general values and policy inclinations. Note how

Director Noveck framed her summary of the results of the Phase I brainstorming:

Today, we want to share with you a little about what we've learned from you about transparency. Transparency is of vital importance. As the President emphasized in his *Memorandum on the Freedom of Information Act*: "A democracy requires accountability, and accountability requires transparency. As Justice Louis Brandeis wrote, 'sunlight is said to be the best of disinfectants.' . . . At the heart of that commitment is the idea that accountability is in the interest of the Government and the citizenry alike." (Noveck 2009)

In other words, the first outcome of brainstorming on transparency was to reaffirm what President Obama had already said about transparency.

But a comparison of the public input on both the open government directive and the President's declassification order with the actual documents promulgated by the administration supports the possibility that public input was influential. For example, the formal output on open government was a December 8, 2009, memo from the director of the Office of Management and Budget, Peter Orszag, to the heads of executive departments and agencies, which stated a general philosophy regarding openness, transparency, and public participation and imposed on the agencies a set of specific implementation requirements.[3] Not surprisingly, there is a close resonance between the public input on general principles and the more philosophical portions of the order.[4] But there are also more specific resemblances. For example, the public recommenders urged: "The CTO should promote a common data & metadata format to be used across all public data production. The format should be part of the specifications of requirements to data-producing federal programs, so that data consumers can trust APIs and bulk files to be consistent over time and across agencies."[5] Section 1(b) of the order provides:

To the extent practicable and subject to valid restrictions, agencies should publish information online in an open format that can be retrieved, downloaded, indexed, and searched by commonly used web search applications. An open format is one that is platform independent, machine readable, and made available to the public without restrictions that would impede the re-use of that information.

It may be that the government drafters of 1(b) would have come up with the same idea even without the provocation of public input, but this example—and others like it—at least raise the possibility that public participation was meaningful.

The same is true of the Obama December 2009 executive order on classified information.[6] Participation in the online declassification forum was fairly narrow. The forum remained open for comments through July 19, 2009, even though the Public Interest Declassification Board was committed to making its recommendations to the President the following week. This does not suggest a lengthy deliberation within the board about whatever suggestions the forum might elicit, especially in its final days.

On the other hand, it is not hard to find many fairly close resonances between a range of public suggestions and what the Obama executive order requires. For example, one public suggestion was that "Information may continue to be classified only if the need to protect such information outweighs the public interest in disclosure of the information" (National Archives 2009, 11). Section 3.1(d) of the new order actually says:

It is presumed that information that continues to meet the classification requirements under this order requires continued protection. In some exceptional cases, however, the need to protect such information may be outweighed by the public interest in disclosure of the information, and in these cases the information should be declassified.[7]

It was likewise suggested that the Information Security Oversight Office "must not only have the authority to declassify; it must also be assigned the affirmative responsibility to seek out and correct classification errors by using its declassification powers" (National Archives 2009, 6). Under section 5.1(b)(4) of the order, the ISOO is given "authority to conduct on-site reviews of each agency's program established under this order, and to require of each agency those reports and information and other cooperation that may be necessary to fulfill [the ISOO's] responsibilities."[8] The order is so lengthy and complex and the suggestions so numerous that a detailed comparison of one or the other would itself require a substantial study. But these are not isolated examples. And although the government drafters of the President's revised order may have developed the same ideas even without public prodding, public participation may well have had a role in shaping what is now official government policy. Indeed, even if one outcome of public participation is to undergird the administration's preexisting policy commitments, it may still be deemed important. Whether the model can play out this straightforwardly on more contentious topics such as health care, tax policy, and environmental regulation remains to be seen.

It is hard to see the scope, energy, and inventiveness of these efforts as anything but positive. Predicting their potential effect on the overall system of democratic discourse in the United States nonetheless raises difficult questions. Some are questions about the specific configurations of power in the United States; others are more generalizable. For example, can governments in power ever be expected to sustain genuine policy dialogues with a contentious public? Or might the primary effect of any regime's online initiatives rather be to solidify the identification with and allegiance to the regime by an ICT-savvy elite who feel "in on the action?" Conversely, it might be asked to what degree online government consultations should be influential. President Obama famously made a campaign promise not to sign nonemergency legislation into law until the passage of a five-day period for public comment (PolitiFact.com 2009). Given that the enactment of legislation typically reflects a long and labyrinthine process of bargaining in which the President was himself likely a significant party, it is not at all clear that the President should feel tempted to modify his views at the last minute because of online public input.

From the "Obama Moment" to a Larger Perspective

To address these and other significant issues, a group of nineteen authors who were physically situated in eight countries and had personal and professional ties to many others worked for over three years on a collaborative study of the phenomenon of online consultation and its relationship, both actual and potential, to democratic discourse and the building of democratic legitimacy. What we have produced, we hope, is not simply an anthology but an integrated discussion of the issues thus broached, with each chapter under the primary stewardship of its identified author or authors.

Our core argument is as follows. A useful understanding of the online consultation phenomenon has to go beyond how particular consultations might or might not affect the outcomes of individual policy making episodes. We need to consider what such consultations provide or could provide to the larger flow of political communication within a society. This also means regarding online consultations as something more than simple two-way dialogues between citizen-participants and public decision makers. Instead, they represent a kind of networked communication involving citizens (both participants and auditors), public decision makers (of both the legislative and administrative sort), bureaucrats, technicians, civil society organizations, and the media generally. Exploring the meaning of online consultations to these diverse actors requires evidence gathering through multiple methods, comparative study, and analysis across a variety of disciplines. We have to appreciate how the experience is constructed by social, political, and legal forces, including the design of the online consultation experience itself. This approach yields an understanding that online consultation can best contribute to democratic practice by inspiring and supporting a reimagining of democratic citizenship—a robust form of citizenship that is enhanced by new forms of information and communication technology.

Both to build and to illustrate the fruits of this argument, the book is organized into three sections. In the first, "Online Consultations and the Flow of Democratic Communication," four essays situate the online consultation phenomenon in a conceptual framework that takes into account our broader media environment, the effect of technology on citizen expression, and the range of discursive practices that online social media now make possible. Chapter 2, "Democracy, Distance, and Reach: The New Media Landscape," by Stephen Coleman and Vincent Price, orients us to thinking about online consultation as an instance of communication that seeks to overcome distances between citizens and between citizen and government. In "Web 2.0: New Challenges for the Study of E-Democracy in an Era of Informational Exuberance" (chapter 3), Andrew Chadwick urges that online consultations be evaluated within a range of online discursive practices that, even if not formally deliberative, have the potential to deepen democratic life.

In chapter 4, "Online Consultations in Local Government: What Works, When, and Why?," Joachim Åström and Åke Grönlund use a case-survey method to aggregate the collective judgments of previous research regarding the effect of online consultations on local democratic practices. Three hypotheses from the literature—claiming that institutional design, democratic intentions, and quality of research are the most important factors behind the reported effectiveness of online consultations—are tested. Finally, for this section, "Neighborhood Information Systems as Intermediaries in Democratic Communities," by Steven J. Balla and Sungsoo Hwang, explores the mobilizing potential for neighborhood information systems, technology innovations that aim to enhance the awareness and participation of stakeholders in local affairs, to operate as intermediaries in democratic information communities.

The second major section of the book provides a multifaceted look at "What Online Consultations Mean to Their Participants." In "Playing Politics: The Experience of E-Participation" (chapter 6), Vincent Price explores the meaning of online consultations for citizen-participants, while Scott Wright, in "The Participatory Journey in Online Consultations" (chapter 7), examines the barriers that inhibit citizen participation. Moving beyond a narrow definition of the digital divide based around access, Wright adopts the metaphor of a participatory journey to help explain the kinds of barriers that citizens might face and that challenge the ideal of inclusiveness.

In chapter 8, "Democratic Consultation and the E-Citizen," Stephen Coleman, Rachel Gibson, and Agnes I. Schneeberger draw on data from a 2005 nationally representative survey of UK Internet users to explore public attitudes toward political consultation, online communication, and political efficacy. Their analysis suggests that the citizen demand to be consulted online coexists with skepticism about the capacity of governing institutions to listen to and learn from the public. In "The Technological Dimension of Deliberation: A Comparison between Online and Offline Participation" (chapter 9), Laurence Monnoyer-Smith uses data from online and face-to-face consultations regarding the Paris water treatment system to argue that the technological stage on which online consultation occurs is not neutral with respect to who participates or how they express themselves. Thus, the meaning of consultation may well differ for citizen participants according to the platform they are offered for self-expression.

Following this extended examination of the citizen experience of online consultation, chapters by Stephen Coleman and Scott Wright (chapter 10), Jeffrey S. Lubbers (chapter 11), and the team of David Lazer, Michael Neblo, and Kevin Easterling (chapter 12) examine the experiences and attitudes, respectively, of third-sector civil-society groups, government bureaucrats, and elected legislators.

The book's third major section, "The Legal Architecture of Online Consultation," reveals how law operates to create both opportunities and constraints for online consultations. This section discusses both the need for laws that empower online consultation and the ways in which law and legal process shape the democratic effects of online consultation. Two chapters by Peter L. Strauss (chapter 13) and Polona Pičman Stefančič (chapter 14), respectively, show how the very different structures of administrative policy making in the United States and European Union create different windows of opportunity for online consultation by administrative agencies to affect actual policy outcomes. Chapter 15, "The Legal Environment for Electronic Democracy," by Peter M. Shane and Polona Pičman Stefančič shows how law imposes opportunities and constraints for online discussion design, with particular attention to how the laws of the United States and European Union delineate the rights and duties of forum sponsors and participants. Finally, in "E-Democracy, Transnational Organizations, and the Challenge of New Technointermediation" (chapter 16), Oren Perez posits that online consultation mechanisms have the potential to legitimate systems of transnational governance that currently suffer from an apparent democratic deficit but sees the underdevelopment of global administrative law as a key impediment to the advent of robust transnational systems of consultation.

The book concludes with an essay by Stephen Coleman (chapter 17) that synthesizes these threads of analysis and takes stock of their implications for the future of online consultation. He argues that the question "What form of online consultation best supports democratic citizenship?" cannot be addressed without acknowledging the contested definition of citizenship itself. For Coleman, the emergence of a more robust democratic life rests on an ideal of what he calls the "actualizing citizen" who is "a social actor characterized by multiple connections, weak ties, a reflexive approach to identity and belonging, a postdeferential attitude toward authority, and a sense that political communication is a two-way street, entailing more than a flow of top-down messages from rulers to ruled." He concludes that governments wishing to engage with this new form of social actor "need to adopt strategies and technologies that can draw on people's eagerness to define their own relationship to society and its relationship to them."

Analyzing online consultations is triply daunting because the practice is international, its implications are interdisciplinary, and the worlds of politics and technology are changing everywhere in Internet time. Whether the Obama moment marks a genuine pivot toward something like the imaginary world of Agora or just another variation on politics as usual is an inquiry that will take on a different cast as years—or perhaps only months—go by. But even as the events that capture today's attention fade into history, the contributors to this volume are hopeful that our international and interdisciplinary investigation will provide an enduring foundation for future analysis. The journey to Agora may be uncharted, but this book suggests what mapmakers should look for.

Notes

1. Deliberative polling is a form of structured deliberation pioneered by James Fishkin. Its aim is to determine what a representative sample of people would

conclude about an issue, given the opportunity to study and discuss the issue prior to registering their views (Fishkin 2009).

2. Memorandum of the President to Executive Departments and Agencies re: Transparency and Open Government, January 21, 2009, accessed September 5, 2010, http://www.whitehouse.gov/the_press_office/Transparency_and_Open _Government.

3. Memorandum from Peter R. Orszag, director, Office of Management and Budget, for the Heads of Executive Departments and Agencies re: Open Government Directive, December 8, 2009, accessed September 5, 2010, http://www .whitehouse.gov/sites/default/files/omb/assets/memoranda_2010/m10-06.pdf.

4. The final wiki input on general principles appears at http://mixedink.com/#/ OpenGov/TransparencyDefinition (accessed September 5, 2010).

5. Available at http://mixedink.com/#/OpenGov/DataTransparency (accessed September 5, 2010).

6. Exec. Order No. 13,526, *Federal Register* vol. 75, p. 707 (2010).

7. *Federal Register* vol.75, p. 713.

8. Ibid., 724.

References

Aun, Fred. 2008. "Over Long Campaign, Obama Videos Drew Nearly a Billion Views." *ClickZ News* (November 7). Accessed September 5, 2010. http://www. clickz.com/clickz/news/1711540/over-long-campaign-obama-videos-drew -nearly-billion-views.

Blumler, J. G., and S. Coleman. 2001. *Realising Democracy Online: Creating a Civic Commons in Cyberspace*. London: Institute for Public Policy Research.

Clark, Jessica, and Patricia Aufderheide. 2009. *Public Media 2.0: Dynamic Engaged Publics*. Washington, DC: Center for Social Media.

Downie, Leonard, Jr., and Michael Schudson. 2009. *The Reconstruction of American Journalism*. New York: Columbia Journalism School.

Faga, Martin. 2009. "Declassification Policy Forum: Introduction." White House Open Government Initiative Blog (June 29). Accessed September 5, 2010. http://www.whitehouse.gov/blog/Declassification-Policy-Forum-Introduction.

Fishkin, James. 2009. *When the People Speak: Deliberative Democracy and Public Consultation*. New York: Oxford University Press.

Free Press. 2009. *Changing Media: Public Interest Policies for the Digital Age*. Washington, DC: Free Press.

Horrigan, John. 2008. *Home Broadband 2008: Adoption Stalls for Low-Income Americans Even as Many Broadband Users Opt for Premium Services That Give Them More Speed*. Washington, DC: Pew Internet and American Life Project.

Jenkins, Henry. 2006. "MySpace and the Participation Gap." *Aca-Fan: The Official Weblog of Henry Jenkins* (June 21). Accessed September 5, 2010. http://www.henryjenkins.org/2006/06/myspace_and_the_participation.html.

Knight Commission on the Information Needs of Communities in a Democracy. 2009. *Informing Communities: Strengthening Democracy in the Digital Age.* Washington, DC: Aspen Institute.

Konga, Jury, and Michael Proudlock. 2010. "Municipal Open Government Framework: A Work in Progress." Accessed September 5, 2010. http://www.slideshare.net/jkonga/municipal-open-gov-framework-work-in-progress.

Mayer-Schönberger, Viktor, and David Lazer. 2007. "The Governing of Government Information." In *Governance and Information Technology*, edited by Viktor Mayer-Schönberger and David Lazer, 290. Cambridge: MIT Press.

McSwain, Dan. 2009. "Wrapping Up the Citizen's Briefing Book." *Change.Gov* (January 16). Accessed September 5, 2010. http://change.gov/newsroom/entry/wrapping_up_the_citizens_briefing_book.

National Archives. 2009. "Summary of Comments Received from the Public for the Review of Executive Order 12958, as Amended: Classified National Security Information." Accessed September 5, 2010. http://www.archives.gov/pidb/summary-public-comments.pdf.

National Center for Education Statistics. 2005. *National Assessment of Adult Literacy (NAAL): A First Look at the Literacy of America's Adults in the Twenty-first Century.* Washington, DC: U.S. Department of Education.

Noveck, Beth. 2009. "Wrap-Up of the Open Government Brainstorming: Transparency." *White House Open Government Initiative Blog* (June 2). Accessed September 5, 2010. http://www.whitehouse.gov/blog/Wrap-Up-of-the-Open-Government-Brainstorming-Transparency.

Obama-Biden Transition Project. 2009. *Citizens Briefing Book.* Washington, DC: Obama-Biden Transition Project. Accessed September 5, 2010. http://www.whitehouse.gov/assets/documents/Citizens_Briefing_Book_Final.pdf.

Peha, Jon M. 2008. *Bringing Broadband to Unserved Communities.* Washington, DC: Brookings Institution.

PolitiFact.Com. 2009. "Barack Obama Campaign Promise No. 234: Allow Five Days of Public Comment before Signing Bills." *PolitiFact.Com.* Accessed September 5, 2010. http://www.politifact.com/truth-o-meter/promises/promise/234/allow-five-days-of-public-comment-before-signing-b.

Public Interest Declassification Board. 2009. "Wrapping Up the Declassification Policy Forum." *Open Government Initiative* (July 27). Accessed September 5, 2010. http://www.whitehouse.gov/blog/Wrapping-up-the-Declassification-Policy-Forum.

Shane, Peter M. 2004. "The Electronic Federalist: The Internet and the Eclectic Institutionalization of Democratic Legitimacy." In *Democracy Online: The*

Prospects for Political Renewal through the Internet, edited by Peter M. Shane, 65–82. New York: Routledge.

Starr, Paul. 2009. "Goodbye to the Age of Newspapers (Hello to a New Era of Corruption)." *New Republic* (March 4).

Sunstein, Cass. 2007. *Republic.com 2.0*. Princeton: Princeton University Press.

Swanson, Christopher B. 2009. *Cities in Crisis 2009: Closing the Graduation Gap*. Bethesda, MD: Editorial Projects in Education.

I
Online Consultation and the Flow of Political Communication

2

Democracy, Distance, and Reach: The New Media Landscape

Stephen Coleman and Vincent Price

To live in a representative democracy is to be spoken to, for, and about through channels of mediation. The sources of political mediation include parliaments, congresses, and town halls, as well as newspaper offices, TV and radio studios, press conferences, and public rallies. Although any of us might occasionally witness some of these directly (via a tour around the legislative chamber, a ticket to participate in a studio discussion, or a seat at an election rally), most of us encounter them only through the media. We are usually one step removed from the live voice of government. Because they are disembodied, mediated relationships place a great premium on trust—in the images projected by politicians and the portrayals provided by the media. The more distant we feel from political leaders, the harder it is to establish trust or feel confident about our capacity to influence them. If political trust and efficacy fall low enough, then citizens often disengage: they stop watching, judging, and voting. The more distant government appears to be from the people, the shakier its claim to democratic legitimacy. Because government responsiveness is central to the ideal of democratic legitimacy, political leaders feel an ongoing normative pressure to close the communicative distance between themselves and the people they claim to speak for.

In many countries, there is a growing sense that governments have lost touch with the people they represent. Distrust of official political voices has become a default position that is encouraged by media institutions that seem to delight in the political disenchantment of their audiences—even though, ironically, the media themselves are victims of this generalized loss of faith in authority. A lack of deference may be good for democracy in that it encourages healthy skepticism toward established power, but without opportunities to exercise political influence, it can easily harden into cynicism or know-nothing populism.

This chapter explores how a public voice in policy making and every-day governance might be enhanced within the context of a changing media landscape. This exploration is developed in three stages. First, we consider the concept of political distance, drawing on recent arguments from geographical theory to help us think imaginatively about what it means for governments to be in touch with the public. In the second stage of our argument, we set out feasible terms of consultative demo-cratic communication that are based on the principles of narrowing political distance and extending two-way reach. In the third stage, we examine the new media landscape and its potential for facilitating a more consultative democratic relationship. Finally, we draw some conclusions about the scope of new media for the reengineering of political distance.

Political Distance

All communication starts with distance and aspires toward reach. Dis-tance is the confounding aspect in all attempts to communicate, and it opens up countless opportunities for mishearing, misunderstanding, neglect, and disrespect. Two people sitting on a park bench can be distant, separated by decades of memories, conditioning, affective dispo-sitions, and modes of expression. Distance can be between a studio presenter and her imagined audience of millions who are somewhere "out there," between a politician and his email recipients, between share dealers operating across time zones, and between readers and writers of love letters. The practice of communicating always entails the wish to reach others across real or metaphorical distance. It is a bridging exercise—a desire to touch through text, sound, gesture, or the pressure of skin on skin. Indeed, the essence of *mediated* communication—the kind that most of us experience in relation to government—is the impossibility of direct interaction and the need for reach to be realized across disembod-ied distance.

Mediated communication acknowledges distance and simulates close-ness. The "dear reader" of the novelist, like the "fellow Americans" of the candidate, is an artifice intended to diminish feelings of apartness. What Scannell (2000, 9) has referred to as "for everyone as someone" structures of communication—such as the pseudo-intimacy of the disc jockey's chatter or the "I understand your life" sincerity pose of the vote-soliciting politician—is central to contemporary forms of media

address. Undistancing itself is now a crucial legitimizing basis for authority. A century ago, power could address its subjects in the second-person
plural, and the "you" of the advertisers' message was an amorphous
mass, fixed at a distance from whatever centers there might be. It was
no accident that Lippmann's (1925) "deaf spectator" sat in the back row,
straining to make sense of the complexities of public affairs. In the 1920s,
the entire public sat in the back row and had to be shouted at from afar.
Before the fireside chat came the political megaphone, a crude but effective instrument of reach. The problem with megaphone mediation is its
insensitivity to the moment of reception—its assumption that the hearer
of a message will not talk back. It is rooted in a particular view of political communication that sees messages as being sent from A to B in the
hope that B will be influenced by A. The geography of communicative
distance is more complicated than that.

We owe to political geographers like Massey (2005), Soja (1971),
Thrift (2008), and Amin (2004) an understanding of space as a relational
concept that is embedded in culturally determined spatialities rather than
a concrete and static entity that can be measured and charted on the
basis of scientific quantification. In their attempts to conceptualize space
as effects of social interaction, these geographers have contributed on
several levels to a rethinking of political distance. First, they alert us to
the danger of seeing communication as a fluid movement of messages
between physically manifest identities. From their perspective, identity is
itself a relational effect that is shaped and reshaped through the transitive
process of reaching out and being reached. For example, an isolated rural
community can be so characterized only if it lacks the means of connecting with urban, central networks of power. When those means are available, the community not only ceases to be isolated but might acquire a
new sense of political efficacy, a broader range of cultural influences,
and perhaps a more fragmented outlook. In short, its relationship to
space changes its identity. Political history is replete with examples of
places that are transformed in their political character as a result of
relational reorientation.

This leads to a second observation—that propinquity is never objective but is negotiated. As Sassen (1998) has shown, the placing of international airports, banking centers, and telecommunications clusters
makes some cities powerful within global space and others less significant. Being inside a network is a major advantage, and outsiders negotiate hard to get in. Where one stands in the sphere of political power is

always a consequence of contestation. Distance is neither natural nor neutral; it is a relational effect that expands and shrinks to a political rhythm.

Third, culture is itself a relational consequence of political space. An example of the distributed nature of reality can be seen in the institution of the postal service. Post offices are local. When there are attempts to close them down, energetic local campaigns tend to arise to preserve them as the heart of an area. Post offices arouse intense place-based loyalties yet can operate only by stretching distance and adopting technologies that reach out to the far-flung, exotic, and inaccessible. Post offices are both inside and outside the local, but the interiority of the local would have no meaning without its integration within a network of externality. The same is true for politics. A local politician can speak only for her small-town constituents by acting in and on the world that is beyond their direct experience. Folksy intimacy at the rhetorical level becomes merely barren parochialism unless the interests and values it speaks for can be projected into distant regions in which hegemonic codes of impersonal, administrative rationality hold sway.

These observations about spatiality suggest that the notion of political distance can be understood meaningfully only in terms that exceed quantitative measurement and acknowledge the ways in which scales of difference are constructed and contested through historical contingency. The principal means of such construction include technologies of political communication, which can be defined as those technical artifacts, bodies of knowledge, and circuits of energy that expand or limit distance and reach between people involved in the authoritative allocation of values. As communicative ecologies have changed over the centuries from talk and sign writing to multimedia digital convergence, so have the ways in which power can be imagined, displayed, articulated, reported, observed, and challenged.

The Terms of Consultative Democracy

Broadcasting, the twentieth-century's dominant communication medium, has severe limitations as a consultative medium. Viewers and listeners can write or call in, vote on issues in countless polls, and even comment in online forums on issues that have stimulated or angered them. But the relationship of even the most active audiences to media production is always asymmetrical. They do not make the shows or news bulletins that they watch. A public debate on television is never much more than an exercise in mass consumption (Coleman and Ross 2010).

Interactive communication technologies, with their capacity for peer-to-peer discussion, would seem to be more suited to forms of public debate that are intended to be genuinely democratic, in the sense of being open to all, free from agenda manipulation, and consequential in their outcomes. But there are huge obstacles to overcome before such a relationship between the Internet and democracy can be realized. Let us suppose that digital divides, knowledge gaps, group fragmentation, and institutional resistance to public input can be overcome. What normative conditions would need to be in place to allow interactive, digital information, and communication technologies to contribute to a more consultative form of democratic governance?

We outline five ideal normative conditions for narrowing political distance and expanding communicative reach. The first is the provision of abundant, pluralistic, and freely accessible information sources. This has long been regarded by media scholars as a central prerequisite for any democratic media system (Blumler and Gurevitch 1995; Dahlgren 1995; Keane 1991). But until the emergence of the Internet, information has tended to be scarce and filtered through a narrow range of well-resourced corporate and state institutions. With the radically reduced costs of content production and dissemination brought about by the capacious space of the Internet, the capacity to both create and receive a wide range of diverse and freely accessible media sources has resulted in media abundance. As Bimber (2003, 92) has put it, "new means for elites to distribute and acquire information, new possibilities for citizens to identify and communicate with one another, changes in the ways that citizens interact with the news system, and the historical preservation of information, among other developments, contribute toward a state of *information abundance* in the political system." Although Paterson (2005) reminds us that the sources of news used by mainstream new media organizations are concentrated in a narrow range of professional agencies, countless blogs and alternative news networks have significantly expanded the field of available news, views, and opportunities for discussion. User-generated news and information expands democratic reach by overcoming traditional divisions between sender and receiver, authoritative voice, and affected audience (Outing 2005).

A second democratic norm concerns the possibility of deliberation. Most democratic theorists would argue that democracy can never be fully realized unless citizens have opportunities to air their opinions in public, exchange ideas with others beyond their immediate circle of acquaintances, and arrive at conclusions or decisions that are influenced by reflective communication (Bohman 1996; Carpini, Cook, and Jacobs 2004; Gutmann and Thompson 1996). Despite the existence of vox pops, talk shows, and call-ins, broadcasters have tended to regard public voices as an appendage to the professionally orchestrated, studio-centered productions that are consistent with their monological tradition (Coleman and Ross 2010). Innovations in public deliberation have tended to take place beyond and around the mass media in face-to-face events such as town meetings, citizens' juries, and consensus conferences.

Increasingly, however, exercises in public deliberation have moved online, often as pilot projects or experiments but with some promise of becoming integrated into the wider civic culture. Evaluations of these exercises suggest that online deliberation might have at least four democratic benefits. First, by transcending geographical confines and enabling Internet users to connect with a broader range of perspectives than they would encounter through face-to-face communication, citizens online are more likely to be exposed to heterogeneous opinions, preferences, and values than tends to be the case in offline political discussion (Albrecht 2006; Graham and Witschge 2003; Janssen and Kies 2005; Kelly, Fisher, and Smith. 2005; Muhlberger 2005; Price and Cappella 2002). Second, by eliminating the presence of social status cues, online deliberation reduces the likelihood of contributors being judged on the basis of what they look or sound like: the potential for discrimination is reduced (Kenny, Swee, Lim, Detenber, and Alsagoff 2008; McKenna and Bargh 2000; Stromer-Galley 2002). Third, online deliberative interaction offers greater opportunities for knowledge sharing and long-term community building than many forms of offline deliberation (De Cindio and Schuler 2007; Kaye and Johnson 2002; Plant 2004). Finally, some studies have found that online deliberation has mobilization and efficacy-building effects that take people beyond shared reflection to collective action and forms of civic participation conducive to healthy democracy (Horrigan, Garrett, and Resnick 2004; Johnson and Kaye 1998; Price and Cappella 2002; Shah, Kwak, and Holbert 2001). Each of these benefits reflects a diminution of territorial, cognitive, and affective distance and new possibilities of democratic reach within and between dispersed communities.

Third, it is clear from the history of broadcasting that without well-resourced and protected public spaces dedicated to the purpose of civic interaction, public communication is likely to be enervated by the dominance of media spaces owned or controlled by corporate and political elites. Public-service broadcasting, where it has been tried, has tended to resist some of the worst forms of distracting agenda cutting associated with the media marketplace. Public-sphere norms stand in stark tension with the anarchic ethos of the Internet, the evolution of which has left little room for the conscious nurturing of cross-cutting networks (Mutz 2002; Sunstein 2001) or direct channels between citizens and the local, national, and transnational institutions that govern them (Coleman and Blumler 2009).

Linked to this is a fourth norm—that governments should be sensitive and responsive to public input to media debates. In recent years, democratic governments have become increasingly aware of the need to open up interactive communication channels with those they represent (OECD 2001). A wide range of experiments in e-democracy have been implemented, with varying degrees and standards of success (Albrecht 2006; Coleman and Gøtze 2001; Coleman and Norris 2004; Jankowski and Van Os 2004; Monnoyer-Smith 2007; Wright 2006). In most cases, reluctance or unreadiness on the part of politicians and officials has limited the effects of online deliberation. Although citizens have found the experience of online consultation useful as a means of exchanging ideas and telling their stories, their sense that governmental institutions remained distant from them resulted in feelings of reduced political efficacy. So although the Internet does appear to open up a space in which norms of information availability and public deliberation might be realized, thereby expanding and enhancing democratic reach, institutional practices regarding public space and government responsiveness remain culturally distantiated and impervious to democratic normative requirements. These aspects of the communication ecology are likely to be best addressed at the policy level, although that will call for a cultural shift that goes against the current grain of spatial privatization and bureaucratic unaccountability.

Ultimately, extending democratic reach is a moral enterprise. As Roger Silverstone, who better than anyone grasped the nature of the dialectic of reach and responsibility, has put it:

the media, as indeed other technologies, enable the stretching of action beyond the face-to-face, and consequently undermine the expectation of responsibility and reciprocity that action and communication in face-to-face settings conventionally require. Technologies disconnect as well as connect. The distance they create between interlocutors, between subject and subject, is a precondition, as many have argued, for the erosion of any sense of responsibility that individuals would be expected to have for the other. (Silverstone 2007, 11)

In this sense, communication entails more than messages between senders and their intended recipients. It also encompasses those unsaid, unacknowledged, and unspeakable dimensions of public interaction that all too often take the form of awkward silences, embarrassed evasions, and conspicuous gaps in the agenda. This fifth norm of media democracy is perhaps the most opaque, is certainly the most elusive, but surely presents the most pressing ethical challenge to online consultation and policy deliberations. Can online discussion both include a representative section of the population (which is a tall order) and also represent the voices of those traditionally unrepresented, ignored, and even feared? Silverstone's response to this challenge was to invoke the concept of "proper distance," which "refers to the importance of understanding the more or less precise degree of proximity required in our mediated inter-relationships if we are to create and sustain a sense of the other sufficient not just for reciprocity but for duty of care, obligation and responsibility" (Silverstone 2007, 47). Within the new geography of distance and reach that have been discussed in this chapter, the capacity to speak to and with others has increased dramatically, making all but global relationships seem somewhat parochial, while news agendas remain locked into national discourses that appear increasingly cramped and unambitious. Whereas government-run consultations have tended to focus citizens' attention on national agendas, grassroots online discussion has tended toward transnational, cross-cutting, and internetworked modes of speaking and acting (Bennett 2003). Might it be through these globally discursive online networks—around global warming, third-world debt, the wars in Iraq and Afghanistan, and the Internet itself—that a new sense of moral reach is being realized? If so, it is through these exercises in the stretching of political distance (rather than any bureaucratically conceived schemes for government-shaped e-democracy) that the new media ecology is most likely to be democratically nurtured.

Media Transitions

Recent years have brought enormous changes to communication systems, and young media consumers today find it difficult to grasp how limited a set of media choices their parents and grandparents enjoyed at their age. In the past thirty years, the number of media devices available to consumers has more than tripled, and a number of new media introduced in that time—for example, mobile phones, personal computers, compact discs, and digital video disks—have penetration rates above 50 percent of U.S. households (Veronis Suhler Stevenson 2008). Digital transmission and storage technologies, expanded cable networks, and broadband Internet access have combined to increase by orders of magnitude the range of available news and entertainment options. Consequently, it would appear that the first of the conditions outlined above for narrowing political distance and expanding communicative reach—the provision of abundant, pluralistic, and accessible information—is better satisfied today than at any other time in history.

The widespread availability of diverse media sources, however, does not necessarily translate into a better informed citizenry or even into larger audiences for news. Recent trends in news consumption show a complex and dynamic pattern. Here we draw examples primarily from the American system, but the trends have been worldwide in scope. Newspapers have suffered dramatic losses of both advertising revenues and readership, which have declined at a steady rate. The remarkable growth in television cable news has come largely at the expense of traditional broadcast news, with both national network news and local TV news losing significant shares of the viewing audience. Meanwhile, use of the Internet for obtaining news has risen sharply in recent years, and many "soft news" alternatives—talk shows, opinionated discussion formats, and entertainment-oriented news—have drawn off sizable portions of the traditional news audience (e.g., Baum 2005; Patterson 2001; Pew Research Center for the People and the Press 2006, 2008a). Consumers are, in general, shifting from traditional to digital media. Veronis Suhler Stevenson (2008) projects that over the next five years, broadcast TV, radio, and newspapers will all show significant declines in hourly use, while cable and satellite TV, videogames, the Internet, and mobile communications will exhibit the largest gains. Similarly, advertising spending has been migrating and will continue to move away from traditional print and broadcast outlets and toward online and alternative out-of-home venues.

Many of the most important changes are in the television landscape, where cable news channels have made large gains in audience over the broadcast networks. In the 1990s, large majorities of the news audience, as assessed in polls and surveys, were regular consumers of national TV network news (60 percent in 1993), and even more reported regular consumption of local news (77 percent in 1993) (Pew Research Center for the People and the Press 2006). Since then, regular viewership of network news has fallen dramatically, and so has that of local news. At first, Cable News Network (CNN) made inroads, with close to a third of poll respondents saying they were regular consumers in the 1990s, but with the arrival of MSNBC, the Fox Broadcasting Company, and others, Pew Center surveys now find more people reporting that they regularly follow news on cable (39 percent) than on the broadcast networks (28 percent). Fox is now reported to be a regular source of news for about a quarter of respondents in the most Pew surveys, slightly ahead of CNN. The audience share for network news has been halved since 1970, while ratings are half what they were in 1980. According to the Pew Center (2010), barely half of Americans now report watching local TV news on a regular basis. The upshot of these trends is that the audience for TV news has fragmented and become spread more thinly across a much larger array of diverse outlets, many of them cable channels.

Newspaper readership has declined significantly over the past few decades, and most major newspapers in the United States have lost both circulation and advertising revenues. Although about half of survey respondents say they regularly get news from a daily newspaper, only about a third of survey respondents indicated in 2008 that they read a newspaper during the preceding day (Pew Research Center for the People and the Press 2008b). As newspaper circulation has declined, however, online news has grown. Almost 30 percent of Americans now say they get news regularly online (ibid.). Although most online news is obtained from traditional media outlets, media companies are not able to recoup their lost advertising revenues online, given that the cost per thousand readers or viewers of Internet advertising is a small fraction—less than a fifth—of the cost of advertising on TV or in newspapers.

The Internet is growing as a source of political campaign information. According to the Pew Center (2008a), nearly a quarter of Americans (24 percent) said they regularly learned something about the 2008 presidential campaign from the Internet, almost double the percentage at a comparable point in the 2004 campaign. The Internet emerged as second only to TV as the main reported source of election news (though a distant second, with 15 percent reporting that their main source is the Internet, compared with 60 percent naming TV).

Online news is just one of the Internet-related innovations in public affairs information witnessed in the past decade. The blogosphere is a vast array of personal journals or weblogs that feature ongoing commentary on public affairs and elections, with links to other blogs and information sites. Popular sites—for example, Glenn Reynolds's *Insta-pundit,* Markos Moulitsas's *Daily Kos,* and Josh Marshall's *Talking Points Memo*—have hundreds of thousands of hits daily and post a continuous stream of political observations and arguments. So do Web magazines, such as *Salon.com,* the *Drudge Report, Columbia Journalism Review Campaign Desk,* and the *Huffington Post.* Blogs and Web magazines share several distinguishing features. They are thoroughly interlinked, with larger sites driving hits to others. These links also force blogs up the "Googlearchy," which values links as indicators of importance. Second, they have the general character of insider talk, as bloggers trade tales of the story behind the story, fleshing out and critiquing the work of traditional news media, and occasionally pressing them to cover stories that would not otherwise have appeared on the news agenda (such as U.S. Senator Trent Lott's racially tinged comments at colleague Strom Thurmond's hundredth birthday party and forged documents used by CBS News, each of which ultimately triggered high-profile resignations).

Joining online news and blogs in the mix of significant political communication media are social-networking sites, such as Facebook (now claiming 500 million active monthly users), Myspace (with about 60 million users), and video-distribution sites such as YouTube (with over 70 million users). Substantial numbers of young people—more than a quarter of those younger than age thirty, including 37 percent of those ages eighteen to twenty-four—said that they received information about the 2008 U.S. presidential election from social networking sites (Pew Research Center for the People and the Press, 2008a). This practice was almost exclusively limited to young people. The Pew Center reported that only 4 percent of Americans in their thirties and 1 percent of those ages forty and older received news about the campaign in this way. And finally, developments in mobile technologies permit geospatial mapping of friends and organization of semispontaneous meet-ups.

These changes in the media landscape have raised a number of democratic hopes. The highly interactive nature of many of these technologies has fueled expectations that larger and more diverse segments of the population might talk politics online and become more thoughtfully engaged in issues of the day. Viewed in this light, new media advance the possibility of deliberation—the second condition for narrowing political distance and extending reach. However, although political talk online is growing, it is still not common. Surveys tend to find that most people interact online with professional associations or hobby-based groups, not political or civic groups, and few of the latter are cited as primary online communities (Horrigan 2001). Few people report engaging in online debates in their communities, and most locally focused Internet use is related to commercial information or local events. So online discussion of political issues might engage about 10 percent of Internet users, which is perhaps 7 percent of the general population. At present, widespread deliberation carried via new electronic media—outside of formal consultation programs launched by academic, public-interest, or governmental organizations—appears to be more a possibility than a reality.

What about the third condition for closing political distance—well-resourced and protected public spaces dedicated to civic interaction? As noted earlier, several significant efforts have been made by governments, particularly in Europe and North America, to create open, Web-based platforms for civic engagement with a variety of policy issues (see the chapters in this volume by Joachim Åström and Åke Grönlund; Stephen Coleman, Rachel Gibson, and Agnes Schneeberger; Laurence Monnoyer-Smith; Polona Pičman Štefančič; Peter M. Shane and Polona Pičman Štefančič; and Peter L. Strauss). Even the most well-funded and expansive of these efforts have captured only a small proportion of the local, regional, or national constituencies invited to engage. Of broader potential reach are a number of nongovernmental avenues, both not-for-profit and commercial platforms, for citizens to interact. Blogospheres, collaborative wiki technologies that permit dispersed readers and writers to share and edit documents online, and emerging mobile technologies have all raised hopes for a more widely participative, citizen-produced form of political communication.

A notable example is *OhmyNews.com*, a South Korean online newspaper with the motto "Every citizen is a reporter." Founded in 2000, the online service accepts, edits, and publishes articles from its readers in an open-source style of news reporting, with about 20 percent of the site's content written by a professional staff and the balance contributed by others, mostly ordinary citizens. *OhmyNews* was reportedly influential in determining the outcome of the South Korean presidential elections in late 2002. Roh Moo Hyun, who won the election, granted his first interview afterward with the paper. This kind of open editing encourages democratic use of the Web and promotes the open contribution and composition of material by widely distributed, nontechnical users. At the same time, it brings with it problems of verifiability, and in the absence of an effective editorial mechanism, it can incite public passions with misinformation as easily as it can engage productive public opinion based on accurate information. Open systems also can become subject to vandalism and other potentially malicious forms of hijacking. As Rheingold (2008) put it, "a smart mob is not necessarily a wise mob." The challenge is one of harnessing the democratic potential of citizen journalism while retaining the critical intelligence-gathering and information-vetting functions of traditional journalism.

The intelligence of public input into media debates will no doubt influence the likelihood that governments will be sensitive and responsive to that input—the fourth condition for decreasing political distance. There is, in this connection, another fundamental concern related to the authenticity of blogs or citizen journalism as new public voices. The democratic hope is that new sources outside the mainstream media will enable public control over news agendas, which have to date largely been negotiated between governing elites and the major news media (particularly television news). Politicians and other political elites are adept at capitalizing on the bureaucratic methods of journalists and supply a continuous stream of inexpensive news to the media that is constructed in ways that serve suppliers' and journalists' mutual interests. Thus, conventional media systems maintain or even extend rather than close the distance between politicians and journalists on the one hand and citizens on the other.

With a diversified media environment and an active blogosphere, some would argue that an elite control of the agenda is more difficult and less predictable. Whether the news agenda has opened up along these lines is debatable, however, for several reasons. First, elites still have active back-channel ties to many of the major bloggers (who are themselves overwhelmingly elite—predominately white, male, and highly educated and from the journalistic and legal professions) (Hindman 2009). Second, the mainstream media are still needed to reach mass audiences. Information from bloggers might diffuse broadly via word of mouth, social-networking sites, or email, but such diffusion, at least on any scale comparable to mass media, has not been established. The reverse pattern—that material generated by mainstream media is widely circulated via the Internet—seems more common (as when Katie Couric's *CBS Evening News* interview with 2008 vice-presidential candidate Sarah Palin became available to millions via YouTube and other sites). Some research indicates that blogs rely heavily on professional news media, preserving and reinforcing traditional journalistic norms and providing a secondary market for mainstream news (Reese, Rutigliano, Hyun, and Jeong 2007).

Government responsiveness to debate carried in the media therefore represents responsiveness to the public only insofar as the media are successful in representing the full range of public voices. The fifth condition required for closing the communicative distance between governors and the governed is a media system that is capable of adequately representing those who are traditionally disenfranchised, apathetic, ignored, or feared. Does the new media ecology widen the embrace of such outsiders or bystanders? Novel interactive technologies do seem to offer political outsiders unprecedented points of entry to public debate, but these new modes of communication will likely draw participants from a limited reservoir of citizens who are available for such engagement. Although there are exciting new developments on the scene, television remains the mainstay of public information, and most citizens continue to live in an offline news environment.

Still, the interrelated developments in media technology noted above have transformed the news audience—the potential public—in several important ways. Generational transitions, the increase in competing sources of news, and the increase in attractive entertainment options for people less interested in public affairs have stratified the news audience along several dimensions. Again, these transformations are perhaps most visible in the American context:

Age   Older viewers and readers have stayed with printed newspapers and television broadcast news, while younger cohorts splinter into myriad audiences for cable programming, online news, and social-networking sites. People over age forty read newspapers and watch network television at twice the rate of those under thirty (Pew Research Center for the People and the Press 2008b, 2010). As noted above, the practice of obtaining news from social networking sites is limited almost exclusively to those under age forty.

Partisanship   Conservatives and those who identify with the Republican Party have migrated to conservative programming on radio and cable (such as Fox News), while the audiences for other outlets, such as MSNBC, are increasingly composed of primarily liberal and Democratic-leaning people (Pew Research Center for the People and the Press 2009).

Trust   Audiences are increasingly skeptical of the news, and their trust in most traditional news outlets has declined significantly over the past decade. Trust has also taken on increasingly partisan overtones. Partisans tend to discriminate between trusted and nontrusted sources more than moderates and nonpartisans do. Conservatives are particularly mistrustful of the media, and this has become more pronounced in recent years as partisan credibility gaps, particularly in ratings of cable news outlets, have widened (Pew Research Center for the People and the Press, 2008b).

In recent Pew polls, about a quarter of respondents say they prefer news that reinforces their beliefs over balanced news, with conservatives being somewhat more likely to tell survey researchers they like news that reflects their views (Pew Research Center for the People and the Press, 2010). Compared to a decade ago, trust is now lower, much more partisan, and more highly differentiated across different outlets and audience segments.

Knowledge   There is also increasing differentiation in the selection of channels by political information levels, particularly among younger citizens. Among those under age thirty, surveys find much higher political knowledge among regular newspaper readers than among nonreaders and higher knowledge among cable TV viewers than nonviewers (but smaller knowledge differences between network TV viewers and nonviewers). Some comedy programs (notably, *The Daily Show* with Jon Stewart) draw an audience as knowledgeable as those who are regular newspaper readers or cable news viewers.

Prior (2005) estimates that, even though the total volume of news consumed by the public has grown, the number of people consuming news has actually dwindled. For younger cohorts, self-reported time spent with news was down by nearly 20 percent among those under thirty over the last decade. So where are news audiences going? Most of the content that has been made available to people through the dramatic expansion of media options is entertainment. To hold their audiences, providers of news have turned to "infotainment" programming, and the news has become softer (focusing on stories about hobbies and entertainment). The few studies that have been done of news consumer selections suggest that online users, for example, opt for softer story topics over hard news. In years past, the limited availability of alternatives to news programming, particularly during the dinner hour and early prime time, held some audiences captive to public affairs programming. Now that many more appetizing alternatives available, these less interested media consumers (many of them young) have turned to entertainment or infotainment instead. The upshot is increased variance in information holding in the population, with those people interested in public affairs consuming far more news and those less interested consuming much less (Prior

2005). Significant numbers of people—of the sort who in the past would have encountered a modicum of news through national outlets such as network TV—now consume little or none, and what they do consume is likely to be couched in soft-news and infotainment formats.

Conclusion

Citizens who are consulted online are informed by long-held habits of civic engagement or disengagement, political interest or apathy, and information seeking or avoidance. These habits are socialized by family, school, community, and the media environment.

As noted in the introduction to this volume, online consultations have the potential to buttress the legitimacy of government by advancing both political freedom and political equality. Our review of recent changes in the media landscape suggests that, with respect to the poles of freedom and equality, tendencies in news consumption have been toward the former without necessarily advancing and perhaps even retarding the latter. Although those interested in online consultation seek to close the gaps in knowledge, opinion, and influence that separate political elites and the mass of citizens, these efforts work in tension with larger trends that may well be pulling in an opposite direction. Powerful expansions of media opportunity have opened up predictable communication-effects gaps that allow the people who are best positioned—by way of socioeconomic resources, political power, and education—to extract value from media innovations at a much more rapid pace than those less well situated (Rogers 2004; Tichenor, Donohue and Olien 1970).

In the midst of change, much is unclear. One important question concerns the potential destabilizing effects of a multiplex media system. These systems have always been in a state of dynamic tension between centripetal forces (mass-market imperatives and cultural forces that drive toward social integration) and centrifugal forces (outlets that express minority interests, appeal to differentiated communities, and build ingroup solidarity). For decades, many critics of American journalism worried about overcentralization and overly mediated campaigns that were dominated by sound-bite TV journalism. The reduction of politics to a single-source, mass-consumed stream of TV news stories was seen as highly problematic. Today people seem to be in a mood to mourn the loss of the network era, fearing a new era of increased polarization and the evacuation of places—even the network news—where minds could meet their opposition (Sunstein 2001). James Carey, in a perceptive 1969 essay on the rise of the media professional, attributed the "objective reporting" model to the market-related demands of mass news media (Carey 1969). He described a transition that took place in the twentieth century from a partisan press system into a highly centralized system and that was driven by complex relationships between technological developments and social-political trends, principally the rise of progressivism. We may be shifting back to a more partisan system, driven again by technological changes but changes that today are segmenting rather than assembling mass audiences. Stroud (2008) found some evidence that the partisan character of audiences for news programs may lead to more polarized public opinion. Moreover, users of partisan news develop significantly different issue agendas depending on the media they consume (for example, Fox News versus CNN or MSNBC).

In the light of these findings, it would be unwise to adopt an uncritically sanguine approach to the prospects of online or digital democracy. Distances between governments and governed can be just as intractable in the sphere of virtual communication as in other mediated contexts. But it would be equally injudicious—perhaps even irresponsible—to draw simplistic conclusions based on overdetermined notions of new media relationships. Our starting point in this chapter was a recognition that political distance is an effect of sociopolitical positionings. The policy question following from this is whether alternative ways of conducting political communication, identifying the roles of its key actors, and developing institutional responsiveness can forge a space for a more discursive and consultative democracy.

References

Albrecht, S. 2006. "Whose Voice Is Heard in Online Deliberation? A Study of Participation and Representation in Political Debates on the Internet." *Information Communication and Society* 9, no. 1:62–82.

Amin, A. 2004. "Regions Unbound: Towards a New Politics of Place." *Geografiska Annaler. Series B, Human Geography* 86:33–44.

Baum, M. A. 2005. "Talking the Vote: Why Presidential Candidates Hit the Talk Show Circuit." *American Journal of Political Science* 49, no. 2:213–234.

Bennett, W. J. 2003. "New Media Power: The Internet and Global Activism." In *Contesting Media Power: Alternative Media in a Networked World*, edited by Nick Couldry and James Curran, 17–37. Lanham, MD: Rowman & Littlefield.

Bimber, B. 2003. *Information and American Democracy: Technology in the Evolution of Political Power*. New York: Cambridge University Press.

Blumler, J. G., and M. Gurevitch. 1995. *The Crisis of Public Communication.* London: Routledge.

Bohman, J. 1996. *Public Deliberation: Pluralism, Complexity, and Democracy.* Cambridge: MIT Press.

Carey, J. W. 1969. "The Communications Revolution and the Professional Communicator." *Sociological Review. Monograph* 13 (January):23–38.

Carpini, M. X. D., F. L. Cook, and L. R. Jacobs. 2004. "Public Deliberation, Discursive Participation, and Citizen Engagement: A Review of the Empirical Literature." *Annual Review of Political Science* 7, no. 1:315–344.

Coleman, S., and J. G. Blumler. 2009. *The Internet and Democratic Citizenship: Theory, Practice and Policy.* Cambridge: Cambridge University Press.

Coleman, S., and J. Gøtze. 2001. *Bowling Together: Online Public Engagement in Policy Deliberation.* London: Hansard Society.

Coleman, S., and D. Norris. 2004. *The New Agenda for e-Democracy: Lessons from Initiatives round the World.* New York: Oxford.

Coleman, S., and K. Ross. 2010. *The Media and the Public: "Them" and "Us" in Media Discourse.* Oxford: Wiley-Blackwell.

Dahlgren, P. 1995. *Television and the Public Sphere: Citizenship, Democracy and the Media.* London: Sage.

De Cindio, F., and D. Schuler. 2007. "Deliberation and Community Networks: A Strong Link Waiting to Be Forged." Paper presented at the CIRN Conference on Communities and Action, 6 November, Prato, Italy.

Graham, T., and T. Witschge. 2003. "In Search of Online Deliberation: Towards a New Method for Examining the Quality of Online Discussions." *Communications* 28, no. 2:173–204.

Gutmann, A., and D. F. Thompson. 1996. *Democracy and Disagreement.* Cambridge: Belknap Press of Harvard University Press.

Hindman, M. S. 2009. *The Myth of Digital Democracy.* Princeton: Princeton University Press.

Horrigan, J. 2001. "Online Communities: Networks That Nurture Long-Distance Relationships and Local Ties." Accessed November 29, 2010. http://www.pewinternet.org/~/media//Files/Reports/2001/PIP_Communities_Report.pdf.pdf.

Horrigan, J., K. Garrett, and P. Resnick. 2004. "The Internet and Democratic Debate." Accessed November 29, 2010. http://www.pewinternet.org/Reports/2004/The-Internet-and-Democratic-Debate.aspx.

Jankowski, N. W., and R. Van Os. 2004. "Internet-based Political Discourse: A Case Study of Electronic Democracy in Hoogeveen." In *Democracy Online: The Prospects for Political Renewal through the Internet*, edited by Peter M. Shane, 181–194. New York: Routledge.

Janssen, J., and R. Kies. 2005. "Online Forums and Deliberative Democracy." *Acta Politica* 40, no. 3:317–335.

Johnson, T., and B. Kaye. 1998. "A Vehicle for Engagement or a Haven for the Disaffected: Internet Use, Political Alienation and Voter Participation." In *Engaging the Public: How Government and the Media Can Reinvigorate American Democracy*, edited by T. Johnson, C. Hays, and S. Hays, 123–135. New York: Rowman and Littlefield.

Kaye, B. K., and T. J. Johnson. 2002. "Online and in the Know: Uses and Gratifications of the Web for Political Information." *Journal of Broadcasting and Electronic Media* 46, no. 1:54–71.

Keane, J. 1991. *The Media and Democracy*. London: Polity.

Kelly, J., D. Fisher, and M. Smith. 2005. "Debate, Division and Diversity: Political Discourse Networks in USENET Groups." Paper presented at the Online Deliberation conference, May 20–22, Stanford University.

Kenny, W. P., D. Swee, C. Lim, B. H. Detenber, and L. Alsagoff. 2008. "The Impact of Language Variety and Expertise on Perceptions of Online Political Discussions." *Journal of Computer-Mediated Communication* 13, no. 1:76–99.

Lippmann, W. 1925. *The Phantom Public*. New York: Harcourt.

Massey, D. B. 2005. *For Space*. London: Sage.

McKenna, K. Y. A., and J. A. Bargh. 2000. "Plan 9 from Cyberspace: The Implications of the Internet for Personality and Social Psychology." *Personality and Social Psychology Review* 4, no. 1:57–75.

Monnoyer-Smith, L. 2007. "The Public Debate Enacted: A French Learning Process." *Hermes* 47:21–28.

Muhlberger, P. 2005. "Lessons from the Virtual Agora Project: A Research Design for Studying Democratic Deliberation." *Journal of Public Deliberation* 1, no. 1. http://services.bepress.com/jpd/vol1/iss1/art5.

Mutz, D. C. 2002. "The Consequences of Cross-Cutting Networks for Political Participation." *American Journal of Political Science* 46, no. 4:838–855.

OECD. 2001. *Citizens as Partners: Information, Consultation and Public Participation in Policy-Making*. Paris: PUMA, OECD.

Outing, S. 2005. *The Eleven Layers of Citizen Journalism*. June 13, updated June 15. Accessed March 25, 2011. http://www.poynter.org.

Paterson, C. 2005. "News Agency Dominance in International News on the Internet." In *Converging Media, Diverging Politics: A Political Economy of News Media in the United States and Canada*, edited by David Skinner, James Robert Compton, and Mike Gasher, 145–164. Lanham, MD: Lexington Books.

Patterson, T. E. 2001. *Doing Well and Doing Good*. Cambridge: Harvard University, John F. Kennedy School of Government.

Pew Research Center for the People and the Press. 2010. "Ideological News Sources: Who Watches and Why—Americans Spending More Time Following News." Accessed November 29, 2010. http://people-press.org.

Pew Research Center for the People and the Press. 2009. "Partisanship and Cable News Audiences." Accessed November 29, 2010. http://pewresearch.org/pubs/1395/partisanship-fox-news-and--other-cable-news-audiences.

Pew Research Center for the People and the Press. 2008a. "Internet's Broader Role in Campaign 2008: Social Networking and Online Videos Take Off" Accessed November 29, 2010. http://people-press.org.

Pew Research Center for the People and the Press. 2008b. "Key News Audiences Now Blend Online and Traditional Sources." Accessed November 29, 2010. http://people-press.org.

Pew Research Center for the People and the Press. 2006. "Online Papers Modestly Boost Newspaper Readership." Accessed November 29, 2010. http://people-press.org.

Plant, R. 2004. "Online Communities." *Technology in Society* 26:51–65.

Price, V., and J. Cappella. 2002. "Online Deliberation and Its Influence: The Electronic Dialogue Project in Campaign 2000." *IT and Society* 1, no. 1:303–329.

Prior, M. 2005. "News vs. Entertainment: How Increasing Media Choice Widens Gaps in Political Knowledge and Turnout." *American Journal of Political Science* 49:577–592.

Reese, S. D., L. Rutigliano, K. Hyun, and J. Jeong. 2007. "Mapping the Blogosphere." *Journalism* 8, no. 3:235–261.

Rheingold, H. 2008. "Using Participatory Media and Public Voice to Encourage Civic Engagement." In *Civic Life Online: Learning How Digital Media Can Engage Youth*, edited by W. L. Bennett, 97–118. Cambridge: MIT Press.

Rogers, R. 2004. *Information Politics on the Web*. Cambridge: MIT Press.

Sassen, S. 1998. *Globalization and Its Discontents : Essays on the New Mobility of People and Money*. New York: New Press.

Scannell, P. 2000. "For-Anyone-as-Someone Structures." *Media Culture and Society* 22, no. 1:5–24.

Shah, D. V., N. Kwak, and R. L. Holbert. 2001. "'Connecting' and 'Disconnecting' with Civic Life: Patterns of Internet Use and the Production of Social Capital." *Political Communication* 18, no. 2:141–162.

Silverstone, R. 2007. *Media and Morality: On the Rise of the Mediapolis*. Cambridge: Polity Press.

Soja, E. W. 1971. *Political Organization of Space*. Washington DC: Association of American Geographers.

Stromer-Galley, J. 2002. "New Voices in the Public Sphere: A Comparative Analysis of Interpersonal and Online Political Talk." *Javnost/The Public* 9:23–42.

Stroud, N. J. 2008. "Media Use and Political Predispositions: Revisiting the Concept of Selective Exposure." *Political Behavior* 30, no. 3:341–366.

Sunstein, C. R. 2001. *Republic.com*. Princeton: Princeton University Press.

Thrift, N. J. 2008. *Non-representational Theory: Space, Politics, Affect*. London: Routledge.

Tichenor, P. J., G. A. Donohue, and C. N. Olien. 1970. "Mass Media Flow and Differential Growth in Knowledge." *Public Opinion Quarterly* 34, no. 2:159–170.

Veronis Suhler Stevenson. 2008. Communications Industry Forecast and Report. New York.

Wright, S. 2006. "Government-Run Online Discussion Fora: Moderation, Censorship and the Shadow of Control." *British Journal of Politics and International Relations* 8, no. 4:550–568.

3

Web 2.0: New Challenges for the Study of E-Democracy in an Era of Informational Exuberance

Andrew Chadwick

Being at the margins of the formalized procedures grants improvisers an added element of liberty, and sometimes of play, about the choices of which resources to harness and how. If these approaches look rough compared to neat and tidy formal procedures, they are on the other hand highly situated: they tend to include an added element of ingenuity, experience, and skill belonging to the individual and their community (of practice) rather than to the organizational systems. Finally, they all seem to share the same way of operating: small forces, tiny interventions, and on-the-fly add-ons lead, when performed skillfully and with close attention to the local context, to momentous consequences, unrelated to the speed and scope of the initial intervention. These modes of operation unfold in a dance that always includes the key aspects of localness and time (the "here and now"); modest intervention and large-scale effects; on-the-fly appearance but deeply rooted in personal and collective skill and experience.
—Claudio Ciborra, *The Labyrinths of Information* (2002, 48)

Claims regarding the Internet's potential to reshape democratic life have been made for nearly twenty years. Scholarship has proceeded through several waves—early enthusiasm (for example, Corrado 1996; Dahlberg 2001; Morris 1999), pessimistic reactions (for example, Hill and Hughes 1998; Margolis and Resnick 2000; Wilhelm 2000), and recent more balanced and empirically driven approaches of the post-dotcom era (for example, Price 2009; Shane 2004). Despite the increasing maturity of e-democracy scholarship, one inescapable fact remains: the reality of online deliberation (whether judged in terms of its quantity, its quality, or its effect on political behavior and policy outcomes) is far removed from the ideals set out in the early to mid-1990s.

This chapter seeks to broaden the debate about e-democracy. Since the emergence of the e-democracy movement, most projects and analyses have used rich and sustained deliberation on an often romanticized Athenian or public-sphere model as a yardstick to judge and measure outcomes. This approach, heavily influenced by an ideal of rational critical discourse, has proved difficult to embed in political organizations. As a consequence, the use of digital network technologies to shape public policy is generally met with incredulity by most politicians, public servants, and citizens. Following a brief critique of the assumptions underlying the literature to date, the chapter sketches out an alternative approach—one based on the incentive structures that seem to shape how public servants and citizens now behave online. The approach is derived from preliminary observations of the low-threshold coproduction behavior characteristic of what has come to be known as Web 2.0. Although it may not live up to the high ideals of the deliberative public sphere, some of this behavior has real value in online consultation and public policy making. We should acknowledge that successful e-democracy programs may require a plurality of different sociotechnical values and mechanisms.

The Deliberative Assumption

The push for Internet-enabled e-democracy emerged in the early to mid-1990s as Internet diffusion began to take off in the developed world. Although it is not often mentioned, the movement is situated in the broader context of the revival of participatory democracy that took place during the 1960s and 1970s (Chadwick 2006, 84–89). Inspired in part by oppositional social movements as well as a reappraisal of the direct democracy of Rousseau, political theorists—notably Barber, Macpher son, Pateman, and Habermas—established a new agenda that has persisted into the twenty-first century (Barber 1984; Habermas 1989 [1962]; Macpherson 1977; Pateman 1970).

At the same time, some empirical political scientists, most notably Fishkin, contributed to the deliberative turn by advocating new forms of opinion polling that rested on discussion. Echoing themes in Barber's (1984) model of "strong democracy," Fishkin suggested that "deliberative polling" has an educative effect that forces citizens to reconsider preconceived opinions and is thus superior to the individualist methodology that dominates traditional opinion polling (Fishkin 1991).

For participatory democrats, political deliberation (if—and it is a big *if*—it fulfills certain criteria) can have a transformational influence on citizens. Contrary to liberal individualist perspectives that assume that citizens' political views are predetermined by their interests, deliberative democrats argue that we discover legitimate solutions to political problems only by engaging in sustained, reflective discourse.

Perhaps the most influential approach to the role of communication in citizen engagement over the last several decades is Habermas's concept of the "public sphere" (Habermas 1989). In 1962, Habermas argued that the development of early modern capitalism during the eighteenth century heralded a new era of communication based on a culture of enlightened, critical, and reasoned public debate. This culture, which was restricted to the propertied, was based on an independent, privately owned press, the reading of political periodicals, and rich political discussion in physical spaces such as coffee houses, salons, and pubs. It encouraged critical and reasoned forms of political deliberation away from direct political control and allowed public opinion to develop (1989, 27). Most scholars have deserted Habermas's empirical claims and use the public sphere as a normative ideal to judge the existing communication structures of contemporary societies. Often this approach involves bringing in concepts from Habermas's more general theories of discourse and deliberation in attempts to provide criteria for rational-critical discourse (for example, Chambers 1996; Curran 1991; Dahlberg 2001; Dryzek 1990; Friedland 2001).

The ideal of the deliberative public sphere is probably the most influential concept in the scholarly writing on e-democracy (Chadwick 2006, 83–113; Papacharissi 2002). The Internet emerges as a communication medium uniquely suited to providing arenas for public debate that are relatively spontaneous, flexible, and self-governed (Dahlgren 2000). Citizens that have progressively shrunk into their respective private spheres as the historical public sphere collapsed are, in the Habermasian interpretation, once again able to emerge as a public force.

There are many potential examples of how these normative assumptions underpin both practice and interpretation, but by way of illustration, consider the work of three scholars—Lincoln Dahlberg, Michael Froomkin, and Stuart Shulman. Dahlberg (2001) extracts six main conditions that e-democracy must fulfill if is to create a genuinely deliberative public sphere—autonomy from state and economic powers, reason rather than assertion, reflexivity, ideal role taking, sincerity, and discursive inclusion and equality. Froomkin suggests that "new technology may enhance the quantity and especially the quality of mass participation in a representative democracy. . . . internet tools may enrich political debate [and] improve the quality and deliberativeness of both geographic communities and communities of practice" (Froomkin 2004, 3; see also Froomkin 2003). Finally, Shulman, a scholar of e-rulemaking, is highly critical of the role played by interest organizations in supplying Web forms and email templates that enable citizens to lobby government agencies. His empirical investigations are framed in such a way that he sees no "signs of deliberation . . . , inclusion of difference, respect for a variety of positions, transformation of preferences, as well as expanding and authentic discourse . . . to move the process to a higher deliberative plane" (Shulman 2006, 44–45).

Romanticized ideals of deliberative democracy and "thick" citizenship underlay most of the e-democracy literature, whether critical or not (Chadwick 2006, 83–113; Tambini 1999). These are rarely stated, but they are important because they value certain types of activity over others, even though recent—and in my view significant—developments in online political behavior may have little to do with these ideals.

I share the concerns over the future of civic engagement, and it is indisputable that we should continue to strive for more deliberative forms of political communication. But we should not lose sight of the many other forms of behavior that less easily fit with the deliberative assumption. The 1990s e-democracy paradigm was preoccupied with the creation of deliberative spaces, particularly discussion forums. It was assumed that they would provide for rich, critical, self-reflective, toler-ant, and sustained citizen engagement elegantly expressed through the medium of the written word. They would allow citizens to deliberate free from the constraints of time and space and would provide additions to traditional policy making structures. They would be autonomous, self-governing, flexible, unconstrained, and self-consciously designed not to limit or narrowly channel citizen expression. Overall, these criteria and expectations were, as Vedel writes, in a classic piece of understate-ment, "very demanding" (Vedel 2006, 232). Given the particular models of citizen behavior privileged in these approaches, we should not be surprised that e-democracy often failed to live up to expectations.

Assumption Meets Realities

The deliberative assumption would not be so damaging had it not so powerfully shaped governments' largely negative responses to e-democ-racy. The empirical evidence we have on online deliberative forums reveals a familiar set of themes that any researcher working in the field will instantly recognize (Chadwick 2011). First, there is the basic factual point that in the majority of online policy-oriented consultations to date, only very small groups of citizens chose to participate. In the United Kingdom, for example, the Hansard Society and the Ministry of Justice's

Digital Dialogues program ran from 2006 to 2008 and included several online deliberative forums (along with blogs, webchats, expert panels, and online questionnaires). Participation rates in the forums were low (table 3.1). Second, elected officials and public-sector bureaucrats have been reluctant to enshrine deliberative online consultation into their routine modes of operation. This has been attributed to a range of factors—lack of time and financial resources due to the need to moderate online forums; fear of litigation; intra- and interbureaucratic rivalries that pit government agencies and departments against each other; concerns about marginalizing elected legislators and established interest organizations; criticisms of the lack of careful reflection on the design of online environments, specifically how they may undermine deliberation by reducing interactivity; a generalized fear of losing control over the policy agenda and opening up the floodgates by raising citizens' expectations about policy influence; concerns about journalists who quote citizen comments out of context as a means of framing stories in the mainstream media; concern over the representativeness and expertise of forum participants, especially where small numbers are involved;

Table 3.1
Forum participation rates in the *Digital Dialogues* e-democracy program, United Kingdom, August 2006 to August 2007

Forum	Duration (months)	Number of citizen posts
Department of Communities and Local Government forum	6	411
Department for Constitutional Affairs Family Justice Division forum	3.5	172
Department for Constitutional Affairs Family Justice Division forum (Children and Young People)	2	26
The Review of the Funding of Political Parties forum	2.5	217
Foreign and Commonwealth Office European Youth Parliament forum	1.5	57
Planning Portal forum	4	67
Law Commission Tenth Programme of Law Reform forum	1.75	43

Source: Hansard Society (2007).

concern over the digital divide shaping citizen participation, not just in the sense of physical access to the Internet but also media or electronic illiteracy weighing heavily on top of more traditional stratifiers of political engagement, such as education, socioeconomic status, age, race, and ethnicity.

This is not the whole story. There are examples of e-democracy that have proved valuable for citizens and government, but these are in the minority, and their value was not necessarily derived from their deliberative nature. Probably the largest and most rigorous empirical study of online deliberation to date—Price and Cappella's *Electronic Dialogue* and *Healthcare Dialogue* experiments—were broadly successful, but they were "not intended to be formally deliberative exercises; instead, group members were simply invited to discuss a number of topics" (Price 2009, 45; Price and Cappella 2002). And in these cases, the discussions were probably not inclusive enough to satisfy the deliberative assumption. "Argument repertoire" was the best predictor of participation in online discussion. This measure of political sophistication—based on the number of different arguments that citizens are able to mobilize in support of their opinions—was strongly correlated with age and education (older and more highly educated individuals were significantly more likely to participate than others). Quantity of contributions increased with levels of political knowledge and educational attainment. Although we need to recognize that these experiments did lead to interactive discussion and an increase in political knowledge among participants, these were not classical deliberative encounters.

The characteristics that shape the success or failure of e-democracy are manifold and complex, and there is insufficient space to discuss them here (see Chadwick 2011). But scholars ought to be interested in why programs succeed and why they fail, and this might have something to do with unrealistic assumptions about the incentives that shape political behavior in the online environment.

My aim in this chapter is not to echo the argument that the online environment's disinhibiting effects or the absence of informal or formal sanctions for those seeking to undermine debate render it a poor relation of face-to-face discussion. Again, this is empirically contested. For every criticism of the online environment, there is a counterpoint about its capacity to reduce constraints on the voices of the less powerful and many concerns about the quality of traditional face-to-face political interaction. More fundamentally, I am not seeking to fortify the generalization that citizens lack the motivation to think about and discuss politics (Vedel 2006, 232). These points are empirically disputed, and it is also unnecessary to assume that citizens should be highly informed and highly motivated (Delli Carpini, Cook, and Jacobs 2004). Most citizens will fall into categories along a continuum, and it is unlikely that they will remain in one category in perpetuity. Most of us occupy positions between these two extremes, depending on our contexts. It is my hypothesis that sociotechnical environments that have this level of granularity designed in—to enable citizens to demonstrate citizenship in diverse ways—are more likely to be successful than those that do not.

Politics: Web 2.0

Before attempting to understand what Web 2.0 offers for e-democracy, we need some way of defining it and of teasing out its broader implications for political behavior in a way that stays close to its technological characteristics without reducing it to those characteristics. Space limits preclude a full discussion, but here I build on Tim O'Reilly's (2005) seminal outline, arguably the most influential discussion of the term to date.[1]

O'Reilly's technology-centered approach defines Web 2.0 in terms of seven key themes. Some of these are more relevant to my purposes than others, and some require extra theoretical work to render them meaningful for this discussion.[2] Nevertheless, the seven principles are the Internet as a platform for political discourse; the collective intelligence emergent from political Web use; the importance of data over particular software and hardware applications; perpetual experimentalism in the public domain; the creation of small-scale forms of political engagement through consumerism; the propagation of political content over multiple applications; and rich user experiences on political Web sites.

The first principle—the Internet as a platform for political discourse—means that the Web has moved from the older model of static pages toward a means of enabling a wide range of goals to be achieved through networked software services. The archetypal Web 2.0 Web-as-platform service is Google, whose value depends almost entirely on the interface of its distributed advertising network, its search algorithm, and its huge database of crawled pages. Two key features of this aspect of Web 2.0 are particularly salient—the power of easily scalable networks and the "long tail." Easily scalable networking involves an organization's ability to adapt to sudden growth surges and ad hoc events that increase demand for its services. The theory of the long tail (Anderson 2006) is that online distribution is changing the political economy of content creation as online storage and distribution significantly reduce the costs and increase the market for diverse content, resulting in a sales and products curve with a "head" of mass market products and a long "tail" of niche products. The Internet thus contributes to a more diverse and pluralistic media landscape.

These Web-as-platform principles can be seen at work in a range of political arenas. The 2004 primary and presidential campaigns in the United States saw the emergence of a campaigning model based on online venues loosely meshed together through automated linking technologies, particularly blogs (Chadwick 2007a; Hindman 2005). However, nowhere is the idea more strongly embodied than in the recent shift toward online social networking on platforms such as Facebook and Myspace and social media sites such as YouTube. The symbolic moment came in January 2007, when John Edwards and Barack Obama announced their candidacies for the Democratic presidential nomination via brief and informal video postings on YouTube, but the U.S. midterms of November 2006 had already witnessed an explosion of political activity on social-networking sites, as well as the intensification of blogging by candidates and a long tail of amateur pundits (Williams and Gulati 2007).

The second theme of Web 2.0 is collective intelligence. The core idea is that a distributed network of creators and contributors, the majority of them amateurs, can use simple online tools to produce information goods that may outperform those produced by so-called authoritative, concentrated sources. Examples of this abound, but two stand out as having caught the political imagination—free and open-source software projects and user-generated content sites. The underlying model of online collaboration that produces these vast collections of human intelligence has been much debated. Opinions differ, for instance, over the extent to which hierarchy matters in these environments. Some, such as Weber (2004), suggest that it accounts for a great deal, while others, such as Weinberger (2007), downplay its importance. These debates aside, it seems safe to suggest that Web 2.0 rests in part on a broadly voluntarist model of knowledge creation.

At a basic level, many interesting and significant developments in online collective action have been enabled by free and open-source software creations, providing a good example of elective affinity between political values and technological tools. Wikipedia itself has become a political battleground, as supporters of candidates, causes, groups, movements, and even regimes engage in incessant microscopic "edit wars" over entries. Beyond this, the principle of collective intelligence now animates politics in a variety of arenas. The blogosphere has enabled ongoing citizen vigilance on a grand scale. Political actors and media elites now exist in an always-on environment in which it is impossible to escape the "little brother" surveillant gaze of citizen-reporters—from easily assembled Flickr photostreams of marches and demonstrations ignored by mainstream media, to video bloggers such as Connecticut Bob, who took to the streets with his home movie camera to track Senator Joseph Lieberman's less guarded moments during the 2006 U.S. midterm elections.

The third principle of Web 2.0 is the importance of data. The central claim is that the current era is characterized by the aggregation of huge amounts of information. Those who can successfully mine, refine, and subsequently protect it are likely to emerge as dominant. Most of these data have been created from the concentrated labor of volunteers, or they may be the by-products of countless distributed and coincidental interactions. But the key point is that informational value emerges from the confluence of distributed user-generated content and its centralized exploitation.

This principle points to the ongoing importance of long-standing controversies surrounding privacy, surveillance, and the commercial and political use of personal information (Howard 2006). The ease of connection in the social-networking environments of Web 2.0 offers a multitude of possibilities for automated gathering, sorting, and targeting. In the early days of the Web, political actors would often complain that they had "no control" over the online environment or that they did not know how to target particular groups or supporters (Stromer-Galley 2000). The applications of Web 2.0 render these tasks much more manageable as individuals willingly produce and reveal the most elaborate information about their tastes and preferences within enclosed technological frameworks. In the realm of political campaigns, e-government and e-democracy, social-networking sites thus offer political actors many advantages over the open Web.

The fourth theme is perpetual experimentalism in the public domain. As indicated above, the attraction of O'Reilly's model is that it captures literal, quite narrow developments in technological practice, but it can also be used at a metaphorical level to capture social and political behaviors. Web 2.0 applications have been characterized by an unusual amount of public experimentalism. This is most obviously illustrated by the "perpetually beta" status of many of the popular services. Although this is a symptom of the requirements of building and testing scalable Web applications on meager resources, it also reflects a value shift away from tightly managed development environments and toward those characterized by fluidity and greater collaboration between developers and users.

This sense of democratic experimentalism has been one of the driving values of the Internet since its earliest days (Chadwick 2006, 38–48), and I have argued elsewhere that this principle should be at the center of the development of e-government systems because it encourages participation by democratically conscious software engineers (Chadwick 2003). But Web 2.0 has seen democratic experimentalism proliferate across a surprising range of political activities. Election campaigns in the United States are now characterized by obsessive and continuous recalibration in response to instant online polls, fundraising drives, comments lists on YouTube video pages, and blog posts. But there is perhaps no better example of the effects of the permanent beta in politics than the British prime minister's e-petitions initiative, which was launched in November 2006. The site remained in beta for several years and has recently metamorphosed into another service. Adding the beta stamp to an e-government initiative at the heart of the executive machinery of one of the world's oldest liberal democracies tells us just how far the penetration of these values and working practices has gone.

The next two Web 2.0 themes—the creation of small-scale forms of political engagement through consumerism and the propagation of political content across multiple applications—are more specialized but still reveal important aspects of the new politics. Many data cannot be sealed off from public use because it would be politically unacceptable, or a business model might depend on open access. Web 2.0 is characterized by the mashing together of different data in pursuit of goals that differ from those originally intended by the producers of those data. This practice may grant increased power to citizens. For example, the British activist volunteer group MySociety has run a number of sites (such as TheyWorkForYou and FixMyStreet) that combine publicly accessible government data with user-generated input. TheyRule allows users to expose the social ties among political and economic elites by mapping out the network structures of the corporate boards of multinational firms. Meanwhile, mobile Internet devices are increasingly important, again with a distinct user-generated inflection through practices such as video and photoblogging, as well as mainstream news organizations' increasing reliance on amateur "witness reporters" (Stanyer 2009).

The final theme of Web 2.0 is rich user experiences on political Web sites. In the narrow technical sense, this refers to the development of applications designed to run code (specifically, asynchronous JavaScript and XML, or AJAX) inside a Web browser in ways that facilitate interactivity and the rapid retrieval, alteration, and storage of data. Most of the successful Web 2.0 applications combine such capabilities with back-end databases that store user-generated content able to be modified by others. Although valuable information is created by such actions, these are often not the result of heroic individual efforts but of aggregated small-scale, low-threshold forms of behavior—seemingly "happy accident" outcomes of thousands of individual interactions (Bimber, Flanagin, and Stohl 2005, 372; Chadwick 2007a, 290). But these are not entirely accidental. Many Web 2.0 systems are designed to capture useful aggregated data from even the most minimal of user activities. This occurs on sites that encourage users to create original content but that also offer readers the chance to edit it or rate it. Highly rated pieces rise to the top of the recommended diaries feature on the *Daily Kos* home page, while MoveOn's *Action Forum* contains a similar mechanism for prioritizing issues.

Perhaps the most significant aspect of Web 2.0 politics as rich user experience has emerged in the form of online video. This took most commentators by surprise. Past predictions of media convergence generally argued that an abundance of bandwidth would make the Internet a more televisual, large-screen experience. YouTube may eventually metamorphose into a fully converged large-screen online broadcasting network, but the indications so far are that it will not, primarily because it has generated a huge user base that savors its small-screen, DIY format.

In the political sphere, YouTube has made a sizeable dent in earlier predictions of the emergence of slick, professionalized televisual political communication that can be resourced only by government and wealthy politicians (Margolis and Resnick 2000). This is clearly wide of the mark when both political elites and citizens perceive that the visual genres of an effective YouTube video do not depend on professional media production techniques. The cynical may decry the rise of YouTube campaigning on the grounds that it is inauthentic spin based on manufactured folksy imagery. In the United Kingdom, the Conservative Party leader David Cameron was widely criticized by the mainstream media for this approach on his site Webcameron, launched in 2006. And yet the impressionistic evidence suggests that the method attracts members of the public, evidenced by more than 30,000 citizen postings during his forum's experimental lifespan between May and December 2007 (Cameron 2007). In important ways, each new digital technology that captures public attention quickly becomes politicized. YouTube has become one of the most popular online applications—essentially a tool for content distribution by politicians.

Technologies possess inherent properties that shape and constrain political norms, rules, and behavior, but these must be situated within political contexts (Chadwick 2006, 17–21). The seven themes of Web 2.0 discussed above are by no means exhaustive and only begin to provide analytical purchase on the changes currently underway. Yet it would be a mistake to dismiss Web 2.0 as solely the creation of marketing departments. We need to try to make sense of the sometimes remarkable pace of these recent changes while also recognizing the continuities with the Internet's earlier phases. The area of e-democracy should be no exception.

In the rest of this chapter, I try to identify what we might seek to learn about the values and incentive structures that seem to characterize political behavior in these environments and to what extent these may have value for e-democracy. I organize this into two broad sections. First, I approach the problem from what might be termed the demand side—the perspective of citizens. Then I approach it from the supply side—the perspective of government organizations (for a similar approach, see Margetts 2006; Margetts and Dunleavy 2002).

Learning from Web 2.0: Citizens

What can we learn from citizen behavior in Web 2.0 environments?

Usability

The leading Web 2.0 applications are dominated by a distinctive usability ethos that was often absent from the earlier phases of the Web's development. Early critical accounts of Internet-mediated politics often bemoaned the growth of a digital divide between DIY Web sites and the glitzy, "professionalized" sites of the wealthy and powerful. Although it would be a mistake to ignore the powerful back-end technologies that enable Web 2.0 sites to function, the usability doctrines of figures such as Nielsen (1999) have had a major influence on the look and feel of the Web 2.0 environment. Extremely simple messaging platforms such as tumblelogs or Twitter are testimony to this approach, where accessibility and ease of use are the core principles that drive the services. The UK's MySociety projects are based on the principle of "small is beautiful" and of enabling citizens to do one simple thing easily and elegantly. They-WorkForYou, for example, provides an intuitive searchable interface to Hansard, the record of all UK parliamentary proceedings. Debates are listed in an easy-to-follow format and allow for citizen comments on specific parliamentarians' speeches. Once submitted, citizen comments appear alongside the original parliamentary speech. Citizens are also able to comment on the comments of others. The site also provides citizens with the opportunity to learn about the views and behavior of members of Parliament, including their voting records, speeches, committee membership, and entries in the register of members' interests (TheyWorkForYou 2008). In Web 2.0 sociotechnical environments, the complexity often emerges from the aggregation of many simple contributions.

Thresholds

Many Web 2.0 services rely on large numbers of individuals behaving with regularity in low-threshold ways. A threshold is here understood to be a function of an individual's calculation about the expected utility of participating in a given activity, based on the likelihood of participation by others (Granovetter 1978; Miller and Page 2004; Olson 1965, 164). But the key point about political behavior online is that much of the technological architecture of Web 2.0 applications designs is in low- *and* high-threshold activities and many variants in between. An example is the division of labor typified by many news aggregators and blogs such as Digg, *BBC News Online*, or *AOL News*. This user-generated content circulates around a reactive, story-telling model. Citizens write stories, and a sample of these is opened up to comments and ratings. Some tell the stories, others make brief comments, and others rate both the story and the comments with a simple button click. Highly rated stories rise to the top of the list. Many of these stories begin life as stories about other stories—remixed versions of the content of others. A good policy example comes in the form of "Frank: Your Stories," which is a user-generated element on the UK government's drugs awareness site for young people (Frank: Your Stories 2008). The page allows users to write and upload their own stories, providing an interesting combination of an information site (with a public health agenda) that is now relying on user content to help it fulfill its role. The popularity of this approach is explained by the fact that it is not an all-or-nothing model. Quantitatively and qualitatively different forms of contribution are facilitated by the technological architecture. Many citizens seem to find mixing together sources of digital content originally created by others to be a compelling and worthwhile experience in its own right. It would be an exaggeration to say that the political economy of political content creation has been transformed, but it seems to have shifted in significant ways.

Trusted Governance

Trust is one of the most valuable and one of the most elusive forces in online politics. Anonymity and pseudonymity may encourage freedom of expression, but they also constantly undermine sustained collaboration in problem solving. Government-run online consultations have been criticized for their insensitivity to how the sociotechnical environment encourages or undermines trust (Wright 2006). Web 2.0 environments do not solve these problems, but in recent years some interesting models have emerged for sustainable coproduction, reflecting an interesting blend of self-governance and regulation (Benkler 2006). Three examples include Wikipedia, eBay, and Digg.[3] Wikipedia relies on a blend of spontaneous self-correction by the army of volunteer Wikipedians and an expanding conception of hierarchy (entries are now frequently locked down, and prominent warnings are increasingly displayed at the top of contentious or incomplete entries). EBay is temporally pre-Web 2.0, but its mechanisms for generating sufficient trust for online transactions to occur (low threshold buyer and seller ratings) have provided the inspiration for many Web 2.0 projects. Digg, the "editorless" user-generated news site, relies on individuals to submit links to interesting stories. Submissions are given a simple positive or negative rating by users and rise or fall on this basis. Users may add brief textual comments to substantiate their decision to "digg" or "bury" a story, adding a very low threshold deliberative element.

Policymakers have started to experiment with such mechanisms. In 2007, the New Zealand Police Service was required to draft a submission of the Police Act for renewal. The service decided to undertake this process using a wiki that was open to all members of the public. The experiment was a success and attracted much international interest. According to information on the project on its (now archived) Web site, the result of the consultation shaped the final version of the bill, which was introduced to the New Zealand Parliament (New Zealand Police 2008).

It would be naïve to suggest that coproduction environments such as Wikipedia, eBay, and Digg create the high levels of trust that are typical of face-to-face encounters such as deliberative polling. But they seem to encourage voice and loyalty and discourage exit (Hirschman 1970). In this sense, the small-scale interactions in these environments offer potentially valuable lessons for online consultation, where ease of exit has long been perceived as a barrier to citizen and government participation.

Third Places

Social-networking sites such as Facebook differ in important respects from the open Web. They provide areas in which individuals express many different facets of their identities and in which diverse lifestyles and values play out. The affordances of social-networking environments encourage us to build our lives online. It has been argued that the Internet is a purposive medium and is therefore less likely to have by-product learning effects in comparison with other media such as television, where serendipitous encounters with political information occur in the context of entertainment (Prior 2007; for the original argument, see Downs 1957). For some, this reinforces traditional stratifiers of political engagement (Bimber and Davis 2003).

But although this may have been true of earlier phases of the Internet, the emergence of social-networking applications has altered the context. Political life in Facebook "piggybacks" on the everyday life context of the environment in much the same way as "third places" away from the home and the workplace function in community-building, social capital, and civic engagement (Oldenburg 1997). Politics here aligns itself with broader repertoires of self-expression and lifestyle values. Politics in Facebook goes to where people are, not where we would like them to be. When the company opened up its code in 2007 as a means of encouraging programmers to create extra features, it unleashed a wave of new applications, the majority of which concerned the expression of lifestyle choices and consumerism. But also significant are the growing numbers of directly political applications (over 500 within a year of Facebook opening up its code), such as Causes, which by early 2008 averaged 114,000 daily active users (Facebook Causes 2008). Many Facebook profile pages are now a mish-mash of content and genres, where music, film, and fashion sit alongside political campaigns, donation drives, sloganeering, and so on. Once again, a low-threshold deliberative environment, with features such as The Wall and Groups, allows users to comment on others' profiles and to hold ongoing conversations in semi-public spaces.

The Affective Turn

Much of the commentary on Web 2.0 has focused on the rise of highly individualized forms of online expression and the ways that these may contribute to a broader social narcissism (Keen 2007). Much of the writing about blogs and YouTube, for example, has criticized what are perceived to be self-obsessed, egotistical communication genres. Some lament the rise of audiovisual content online, complaining that it signals the end of an innocent ideal of text-based communication free from the constraints of physical markers such as ethnicity, appearance, accent, and social class (Chadwick 2007b). Many of the early advocates of e-democracy celebrated the egalitarian quality of textual computer-mediated communication.

Visual communication genres online seem to present challenges to our understanding of e-democracy. But is the news all bad? Over the last decade or so, some have broadened the concerns of social and political theory to encompass the role of affective dimensions in the regulation of social life. Giddens (1999, 63) has called for a "democracy of the emotions in everyday life," while Young has written of political deliberation's "internal" exclusionary dynamics, which subtly devalue informal and emotional discourse (Young 2000). More recently, Papacharissi (2009), drawing on Inglehart and Welzel (2005), has pointed to a "civically motivated narcissism" in which "Self-expression values are connected to the desire to control one's environment, a stronger desire for autonomy, and the need to question authority" and has concluded that "self-expression values are not uncivic." Citizen-produced audio and video deviate from the ideal of textual deliberative discourse, but in the genres of YouTube they arguably democratize political expression by creating a new grassroots outlet for the affective in politics.

Certain policy sectors might be more attuned to this style of discourse than others. The site of the United Kingdom's National Health Service review, which ran from 2007 to 2008, included a Have Your Say section (which featured a news and announcements blog that allowed public commenting), Lord Darzi's personal blog (which also allowed commenting), online surveys for both NHS stakeholders and members of the public, and an accompanying YouTube stream (UK National Health Service 2008).

Although much empirical work remains to be done in this area, we can hypothesize that many citizens are at ease uploading a quickly recorded video delivered in an informal, conversational style but that they are less confident if asked to deliberate formally. Thus, although we may be losing the egalitarian effects of text-based computer-mediated communication, audiovisual online culture might not have entirely negative effects on citizen engagement.

Numbers

Finally, there is the basic, often elided, question of numbers. Faced with low participation rates, many e-democracy programs have fallen back on the argument that numbers do not matter and that it is the quality of political deliberation that counts. The best-known formal deliberative schemes have never grown beyond communities of a few hundred. To revisit a point made earlier in this chapter, critics have questioned the reliance by interest organizations on form emails and Web templates that enable many thousands of citizens to send comments to policy makers (Shulman 2006).

But should we devalue large numbers of individual citizen actions, even if those actions carry very little cost? Web 2.0 environments are significant because they enshrine participation by thousands or even hundreds of thousands in scalable ways. The most powerful Web 2.0 applications—particularly at online social networking sites such as Facebook and Twitter—derive their value from the predictable network effects associated with large numbers of participants. Because they are not tied to a heavily deliberative model, political networks in Facebook and Twitter are able to grow comparatively quickly, and as more people participate, there is more value is in the network. The first signs of this dynamic emerged during the 2004 U.S. presidential primaries when many citizens added simple one-line comments to blog posts. Another good example is the *Daily Kos* blog, which frequently receives thousands of comments on individual blog posts, and there may be several such blog posts in any given day.

Although it has been criticized for its lack of deliberative mechanisms, if judged in terms of the number of participants, the UK prime minister's E-Petitions Web site is one of the must successful e-democracy projects of all time. In its first year, over 29,000 petitions were submitted. Accepted petitions attracted 5.8 million signatures from 3.9 million unique email addresses (UK Prime Minister's Office 2008). E-petitions have quickly become part of the online repertoire of citizen groups in the United Kingdom and have viral characteristics. For example, a search on Facebook reveals a number of groups that have been formed around specific petitions (Facebook Downing Street E-Petitions 2008).

Learning from Web 2.0: Government

Finally, I turn to what Web 2.0 potentially offers government.

More Granularity, Less Risk

Just as Web 2.0 environments lower thresholds for citizens, so they also lower them for government. A major disadvantage of the deliberative forum model is its high-profile, one-size-fits-all approach. Many risk factors present themselves in this environment, but three are particularly salient. First, forum participation rates will be low, which over time deters citizens from entering the forum for fear of standing out as well as attracting negative media coverage. Second, the forum descends into irrelevance or flame wars and becomes heavily censored or an embarrassment. Third, the forum's sponsors lose control of its agenda and either overmoderate it or disown it.

The more granular Web 2.0 environments, where different repertoires of engagement—including postings, comments, ratings, and wiki editing—sit side by side do not eliminate these risks, but they may reduce them. Consider, for example, the UK Foreign Office's group blog (UK Foreign Office 2008). This features entries by the UK's foreign minister, junior ministers, and career civil servants and occasionally guest writers. Under the Labour administration of 2005–2010, two writers—Jim Murphy (minister for Europe) and David Miliband (foreign secretary, who began blogging while a minister at the Department of the Environment)—concentrated on policy and their roles as ministers. This shed light on the civil service and allowed the public to interact with what are usually anonymous officials. The entries rarely received large numbers of comments, although many people read them (Hansard Society 2007). But the advantage of the blog format is that comments and interaction are not pivotal to the experience. Many blogs have no comments, but this seems to be generally accepted as part of the blogging ecosystem and seemingly does not deter their authors. The general sense of an ongoing flow of material in a conversational style also avoids the perception that this is a high-stakes, tightly managed environment. The amount of time and staff resources required to run a group blog are also fewer than those required to run a deliberative forum.

Jack Kingston is Republican congressman for the First District of Georgia. Kingston has long encouraged constituents to upload questions to YouTube and send him the link via his Web site. He then responds via YouTube. Kingston also leaves the comment board open on his videos and streams, and they can be rated by users. Kingston's personal Web site has long had an excellent blog, which has a fully open comment policy (Kingston 2008a, 2008b).

The theme may be extended to cover the presentation of politicians' and officials' online personas. Politicians' blogs and personal YouTube videos tend to avoid formal stump-speech and press-release jargon. The microblogging services such as Twitter, which permits individual messages only 140 characters long, take this informality to extremes. Yet some politicians seem to have adopted it with relish. Stuart Bruce, one-time director of communications in the UK Department of Health said of his minister Alan Johnson: "Using Twitter clearly shows that he's an ordinary guy" (Jones 2007). In Australia, the state of Victoria's Public Service Continuous Improvement Network describes itself as "a whole of government network" that "includes 2601 members across the Victorian Public Sector" (Australian State of Victoria Government 2008). The network's Web site takes the form of an open comment blog with regular postings by staff. Discussion centers on ideas related to public-service delivery and organizational change but is conducted in a highly informal style.

A final point here concerns the shift away from the open Internet toward the more enclosed environments that are characteristic of social-networking sites. These have been criticized for their privacy pitfalls. However, from the perspective of government, the inauthenticity of online discourse has long been a significant hurdle to online consultation. Some of the online mechanisms of Web 2.0—the use of real names, continuous presence, clear archives, the inclusion of photos, and address details—are designed to encourage greater trust. These provide for a richer, though still admittedly thin, representation of a citizen's real-life identity. Interactions among citizens in these enclosed environments are a long way from the free-wheeling libertarian ethos of USENET, which was much admired by the early e-democracy movement. But they reduce the risk of politically embarrassing comments, and they offer public servants a greater sense of control over the terms of engagement.

Less Indegree Centrality, More Outdegree Centrality

Emerging work in e-government (Escher, Margetts, Petricek, and Cox 2006) explores the concept of *nodality*, described by C. Hood and H. Margetts as "the property of being in the middle of an information or social network" (Hood and Margetts 2007, 5). In quantitative social-network analysis, the more common concept is *centrality*, which can be defined and measured in a number of ways. The most basic of these is *degree centrality*, which refers to the number of links a node has to others. Those with more links to others are in a more central position in an information network. However, a further measure of network centrality illustrates the importance of the direction of information flows. *Indegree centrality* refers to the number of incoming links to a node, while *outdegree centrality* refers to the number of outgoing links. Web sites with high indegree centrality are more popular than those with low indegree centrality, while sites with high outdegree centrality are better at situating themselves within a wider network of sites. Both of these measures of centrality (along with others not considered here—see Wasserman and Faust 1994) are relevant for empirically assessing the extent to which a Web site enjoys an influential position.

We can hypothesize that many government departments and agencies will naturally aspire to high indegree centrality because they wish to be authoritative. The evidence that they achieve this is mixed, with reports of low take-up rates for some e-government services, information sites, and e-democracy sites (UK National Audit Office 2007). However, we may assume that it is also in a government department's interest to score highly in terms of outdegree centrality. This gives a stronger impression that policy making is pluralistic and inclusive because the department considers a wide range of organizations and information sources to be worthy of a link. Again, the evidence we have for this surprisingly under-researched phenomenon reveals low incidence of linking to outside organizations in general (Chadwick with May 2001) and much variability across government agencies (Escher et al. 2006).

For government, strengthening linkages with external organizations allows it to take advantage of the huge reservoirs of material created by the informational exuberance of countless citizens. The *Power of Information Report* produced for the UK Cabinet Office takes this as its central theme, arguing for "experimental partnerships between major departments and user generated sites in key policy areas" (Mayo and Steinberg 2007, 5). Similar ideas are at play in the work of companies such as the online market-research body Neighborhood America. There is much scope for distributing government information among these online communities. But more important, government can learn from the many thousands of daily interactions, most of them low threshold, on sites such as Netmums, the popular parenting and health-advice community with 275,000 users by 2007 (Mayo and Steinberg 2007, 4), and TheStudentRoom, which by 2008 had forums containing upward of 8 million messages and an 8,000-page user-generated wiki covering a wide variety of topics related to higher education.

An initial foray into this new area can be seen at Governmentdocs. org, a project of U.S. civil-society organizations including the Sunlight Foundation and the Electronic Frontier Foundation (Governmentdocs 2008). The site provides an online repository "allowing users to browse, search, and review hundreds of thousands of pages acquired through the Freedom of Information Act (FOIA) and other public disclosure, or 'sunshine,' laws." It encourages citizen reviewers to tag, rate, and comment on documents. Comments are stored with each document, and both can be linked to from blogs and other Web sites.

Government agencies cannot compete with self-organizing sites in terms of numbers, but they could harness this information to shape policy decisions and could tap into these communities to conduct consultations based on the terms of interaction that are the norm for these sites rather than what Whitehall or Washington thinks best.

Behavioral Feedback

As discussed above, Web 2.0 environments tend to design in outcomes based on aggregated individual behavior. A record of the interactions in these environments—the simple posting of a one-line message or the tagging of a video—is a valuable commodity in itself. The data can be used to sell advertising space or refine a service. The basic informational value of citizens' feedback on government sites is and should be seen as an important component of e-democracy, even though it does not conform to the deliberative ideal. Although feedback may take the familiar form of completing Web questionnaires and so on, data on the ways in which citizens navigate around sites and the information they perceive as most valuable (measured by the time they spend, the clicks they perform, and the documents they download) can be used to shape the design and delivery of services (Chadwick 2003, 452). Text data from deliberative forums are valuable but labor-intensive to analyze in large quantities. Data from small-scale interactions such as ratings and polls are more amenable to statistical analysis. All of this predates Web 2.0, but Web 2.0 extends the principle through an emphasis on aggregating data based on user behavior rather than substantive textual commentary.

Conclusion

Where does this leave e-democracy research? Although the study of online deliberative forums should continue, it needs to be joined by analyses of the phenomena outlined in this chapter. We need empirical and normative means of deciding on the democratic value of forms of engagement that citizens take seriously as part of their repertoire of political expression. In the remainder of this conclusion, I set out two sets of issues that are important for such a project.

First, there is the question of the distribution of political power. Granular online engagement implies a diffusion of power, although this is a matter for empirical exploration and requires rethinking a range of firmly embedded assumptions about representation and the role played by intermediaries in liberal democratic political practice. As I argued earlier in this chapter, unseating the deliberative assumption does not require that we also unseat the assumption of a politically motivated citizenry. Schudson (1999) has argued for the concept of the monitorial citizen—one aware of the need to keep a watchful eye on politics but content to allow leaders of intermediary institutions (the professional media, parties, voluntary associations) to play the most important role. As Oren Perez's chapter (chapter 16 in this volume) shows, this influential view has found allies in a range of empirical literature on citizens' cognitive limitations, in which the importance of intermediary groups is seen as paramount for democratic stability (Graber 2004).

At first glance, the sociotechnical environments described above seem to form a perfect habitat for the monitorial citizen, particularly in their low threshold incarnations. But in the era of Web 2.0 politics, are intermediaries as important as Schudson suggests? There will always be a need to organize, aggregate, filter, and channel, but Web 2.0 has demonstrated, albeit tentatively so far, that these functions may be distributed among networks as well as concentrated in formalized leaderships. This leads to a range of questions, both normative and empirical: Will the number of intermediaries radically increase, diversify, and become more evenly distributed? Will the aggregate sociotechnical environments created by the informational exuberance of citizens continue to multiply, rendering intermediaries less important overall? If political representatives are expected to immerse themselves in these environments, what does this mean for the legitimacy of decision making processes? How can we balance the well-meaning informational exuberance of political amateurs against the expertise of professional journalists and elected and unelected public servants? Are such categories as meaningful as they once were, now that online coproduction is becoming embedded in political life? In short: who governs, and who ought to govern?

The second set of questions relates to a long-standing problem of e-democratic practice that is now potentially an even greater challenge: how can we provide mechanisms that connect the granular information environments of Web 2.0 citizen activity with real policy making? My aim in this chapter has been to illustrate conceptual points with examples of where this connection is being made, but these constitute just a small part of a much larger universe of political activity, and they are far from perfect. There are several central questions: Can the spirit of public experimentalism lead to sustained patterns of interaction between citizens and governors, or is it likely to supply government with a new set of excuses for prematurely ending initiatives? Can we escape the one-size-fits-all mentality of deliberative forums? To what extent and under what conditions are policy makers likely to engage with the third places of online social networks, and to what extent and under what conditions will citizens welcome policy makers? Do these new environments actually encourage voice and loyalty and discourage exit?

Many other questions could be raised. This chapter has attempted to interpret some of the ways in which recent changes in the online environment present challenges to the dominant assumptions of e-democracy practice and research. But it would be a mistake to suggest that everything Web 2.0 is new: there are important continuities with earlier phases of online politics. At the same time, it would also be a mistake to lose sight of the real shifts, both quantitative and qualitative, that the present era heralds for the evolution of democracy.

Acknowledgments

I am extremely grateful to the following: Vincent Price and Oren Perez for their helpful comments and suggestions on an earlier version of this chapter; Nick Anstead for his careful research assistance; and the Moritz College of Law and the Mershon Center for National Security Studies at The Ohio State University for their financial support. An earlier version of this chapter was published as Andrew Chadwick, "Web 2.0:

New Challenges for the Study of E-Democracy in an Era of Informational Exuberance," *I/S: A Journal of Law and Policy for the Information Society* 5, no. 1 (2009): 9–41.

Notes

1. This section draws in part on Chadwick and Howard (2009).

2. O'Reilly's original principles are "the web as platform"; "harnessing collective intelligence"; "data is the next 'Intel inside'"; "the end of the software release cycle"; "lightweight programming models"; "software above the level of a single device"; and "rich user experiences" (O'Reilly 2005).

3. The three examples were discussed in more detail at a workshop on Engaging with the "Google Generation" at the Oxford Internet Institute, December 19, 2006, in which I participated (see the report by Dutton and Peltu 2006, 15).

References

Anderson, C. 2006. *The Long Tail: How Endless Choice Is Creating Unlimited Demand*. London: Random House.

Australian State of Victoria Government. 2008. Victorian Public Service Continuous Improvement Network Website. Accessed April 14, 2008. http://www.vpscin.org.

Barber, B. 1984. *Strong Democracy: Participatory Politics for a New Age*. Berkeley: University of California Press.

Benkler, Y. 2006. *The Wealth of Networks: How Social Production Transforms Markets and Freedom*. New Haven: Yale University Press.

Bimber, B., and R. Davis. 2003. *Campaigning Online: The Internet in U.S. Elections*. New York: Oxford University Press.

Bimber, B., A. J. Flanagin, and C. Stohl. 2005. "Reconceptualizing Collective Action in the Contemporary Media Environment." *Communication Theory* 15, no. 4:365–388.

Cameron, D. 2007. Webcameron Website. Accessed December 15, 2007. http://www.webcameron.org.uk.

Chadwick, A. 2003. "Bringing E-Democracy Back In: Why It Matters for Future Research on E-Governance." *Social Science Computer Review* 21, no. 4:443–455.

Chadwick, A. 2006. *Internet Politics: States, Citizens, and New Communication Technologies*. New York: Oxford University Press.

Chadwick, A. 2007a. "Digital Network Repertoires and Organizational Hybridity." *Political Communication* 24, no. 3:283–301.

Chadwick, A. 2007b. "Web 2.0 Politics: Three Things We Should Celebrate, and Three Things We Shouldn't." Paper presented at The Social Impact of the

Web: Society, Government and the Internet, RSA special conference, London, May 25.

Chadwick, A. 2011. "Explaining the Failure of an Online Citizen Engagement Initiative: The Role of Internal Institutional Variables." *Journal of Information Technology and Politics* 8, no. 1:21–40.

Chadwick, A., and P. N. Howard. 2009. "Introduction: New Directions in Internet Politics Research." In *The Handbook of Internet Politics*, edited by A. Chadwick and P. N. Howard, 1–9. New York: Routledge.

Chadwick, A., with C. May. 2001. "Interaction between States and Citizens in the Age of the Internet: 'E-Government' in the United States, Britain and the European Union." Paper presented at the American Political Science Association Annual Meeting, San Francisco, August 30.

Chambers, S. 1996. *Reasonable Democracy: Jurgen Habermas and the Politics of Discourse*. Ithaca: Cornell University Press.

Ciborra, C. 2002. *The Labyrinths of Information: Challenging the Wisdom of Systems*. Oxford: Oxford University Press.

Corrado, A. 1996. "Elections in Cyberspace: Prospects and Problems." In *Elections in Cyberspace: Toward a New Era in American Politics*, edited by A. Corrado and C. M. Firestone, 1–31. Washington, DC: Aspen Institute.

Curran, J. 1991. "Mass Media and Democracy: A Reappraisal." In *Mass Media and Society*, edited by J. Curran and M. Gurevitch, 82–117. London: Edward Arnold.

Dahlberg, L. 2001. "The Internet and Democratic Discourse: Exploring the Prospects of Online Deliberative Forums Extending the Public Sphere." *Information Communication and Society* 4, no. 1:615–633.

Dahlgren, P. 2000. "The Internet and the Democratization of Civic Culture." *Political Communication* 17, no. 4:335–340.

Delli Carpini, M., F. L. Cook, and L. Jacobs. 2004. "Public Deliberation, Discursive Participation, and Citizen Engagement: A Review of the Empirical Literature." *Annual Review of Political Science* 7:315–344.

Downs, A. 1957. *An Economic Theory of Democracy*. New York: Harper and Row.

Dryzek, J. S. 1990. *Discursive Democracy: Politics, Policy, and Political Science*. New York: Cambridge University Press.

Dutton, W. H., and M. Peltu. 2007. *Reconfiguring Government-Public Engagements: Enhancing the Communicative Power of Citizens*. Oxford: Oxford Internet Institute.

Escher, T., H. Margetts, V. Petricek, and I. Cox. 2006. "Governing from the Centre? Comparing the Nodality of Digital Governments." Paper presented at the Annual Meeting of the American Political Science Association, Philadelphia, August 31.

Facebook Causes. 2008. Facebook Causes Application. Accessed April 14, 2008. http://www.facebook.com/causes.

Facebook Downing Street E-Petitions. 2008. Facebook Downing Street E-Petitions Search. Accessed April 1, 2011. http://www.facebook.com/search/?q= downing+street+petition&n=-1&k=200000010&init=r.

Fishkin, J. S. 1991. *Democracy and Deliberation: New Directions for Democratic Reform.* New Haven: Yale University Press.

Frank: Your Stories. 2008. Frank: Your Stories Website. Accessed April 14, 2008. http://www.talktofrank.com/article.aspx?id=244.

Friedland, L. A. 2001. "Communication, Community and Democracy: Toward a Theory of the Communicatively Integrated Community." *Communication Research* 28, no. 4:358–391.

Froomkin, A. M. 2003. "Habermas@Discourse.net: Toward a Critical Theory of Cyberspace." *Harvard Law Review* 116, no. 3:751–873.

Froomkin, A. M. 2004. "Technologies for Democracy." In *Democracy Online: The Prospects for Political Renewal Through the Internet*, edited by P. M. Shane, 3–20. New York: Routledge.

Giddens, A. 1999. *Runaway World: How Globalization Is Reshaping Our Lives.* London: Routledge.

Governmentdocs. 2008. Governmentdocs Web site. Accessed April 14, 2008. http://www.governmentdocs.org.

Graber, D. 2004. "Mediated Politics and Citizenship in the Twenty-First Century." *Annual Review of Psychology* 55:545–571.

Granovetter, M. S. 1978. "Threshold Models of Collective Behavior." *American Journal of Sociology* 83, no. 6:1420–1443.

Habermas, Jurgen. 1989. *The Structural Transformation of the Public Sphere.* Cambridge: MIT Press.

Hansard Society. 2007. *Digital Dialogues Second Phase Report August 2006–August 2007.* London: Hansard Society.

Hill, K. A., and J. E. Hughes. 1998. *Cyberpolitics: Citizen Activism in the Age of the Internet.* New York: Rowman and Littlefield.

Hindman, M. 2005. "The Real Lessons of Howard Dean: Reflections on the First Digital Campaign." *Perspectives on Politics* 3, no. 1:121–128.

Hirschman, A. O. 1970. *Exit, Voice, and Loyalty: Responses to Decline in Firms, Organizations, and States.* Cambridge: Harvard University Press.

Hood, C., and H. Margetts. 2007. *The Tools of Government in the Digital Age.* London: Palgrave.

Howard, P. N. 2006. *New Media Campaigns and the Managed Citizen.* Cambridge: Cambridge University Press.

Inglehart, R., and C. Welzel. 2005. *Modernization, Cultural Change and Democracy.* London: Cambridge University Press.

Jones, L. 2007. "Member of the Twittering Classes." *The Guardian,* May 17.

Keen, A. 2007. *The Cult of the Amateur: How Today's Internet Is Killing Our Culture and Assaulting Our Economy*. London: Nicholas Brealey.

Kingston, J. 2008a. Jack Kingston's Blog. Accessed April 14, 2008. http://kingston.house.gov/blog.

Kingston, J. 2008b. Jack Kingston's MailTube. Accessed April 14, 2008. http://www.youtube.com/user/JackKingston.

Macpherson, C. B. 1977. *The Life and Times of Liberal Democracy*. Oxford: Oxford University Press.

Margetts, H. 2006. "E-Government in Britain: A Decade On." *Parliamentary Affairs* 59, no. 2:250–265.

Margetts, H., and P. Dunleavy. 2002. *Cultural Barriers to E-Government*. London: HMSO.

Margolis, M., and D. Resnick. 2000. *Politics as Usual: The Cyberspace "Revolution."* London: Sage.

Mayo, E., and T. Steinberg. 2007. *The Power of Information: An Independent Review*. London: Cabinet Office.

Miller, J. H., and S. E. Page. 2004. "The Standing Ovation Problem." *Complexity* 9, no. 5:8–16.

Morris, D. 1999. *Vote.com: How Big-Money Lobbyists and the Media Are Losing Their Influence, and the Internet Is Giving Power Back to the People*. Los Angeles: Renaissance Books.

New Zealand Police. 2008. Wiki Police Act Consultation Website. Accessed April 1, 2011. http://www.policeact.govt.nz.

Nielsen, J. 1999. *Designing Web Usability: The Practice of Simplicity*. Indianapolis: New Riders.

Oldenburg, R. 1997. *The Great Good Place: Coffee Shops, Bookstores, Bars, Hair Salons, and Other Hangouts at the Heart of a Community*. 2nd ed. New York: Marlowe.

Olson, M. 1965. *The Logic of Collective Action: Public Goods and the Theory of Groups*. Cambridge: Harvard University Press.

O'Reilly, T. 2005. "What Is Web 2.0? Design Patterns and Business Models for the Next Generation of Software." Accessed April 14, 2008. http://oreilly.com/lpt/a/6228.

Papacharissi, Z. 2002. "The Virtual Sphere: The Net as a Public Sphere." *New Media and Society* 4, no. 1:5–23.

Papacharissi, Z. 2009. "The Virtual Sphere 2.0: The Internet, the Public Sphere and Beyond." In *The Handbook of Internet Politics*, edited by A. Chadwick and P. N. Howard, 230–245. New York: Routledge.

Pateman, C. 1970. *Participation and Democratic Theory*. Cambridge: Cambridge University Press.

Price, V. 2009. "Citizens Deliberating Online: Theory and Some Evidence." In *Online Deliberation: Design, Research, and Practice*, edited by T. Davies and S. P. Gangadharan, 37–58. Chicago: University of Chicago Press.

Price, V., and J. N. Cappella. 2002. "Online Deliberation and Its Influence: The Electronic Dialogue Project in Campaign 2000." *IT and Society* 1, no. 1:303–329.

Prior, M. 2007. *Post-Broadcast Democracy: How Media Choice Increases Inequality in Political Involvement and Polarizes Elections*. New York: Cambridge University Press.

Schudson, M. 1999. *The Good Citizen: A History of American Civic Life*. Cambridge: Harvard University Press.

Shane, P. M., ed. 2004. *Democracy Online: The Prospects for Political Renewal through the Internet*. New York: Routledge.

Shulman, S. 2006. "Whither Deliberation? Mass E-Mail Campaigns and U.S. Regulatory Rulemaking." *Journal of E-Government* 3, no. 3:41–64.

Stanyer, J. 2009. "Web 2.0 and the Transformation of News and Journalism." In *The Handbook of Internet Politics*, edited by A. Chadwick and P. N. Howard, 201–213. New York: Routledge.

Stromer-Galley, J. 2000. "Online Interaction and Why Candidates Avoid It." *Journal of Communication* 50, no. 4:111–132.

Tambini, D. 1999. "New Media and Democracy: The Civic Networking Movement." *New Media and Society* 1, no. 3:305–329.

TheyWorkForYou. 2008. TheyWorkForYou Web site. Accessed April 14, 2008. http://www.theyworkforyou.com.

UK Foreign Office. 2008. FCO Bloggers: Global Conversations. Accessed April 1, 2011. http://blogs.fco.gov.uk/roller.

UK National Audit Office. 2007. *Government on the Internet: Progress in Delivering Information and Services Online*. London: HMSO.

UK National Health Service. 2008. Our NHS, Our Future: Have Your Say Website. Accessed April 1, 2011. http://www.ournhs.nhs.uk.

UK Prime Minister's Office. 2008. E-Petitions Website. Accessed April 14, 2008. http://petitions.number10.gov.uk.

Vedel, T. 2006. "The Idea of Electronic Democracy: Origins, Visions and Questions." *Parliamentary Affairs* 59, no. 2:226–235.

Wasserman, S., and K. Faust. 1994. *Social Network Analysis: Methods and Applications*. Cambridge: Cambridge University Press.

Weber, S. 2004. *The Success of Open Source*. Cambridge: Harvard University Press.

Weinberger, D. 2007. *Everything Is Miscellaneous: The Power of the New Digital Disorder*. New York: Holt.

Wilhelm, A. G. 2000. *Democracy in the Digital Age: Challenges to Political Life in Cyberspace*. New York: Routledge.

Williams, C. B., and J. Gulati. 2007. "Social Networks in Political Campaigns: Facebook and the 2006 Midterm Elections." Paper presented at the Annual Meeting of the American Political Science Association, Chicago, August 30.

Wright, S. 2006. "Government-run Online Discussion Fora: Moderation, Censorship and the Shadow of Control." *British Journal of Politics and International Relations* 8, no. 4:550–568.

Young, I. M. 2000. *Inclusion and Democracy*. New York: Oxford University Press.

4

Online Consultations in Local Government: What Works, When, and Why?

Joachim Åström and Åke Grönlund

Many people are concerned that local democracy is not what it once was or should be. Declining interest in traditional forms of participation, manifested by distrusting citizens and declining social capital, afflict government at all levels. However, local government is one of the cornerstones on which subsequent participation develops. It has been argued that the vitality of broader democratic practices is contingent on the strength of local democracy and that local arenas are critical for learning the skills necessary for democratic practice. Another argument maintains that the issues demanding the most pressing political responses are everyday concerns that are the responsibility of local officials (Phillips 1996; Loughlin 2001). For these reasons, local politics have a key role to play in "reconnecting democracy." Although local democracies across the world differ in many ways—there are variations in local autonomy, state traditions, and political and governance institutions—similar complaints about democratic deficits are taken as starting points for reform in many places, with remarkable similarities across quite different systems (Daemen and Schaap 2000). In an attempt to regain ground, we witness the emergence of local participatory approaches far and wide. *Participation* has become a key political buzzword, and online consultations are the latest fashion or perhaps hope.

The degree of attention being given to expanding citizens´ role in the policy process points to the need to consider what effects these processes might have on policy decisions and the number of people who participate in them. Indeed, a growing body of literature pays attention to the *failure* of participatory governance (cf. Jessop 2000). Many online consultation experiments have been conducted and evaluated recently, resulting in diverse insights on a variety of situations. However, these studies usually do not enhance the understanding of what may work, when, and why. To answer these types of questions, research must move from descriptions of isolated projects toward comparative evaluation (Demo-net 2008b). The aim of this chapter is to take one step in that direction. A case-survey method is used to aggregate the collective judgments of researchers regarding the effect of online consultations on local demo-cratic practices. We also seek to identify some of the contextual and procedural attributes that relate to success. The literature is replete with comments about the success and failure of consultations, but few if any comparative studies investigate results in a systematic way. On the basis of fifty-eight European and U.S. case studies, this chapter explores three specific claims.

The first, made by Archon Fung (2003), argues that the success of online consultations and their consequences for democratic governance depend on "the details of their institutional construction." In Fung's view, the methods by which participants are selected, the timing of con-sultations within the policy cycle, and the mode of communication adopted set a decisive context for participant interaction. The second claim, presented by Ricardo Blaug (2002), is that democracy is an ongoing struggle rather than one standard recipe of institutional designs. Successful consultations can occur only if deliberative changes are made in the structures of political power. The third claim, made by Ann Macin-tosh and Angus Whyte (2006), is that the reported successes or failures of consultations depend on the focus and quality of research perspectives, not on design choices or power struggles.

The chapter begins with a discussion of the advantages and limitations of the case-survey method and then presents the theoretical framework, including a first glance at the effects of online consultations through the lenses of our three claims. Logistic regressions are thereafter used to analyze the extent to which various contextual factors affect the prob-abilities of success. Finally, the conclusion draws together various lines of analysis and discusses empirical evidence that supports optimism or pessimism concerning the democratic potential of online consultations.

The Case-Survey Method

Local government is the online consultation laboratory. In most coun-tries, experimentation, if there is any, takes place primarily at this level. Europe's many government-initiated e-democracy projects have tended to have a clear local government orientation (Demo-net 2008a). The United States has had comparatively fewer government-led trials at the local level. This focus on local-level experimentation offers researchers two potential advantages—propinquity and numerosity (John 2006). *Propinquity* denotes the closeness of local political and social actors to each other and to the social processes that affect localities. Propinquity makes the effects of new processes more readily observable to those who govern localities and to researchers than to those at higher levels of governance. *Numerosity* refers to the many local governments within nations, which are advantageous for a number of reasons, particularly when it comes to generalizing results. The advantages of numerosity and propinquity are seen in two kinds of research design—one statistical and inferential and the other qualitative and interpretive. However, a case survey is well suited to draw on both of these approaches by combining large numbers with qualitative dimensions.

The case-survey method (also referred to as *meta analysis* or *structured content analysis of cases*) applies a structured investigation protocol to several case studies to generate cumulative findings. This is particularly useful in a situation where the existing research is mainly case studies and where it is difficult to do structured primary research across cases. The strength of the method lies in its capacity to integrate the research findings of diverse studies. It is a flexible method in which many different types of case studies can be brought together to observe patterns among them. Since these studies are typically information rich, involving many factors and qualitative data, the case survey can also benefit from addressing other factors than can typically be included in traditional surveys. Nonetheless, the quality of the data in any case survey is only as good as the quality of the case studies from which the data come. Also, since the original case studies are produced by different authors and for different purposes, they tend to leave gaps in the data. Yet another limitation is that the case survey is unlikely to produce results on which strict statistical generalization may be based because there is no way to determine the degree to which the existing case studies are representative. Generalization is thus impeded because the selection of individual case studies is beyond the control of the secondary analytical investigator but instead is limited to studies that were done by others (Lucas 1974; Larsson 1993; Yin and Heald 1975).

Basically, there are two ideal strategies for choosing cases for comparison. The first is to select cases that are as similar as possible (in terms of their contextual characteristics) and to analyze the differences in outcomes, isolating the factors that explain these differences. The second is to select cases as different as possible from one another and then analyze their commonalities—that is, the common explanatory variables of otherwise diverse cases that explain similar outcomes. We have used the second approach—a most-different strategy—to test the three claims outlined above. For this reason, we included cases from various countries in which different methods were used both for the actual implementation and for subsequent research on them. We also selected cases that were conducted on different scales—some very small and some quite large. This should increase the probability that the relationships and patterns we find are significant and not due to local specificities.

The study originally aimed to include fifty European and fifty U.S. case studies. These were found through traditional channels, such as online libraries, conference proceedings, Google Scholar, and other Web search tools. We also surveyed networks of scholars in the e-participation field, particularly those organized in the Demo-net network. Somewhat surprisingly, we found far fewer case studies in the United States than in Europe. Considering the overwhelming community of Internet users in the United States, one might expect plenty of incentive for local governments to provide new ways of participating online (Peart and Diaz 2007). However, a possible reason for the lack of initiatives in the United States is the society-centered approach to understanding politics whereby state institutions are played down and debate is more about the distribution and exercise of power among different groups (Loughlin 2001, 6).

Making sure that apples are not compared to oranges, we included only cases characterized by some online activity, proximity in time, and the existence of comprehensive research evaluation. Because some cases stretch over several years, we could not impose a strict time limit, but we focused on cases after the year 2000. Our final selection included forty-eight European and ten U.S. cases. Each case was coded by one of two PhD students or by both. To ensure consistent coding at the outset, we conducted an intercoder reliability test in which both researchers initially read and coded the same subset of case studies independently. The process was repeated until the reliability test showed greater than 80 percent agreement, a level of reliability regarded as satisfactory in the literature (Larsson 1993).

A number of theoretical criteria have been advanced to determine whether consultations work. Often these include characteristics such as representativeness, early involvement, transparency, independence, and influence (Rowe and Frewer 2004). Since new forms of democracy may affect the decision making structure as a whole, there is also a discussion on what new roles citizens, politicians, and civil servants might develop. Indeed, in the introduction of this book, Peter M. Shane argues that "an analysis of the e-democracy phenomenon requires us to understand online consultation as part of the way governments more generally are repositioning themselves in the information flows of the communities they serve." From such a broader perspective, online consultations might be expected to produce their effects in a variety of ways, some of them indirect or hidden. Indeed, the most important effects might be the least accessible to observation, thereby presenting empirically minded scientists with a neat paradox.

Taking empirical work as a point of departure, as we do in this chapter, it is not surprising that a somewhat narrower perspective emerges. We focus on *participation* (whether the process attracts a large number of citizens), *deliberation* (whether the process provides open dialog and a space to understand and frame issues), and *policy influence* (whether the process has the ability to influence policy and decision making). A majority of the case studies we have examined evaluate these three criteria to varying degrees and therefore are suitable for our purposes. Even so, whether a consultation's participation, deliberation, and policy influence were high or low is not easy to determine. Such a judgment often requires knowledge of local circumstances. Therefore, we have coded explicit qualitative judgments of primary researchers, not our own reading of facts and numbers. On the basis of evaluations of primary researchers, our three criteria were measured using a scale of low, medium, high, and "not measured." The last category was important since the case coder had to be given the alternative of answering that a case study did not contain an explicit qualitative judgment to answer the question. In the analysis below, the scales have been recoded into dichotomous variables (0 = low, 1 = medium/high).

A few case examples can illustrate what has been coded as high and low. When it comes to the level of participation, Hilton argues that "amongst all of the e-democracy initiatives that Bristol has piloted, e-petitions have attracted the highest level of support amongst elected Members and citizens. More than 12,000 people have participated. The exit poll that participants complete after using the e-petitioner indicates a wide spread from all parts of the city and that a significant proportion, 20 percent, have never signed a petition before" (Hilton 2006, 422). Hence, this case has been coded as *high* on participation. When it comes to the quality of deliberation, the study by Märker, Hagedorn, Trenel, and Gordon (2002, 14) was regarded as *high* given the authors' conclusion that "the good quality of the resulting discussion is evidenced by both the relatively high degree of cross-references among the contributions—'interactive communication' is not at all typical in Internet discussion forums—and the constructive dialog between the opponents of the development project and the city's planning department." Finally, one of the conclusions by Jankowski and van Os (2004, 1) in their evaluation was that the government officials responsible for the consultation "were primarily interested in the organizational aspects of the event as opposed to the content of the discussions and the contribution of these discussions to policy formation." Consequently, this case was coded *low* on policy impact.

A Framework for Understanding Online Consultations

Those who work in the field of public engagement and online consultations describe their efforts and motivations in similar terms: they are seeking to enhance participation, create deliberative democracy, and make government more accountable. However, these similarities should not obscure the rich and multidimensional variations that are evident in their endeavors. The mechanisms that are used to encourage participation are diverse, and they include the traditional (such as public hearings), the novel (such as online referenda), those mechanisms that seek responses from participants acting alone (such as e-surveys), and those involving deliberation among participants acting in groups (such as online deliberations) (Rowe and Frewer 2004). Considering this variation in mechanisms, how can we understand the effectiveness of online consultations?

First Claim: Institutional Design Is the Key

For some analysts, the success of consultations and their consequences for democratic governance depend on "the details of their institutional construction" (Fung 2003). Because designs set the context and conditions of participant interaction, we need to understand which designs work best in relation to what goals and why. Many scholars find that information and communication technology (ICT) improvements in our communication opportunities could be a vital force in fostering a closer relationship between citizens and their governments. The unprecedented interactivity offered by new information and communication technologies has the potential to expand the scope of government consultations with citizens and other key stakeholders during policy making. This means that e-participatory techniques could provide one ingredient for making participatory policy making more effective.

In this study, we look at four design choices and their consequences. The first concerns how participants are selected for the online consultation. The most common mechanism is voluntary self-selection. Forty percent of the consultations included in our case survey are open to everyone who wishes wish to attend. This is sometimes complemented with mechanisms for selecting individuals who occupy positions in local government, such as politicians and expert administrators. The Danish Nordpol.dk (Jensen 2003) and the Bollnäs Dialogue in Sweden (Åström 2004) represent two cases where certain politicians were hand-picked to initiate debates that led to discussions with citizens. Other groups have strategically recruited participants from subgroups that are less likely to engage or have tried to enhance representativeness through random selection. The city of Bristol in the United Kingdom, for instance, used a market-research company to recruit members to their e-panel in combination with street recruitment, newspaper advertisements, online advertisements, email newsletters, and widely distributed promotional material (Hayward 2005). When comparing the failure rates of e-consultations based on voluntary self-selection to those that employed other methods of recruitment, we observe a slightly higher failure rate among the former, especially in the quantity of participation (47 percent compared to 35 percent) and the quality of deliberation (47 percent compared to 34) (table 4.1).

A second design choice that is discussed when researchers are considering where e-consultations are most appropriate in the policy process is a framework for differentiating stages in the policy life cycle. These stages are more or less in line with Dunn's five-stage model (1994), which includes agenda setting, policy analysis, policy decision, implementation, and evaluation. According to the OECD (2001), public consultation and active participation should be undertaken as early in the policy process as possible to allow a greater range of policy solutions to emerge. At this stage, it is argued, the process is most open to suggestions from citizens and is also characterized by a significant degree of public deliberation—which many new ICT tools are designed to facilitate. In line with this recommendation, the results of this study show that the majority of case studies describe e-consultations that take place at the agenda-setting stage. These consultations are sometimes targeted to collect ideas for the development of a strategic vision of a city, as in the DEMOS debate in Hamburg 2003 (Albrecht 2006). In other cases, they are related to different topics, such as business conditions, health issues, or education, and citizens are supposed to identify issues of interest to them (Jensen

Table 4.1
A summary of online consultation failures (percentage)

		Participation failure (%)	Deliberation failure (%)	Effect on policy failure (%)
	All cases	41 (*n* = 42)	39 (*n* = 46)	49 (*n* = 45)
Participant selection	*Voluntary*	47 (*n* = 19)	47 (*n* = 17)	50 (*n* = 20)
	Strategic/ random	35 (*n* = 23)	34 (*n* = 29)	48 (*n* = 25)
Stage in the policy cycle	Early *stage*	57 (*n* = 31)	39 (*n* = 33)	58 (*n* = 31)
	Analysis/ decision stage	9 (*n* = 11)	38 (*n* = 33)	29 (*n* = 14)
Deliberative mode	*Express preferences*	47 (*n* = 19)	57 (*n* = 21)	63 (*n* = 22)
	Deliberative/ aggregative	35 (*n* = 23)	24 (*n* = 25)	35 (*n* = 23)
Media Mix	*Online only*	57 (*n* = 21)	29 (*n* = 24)	65 (*n* = 23)
	Online and offline	24 (*n* = 21)	50 (*n* = 22)	32 (*n* = 22)
Democratic intentions	*Mixed*	50 (*n* = 24)	54 (*n* = 26)	56 (*n* = 27)
	Strong	28 (*n* = 18)	22 (*n* = 18)	29 (*n* = 18)
Timing of evaluation	*Early* project	40 (*n* = 20)	35 (*n* = 23)	71 (*n* = 21)
	Mature project	35 (*n* = 20)	44 (*n* = 23)	27 (*n* = 22)
Research involvement	*Independent research*	50 (*n* = 20)	44 (*n* = 25)	59 (*n* = 27)
	Involved research	33 (*n* = 21)	35 (*n* = 20)	29 (*n* = 17)
Content analysis	*Not used*	42 (*n* = 24)	46 (*n* = 28)	40 (*n* = 30)
	Used	39 (*n* = 18)	28 (*n* = 18)	67 (*n* = 15)

2003). At first glance, the results indicate that initiatives relating to the policy-analysis or decision stages are more effective in attracting participants and influencing policy than those dedicated to agenda setting. For instance, only 9 percent of the studies conducted on consultations at the policy-analysis or decision stage refer to the small number of participants, whereas 57 percent of the studies at other stages do.

A third institutional design choice concerns the mode of communication in a consultation. Many e-consultations are designed around the physical limitations of traditional technologies. Public meetings occupy a fixed time and place, limiting the attendance of citizens and their opportunities to speak. The use of consultation documents is limited by the amount of paper handling. These constraints are not the same for apparently equivalent online processes. People need not to be together in the same place or at the same time. Instead, people are encouraged to express their preferences online (Morrison and Newman 2001). Other consultations are more ambitious, attempting to translate the views or preferences of participants into a collective view or decision by the use of deliberative mechanisms (Fung 2006). Research results suggest that this does not necessarily increase the number of participants in the consultation, but it does seem to increase considerably the quality of deliberation and the probability of policy impact.

Finally, many commentators on institutional design for online consultations highlight the importance of ensuring the integration of online and traditional methods for citizen engagement in policy making. Our results show that an approach based on multiple channels is more likely to succeed in engaging citizens than reliance on a single medium is.

In summary, we find support for the claim that institutional designs affect the outcome of e-consultations and that different design factors influence different goals. When it comes to the goal of increasing the volume of participation, the most important design decisions seem to be which stage in the policy cycle to choose and whether to integrate online and offline mechanisms. Cases where the consultation takes place in the policy analysis or decision making stage and where online and offline methods have been integrated show many fewer failures. When it comes to the quality of deliberation, on the other hand, the mode of communication matters the most. Deliberation is considered more effective when people are expected to express their preferences and also are encouraged to deliberate on their preferences. The figures also indicate that deliberation may actually function better online than offline since integrated efforts have resulted in more reports of low-quality deliberations. The effects on policy, finally, are positively related to the analysis and decision making stage in the policy cycle, a deliberative mode of communication, and an integration of online and offline methods.

Second Claim: Democratic Intention Is the Key

A second strand in this debate about online consultations suggests that democracy building is an ongoing process of struggle and contestation rather than the adoption of a standard recipe of institutional designs.

According to Ricardo Blaug (2002), democracy is an uneasy marriage between two contrasting projects with different locations in the structure of power. When viewed from the periphery, democracy is a method of challenging existing institutions. When viewed from the center, democracy appears as a set of institutions to be valued, protected, and improved. As Stephen Coleman argues in the final chapter in this book, the very notion of the democratic citizen is culturally constructed and open to a number of competing interpretations, each of which is politically framed. For the prospects of online consultations, this has two important implications. First, where online consultations are based on the compatibility of these projects, they may be seriously misplaced. The initiators must accept divergence between their own hopes and the actual outcome. Only by doing so might they become involved in a process of self-creation that reflects the norms of critical democratic theory. Second, where democratic initiatives promote a particular understanding of democracy and a particular set of organizational assumptions, they risk failure. Let us dwell on these points a little.

According to Blaug, citizen participation is about power and its exercise by different social actors in the spaces created for the interaction between citizens and local authorities. However, the control of the structure and processes for consultations is usually in the hands of governmental institutions, which may become barriers for effective involvement of citizens. First, the attractiveness of consultations for elites does not always reside in its potential to shift sovereignty from politicians and professionals to deliberating citizens. Although the ethos of responsiveness may put citizens at the center by inviting their input, there is still often a desire to keep them away from the administrative work and actual decision making centers. A second and related problem is that consultation initiatives often are the carrier of a particular organizational paradigm—hierarchism (Blaug 2000). They embody the assumption that effectiveness is something that can be attained only through leadership, bureaucracy, and centralized control. Attempts to communicate democracy to citizens therefore entail the simulation of organizational methods that, although obvious for the sender, may be quite different from those of the receiver:

Speaker and receiver understand their democratic activities very differently, and the provision of assistance thus amounts to requiring receivers to change their practices to fit those of the speaker. Democracy, assumed to be one object, is given to receivers in such a way as to make them obey the organizational assumptions of those located nearer the centre of institutionalized political power. This is a profound breakdown in communication, one that may indicate why such initiatives so often fail to produce more democracy. (Blaug 2002, 109)

In this view, the democratic intentions of the sender are the key to understand the degree to which online consultations manage to attract participants, foster deliberation, and influence policy. Some reports in this study highlight the difficulty of knowing whether the participatory initiative is genuine or if "deadlines and rigid targets set by central government cause councils to pay lip service to participation initiatives" (Karakaya Polat 2005). Democratic intentions are nonetheless often put forward as a key factor affecting the success or failure of consultations. In relation to Milwaukee's neighborhood strategic planning process, Ghose (2005, 70) argues that "a number of disempowering traits compromise the potential for citizen participation." Despite the fact that the city council was repeatedly encouraged to participate in the online hearing in the city of Esslingen, this project failed to motivate any politician at all to contribute (Märker et al. 2002). In their study of a Norwegian online forum, Rose and Sæbø (2005) argue that the biggest problem was conflicting interests between politicians and citizens. In a majority of the case studies we have examined, there are similar complaints of political unwillingness, limited government commitment, and conflicting interests. But there are also reports describing the opposite. The overall conclusion about the debate of Nordpol.dk, for instance, was that politicians participated and "showed great responsiveness" to the citizens" postings, which strongly contributed to "democratic success" (Jensen 2003).

Table 4.1 indicates that democratic intentions affect the outcomes of online consultations. In cases of strong intentions, there are substantially fewer reports of a low volume of participants, a low quality of deliberation, or a lack of policy effects. This contrasts with cases in which intentions are mixed. When it comes to the volume of participation, the difference between cases with strong democratic intentions and those with mixed intentions is 22 percent, while corresponding numbers in relation to the quality of deliberation and policy effects are 32 and 17 percent, respectively. Cross tabulations suggest that the effects of institutional design and democratic intentions are interrelated. In general, they seem to reinforce each other and may therefore be seen as complementary analytical frameworks that in combination help to explain why online consultations succeed or fail. When it comes to the volume of participation, for instance, strong intentions in combination with a strategic or random selection of participants, a consultation at the policy analysis or decision making stage, a deliberative mode of communication, or an integration of online and offline methods all have a failure rate below 22 percent. When intentions are mixed and participant selection is voluntary, the consultation is conducted in another phase of the policy cycle, the communicative mode is about expressing preferences, or only online methods are used, the failure rate is between 56 and 64 percent.

Third Claim: The Role of Research Is the Key

A third claim to be considered about online consultations is that too little empirical independent scientific evidence demonstrates the use, success, and failure of e-consultation in practice. Instead, there is much anecdotal evidence, usually drawn from the most successful cases and developed from limited analytical frameworks. According to Macintosh and Whyte (2006), the study of e-consultations is still in its infancy and must be developed if we are even to begin to determine whether e-consultations are renewing local democracy. This is a challenging thought. Perhaps the reported success and failure of e-consultations is not primarily the result of institutional designs and power struggles on the ground but on the quality of research.

A strength of the case-survey method lies in the opportunity to test how research quality affects outcome variables. The reviewer can introduce case-quality variables and characterize them according to methodological and other concerns. In this way, a priori research assumptions can be turned into empirical questions and testable hypotheses (Lucas 1974; Larsson 1993; Yin and Heald 1975). We had the opportunity to test whether the practical involvement of researchers affected e-consultation outcomes. In the past, the overwhelming rationale of the social sciences has been based on the study of well-established phenomena, with social scientists observing from a distance and then telling policy makers where they went wrong. The temptation for researchers examining the use of electronic forums is to jump into the struggle over defining what they are really for and to help forge new uses. Although knowledge about these issues is still very limited, researchers can certainly play a helpful role in the development and improvement of policy making processes. The results of their interventions could even yield positive benefits for democracy. The problem is, however, that research may become somewhat tainted and less critical (Olsson and Åström 2006). Researchers that are practically involved in consultations may have a vested interest in supporting them as a means of strengthening the role of new media in a changing political landscape.

In our study, 44 percent of the researchers we considered had been practically involved in the cases they evaluated. They had been members of the project teams that planned the consultation, developed software, and moderated debates. In table 4.1, it is clear that researchers who were involved in the subject of their studies had a tendency to rate consultation effects higher than those who were independent. Whether this was a consequence of vested interests, more successful consultations, or both is a trickier question. On the one hand, the results show that consultations are more often designed successfully when researchers were involved, deliberative mechanisms were used, consultations occurred at the analysis or decision stage, and there was integration of online and offline methods. On the other hand, the results show that independent researchers are somewhat more critical in their judgments, even after controlling for institutional designs.

It is possible to make an empirical examination of the relationship between consultation effects and the various methodologies and data-collection procedures used by researchers to generate their observations. According to Lipsey (2000), evaluators' findings about effects are often influenced as much by the evaluator's methodological choices as by the actual effectiveness of the intervention. Therefore, when it comes to evaluating the quality of deliberation, for instance, it might be good to know whether a content analysis of online discussions has been carried out. As table 4.1 indicates, in a majority of the studies this was not the case. Deliberation also was more often judged to have failed when no content analysis was conducted. Another potentially interesting variable is the timing of the study. Although early evaluations may check that a project is doing what it planned to do and identify improvements along the way, a more mature evaluation is often in a better position to reveal the project's effects. The results in table 4.1 indicate that this is especially true in the assessment of impact on policy. Both these patterns thus provide an important finding about the online consultation literature: perhaps contrary to what one might expect, higher-quality evaluations are associated with more successful cases of consultation. Whether this is because results are tainted by research approaches or because one of the by-products of successful innovation is the ability to stand up to more stringent research efforts, the fact remains that consultation results are more positive when research quality is higher.

Predicting the Odds for Success

Our first inspection of the data reveals that the failure rate is high in relation to all three criteria—institutional design, democratic intent, and research availability. Furthermore, the case studies show clear similarities, despite the fact that they took place in different contexts. When comparing the figures in relation to design choices, democratic intentions, and research, systematic patterns are evident. In fact, all three claims are somehow supported by the data. Taken together, this encourages us to find out which factors—when controlling for all other variables—are most important and how the odds for online consultations might possibly change. Since we are dealing with a relatively limited number of cases, the use of more advanced statistical techniques is somewhat precarious. But with the caveat that the results should be interpreted with caution, we report results from a series of logistic regression tests.

In table 4.2, the regression coefficients are reported with participation (0 = low, 1 = high) as a dependent variable. The crucial value here is Exp (B), which is an indicator of the change in odds. From these values, we find that stage in the policy life cycle is by far the strongest predictor among the variables. In probability terms, we can say that the chances for success in participation, when controlling for other variables, are almost nine times higher when implementing the consultation in the analysis or decision making stage. The result is statistically significant at the 0.1 level. The ways that participants are selected and the mix of

Table 4.2
Model estimates and model summary: Odds for a high number of participants

Model estimates	Coefficient	Significance	Exp(B)
Constant	−1.007	.130	.365
Participant selection	.901	.222	2.462
Stage in policy cycle	2.171	.064	8.768
Offline and online mix	1.071	.150	2.918
Model summary	Value	Significance	
Chi-square	10.646	.014	
Cox-Snell R-square	.224		
Nagelkerke R-square	.302		

online and offline methods changed the odds in the way we would expect, even though these results were not statistically significant.

Taking the analysis one step further, we examined the predicted probabilities for an online consultation to reach a successful rate of participation in different stages in the policy cycle when the other variables were held at their mean (by using the prtab function in STATA). This analysis showed that online consultations in early stages of a policy process had a probability of 51 percent to attract a high number of participants and that online consultations in later stages showed a probability of 90 percent. This interesting result probably reflects the exploratory or experimental nature of many agenda-setting initiatives. As Jankowski and Van Os (2004) state in relation to online deliberations in the city of Hoogeveen, government officials were more interested in the organizational aspects of the event than the content of the discussions and their contribution to policy formation. According to public-choice theory, one obstacle to citizen participation under these circumstances is the phenomenon of *rational ignorance* (Rydin and Pennington 2000; Downs 1957). The point is that collecting and processing information takes time, effort, and resources. It has a cost. Therefore, actors have to ensure that it is worthwhile expending these resources in terms of the likely benefits. In cases where the outcome of individual participation in the policy process is uncertain, it is simply not worthwhile taking part. This should not be taken as evidence that people are apathetic or content with the status quo. On the contrary, when political issues and stakes are made clear, the probabilities that citizens will engage become much higher.

Although the debate on online deliberation has veered between exuberant optimism and ominous pessimism, Wright and Street (2007) have argued in favor of a third position. According to them, the form and character of Web sites and the political processes they make possible cannot be assumed. Instead, the designs of Web sites shape whether the result will be deliberative. The results in table 4.3 support their argument. Modes of communication turn out to be the most important variable, increasing by nine times the chances for deliberations to work in moving from consultations that are about expressing preferences to those adopting a deliberative mechanism. We also find that participant selection is a strong predictor, making the odds for deliberation five times higher in strategic or random selection than in voluntary self-selection. Taken together, the predicted probabilities of these two design variables lend fairly strong support to the assumption that deliberation is possible

Table 4.3
Model estimates and model summary: Odds for high-quality deliberation

Model estimates	Coefficient	Significance	Exp(B)
Constant	1.071	.440	2.919
Participant selection	1.673	.065	5.329
Modes of communication	2.142	.017	8.519
Democratic intentions	1.730	.053	5.640
Content analysis research	2.034	.038	7.643
Model summary	Value	Significance	
Chi-square	15.106	.004	
Cox-Snell R-square	.280		
Nagelkerke R-square	.379		

when circumstances are right. A consultation that is designed for self-selected participants and aimed at expressing preferences has a predicted probability of 18 percent to become deliberative. When there is a strategic or random selection and some sort of deliberative mechanism involved, the probability rises to 91 percent.

Regardless of design, democratic intentions are not easily hidden in open forums. The strong idealization of the conditions for open and fair deliberation offer a critical standard by which it is possible to assess the democratic quality of a particular interaction and analyze the many ways in which real instances of deliberation are distorted by power. When arguments offered by some participants go unanswered by others, when information that is required to understand the force of a claim is absent, or when some participants are unwilling to give weight some of the arguments in the debate, then the process becomes less deliberative (Fishkin 1995). That democratic intentions are important in this context is confirmed by table 4.3, which suggests that deliberations are about six times more likely to work when democratic intentions are strong compared to when they are mixed. As mentioned before, one reason for this is the widespread belief that formal decision making related to policy issues should continue to be the prerogative of city council representatives. This is, however, accompanied by reasons referring to the character of online interaction. In contrast to mainstream media, online space usually allows users to contribute or even control content and to initiate contact with other users. The ethos is often one of open-mindedness and

Table 4.4
Model estimates and model summary: Odds for a high impact on policy

Model estimates	Coefficient	Significance	Exp(B)
Constant	−6.184	.003	.002
Participant selection	2.792	.031	16.318
Modes of communication	2.908	.019	18.312
Online and offline mix	2.899	.015	18.154
Timing of study	3.854	.003	47.182
Model summary	Value	Significance	
Chi-square	27.743	.000	
Cox-Snell R-square	.475		
Nagelkerke R-square	.634		

knowledge sharing rather than certainty and party loyalty. On the other hand, the political parties and politicians who are using online space to reconnect with the public may appear to be professionally implicated in the very culture that many online participants seek to transcend (Coleman 2005). Making online deliberation work, therefore, seems to require the strong commitment, openness to change, and self-creation that Blaug is asking for.

In the literature on consultation exercises, it is often argued that their importance for policy is hard to measure or explain (Demo-net 2008b). This is both supported and challenged by our analysis. On the one hand, many studies in the field are engaged with the methodological aspects of participatory initiatives in early stages of experimentation and are therefore less likely to see any effects on policy. Evaluations of more mature projects are forty-seven times more likely than early evaluations to show an effect on policy. On the other hand, when controlling for the timing of evaluations, clear patterns tend to emerge. Three design variables stand out as showing strong predictability, and they are all significant at the 0.05 level—modes of communication, participant selection, and media mix.

Citizen participation is a complex process that goes well beyond providing an official forum for people to voice community concerns. In one way or the other, it must be related to existing political institutions and decision making centers if it is to make a difference. Judging from the data, deliberative mechanisms are crucial in this regard, increasing the chances of affecting policy by eighteen times. Put another way, when controlling for other variables, the predicted probability of affecting policy increases from 22 to 84 percent when turning from consultations that are about expressing preferences to those that adopt more sophisticated mechanisms for informing policy makers. Considering that consultations to strengthen local democracy may be rendered worthless if consultees feel that their views have been ignored, simple "have your say" forums could thus be called into question—especially because local governments struggle to convince people that participating in consultation exercises is worth their time.

Furthermore, political equality is an important concern. Those who already are in some way excluded or less powerful in the political process cannot be further disadvantaged by online consultation. Some have argued that the solution to this classic dilemma of modern democracies is to not consult citizens at all, since this gives voice to previously privileged groups (Gilljam 2003). Others have argued that consultation initiatives involve a different kind of citizen who is more representative of the general population than commonly occurs in other forms of political engagement, such as activism or protesting. Consultations therefore hold the potential of redressing some of the long-running biases in political participation (John 2009). However, the sense of unease seems to continue. Many believe there is a link between inequality in participation and the type of outputs and outcomes consultations produce, probably making them thorny to integrate in formal decision making processes. The results of this study suggest that this problem is often exacerbated by the design of consultations. It is sixteen times less likely that a consultation will affect policy when the participants are self-selected compared to when there has been a selective recruitment or random selection. Actively asking people to get involved might not only influence citizens' decision to participate but also make the exercise more legitimate. A similar pattern is found in relation to the mixing of online and offline methods, which might be helpful in engaging different target audiences and in gaining wider acceptance.

Design is of key importance here. The most substantial difference is found when considering the contingent effect of modes of communication and participant selection, when holding the other variables at their mean (by using the prtab function in STATA). The predicted probability for a consultation to affect policy is 6 percent when it is designed for self-selected citizens to express preferences. When citizens are selected strategically or at random and there is some aggregative or deliberative mechanism, the predicted probability to affect policy is no less than 95 percent.

If this represents a strong support for Fung, where does it leave Blaug? Although not showing statistical significance on its own, democratic intentions are related to designs in that those manifesting strong democratic intentions were more likely than others to have used strategic or random selection, a deliberative mode of communication, and a mix of online and offline methods. There are thus good reasons to believe that designs that offer citizens most control and genuinely affect policy tend to be chosen by those who have the most democratic commitment.

Conclusions

Applying a case-survey approach to online consultations yields some insights into the factors that might allow participatory governance to succeed. Although the results show high overall failure rates, they add an optimistic note to the study of online consultations in clearly indicating that it is possible to succeed and that success is associated with specific design criteria and to democratic intentions. The flip side of this is that without adherence to these factors, online consultations will not be of much use.

Considering that experimentation is taking place in very different contexts, the common traits we have identified are surprisingly consistent. Perhaps differences between countries are not as large as is commonly supposed. Local democracies in most countries share one foundation: they are representative democracies. A key challenge is to find a new balance between participatory and representative forms of democracy. Democratic intentions and commitment to the process are tremendously important to success, not least when it comes to accomplishing open and fair deliberation. In contrast to some earlier suggestions in the literature, this study suggests that consultations have the best odds of success in the analysis or decisional stage of the policy process when issues and stakes are made clear. Although there are exceptions to this (such as the successful uses of e-petitioning systems), many agenda-setting initiatives fail to attract the interest of citizens. Modes of communication seem to be the most important variable for making deliberations work and affecting policy. Simple "have your say forums" have very low odds of success. Furthermore, the chance of affecting policy increases when there is a mix of online and offline methods and a random or strategic selection of participants. In the face of concerns about political equality, such factors tend to influence various groups to participate and also make the exercise more legitimate.

The conclusions from this research offer relatively good news for online consultations. However, if local governments are to reverse the trend of civic disengagement, they need to gain a fuller understanding of online consultation designs and the underlying organizational assumptions that are mediating communications between citizens and policy makers. Although research can be of assistance in such a process, the outcomes are mainly in the hands of political actors.

References

Albrecht, S. 2006. "Whose Voice Is Heard in Online Deliberation? A Study of Participation and Representation in Political Debates on the Internet." *Information Communication and Society* 9, no. 1:62–82.

Åström, J. 2004. *Mot en digital demokrati? Teknik, politik och institutionell förändring.* Örebro Studies in Political Science 9. Örebro: Örebro University.

Blaug, R. 2000. "Blind Hierarchism and Radical Organizational Forms." *New Political Science* 22, no. 3:379–396.

Blaug, R. 2002. "Engineering Democracy." *Political Studies* 50:102–116.

Coleman, S. 2005. "Blogs and the New Politics of Listening." *Political Quarterly* 76, no. 2:272–280.

Daemen, H. H. F. M., and L. Schaap, eds. 2000. Citizen and City: Developments in Fifteen Local Democracies. Delft: Eburon.

Demo-net. 2008a. "Analytical Report on eParticipation Research from an Administration and Political Perspective: A Review on Research about eParticipation in the Institutional Domain." Deliverable D14.1.

Demo-net. 2008b. "eParticipation Evaluation and Impact." Deliverable 13.3.

Downs, A. 1957. *An Economic Theory of Democracy.* New York: Harper.

Dunn, W. N. 1994. *Public Policy Analysis: An Introduction.* 2nd ed. Englewood Cliffs: Prentice-Hall.

Fishkin, J. 1995. *The Voice of the People.* New Haven: Yale University Press.

Fung, A. 2003. "Recipes for Public Spheres: Eight Institutional Design Choices and Their Consequences." *Journal of Political Philosophy* 11, no. 3:338–367.

Fung, A. 2006. "Varieties of Participation in Complex Governance." Special issue. *Public Administration Review* (December):66–75.

Ghose, R. 2005. "The Complexities of Citizen Participation through Collaborative Governance." *Space and Polity* 9, no. 1:61–75.

Gilljam, M. 2003. "Deltagardemokrati med förhinder." In *Demokratins mekanismer,* edited by M. Gilljam and J. Hermansson, 185–211. Malmö: Liber.

Hayward, C. 2005. *Introducing e-Enabled Citizens' Panels.* http://www.bristol .gov.uk/ccm/cms-service/download/asset/?asset_id=33463229.

Hilton, Stephen. 2006. "Developing Local e-Democracy in Bristol." *New Information Perspectives* 58, no. 5:416–428.

Jankowski, N. W., and R. Van Os. 2004. "Internet-Based Political Discourse: A Case Study of Electronic Democracy in Hoogeveen." In *Democracy Online,* edited by P. Shane, 181–194. New York: Routledge.

Jensen, J. L. 2003. "Virtual Democratic Dialogue? Bringing Together Citizens and Politicians." *Information Polity* 8:29–47.

Jessop, B. 2000. "Governance Failure." In *The New Politics of British Local Governance,* edited by G. Stoker, 11–32. Basingstoke: Macmillan.

John, P. 2006. "Methodologies and Research Methods in Urban Political Science." In *The Comparative Study of Local Government and Politics: Overview and Synthesis,* edited by H. Baldersheim and H. Wollman, 67–82. Opladen: Budrich.

John, P. 2009. "Can Citizen Governance Redress the Representative Bias of Political Participation?" *Public Administration Review* (March–April): 494–503.

Karakaya Polat, R. 2005. "The Internet and Democratic Local Governance: The Context of Britain." *International Information and Library Review* 37:87–97.

Larsson, R. 1993. "Case Survey Methodology: Quantitative Analysis of Patterns across Case Studies." *Academy of Management Journal* 36, no. 6:1515–1546.

Lipsey, M. W. 2000. "Meta-Analysis and the Learning Curve in Evaluation Practice." *American Journal of Evaluation* 21:207–212.

Loughlin, J. 2001. *Subnational Democracy in the European Union: Challenges and Opportunities.* Oxford: Oxford University Press.

Lucas, W. 1974. *The Case Survey Method of Aggregating Case Experience.* Santa Monica: RAND.

Macintosh, A., and A. Whyte. 2006. "Evaluating How eParticipation Changes Local Democracy." Paper presented at the eGovernment Workshop '06, Brunel University, West London, September 11.

Märker, O., H. Hagedorn, M. Trenél, and T. Gordon. 2002. "Internet-Based Citizen Participation in the City of Esslingen. Relevance: Moderation Software." In *Who Plans Europe's Future?,* edited by M. Schrenk, 39–45. Vienna: Selbstverlag des Instituts für EDV-gestützte Methoden in Architektur und Raumplanung der Technischen Universität Wien.

Morrison, J., and R. Newman. 2001. "On-line Citizenship: Consultation and Participation in New Labour's Britain and Beyond." *International Review of Law Computers and Technology* 15, no. 2:171–194.

OECD. 2001. "Citizens as Partners: OECD Handbook on Information, Consultation and Public Participation in Policy-making." Paris: OECD.

Olsson, J., and J. Åström, eds. 2006. *Democratic eGovernance: Approaches and Research Directions.* Stockholm: Almqvist & Wiksell.

Peart, M. N., and J. R. Diaz. 2007. *Comparative Project on Local e-Democracy Initiatives in Europe and North America*. Geneva: University of Geneva.

Phillips, A. 1996. "Why Does Local Democracy Matter?" In *Local Democracy and Local Government*, edited by L. Pratchett and D. Wilson, 20–37. London: MacMillan Press.

Rose, J., and Ø. Sæbø. 2005. "Democracy Squared: Designing On-line Political Communities to Accommodate Conflicting Interests." *Scandinavian Journal of Information Systems* 17, no. 2:1–26.

Rowe, G., and L. J. Frewer. 2004. "Evaluating Public-Participation Exercises: A Research Agenda." *Science, Technology and Human Values* 29, no. 4:512–556.

Rydin, Y., and M. Pennington. 2000. "Public Participation and Local Environmental Planning: The Collective Action Problem and the Potential of Social Capital." *Local Environment* 5, no. 2:153–169.

Wright, S., and J. Street. 2007. "Democracy, Deliberation and Design: The Case of Online Discussion Forums." *New Media and Society* 9, no. 5:849–869.

Yin, R. K., and K. A. Heald. 1975. "Using the Case Survey Method to Analyze Policy Studies." *Administrative Science Quarterly* 20, no. 3:371–381.

5

Neighborhood Information Systems as Intermediaries in Democratic Communities

Steven J. Balla and Sungsoo Hwang

Organizations in dozens of municipalities around the United States have developed and implemented neighborhood information systems. Neighborhood information systems bring together and disseminate, via the Internet, regularly updated statistics on births, crime, educational performance, and other vital community conditions (National Neighborhood Indicators Partnership n.d. a; Treuhaft et al. 2007, 26). The basic idea is that these data, when combined with maps and other analytical tools, provide individuals and organizations with a means of monitoring trends and outcomes in geographic areas of interest (Kingsley 1998, 5–11). Neighborhood information systems, in other words, are technology innovations that aim to enhance the participation of diverse sets of local stakeholders—government agencies, civic organizations, small businesses, and individual citizens—in the protection and revitalization of their communities.

The adoption and diffusion of neighborhood information systems is a potentially promising development for democratic political practice at the local level. It has been argued that such practices are best realized when localities become "democratic information communities" (Shane 2008, 1). The notion of a democratic information community is an ideal. It is a normative aspiration that localities can hold for themselves as they promote an "inclusive flow of information designed to support collective problem-solving, the coordination of community activity, public accountability, and connectedness within the community" (Shane 2008, 1).

Inclusive flows of information are best achieved in communities that have, among other key attributes, diverse sets of intermediary institutions.[1] Such intermediaries are devoted to the creation, organization, dissemination, and analysis of information for, broadly speaking, democratic purposes. For example, nonprofit organizations such as universities and civil society institutions can be effective intermediaries in helping communities incorporate information, in inclusive and constructive ways, into collaborative decision making (Shane 2008, 11).

This chapter explores the potential for neighborhood information systems—which are usually administered and supported by nonprofit organizations, such as universities, United Way affiliates, and independent civic institutions (Kingsley and Pettit 2004, 2)—to operate as intermediaries in democratic information communities. The chapter addresses two specific questions. First, under what conditions, both nationally and at the community level, have neighborhood information systems successfully been established and maintained? Second, to what extent have neighborhood information systems promoted inclusive flows of information and served as catalysts for stakeholder mobilization and collaborative practices?

In addressing these issues, the chapter draws heavily on the results of interviews with nineteen individuals who have been leaders in the development and operation of neighborhood information systems. These interviews addressed issues concerning both the creation of neighborhood information systems and the effects of neighborhood information systems on information flows and stakeholder practices.

Taken together, the interviews highlight both the accomplishments and limitations of neighborhood information systems in serving as democratic intermediary institutions. A combination of entrepreneurial activity at the community level and assistance from national organizations is typically required to bring neighborhood information systems into existence. In places where such resources have been marshaled, neighborhood information systems have disseminated information about economic and social conditions in their communities. Neighborhood information systems have also conducted analyses of the information they have assembled, both in response to the needs of community stakeholders and as a means of actively shaping perceptions of local conditions and priorities. In a small number of notable projects, neighborhood information systems have succeeded in mobilizing historically inactive constituencies and facilitating discourses that are, broadly speaking, democratic in their orientation. Recognizing the promise of such projects and outcomes, leaders of neighborhood information systems are increasingly taking steps to catalyze inclusive political practices in ways that are demonstrable and systematic in their orientation.

Neighborhood Information Systems and the Democratization of Data

The idea of using economic and social indicators to set priorities and evaluate public programs has been around for decades (Kingsley 1998, 1). It was not until the early 1990s, however, that municipalities began to develop full-fledged neighborhood information systems (Hwang 2006, 78). These developments were in part the result of advances in computing power and geographic information systems (GIS) software, which have made it increasingly easy for even nonspecialists to produce professional-quality maps and community statistics (Kingsley 1998, 2–5). In addition, municipal agencies have automated and made publicly available many of their records, greatly enhancing the ease with which interested parties inside and outside government can monitor trends and policy outcomes.

An important institutional development occurred in 1995, when representatives of nonprofit organizations from six communities joined with the Urban Institute, a research center located in Washington, D.C., to form the National Neighborhood Indicators Partnership (Kingsley and Pettit 2004, 1, 4). All of these organizations were operating successful neighborhood information systems and were interested in sharing their experiences and encouraging other municipalities to adopt neighborhood information systems of their own. To facilitate these ends, the Urban Institute agreed to perform a variety of functions, including producing guidebooks, holding conferences, and conducting studies of experiences common to numerous communities.

Over the years, the National Neighborhood Indicators Partnership has expanded to the point where there are now members in thirty-one municipalities (National Neighborhood Indicators Partnership n.d. b). Most of these neighborhood information systems are administered by nonprofit organizations (Kingsley and Pettit 2004, 2). For example, the Advanced Policy Institute at the University of California–Los Angeles maintains several neighborhood information systems. One of these platforms is Living Independently in Los Angeles, a GIS-based, interactive information resource database for people with disabilities living in Los Angeles (Toy and Richman 2004).

Although local governments are important collaborators in National Neighborhood Indicators Partnership projects, they are most often not the central decision making organizations or users of these "virtual data warehouses" (Kingsley and Pettit 2004, 2). In one partnership, for instance, Camden Churches Organized for People, an interdenominational group, joined with the Center for Social and Community Development at Rutgers University to explore the negative consequences of the city's large number of abandoned and vacant housing units (Urban Institute 2009). This exploration revealed that crime rates were substantially higher in areas with elevated vacancy rates. Through the effective use of block-level maps, the groups were able to mobilize community residents, attract media attention, and ultimately secure state funding to help seal up and demolish hundreds of empty units.

Although there are neighborhood information systems in operation throughout the country, research suggests that the National Neighborhood Indicators Partnership constitutes some of the "strongest" (Treuhaft et al. 2007, 26) and "most evident" (Hwang 2006, 79) projects that have yet been developed. Their strength and visibility derive in part from the multidimensional process through which National Neighborhood Indicators Partnership projects are selected (National Neighborhood Indicators Partnership n.d. c). Partner institutions must operate sophisticated neighborhood information systems, but they also must take steps to ensure that their systems are of practical use to community leaders and policy makers, especially those working in distressed neighborhoods. In addition to these substantive restrictions, the National Neighborhood Indicators Partnership selects only one project per municipality and limits expansion to no more than four new projects per year.

In sum, neighborhood information systems are technology innovations that pursue, through the "democratization of data," the enhancement of economic and social conditions in needy communities (Sawicki and Craig 1996, 512). Such revitalizations are driven not by governments acting in isolation but by collaborations involving broad arrays of stakeholders—public officials, nonprofit intermediaries, small businesses, and individual citizens who live and work in affected neighborhoods. Institutionally, the National Neighborhood Indicators Partnership brings together many of the most advanced neighborhood information systems in an ongoing forum for conducting research and disseminating information about programs and best practices. The centrality of the National Neighborhood Indicators Partnership in the development and diffusion of neighborhood information systems raises a pair of organizational and operational questions. What local activities and national resources have facilitated the creation and maintenance of neighborhood information systems deemed strong enough to join the National Neighborhood

Indicators Partnership? To what extent have National Neighborhood Indicators Partnership projects altered information flows and transformed stakeholder practices in communities where they have been established?

National Neighborhood Indicators Partnership Projects

The communities where founding projects of the National Neighborhood Indicators Partnership are located are Atlanta, Boston, Cleveland, Denver, Oakland, and Providence.[2] In 1998, Washington, D.C., became the seventh municipality to have a project, when the DC Agenda Project joined the National Neighborhood Indicators Partnership (Kingsley 1998, 19).[3] Table 5.1 provides a list of the communities where National Neighborhood Indicators Partnership projects are currently in operation, as well as three demographic attributes of these cities (as of 2000).

As the list demonstrates, neighborhood information systems have been established in diverse locations around the country—New England, the West Coast, the Midwest, and the southern tier of states. The National Neighborhood Indicators Partnership has a presence in twenty-four states, including the District of Columbia. In addition to this geographic diversity, project communities vary significantly in the size of their populations. The National Neighborhood Indicators Partnership has projects in New York, Los Angeles, and Chicago, which are the three largest cities in the United States. At the other extreme, seven municipalities, including founding member Providence, have fewer than 200,000 residents. Camden, the smallest project community, counted 79,904 residents in the 2000 Census.

Camden is also distinctive in that it has the smallest proportion of white residents, 16.84 percent, of any community where there is a National Neighborhood Indicators Partnership project. On the one hand, about half of the project municipalities do not have majority white populations. On the other hand, in a number of communities one third or fewer residents are black, Asian, or Hispanic or from other nonwhite backgrounds. The population of Des Moines, for example, is more than 80 percent white.

Des Moines and Providence offer an illustrative contrast when it comes to the density of their populations. Both communities have populations approaching 200,000 residents. Providence, however, has nearly four times as many residents per square mile as Des Moines. National Neighborhood Indicators Partnership projects have been established

Table 5.1
National Neighborhood Indicators Partnership communities, demographic attributes as of 2000

Municipality	State	Population size	Percent white	Population density
New York	New York	8,008,278	44.66	26,403.8
Los Angeles	California	3,694,820	46.93	7,876.4
Chicago	Illinois	2,896,016	41.97	12,752.2
Philadelphia	Pennsylvania	1,517,550	45.02	11,232.8
Dallas	Texas	1,188,580	50.83	3,470.3
Indianapolis	Indiana	781,870	69.09	2,162.8
Columbus	Ohio	711,470	67.93	3,383.1
Baltimore	Maryland	651,154	31.63	8,058.8
Memphis	Tennessee	650,100	34.41	2,327.6
Milwaukee	Wisconsin	596,974	49.98	6,212.0
Boston	Massachusetts	589,141	54.48	12,172.3
Washington	District of Columbia	572,059	30.78	9,316.9
Seattle	Washington	563,374	70.09	6,714.8
Denver	Colorado	554,636	65.30	3,615.6
Nashville	Tennessee	545,524	65.91	1,152.6
New Orleans	Louisiana	484,674	28.05	2,683.7
Cleveland	Ohio	478,403	41.49	6,165.0
Atlanta	Georgia	416,474	33.22	3,162.3
Sacramento	California	407,018	48.29	4,187.4
Oakland	California	399,484	31.29	7,120.9
Minneapolis	Minnesota	382,618	65.13	6,969.4
Miami	Florida	362,470	66.62	10,153.2
Pittsburgh	Pennsylvania	334,563	67.63	6,017.3
Louisville	Kentucky	256,231	62.94	4,126.1
Des Moines	Iowa	198,682	82.29	2,621.1
Grand Rapids	Michigan	197,800	67.30	4,435.0
Providence	Rhode Island	173,618	54.53	9,384.8
Chattanooga	Tennessee	155,554	59.71	1,150.5
New Haven	Connecticut	123,626	43.46	6,541.1
Hartford	Connecticut	121,578	27.72	7,027.6
Camden	New Jersey	79,904	16.84	9,080.0

Note: Population density is measured as the number of residents per square mile.
Source: U.S. Census Bureau, *County and City Data Book: 2000* (2000), accessed April 9, 2009, http://www.census.gov/prod/www/abs/ccdb.html.

both in densely populated municipalities (such as Boston and Philadelphia) and in cities where residents are spread out to a much greater extent (such as Nashville and Chattanooga).

The bottom line is that the adoption of neighborhood information systems has occurred in communities that vary along a number of dimensions. This diffusion raises the following question: what circumstances have led to the development of National Neighborhood Indicators Partnership projects in this particular set of municipalities?[4]

The Activities of Nonprofit Entrepreneurs

To enhance understanding of the creation, maintenance, and operation of neighborhood information systems, interviews were conducted with individuals who have been leaders in the National Neighborhood Indicators Partnership. These individuals were identified through a list of project contacts provided on the Web site of the National Neighborhood Indicators Partnership (National Neighborhood Indicators Partnership n.d. b).[5] The interviews were semistructured in format. The aims of the interviews were to bring to light the considerations, both national and local, that led to the formation of the National Neighborhood Indicators Partnership and the subsequent processes through which neighborhood information systems have spread across municipalities.

Overall, the interviews point to the importance of the availability of resources for overcoming barriers—financial, institutional, and otherwise—to the adoption of neighborhood information systems. Four of the six founding members of the National Neighborhood Indicators Partnership—Boston, Cleveland, Denver, and Oakland—had previously been participants in the Rockefeller Foundation's Community Planning and Action Project. This project, which operated from 1987 until 1992, drew attention to the problem of persistent poverty, which is the proliferation of inner-city neighborhoods "characterized by a growing separation from the rest of society, its norms, and especially its resources" (Rockefeller Foundation 1987, 43).[6]

These locations were chosen because, in the words of the Rockefeller Foundation, "each city offers outstanding institutions or leaders and in some cases the promise of collaboration with local foundations or other financial supporters" (Rockefeller Foundation 1987, 44). These communities, in other words, possessed internal resources for overcoming obstacles to identifying and characterizing the persistent poor and taking actions to address the root causes of hard-core poverty. In its first year of operation, for example, the Boston project demonstrated that under-employment can be as problematic for the persistent poor as not having a job at all. In Denver, the project targeted two of the city's poorest neighborhoods for a particularly intensive effort, working closely with school officials to develop strategies for improving elementary education in these areas (Rockefeller Foundation 1989).

By the early 1990s, the Community Planning and Action Project had begun to facilitate the "regular exchange of information and experiences" among participants (Rockefeller Foundation 1991, 38). Project members took part in a national campaign to assist low-income families in applying for the Earned Income Tax Credit, a rebate that was at the time worth as much as $1,192 per household. The Rockefeller Foundation also brought members together with participants in municipal poverty projects that were simultaneously being sponsored by the Ford Foundation and the Annie E. Casey Foundation (Rockefeller Foundation 1991).

These external activities were fundamental in laying the groundwork for the formation of the National Neighborhood Indicators Partnership. When interviewed, founding members without fail mentioned their prior involvement in the persistent-poverty project.[7] This involvement was described as being crucial in two respects. First, contacts discussed how the Community Planning and Action Project emphasized the combining of data analysis with an orientation toward action at the neighborhood level. Second, contacts highlighted the fact that a staff member at the Rockefeller Foundation who was central to the Community Planning and Action Project eventually took a position at the Urban Institute. The Urban Institute therefore emerged as a natural institutional setting for the continued advancement of these municipalities' efforts in understanding and remedying persistent poverty.

Since its inception, one of the main goals of the National Neighborhood Indicators Partnership has been to facilitate the development and integration of neighborhood information systems beyond the founding communities. The Urban Institute, in tandem with partner organizations such as the Annie E. Casey Foundation, has fostered this diffusion in a number of ways. In some instances, staff members have approached already existing neighborhood information systems about becoming members of the National Neighborhood Indicators Partnership. In 2002, the Greater New Orleans Community Data Center launched a Web site that presents and makes available for analysis demographic information at the neighborhood level. After this launch, the Data Center was contacted about joining the National Neighborhood Indicators Partnership.[8] The Center for Urban and Regional Affairs, in Minneapolis–St. Paul, is another example of an already operating neighborhood information system that was invited into the National Neighborhood Indicators Partnership.[9]

In other communities, the National Neighborhood Indicators Partnership has played an active role in bringing about the creation of neighborhood information systems. In 1998, the Annie E. Casey Foundation began to explore, along with the Association of Baltimore Area Grantmakers, the possibility of developing a neighborhood information system in Baltimore. This exploration kicked off an extensive planning process that involved government officials, neighborhood associations, and a variety of nonprofit organizations. The end result was the formation, in 2000, of the Baltimore Neighborhood Indicators Alliance, which has since operated as the city's member in the National Neighborhood Indicators Partnership (Baltimore Neighborhood Indicators Alliance n.d.; National Neighborhood Indicators Partnership n.d. d).

Similarly, in 1999, the Annie E. Casey Foundation awarded a planning grant that led to the development of CAMConnect, Camden's National Neighborhood Indicators Partnership project (National Neighborhood Indicators Partnership n.d. e). The foundation then provided ongoing assistance to CAMConnect through 2006, after which it sought to help the project become financially self-sufficient. In this regard, CAMConnect's operations are currently funded by member dues, fee-for-service arrangements with data clients, and the sponsorship of the Cooper Health System's Department of Family Medicine.[10]

The diffusion of neighborhood information systems has taken place not only as a byproduct of the activities of national organizations but also through the learning and emulation that have occurred between National Neighborhood Indicators Partnership members and prospective municipalities. In 2000, the City of Columbus, the United Way of Central Ohio, and the John Glenn Institute for Public Service and Public Policy at Ohio State University founded Community Research Partners (National Neighborhood Indicators Partnership n.d. g,). This neighborhood information system was explicitly modeled on the Northeast Ohio Community and Neighborhood Data for Organizing project, a data indicators initiative operated by the Center on Urban Poverty and Community Development, the Cleveland member of the National Neighborhood Indicators Partnership (National Neighborhood Indicators Partnership n.d. f).[11] This emulation ultimately led Community Research

Partners to approach the Urban Institute about being considered for selection into the National Neighborhood Indicators Partnership.[12]

Other neighborhood information systems have also sought out membership in the National Neighborhood Indicators Partnership. The Advanced Policy Institute, for example, approached the National Neighborhood Indicators Partnership about being designated as the Los Angeles member, a request that was granted in 2002.[13] Such designation is valuable to neighborhood information systems for a variety of reasons. Many contacts pointed to the sharing of expertise and experiences across neighborhood information systems as a principal benefit of involvement in the National Neighborhood Indicators Partnership. One community might advise another on, say, what company it hired to redesign its Web site or how it was able to quickly procure government data on foreclosures.[14] Contacts also highlighted the local credibility that being a member of a national partnership confers on their neighborhood information systems.[15] One indicator of this benefit is the fact that a number of municipalities advertise their involvement in the National Neighborhood Indicators Partnership on their home page or in another prominent location on their Web site (e.g., Ochs Center for Metropolitan Studies n.d.; SAVI Community Information System n.d.).

In sum, the interviews and documentary materials demonstrate that there is no single pathway to the development of neighborhood information systems. The founding members of the National Neighborhood Indicators Partnership were among the first municipal projects to bring systematic data analysis to bear on the problem of persistent poverty. Since the formation of the National Neighborhood Indicators Partnership, additional neighborhood information systems have become members through entrepreneurial activities at both the national and local levels. The community innovation and the sponsorship of organizations such as the Urban Institute and Annie E. Casey Foundation have fostered the diffusion of expertise, experience, and other critical resources. Such resources have made it possible for projects to overcome barriers to adoption that are naturally present even in communities broadly conducive to the development of neighborhood information systems.

Data Provision, Analysis, and Neighborhood Information Systems

In communities where the National Neighborhood Indicators Partnership has established projects, how have neighborhood information systems affected information flows? The interviews indicate that neighborhood information systems have, on the whole, succeeded in democ-ratizing data. A fundamental attribute of neighborhood information systems has been the creation of Web-based repositories of information on social and economic conditions.

These repositories typically consist of two main components.[16] The first component is the presentation of information extracted from orga-nizations such as the U.S. Census Bureau and state and local government agencies. For example, in September 2008, the Greater New Orleans Community Data Center disseminated information, collected by the Louisiana Department of Education, about city schools that were in operation at the start of the 2008–2009 academic year (Greater New Orleans Community Data Center 2009).

The second information provision component is oriented toward enabling interested parties to interact with community data in ways of their own choosing. A common instrument in this regard is the use of maps. MetroBoston DataCommon allows users to "create a customized map of the region, a city and town, Boston neighborhood, or one Census Tract" (MetroBoston DataCommon n.d.). Similarly, as figure 5.1 illus-trates, Analyze Dallas makes it possible to generate information, both in numeric and graphical form, tailored to community attributes and geo-graphic levels of interest.

In addition to maintaining data warehouses, National Neighborhood Indicators Partnership projects routinely carry out analyses of the infor-mation they have assembled and disseminated. In some instances, these analyses address topics about which neighborhood information systems have been approached by clients or stakeholders. In Minneapolis–St. Paul, communities submit queries to the Center for Urban and Regional Affairs, which then decides which projects to carry out.[17] For proposals that are selected, the Center for Urban and Regional Affairs hires gradu-ate students in relevant fields at the University of Minnesota to work closely with stakeholders. In one example, a landscape architect student conducted research for a town in central Minnesota that was interested in redesigning its downtown neighborhood.

In other instances, neighborhood information systems carry out analy-ses of their own choosing. One aim of these analyses is to provide infor-mation about the general state of community affairs, as well as circumstances in particular areas of public concern. In Denver, *The Piton Perspective*, a newsletter that is published periodically, addresses poverty issues from a variety of vantage points, including homeownership, pre-school options, and prisoner reentry (Piton Foundation n.d.). In a similar

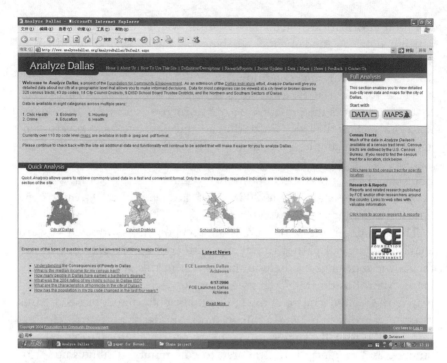

Figure 5.1
Interactive data at *Analyze Dallas*. *Source:* http://www.analyzedallas.org/
AnalyzeDallas/Default.aspx (screen shot taken by the authors October 10, 2008).

vein, *Communities Count,* a report issued by Seattle's Assessment, Policy
Development, and Evaluation Unit, is oriented toward influencing perceptions of community conditions and priorities.[18] For example, in 2008,
the report drew attention to the interconnectedness of affordable housing,
transportation accessibility, commuting times, and the quality of life of
Seattle's poorest residents (Communities Count Partnership n.d.).

Who are the consumers of the information that National Neighborhood Indicators Partnership projects disseminate and analyze? Contacts
mentioned two sets of users with by far the greatest frequency. The first
set consists of nonprofit organizations. These groups are often drawn to
neighborhood information systems when working on grant applications.[19] In this regard, neighborhood information systems serve as
resources for data that are useful in supporting requests for funding.

The second main set of consumers is employees of federal, state, and
local government agencies.[20] These officials range from policy makers in

school districts to social workers, public health nurses, and other street-level bureaucrats (Lipsky 1983). In many instances, these officials turn to neighborhood information systems as sources for data that were originally assembled by the agencies in which they work. Given that National Neighborhood Indicators Partnership projects bring together data about health, transportation, and many other areas of public concern, it is not unusual for agency employees to use this information in analyses that cut across lines of jurisdiction.[21]

Beyond nonprofit organizations and government agencies, contacts highlighted journalists, researchers, small businesses, and the general public as regular users of the resources of neighborhood information systems.[22] Across these disparate stakeholders, the interviews suggest that, even where neighborhood information projects have not directly altered municipal agendas, National Neighborhood Indicators Partnerships projects have made it easier for community interests to pursue their chosen courses of action.[23] But have neighborhood information systems facilitated the mobilization of new stakeholders or the flourishing of discursive democratic practices?

Stakeholder Mobilization and Collaboration

When asked about issues of transformational stakeholder activities, contacts typically responded that such questions are "difficult to answer."[24] Many leaders in the National Neighborhood Indicators Partnership intuit, on the basis of their experiences, that neighborhood information systems have had various effects on community decision making. These effects include increasing stakeholder awareness of the need for and use of data in local governance.[25] For example, neighborhood information systems have influenced the way in which grant making is approached by both applicants and funding organizations. In Washington, D.C., the Washington Area Women's Foundation provides grants to female-headed households. Data and analysis generated by NeighborhoodInfo DC has informed the needs and projects the foundation has focused on in recent years.[26]

In a more general sense, as one contact put it, "In my opinion, the 15 years that we have been providing this information free to neighborhood residents and community based organizations here in Northeast Ohio has changed their level of influence on local government and led to important collaborations."[27] Consistent with this viewpoint, the interviews draw attention to a handful of examples of stakeholder mobilization and collaborative practices that have emerged as a result of changes in information flows.

In Boston, the process of establishing community indicators occurs through a collaborative, discursive series of events.[28] The Boston Foundation assembles hundreds of stakeholders from corporations, grassroots organizations, government agencies, and neighborhood associations. These stakeholders are divided into groups that bring together individuals from diverse backgrounds and sectors. For example, university leaders might be paired with people working in early childhood education, or the regional director of the Department of Housing and Urban Development might be part of a convening on civic health. These groups are then called on to identify broad goals, such as healthy children, for the community to pursue collectively.

Out of these discussions, The Boston Foundation produces a draft framework for its indicators project. This draft is widely circulated for comments and suggestions. In the end, The Boston Foundation settles on a comprehensive array of measures that covers traditional areas of concern (such as housing) as well as arts and culture. These indicators then serve as the basis for The Boston Foundation's archival and analytical work over a two-year period, after which another round of collaboration and subsequent updating occurs.

In communities where sophisticated indicators projects have been established, transformational stakeholder practices have on occasion followed. On the south side of Dallas, which is relatively impoverished, there can be distances of up to five miles between grocery stores. Furthermore, these stores tend to be small markets rather than major chains. As a result, residents have less access to fresh produce, meats, dairy, and healthy foods than their relatively wealthy counterparts on the north side of the city. In response to the circulation of information about these disparities, a group of women (including a pastor's wife and the leader of a neighborhood association) who are not part of the traditional power structure in Dallas took a series of steps, such as trying to arrange meetings with grocery chain representatives, to change this state of affairs. One dividend occurred when Walmart agreed to build a store in an area that straddles the north and south sides of Dallas.[29]

In Cleveland, the Center on Urban Poverty and Community Development has been influential in assisting local activists and organizations to take steps, often through novel collaborations, to revitalize neighborhoods suffering from shrinking populations, poor job markets, and the abandonment of housing units. In 2005, Neighborhood Progress Incorporated, a nonprofit intermediary, launched a project designed to stimulate recovery in the housing markets of six distressed neighborhoods (Cowan 2007, 3). This project, the Strategic Investment Initiative, targets neighborhoods that are relatively well positioned for revitalization, in that these communities possess assets such as parks, cultural institutions, and land parcels suitable for anchor projects of "sufficient scale to catalyze additional private development" (Treuhaft and Kingsley 2008, 18; Neighborhood Progress n.d.).

Throughout the course of the Strategic Investment Initiative, data and maps generated by the Center on Urban Poverty and Community Development have fundamentally shaped the project's direction. Neighborhood Progress Incorporated has relied on the Center on Urban Poverty and Community Development to assemble information about properties being targeted for anchor project acquisition in each of the six neighborhoods (Case Western Reserve University Center on Urban Poverty and Community Development n.d.). Specifically, the Center on Urban Poverty and Community Development has produced lists of blighted buildings and information about properties where water usage is particularly low, the latter of which serves as an indicator of residences and businesses that "have become vacant or are at risk of abandonment" (ibid.).

One community that has been targeted by the Strategic Investment Initiative is Slavic Village, a neighborhood that was originally settled by Polish and Czech immigrants in the mid-nineteenth century (Treuhaft and Kingsley 2008, 19). In recent years, Slavic Village's housing market has fallen into disarray, and at one point, the neighborhood had more foreclosure filings than any other community in the country (Christie 2007). The cornerstone of Slavic Village's revitalization is the acquisition of properties and the improvement of existing homes in areas adjacent to a new, market-rate residential development and multi-use linear park (Treuhaft and Kingsley 2008, 21).

Not only has the Strategic Investment Initiative affected Slavic Village and its redevelopment, but it has also catalyzed stakeholder activism that is beginning to transform practices of community collaboration. More than thirty residents have formed the Vacant Property Task Force, an organization that fights against mortgage fraud, property flipping, and other housing-market abuses (Treuhaft and Kingsley 2008, 21). In an innovative collaboration, the Vacant Property Task Force worked closely with the Center on Urban Poverty and Community Development to conceive of new ways of identifying individuals who misuse financing, foreclosure, and other housing laws and regulations. As a result of this combination of data provided by a neighborhood information system and action taken by community residents, the county prosecutor initiated legal proceedings against a pair of property flippers whose schemes were saddling Slavic Village's already distressed market with an ongoing string of vacant properties (Treuhaft and Kingsley 2008, 21).

In Rhode Island, the work of the Providence Plan, a member of the National Neighborhood Indicators Partnership, has been instrumental in mobilizing new stakeholders, precipitating democratic action, and changing public policy. Historically, the Rhode Island Constitution prohibited convicted felons from voting in elections until the completion of their prison sentences, probations, and parole periods. A few years ago, the Rhode Island Family Life Center, a nonprofit organization that provides assistance to offenders who are in the process of reintegrating into their communities, drew attention to this issue in an effort to amend the constitution and restore voting rights to felons immediately after their release from prison (OpenDoors n.d.).

A seminal moment in this effort came in 2004, when, with the assistance of the Providence Plan, the Rhode Island Family Life Center released a report demonstrating that the ban on felon voting was felt disproportionately across the state and within the city of Providence as well (Rhode Island Family Life Center 2004). In impoverished upper south Providence, for example, 11.2 percent of residents were ineligible to cast ballots. In contrast, in nearby College Hill, where Brown University is located, less than 1 percent of residents were prohibited from taking part in elections. As figure 5.2 illustrates, in addition to presenting this information statistically, the report included a series of color-coded maps that vividly demonstrated how different neighborhoods experienced the ban.

Following the dissemination of this information, a pair of state legislators representing the heavily affected south side of Providence introduced legislation to place a measure on the ballot asking Rhode Island voters to repeal the constitutional prohibition on voting during offenders' probationary and parole periods (Schleifer 2006, 2). This legislative action led to mobilization inside the affected communities. Three former prisoners provided testimony to the state legislature, which quickly approved the measure for inclusion on the 2006 ballot (Schleifer 2006, 2). As the campaign unfolded, more former prisoners, family members, and other Rhode Island residents volunteered their time to work on behalf of the measure's approval. On election day, approximately two hundred volun-

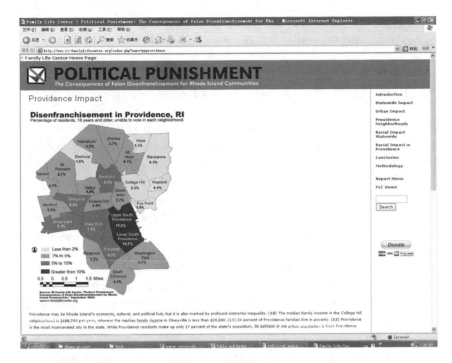

Figure 5.2
Mapping the neighborhood effects of Rhode Island's ban on felon voting. *Source*:
http://www.ri-familylifecenter.org/index.php?name=ppprovidence (screen shot
taken by the authors March 31, 2009).

teers in fifty-three precincts around the state worked to get out the vote
(Schleifer 2006, 3). When the ballots were counted, the measure received
the support of 51.5 percent of voters, and as a result of this combination
of neighborhood information system data and stakeholder mobilization,
an estimated 15,000 offenders had their voting rights restored.

Recognizing the promise of examples such as these, leaders in the
National Neighborhood Indicators Partnership are taking steps to pursue
and demonstrate the participatory possibilities of neighborhood information systems. In Atlanta, where a new National Neighborhood Indicators
Partnership project has been established, one of the organization's fundamental aims is to become a community forum. Project leaders envision
providing stakeholders with opportunities to converse about data and
promote policies around which consensus has emerged.[30] The articulation of such goals presents an opportunity for entrepreneurs at both the
national and local levels to develop metrics that will aid in the evaluation

of whether mobilization and transformational collaborations have followed from the activities of the National Neighborhood Indicators Partnership.

Neighborhood Information Systems and Democratic Discourse

Democratic information communities are ideal places where inclusive flows of information facilitate the mobilization of stakeholders and collaborative approaches to the consideration of public problems (Shane 2008, 1–2). A fundamental question that arises in contemplating such ideals is what roles information and communication technologies might play in helping communities democratize their political practices. Generally speaking, democratization can be fostered through a number of institutional channels, including media outlets that are accessible, diverse, and committed to coverage of local affairs (Shane 2008, 8–10). In addition, nonprofit organizations can play vital intermediary roles in democratic information communities by collecting, organizing, disseminating, and analyzing data in ways that activate stakeholders and advance inclusive decision making.

In this latter regard, the neighborhood information systems that are members of the National Neighborhood Indicators Partnership meet the description, broadly speaking, of democratic intermediaries. These technology innovations are operated and supported mainly by nonprofit organizations such as universities, United Way affiliates, and independent civic institutions.[31] Furthermore, neighborhood information systems perform a variety of democracy-enhancing tasks for the communities in which they operate. These tasks include assembling data from governments and other sources, analyzing these data from a variety of community perspectives, and disseminating these data in ways that allow stakeholders to both consume and configure information in ways that meet their specific needs and interests.

At this stage in their development, neighborhood information systems have, in a small number of notable projects, shaped the composition of interests that participate in local policy making and catalyzed collaborative stakeholder practices. Such aims are not central to the missions of many National Neighborhood Indicators Partnership projects. Variation in the orientations of neighborhood information systems is, in all likelihood, a function of organizational resources. The Boston Foundation, for example, has assets of nearly $900 million (Boston Foundation n.d.). In contrast, CAMConnect employs one full-time staff person and has an annual budget of less than \$100,000.[32] In addition to resource constraints, several contacts highlighted the value that their neighborhood information systems place on operating as neutral data intermediaries.[33] From such a perspective, activities that foster stakeholder mobilization and collaboration can be construed as advocacy efforts that run counter to organizational neutrality.

For those neighborhood information systems with the resources and predispositions to serve as catalysts of transformational stakeholder practices, two attributes are essential for building on the present gains in participation. The first attribute is an articulation of the goals of stakeholder mobilization and collaboration. In the absence of such organizational mission statements, activities that promote these goals are likely to occur on only an ad hoc basis and will be dependent on the inclusive, discursive orientations of individual community stakeholders and leaders in specific National Neighborhood Indicators Partnership projects.

The second attribute is the development of metrics by which the attainment of democracy-enhancing goals can be evaluated. In general, theory has been disconnected from the assessment of deliberative democracy. Many of the expected benefits of democratic theory simply do not materialize when deliberative practices are subjected to empirical scrutiny. According to theorists, such null results indicate only that much empirical inquiry has failed to engage in a meaningful way the key normative principles of deliberation. As one theorist has put it, empiricists sometimes "extract from isolated passages in various theoretical writings a simplified statement about one or more benefits of deliberative democracy, compress it into a testable hypothesis, find or (more often) artificially create a site in which people talk about politics, and conclude that deliberation does not produce the benefits the theory promised and may even be counterproductive" (Thompson 2008, 498–499). Empiricists argue that although many of the claims of deliberative democracy naturally lend themselves to experimentation, theorists often erect artificial barriers by offering "definitions of deliberative democracy that are too broad and that effectively insulate the theory from falsification" (Mutz 2008, 522).

The National Neighborhood Indicators Partnership represents a potential context for reducing this gap between theoretical notions of democratic discourse and empirical practices that are broadly consistent with such notions. Significant hurdles need to be overcome in order to realize this potential. The resource limitations and neutral data intermediary perspectives of many neighborhood information systems can serve as barriers to the development and evaluation of inclusive democratic practices. Furthermore, the task of establishing benchmarks that are both theoretically satisfying and empirically tractable has proven difficult no matter how promising the context. With these limitations in mind, a focus on neighborhood information systems that possess substantial financial resources and established records in the areas of stakeholder mobilization and collaborative practices would seem to be the place for empirically minded democratic theorists to start this effort.

Notes

1. These other attributes include quality journalism and accessible media outlets (Shane 2008, 6–10).

2. The original partner in Atlanta, the Office of Data and Policy Analysis, has recently been replaced by the Atlanta Neighborhood Indicators Project (author interview with Michael Rich of the Atlanta neighborhood information system, June 27, 2008). It is not unusual for this type of institutional replacement to occur among National Neighborhood Indicators Partnership projects. Other communities where such movement has taken place include Baltimore and Miami (author interviews with Matthew Kachura of the Baltimore neighborhood information system and Lisa Pittman of the Miami neighborhood information system, June 19, 2008, and June 23, 2008, respectively).

3. The DC Agenda Project ceased its operations in 2004 (NeighborhoodInfoDC n.d.) and was replaced by NeighborhoodInfo DC, whose Web site appears at http://www.neighborhoodinfodc.org.

4. A related question is the ways that National Neighborhood Indicators Partnership communities are similar to and different from municipalities where National Neighborhood Indicators Partnership projects have not yet been established. This question has been addressed in separate research (Balla 2009).

5. Twenty-nine National Neighborhood Indicators Partnership locations were approached about participating in an interview. Interviews were ultimately conducted with sixteen locations that responded affirmatively. These municipalities were Atlanta, Baltimore, Boston, Camden, Chicago, Cleveland, Columbus, Dallas, Denver, Los Angeles, Miami, Minneapolis–St. Paul, New Orleans, Oakland, Seattle, and Washington, D.C. In addition, an interview was conducted with a staff member at the Urban Institute who is centrally involved in the National Neighborhood Indicators Partnership.

6. The Rockefeller Foundation archives its annual reports at http://www .rockefellerfoundation.org/about-us/annual-reports (accessed November 29, 2010). The reports issued from 1987 through 1992 provide information about the development of the Community Planning and Action Project and the activities of its members.

7. Author interviews with Charlotte Kahn of the Boston neighborhood information system, Claudia Coulton of the Cleveland neighborhood information system, and Junious Williams and Steve Spiker of the Oakland neighborhood information system, June 11–12, 2008, June 18, 2008, and June 24, 2008, respectively.

8. Author interview with Denice Warren of the New Orleans neighborhood information system, June 16, 2008.

9. Author interview with Will Craig of the Minneapolis–St. Paul neighborhood information system, June 16, 2008.

10. Author interview with Derek Ziegler of the Camden neighborhood information system, June 12, 2008.

11. Author interview with Jung Kim of the Columbus neighborhood information system, June 13, 2008.

12. Author interview with Jung Kim of the Columbus neighborhood information system, June 13, 2008.

13. Author interview with Neal Richman of the Los Angeles neighborhood information system, June 19, 2008.

14. Author interviews with Matthew Kachura of the Baltimore neighborhood information system and Matt Barry of the Denver neighborhood information system, June 19, 2008, and July 7, 2008, respectively.

15. Author interviews with Claudia Coulton of the Cleveland neighborhood information system, Tim Bray of the Dallas neighborhood information system, and Denice Warren of the New Orleans neighborhood information system, June 18, 2008, June 11, 2008, and June 16, 2008, respectively.

16. Each of these components is not present in every National Neighborhood Indicators Partnership project. Rather, these components are illustrative of the ways in which neighborhood information systems have delivered data to community stakeholders.

17. Author interview with Will Craig of the Minneapolis–St. Paul neighborhood information system, June 16, 2008.

18. Author interview with Sandy Ciske and David Solet of the Seattle neighborhood information system, June 20, 2008.

19. Author interviews with Derek Ziegler of the Camden neighborhood information system, Tim Bray of the Dallas neighborhood information system, Matt Barry of the Denver neighborhood information system, Denice Warren of the New Orleans neighborhood information system, and Peter Tatian of the Washington, D.C., neighborhood information system, June 12, June 11, July 7, June 16, and July 10, 2008, respectively.

20. Author interviews with Matthew Kachura of the Baltimore neighborhood information system, Claudia Coulton of the Cleveland neighborhood information system, Jung Kim of the Columbus neighborhood information system, Matt Barry of the Denver neighborhood information system, Denice Warren of the New Orleans neighborhood information system, Junious Williams and Steve Spiker of the Oakland neighborhood information system, and Peter Tatian of

the Washington, D.C., neighborhood information system, June 19, June 18, June 13, July 7, June 16, June 24, and July 10, 2008, respectively.

21. Author interview with Matthew Kachura of the Baltimore neighborhood information system, June 19, 2008.

22. Author interviews with Matthew Kachura of the Baltimore neighborhood information system, Claudia Coulton of the Cleveland neighborhood information system, Jung Kim of the Columbus neighborhood information system, Tim Bray of the Dallas neighborhood information system, Denice Warren of the New Orleans neighborhood information system, Junious Williams and Steve Spiker of the Oakland neighborhood information system, and Peter Tatian of the Washington, D.C., neighborhood information system, June 19, June 18, June 13, June 11, June 16, June 24, and July 10, 2008, respectively.

23. Broadly speaking, these interview findings corroborate with the results of a recent nationwide survey of users of neighborhood information systems (Hwang and Hoffman 2009).

24. Author interview with Jung Kim of the Columbus neighborhood information system, June 13, 2008.

25. Author interview with Matthew Kachura of the Baltimore neighborhood information system, June 19, 2008.

26. Author interview with Peter Tatian of the Washington, D.C., neighborhood information system, July 10, 2008.

27. Author interview with Claudia Coulton of the Cleveland neighborhood information system, June 18, 2008.

28. Author interview with Charlotte Kahn of the Boston neighborhood information system, June 11–12, 2008.

29. Author interview with Tim Bray of the Dallas neighborhood information system, June 11, 2008.

30. Author interview with Michael Rich of the Atlanta neighborhood information system, June 27, 2008.

31. The National Neighborhood Indicators Partnership's project directory provides information about the institutional affiliations of members (National Neighborhood Indicators Partnership n.d. b). It is typical for neighborhood information systems to draw organizational and financial resources from an array of national and community groups, thereby making it difficult to classify many members as a distinct type of institution (such as a university center or a United Way affiliate). For example, the Atlanta neighborhood information system is supported by the following organizations: Annie E. Casey Foundation, Atlanta Regional Commission, Atlanta Regional Health Forum, Civic League for Regional Atlanta, Emory University Office of University-Community Partnerships, Georgia State University Fiscal Research Center, The Community Foundation for Greater Atlanta, and United Way of Metropolitan Atlanta (Neighborhood Nexus n.d.).

32. Author interview with Derek Ziegler of the Camden neighborhood information system, June 12, 2008.

33. Author interviews with Denice Warren of the New Orleans neighborhood information system and Peter Tatian of the Washington, D.C. neighborhood information system, June 16 and July 10, 2008, respectively.

References

Balla, Steven J. 2009. "Municipal Environments, Nonprofit Entrepreneurs, and the Development of Neighborhood Information Systems." *I/S: A Journal of Law and Policy for the Information Society* 5, no. 1: 111–134.

Baltimore Neighborhood Indicators Alliance. n.d. "About the Alliance." Accessed November 29, 2010. http://www.ubalt.edu/bnia/about/index.html.

Boston Foundation. n.d. "Financial Information." Accessed November 29, 2010. http://www.tbf.org/AboutTBF/AboutTBFDetail.aspx?id=102.

Case Western Reserve University Center on Urban Poverty and Community Development. n.d. "NEO CANDO in Practice." Accessed November 29, 2010. http://blog.case.edu/msass/2007/10/01/4%20Ford%20and%20Pugh%20-%20%20NEO%20CANDO%20In%20Practice.pdf.

Christie, Les. 2007. "Foreclosures Drift to Sun Belt from Rust Belt: A New Survey Shows Foreclosure Clusters Are on the Move from Industrial Centers to Coastal and Southern States." Accessed April 9, 2009. http://money.cnn.com/2007/06/18/real_estate/foreclosures_hardest_hit_zips/index.htm.

Communities Count Partnership. n.d. "Empowering Local Communities with Timely Information." Accessed November 29, 2010. http://www.communitiescount.org/.

Cowan, Jake. 2007. "Stories: Using Information in Community Building and Local Policy." Manuscript.

Greater New Orleans Community Data Center. 2009. "Open Public Schools in New Orleans for Spring 2009." Accessed November 29, 2010. http://gnocdc.s3.amazonaws.com/maps/orleans_schools.pdf.

Hwang, Sungsoo. 2006. "Role of University in the Partnership for IT Innovations of Community Development: Utilizing Universities' Assets for 'Neighborhood Information System' Development." *Public Administration and Management* 11, no. 2:75–100.

Hwang, Sungsoo, and Mark C. Hoffman. 2009. "In Pursuit of the Effective Neighborhood Information System: User-Friendliness and Training." *Government Information Quarterly* 26 (January):166–173.

Kingsley, G. Thomas. 1998. "Neighborhood Indicators: Taking Advantage of the New Potential." Accessed April 9, 2009. http://www2.urban.org/nnip/pdf/kingsle1.pdf.

Kingsley, G. Thomas, and Kathryn L.S. Pettit. 2004. "Neighborhood Information Systems: We Need a Broader Effort to Build Local Capacity." Accessed April 9, 2009. http://www.urban.org/publications/900755.html.

Lipsky, Michael. 1983. *Street-Level Bureaucracy: Dilemmas of the Individual in Public Service.* New York: Russell Sage Foundation.

MetroBoston Data Common. n.d. "Getting Started." Accessed November 29, 2010. http://www.metrobostondatacommon.org/html/starting.htm.

Mutz, Diana C. 2008. "Is Deliberative Democracy a Falsifiable Theory?" *Annual Review of Political Science* 11:521–538.

National Neighborhood Indicators Partnership n.d. a. "About NNIP." Accessed November 29, 2010. http://www2.urban.org/nnip/about.html.

National Neighborhood Indicators Partnership n.d. b. "NNIP Partners Organizations and Staff." Accessed November 29, 2010. http://www2.urban.org/nnip/loc_list.html.

National Neighborhood Indicators Partnership n.d. c. "NNIP Partners Partner Requirements." Accessed November 29, 2010. http://www2.urban.org/nnip/requirements_p.cfm.

National Neighborhood Indicators Partnership n.d. d. "NNIP Partner Spotlight: Baltimore." Accessed November 29, 2010. http://www2.urban.org/nnip/desc_bal.html.

National Neighborhood Indicators Partnership n.d. e. "NNIP Partner Spotlight: CAMConnect." Accessed November 29, 2010. http://www2.urban.org/nnip/desc_cam.html.

National Neighborhood Indicators Partnership n.d. f. "NNIP Partner Spotlight: Center on Urban Poverty and Community Development." Accessed November 29, 2010. http://www2.urban.org/nnip/desc_cle.html.

National Neighborhood Indicators Partnership n.d. g. "NNIP Partner Spotlight: Community Research Partners." Accessed November 29, 2010. http://www2.urban.org/nnip/desc_col.html.

NeighborhoodInfoDC. n.d. "DC Agenda Is No More!" Accessed November 29, 2010. http://www.neighborhoodinfodc.org/dcaredirect.html.

Neighborhood Nexus. n.d. "About Neighborhood Nexus." Accessed November 29, 2010. http://www.neighborhoodnexus.org/content/about-neighborhood-nexus.

Neighborhood Progress. n.d. "Reinvigorating the Urban Marketplace: Cleveland's Strategic Investment Initiative." Accessed November 29, 2010. http://neighborhoodprogress.org/uploaded_pics/Cleveland%5C's%20Strategic%20Investment%20Initiative_file_1194017511.pdf.

Ochs Center for Metropolitan Studies. n.d. "NNIP." Accessed November 29, 2010. http://www.ochscenter.org/nnip.php.

OpenDoors. n.d. "Home Page." Accessed November 29, 2010. http://www.restorethevote.org/index.php?name=homepage.

Piton Foundation. n.d. "Publications." Accessed November 29, 2010. http://www.piton.org/index.cfm?fuseaction=Content.Publications#THE%20PITON%20PERSPECTIVE.

Rhode Island Family Life Center. 2004. "Political Punishment: The Consequences of Felon Disenfranchisement for Rhode Island Communities." Accessed April 9, 2009. http://www.ri-familylifecenter.org/index.php?name=polpunishhome.

Rockefeller Foundation. 1987. "President's Review and Annual Report." Accessed November 29, 2010. http://www.rockefellerfoundation.org/uploads/files/263421e9-4b17-4b5f-9804-1a28b33162ee-1987.pdf.

Rockefeller Foundation. 1989. "President's Review and Annual Report." Accessed November 29, 2010. http://www.rockefellerfoundation.org/uploads/files/bbb7dcc0-9be9-4cea-bf85-b8866e278325-1989.pdf.

Rockefeller Foundation. 1991. "President's Review and Annual Report." Accessed November 29, 2010. http://www.rockefellerfoundation.org/uploads/files/9fa314bb-a162-4fbb-8165-2163a93a4cba 1991.pdf.

SAVI Community Information System. n.d. "About Us." Accessed November 29, 2010. http://www.savi.org/savii/about/savi.aspx.

Sawicki, David S., and William J. Craig. 1996. "The Democratization of Data: Bridging the Gap for Community Groups." *Journal of the American Planning Association* 62 (Autumn):512–523.

Schleifer, Daniel. 2006. "Unlocking the Vote: Activists and Disenfranchised Former Felons Restore Voting Rights in Rhode Island." Accessed April 9, 2009. http://www.campusprogress.org/articles/unlocking_the_vote.

Shane, Peter. 2008. "Democratic Information Communities." *I/S: A Journal of Law and Policy for the Information Society* 6·95–118.

Thompson, Dennis F. 2008. "Deliberative Democratic Theory and Empirical Political Science." *Annual Review of Political Science* 11:497–520.

Toy, Alan, and Neal Richman. 2004. "Living Independently in Los Angeles (LILA): Lessons from Establishing a Community Information System Built for and by People with Disabilities." Accessed November 29, 2010. http://www.spa.ucla.edu/policyforum/pdfs/LILAReport.pdf.

Treuhaft, Sarah, Arnold Chandler, Joel Kirschenbaum, Melissa Magallanes, and Randall Pinkett. 2007. "Bridging the Innovation Divide: An Agenda for Disseminating Technology Innovations within the Nonprofit Sector." Accessed April 9, 2009. http://www.policylink.org/atf/cf/%7B97c6d565-bb43-406d-a6d5-eca3bbf35af0%7D/BRIDGINGINNOVATIONDIVIDE_FINAL.PDF.

Treuhaft, Sarah, and G. Thomas Kingsley. 2008. "Transforming Community Development with Land Information Systems." Accessed April 9, 2009. http://www.lincolninst.edu/pubs/1356_Transforming-Community-Development-with-Land-Information-Systems.

U.S. Census Bureau. 2000. *County and City Data Book: 2000.* Accessed April 9, 2009. http://www.census.gov/prod/www/abs/ccdb.html.

Urban Institute. 2009. "Stories: Using Information in Community Building and Local Policy." Accessed November 29, 2010. http://www2.urban.org/nnip/pdf/dstory.pdf.

II

What Online Consultations Mean to Their Participants

6

Playing Politics: The Experience of E-Participation

Vincent Price

The idea that public policy should be grounded in public deliberation—in a careful, open search for well-reasoned solutions following a wide-ranging consideration of alternative views—is both intuitively and normatively appealing. Nevertheless, the use of the Internet for citizen consultation and the burgeoning interest in deliberative and participatory democracy have been greeted with skepticism. Notwithstanding impassioned arguments for the value of deliberation and the necessity of engaging ordinary citizens in policy making, critics contend that such arguments rest on wholly unrealistic assumptions about the political interests and capabilities of ordinary citizens. To some, using the Internet for consultation renders the likelihood of productive public consultation even more remote. Against this backdrop, this chapter takes stock of how individuals actually behave in online political discussions, drawing extensively from a series of large-scale field experiments.[1] The empirical review is followed by a speculative discussion of design-related factors that are likely to shape and guide citizen behavior.

Deliberative Dilemmas

Democracy demands informed decisions, which ideally rest on a solid factual foundation but also draw from many competing interpretations of those facts. Most citizens, however, can be experts in the political realm (see chapter 7 in this volume). Because most people feel that politics is rather distant from the pressing matters of everyday life (Lippmann 1922), they focus their attention on those few matters that they deem most relevant. On any given issue, very few people are highly engaged and actively attempt to steer the course of public policy; more citizens follow news about the matter closely and comprise the "issue public"; and most citizens are relatively uninterested and poorly informed

(Converse 1964; Price 1992). Drawing a representative sample of citizens into policy deliberation consequently tends to result in a few knowledgeable participants amid a much greater number of uninterested and ignorant participants.

Democracy thus confronts a central dilemma posed by conflicting desires—to open complicated policy choices to authentic public consultation and simultaneously to maintain intelligence in collective decision making. In seeking to resolve this dilemma, democratic theories have clustered around two distinct poles. Lack of confidence in the ability of ordinary citizens to discriminate intelligently among various policies has led many democratic theorists—among them Lippmann (1922) and Schumpeter (1942)—to fear that democratic catering to a "popular will" would prove at the least inefficient and at the worst disastrously unstable in times of cultural and political stress. In this view, public influence on elected representatives should be strictly limited in favor of an independent, expert bureaucracy that can inform policy choices. In making the case for a "leadership democracy," Schumpeter (1942, 269) proposed that citizens' choices should extend only to periodic selection of "the men who are able to do the deciding." Democracy in this light becomes any system that periodically offers competitive elections, placing considerable distance between the decisions of governing elites and the desires of the masses. Other theorists who share these concerns about the limited capacities of citizens argue that elections by themselves do not ensure a stable and publicly responsive democratic state. Rather, contending minority interests, when they organize and press their claims on elected leaders, are able to bargain for policy accommodations. Such elite-pluralist formulations became ascendant in American political science in the 1950s and 1960s (e.g., Dahl 1956). They emphasize the role of intermediary interest groups—organized into business coalitions, advocacy organizations, and politically active ethnic and religious groups—in maintaining a competitive balance of power and providing a critical linkage function in tying popular wishes to governmental decisions.

Anchoring a different pole in thinking about the capacities of citizens and the ways that elite political decision making and public desires should be linked are participatory and deliberative democratic theorists (e.g., Pateman 1970; Macpherson 1977; Barber 1984). Although specific theoretical formulations vary, writers in these camps generally seek to close the distance between elites and the mass of citizens. They view the latter as being fully capable of active and intelligent self-governance when they are given adequate attention and resources. They challenge pluralists' notion that political power is disaggregated and fairly distributed in society, arguing that social, financial, and political inequities hinder popular mobilization through conventional channels of advocacy. True democracy requires that such inequities be ameliorated and that the active participation of every segment of society be fostered in democratic institutions of all kinds, which must be fully open and publicly accountable (Dryzek 1990; Warren 1992; Mathews 1994). Were people more broadly empowered, this line of argument runs, they would become politically transformed: "They would become more public-spirited, more knowledgeable, more attentive to the interests of others, and more probing of their own interests" (Warren 1992, 8). The act of deliberating—of encountering respectful disagreement from peers—is thought to be especially transformative. It fosters mutual respect and trust, leads to a heightened sense of a person's value as part of an active political community, and stimulates additional forays into political engagement (e.g., Cohen 1997; Gutmann and Thompson 1996).

Even the most ardent deliberative theorists, however, acknowledge that citizens' discursive contributions to public opinion on any given issue will vary considerably from one person to the next. The asymmetric distribution of issue-specific interest and knowledge within the population points to differential abilities to inform and persuade. This is not in principle an impediment to democratic deliberation, as studies in organizational communication have demonstrated. A division of cognitive labor among group members has been found to increase the efficiency and quality of collective decision making (e.g., Hollingshead 1996, 1998; Hollingshead and Brandon 2003). Similarly, at the societal level, deliberation can span knowledge gaps among citizens as multiple issue publics assist one another by alternately leading or following on various issues, efficiently dividing and distributing cognitive and political labor.

This division of labor, however, is a double-edged sword. There is a consequential but blurry line separating informing from dominating. The unbalanced communicative relationships between leaders, experts, and listeners may as easily represent an unjust imposition of will as an efficient distribution of expertise. Without mutual and equal recognition, political discussion can serve as an avenue of demand and acquiescence rather than honest give-and-take. For this reason, some critics view deliberation not as a remedy for what ills contemporary politics but instead as a well-meaning but ultimately harmful intervention that marginalizes or alienates certain citizens—namely, socially powerless and politically disenfranchised groups (e.g., Eliasoph 1998; Hibbing and Theiss-Morse 2002). According to Sanders (1997), more powerful citizens decontextualize and devalue other people's ordinary experiences by dominating the floor, imposing their agenda, and deploying technical jargon. The result can be termed *forced silence,* and its implications are antidemocratic. Citizens feel ineffective, perceive that their opinions are ignored, and lose any sense of self-efficacy and autonomy, which are the soul of democracy. Nor are elites necessarily pleased with forced silence, recognizing that it is hollow and unproductive. It closes off possibilities for effective linkage between the interests and desires of elites and general citizens, fosters mistrust, and undercuts the legitimacy of decisions that are made.

Critics of deliberative democracy (e.g., Sanders 1997; Hibbing and Theiss-Morse 2002) point to several basic problems:

• *Undesirable group pressures*   The notion that group discussion improves the quality of opinion can certainly be questioned. Empirical research of group decision making offers numerous illustrations of opinion polarization, shifts in new and risky directions, and other undesired outcomes (Brown 2000). Groups invite social-normative pressures that can stifle minority views and distort the communication of true preferences (Noelle-Neumann 1984).

• *Dominance by high-status members*   Although the goal of deliberative theory is to embrace all views and empower the disenfranchised, Sanders (1997) argues that deliberative encounters are likely to do just the opposite—discourage participation by those who lack social or political status (such as women or ethnic minorities) or deliberative ability (such as the less well educated) and thus further empower high-status, educated participants. The purportedly egalitarian nature of deliberation cannot be ensured merely by invitation; it must be demonstrated in practice by vocal participation, equitably distributed.

• *Lack of reasonable exchange*   Also open to question is the degree to which citizen discussions will come close to the deliberative ideal of reciprocal, reasonable, and open-minded exchanges (Mendelberg 2002). People may well interact and argue but without giving adequate reasons for their views. Or if reasons are given, they may simply be ignored rather than given a response. People may talk past each other rather than engage in any serious way with the complex issues at stake.

• *The discomfort of disagreement* People, particularly those who are uncertain of their views, may find it uncomfortable to disagree, and many people take political disagreement personally (Mansbridge 1983; Pin 1985; Schudson 1997; Eliasoph 1998). As a result, they may avoid confrontation and real debate. If citizens do air disagreements, they may produce animosities rather than mutual respect and trust. Notwithstanding deliberative theorists' hopes that disagreement will engage citizens, it might induce ambivalence and thus come at the expense of political action (Mutz 2002).

For these and other reasons, the confidence that deliberative theorists place in public consultation might be misplaced. Simply opening policy discussions to ordinary citizens may do little to improve the quality of collective decision making and may not guarantee the true democratization of the process.

Online Opportunities

The Internet and World Wide Web have been greeted by some as cause for optimism about a revitalized public sphere (Poster 1999; Becker and Slaton 2000; Papacharissi 2004) and have given participatory democrats hope for expansive new channels for public consultation. Internet technologies permit group interactions among geographically dispersed and diverse participants, potentially bringing far greater reach, reduced cost, and increased representation to exercises in deliberative democracy. At the same time, some analysts—even those who are committed to deliberation—have questioned whether electronic, text-based interactions are well suited to fruitful political discussion. Their points of concern include the following:

• *Superficiality* Fishkin (2000) argues that text-based exchanges online are probably too superficial to sustain sound political deliberation. Putnam (2000, 177) also remains skeptical of the Internet's capacities for generating social capital, submitting that electronic networks tend to be sparse and unbounded, encouraging "easy-in, easy out" and "drive-by" relationships rather than the close acquaintance promoted by face-to-face contact.

• *Social masking* Computer-mediated communication is often framed as an impersonal phenomenon that deindividuates participants. This renders it poorly suited to getting to know others and encourages uncivil discourse and group-based stereotyping (see the discussion in Kiesler, Siegel, and McGuire 1984; Rice 1993).

• *Hyper-selectivity* Sunstein (2001) warns that the Internet, instead of encouraging reasonable dialog over shared issues, merely encourages "enclave" communication among very like-minded citizens who circulate unfounded and often false information, polarize and intensify opinions, and contribute to widening gaps between those on opposite sides of public issues.

Even if designers of online deliberative programs were able to counter such tendencies, they would still contend with the so-called digital divide—that is, structural inequities in access to computing equipment, in familiarity with its use, in literacy, and in typing ability. The prospects for successful political deliberation online, then, remain unclear.

Despite these potential liabilities, however, online deliberations bring potential benefits, some of which might counter criticisms of deliberative democracy:

• *Reduced social dominance* Studies demonstrate that online discussions are generally much more egalitarian than face-to-face encounters, with reduced patterns of individual dominance and increased contributions by low-status participants (Dubrovsky, Kiesler, and Sethna 1991; Rice 1993; Walther 1995; Hollingshead 1996).

• *Openness* Group decision making experiments generally indicate that online discussions, relative to face-to-face group meetings, generate more open exchanges of ideas (Rains 2005), suggesting considerable utility for deliberative work. Task-oriented groups generate more unique ideas working in computer-mediated settings than when meeting face to face (Gallupe, DeSantis, and Dickson 1988; Dennis 1996).

• *Greater honesty and self-disclosure* Experimental comparisons show that computer-mediated discussions produce more questions, increased self-disclosure, more intimate and direct questions, and fewer peripheral exchanges than face-to-face encounters (Tidwell and Walther 2002). The lack of physical presence and reduction in social cues can be useful rather than limiting. Bargh, McKenna, and Fitzsimmons (2002) find that their experimental participants feel better able to reveal their true selves online than in person.

• *Ease in handling disagreements* Just as social masking may help people reveal themselves to others, it may also reduce some of the anxieties surrounding disagreement. People reported to Stromer-Galley (2003), for example, that they felt better able to discuss political disagreements over the Internet than face to face because it felt more comfortable and less dangerous online.

• *The advantages of writing*   Finally, online encounters may assist people in formulating their thoughts by requiring greater economy of expression, requiring the conversion of inchoate ideas into text, and permitting the review of statements prior to posting.

The distinctive features of political communication online, then, may well prove to help rather than hinder deliberation. By restricting the projection of social status, the reduction in social cues may produce less deferential behavior and so undercut status hierarchies. The ability to input statements simultaneously may assist the sharing of ideas, while anonymity may reduce inhibitions and anxieties about expressing honest views, particularly those that are unpopular.

Empirical Examinations

Despite lively debates about deliberative theory and citizens' ability to deliver useful policy consultations, empirical study of how citizens experience deliberative encounters has been slow in developing and less systematic than we might wish. Most research to date focuses on the outcomes of deliberation, offering little if any concrete evidence about the discursive process itself, about the complex forms of interaction involved (making arguments, absorbing information, rebutting others' arguments, and accommodating or rejecting new viewpoints), and about the perceptions and reactions of participants. Most studies also deal with face-to-face rather than online citizen encounters.

To fill this void, we draw from a series of large-scale field experiments involving extensive survey measures of more than twelve hundred randomly selected participants in close to eight hundred online group discussions.[2] Although not representative of the universe of online interactions that might be implicated in e-consultation programs, these observations offer an opportunity to examine which types of citizens are most likely to attend such online discussions, who is most likely to talk and argue, how different people react to the experience, how they respond to disagreement and challenge, how their opinions are affected by participating, and what patterns of interactions emerge, for instance, between those elites who are knowledgeable and well equipped for discussion and others who bring less formal education or deliberative skill to the encounters.

The Electronic Dialogue Project

The Electronic Dialogue Project was a year-long panel study conducted during the 2000 U.S. presidential election. Its multiwave, multigroup panel lasted roughly one year. All data gathering was conducted over the World Wide Web. The core of the project consisted of sixty groups of citizens who engaged in a series of monthly, real-time electronic discussions about issues facing the country and the unfolding presidential campaign.

Project participants came from a random sample of U.S. citizens age eighteen and older that was drawn from a nationally representative panel of survey respondents maintained by Knowledge Networks, Inc. of Menlo Park, California. The panel was made up of households selected by probability-sampling methods and provided with Internet access and WebTV devices free of charge. Comparisons of the 1,684 Electronic Dialogue study participants with a separate random-digit dialing telephone survey and with U.S. Census data indicated that the study sample was broadly representative, although it tended to slightly overrepresent males and slightly underrepresent those with less than a high-school education, nonwhites, and those with weak interest in politics (Price and Cappella 2002). After completing two baseline surveys in February and March 2000, respondents were randomly assigned to one of three panels:

• *Online discussion panel*   These 915 participants were invited to attend eight, one-hour online group deliberations, roughly once a month, beginning in April 2000 and continuing through December. Members of this panel, regardless of whether they attended discussions, were also asked to complete a series of surveys, one preceding and one following each discussion event, as well as end-of-project surveys in the spring of 2001.

• *Survey-only panel*   These 139 participants were assigned to a survey-only control group and were asked to complete all the monthly surveys and the end-of-project surveys, although they were never invited to attend any online group meetings.

• *Pre- and postelection panels*   As a further control on panel-survey effects, the remaining 630 participants were assigned to a preproject and postproject condition. They were asked to complete the baseline surveys and, one year later, the final end-of-project surveys, but they did not participate in any aspect of the project over the course of the year.

Researchers anticipated less than perfect attendance and formed sixty groups with roughly sixteen invitees per group to produce groups of five to ten participants at each round of discussions. Because of the theoretical interest in the effects of disagreement, three experimental group conditions were created using baseline data—homogeneously liberal groups ($n = 20$), homogeneously conservative groups ($n = 20$), and heterogeneous groups with members from across the political spectrum ($n = 20$). Participants maintained group assignments over the full course of the study.

Discussion groups met live, in real time, with membership straddling several time zones. Participants logged on to their "discussion rooms" at prearranged times using their Web TV devices, television sets, and infrared keyboards. All discussions were carefully coordinated, and moderators worked from preestablished scripts to maintain consistency across groups. Discussions were not intended to be formally deliberative exercises. Instead, group members were simply invited to discuss a number of topics, including which issues ought to be the focus of the campaign; a variety of candidate policy proposals (for example, in areas of education, crime and public safety, taxes, and foreign affairs); the candidates' qualifications; campaign advertising; and the role of the media. In all, nine rounds of meetings were held. The full text of all discussions, including time stamps for each comment posted, was automatically recorded.

The Healthcare Dialogue Project

The 2004 to 2005 Healthcare Dialogue Project shared many of the features of the 2000 campaign study but focused instead on formal policy deliberations about a complex issue—health care reform. It also created online discussions involving health care policy elites in addition to ordinary citizens. Project objectives included examining online deliberation as a means of maximizing public influence in policy making, studying the interaction of policy elites and ordinary citizens in online discussions, and testing hypotheses related to group composition and the quality of deliberations and outcomes.

The project again drew on the Knowledge Networks panel but employed a stratified sampling strategy. The baseline sample of 2,497 participants represented both a general population sample of adult citizens age eighteen and older as well as a purposive sample of 314 health care policy elites with special experience, knowledge, and influence in the domain of health care policy and reform. The general population sample was further stratified into members of "issue publics" who are highly attentive to and knowledgeable about health care issues and ordinary citizens who are less interested. Comparisons of the obtained baseline general population sample to a random-digit dialing telephone sample and to U.S. Census data indicated that the samples were broadly comparable, although project participants were slightly more likely to be middle aged and to follow politics more frequently.

As in the first study, participants were randomly assigned to one of three panels—an online discussion panel, a survey-only panel, or a pre-project and postproject panel. The online discussion panel included 262 health care policy elites, 461 issue-public members, and 768 ordinary citizens who were randomly assigned within strata to participate in a series of four moderated online group discussions over the course of the year. Eighty online groups met twice in the fall of 2004 to discuss health insurance: eight contained only health care policy elites, twelve were homogeneous "issue-public" groups, twenty contained only general citizens, and forty were heterogeneous, mixed across the three strata. Participants who attended at least one of the first two discussions were then reassigned to fifty new groups for another round of two discussions in the spring of 2005, focusing on prescription drugs. In this second round, a random half of the participants remained in homogeneous or heterogeneous groups as before, and half were switched (from homogeneous to heterogeneous groups or vice versa).

Discussion groups were again scripted to ensure consistency across groups, and short briefing materials were made available prior to each online meeting. The full text of all discussions, including time stamps for each comment, was automatically recorded. Following the four discussion waves, an end-of-project survey was conducted in August 2005.

Taken together, these two field studies included close to eight hundred online group discussions involving more than twelve hundred different participants, most of whom attended three or four group meetings over several months. With extensive survey data (nineteen separate survey waves in the 2000 to 2001 project and ten waves in the 2004 to 2005 project), full transcripts of the online interactions, and carefully designed experimental comparisons, we are in a good position to evaluate who attends such discussions, the nature of citizens' online behavior, and the influence of the discussions on knowledge, opinions, and attitudes.

Reading Results

Who Attends Online Discussions?
Generally, about 30 to 40 percent of those invited actually attended the online discussions in both projects, producing groups averaging around

a half dozen persons each. Robust and predictable differences between project attendees and nonattendees emerge, although most such differences are relatively small in magnitude. No significant differences were observed in gender, region of the country, or political leanings; however, people who showed up for the electronic discussions, in both projects, were significantly more likely to be white than those who did not (about a 3 to 4 percent difference), significantly older (by about three years on average), and better educated. The best multivariate models, even those employing as many as thirty predictor variables, account for only small proportions of variance in participation—less than 20 percent in the Electronic Dialogue and less than 10 percent in the Healthcare Dialogue. Most of the variability in attendance among invitees appears to be random rather than systematic, and both projects managed to assemble samples of discussion participants that were highly diverse and broadly representative of the general population.

Many of the phenomena that are thought to stem from engagement in deliberation—trust in other citizens, knowledge, the ability to understand reasons on both sides of issues, civic participation—are also predictors of attendance. Discussion attendees in both projects were significantly higher than nonattendees in their levels of interpersonal trust, regular offline political discussion, political participation, and community engagement. Those who attended the electronic conversations also scored significantly higher than nonattendees on scales measuring political knowledge and interest in public affairs, and in the Healthcare Dialogue project, they were also significantly more knowledgeable about health-related policy issues and more confident in health care institutions. Multiple regressions consistently show that the most powerful predictor of attendance is "argument repertoire"—the list of reasons that a respondent gives in support of his or her opinion on an issue and reasons that other people might disagree. This argument repertoire has proved to be a validated and reliable measure of opinion quality (Cappella, Price, and Nir 2002).

Who "Talks" Online?

Individual participants in both projects contributed on average several hundred words per discussion. Discounting informal small talk at the beginning and end of each discussion and focusing only on the main deliberations, we found that participants in the Healthcare Dialogue project, for instance, averaged just over three hundred words per person. Multiple regressions predicting individual word counts indicate that older participants—who are more likely than younger people to attend discussions—contributed significantly fewer words. Typing skills have a small effect. Although no significant gender differences emerged in the health care deliberations, women contributed significantly more words in the 2000 campaign study. The clearest pattern, though, is the tendency of more politically involved and knowledgeable participants to enter more words into the discussions. In the Healthcare Dialogue deliberations, policy elites contributed significantly more words than members of the health care issue public, who in turn contributed significantly more words than ordinary citizens who are less interested in and knowledgeable about the issues. Again, argument repertoire emerges as one of the strongest predictors of the amount of "speaking."

Despite these biases in favor of more knowledgeable participants, they are small relative to what one might expect from the literature on face-to-face groups. Engagement in the online groups tended to be distributed evenly across participants, with variance across group members typically reaching about 80 percent of its maximum value (Undem 2001). Nor did either project give any indication that those holding minority views are reticent in online discussions. Indeed, those whose issue preferences were furthest from other group members tend to contribute more rather than fewer words.

How Did People Interact Online?

Both qualitative and quantitative analyses of transcripts indicate that the citizen discussions were not especially sophisticated in policy terms but nonetheless were substantive and responsive. This was so even in the Electronic Dialogue discussions, which were not formal deliberations but instead loosely structured discussions about candidates and the issues (see, e.g., Price, Nir, and Cappella 2005; Price and David 2005). People freely and frankly exchanged opinions. In the 2000 campaign discussions, for example, individual participants expressed an average of fifteen statements of opinion about each of the issues discussed.

Perhaps most encouraging to advocates of deliberation, participants tended to explain their opinions, and they were willing to disagree with one another. Close to 40 percent of all pro or con statements came with one or more arguments supporting the position (Price and David 2005). Both opinion expression and argumentation also tended to be equitably distributed across participants. When word counts are controlled, the only variable that shows much relationship to the number of arguments made is the strength with which a participant holds an opinion (Price and David 2005). Analysis of transcripts found that most groups produced a wide range of both pro and con arguments on the issues discussed, and survey responses in both projects indicated that participants felt free to express their views and perceived their group members' opinions to be diverse. Even groups that were homogeneously liberal or conservative produced a reasonable balance of both pro and con arguments on most issues.

How Did Participants Feel about Their Experiences Online?

People generally felt positively about their online experiences (Price and Cappella 2002, 2006). Large majorities in both projects reported that the discussion experience was interesting and enjoyable. In the Electronic Dialogue study, liking of the experience was uniform across liberal, conservative, and mixed groups. In the Healthcare Dialogue deliberations, policy elites expressed slightly less positive reactions than other citizens, but a substantial majority of elites reported liking the experience. Members of the Healthcare Dialogue groups, which concluded their deliberations by voting on priorities for health care policy, expressed high levels of satisfaction with their final choices (Price and Cappella 2006). The vast majority of attendees said that they think "the potential of this technology for good political discussions" is either "good" or "excellent" (Price and Cappella 2002).

Adverse reactions to disagreement were uncommon. Instead, exposure to opposing views appeared to be one of the attractions of the online encounters. Open-ended survey questions invited Electronic Dialogue participants to identify what they liked and disliked about the experience. Almost half of all coded "likes" referred to hearing others' views, interacting with people from different parts of the country, or learning how much they agreed or disagreed with other citizens. By comparison, just over 12 percent singled out the chance to express their views (Undem 2001). Aspects of the discussions that were disliked were fewer in number and most commonly were not the substance of personal interactions but instead were technical issues such as logging in or keeping up with scrolled comments on screen.

Positive reactions to the online experience were common to both members of traditionally empowered political groups and also those traditionally disempowered (that is, women, ethnic minorities, younger people, and less educated participants). Zhang (2008) found that, if anything, members of disempowered groups tended by slight margins to find the discussions more enjoyable than did others. Analysis of open-ended responses to the surveys indicated that different aspects of the experience appealed to more traditionally advantaged groups and those less advantaged. The disempowered tended to report that what they liked most was the opportunity to express their own opinions, and the empowered—whites, males, better-educated participants—said that they most like to opportunity to hear what others had to say (Zhang 2008).

Did People Learn Anything from the Discussions?

Analyzing the effects of deliberation on knowledge, attitudes, and behavior is complicated by the fact that, as noted earlier, the best predictors of attendance proved to be those variables usually cast as theoretical outcomes. Although this can be interpreted as partly confirming the reciprocal relationship between deliberation and good citizenship, it must be taken into account when attempting to gauge the effect of deliberation on attitudes and knowledge. Toward this end, using dozens of measures available from our extensive baseline surveys, we calculated an estimate of each person's propensity to attend and controlled for this propensity score to remove the effects of potential confounding variables (Rosenbaum and Rubin 1983; D'Agostino 1998). Particularly when coupled with separate statistical controls for baseline levels of target outcomes and any variables that may remain imbalanced, this propensity scoring enables fair experimental comparisons to test hypothesized deliberation effects (see Price, Goldthwaite, and Cappella 2002; Price, Feldman, Freres, Zhang, and Cappella 2006).

Analyses of this sort support found that, although there were some gains in objective knowledge—such as knowing that George W. Bush supported government-funded private school vouchers in the 2000 campaign (Price and Cappella 2002)—gains in issue knowledge were modest at best. On the other hand, deliberation did appear to produce significant gains in "argument repertoires"—the range of arguments that people hold both in support of and against their favored positions. Online discussion attendance significantly and positively predicted scores on this argument repertoire measure, controlling for argument repertoire assessed on the baseline survey and for propensity to attend the discussions (Cappella, Price, and Nir 2002). In the Healthcare Dialogue study, analyses indicated that reading the briefing documents affected objective knowledge about health care policy, while attending the online discussions increased argument repertoire (Price, Feldman, and Cappella 2007).

Did the Discussions Influence Participants' Opinions?
Deliberation increases levels of opinion holding. Attendance at the Healthcare Dialogue discussions, for instance, significantly predicted far fewer "don't know" responses to a wide range of policy-opinion questions, controlling for baseline opinion holding and propensity to attend (Price, Feldman, Freres, Zhang, and Cappella 2006).

Deliberation only sometimes produced shifts in policy opinions. Aggregate levels of support or opposition for the policies discussed remained unchanged on many issues; but when group-level opinion did shift, the data suggest generally rational movements in keeping with the pattern of group argumentation (Price and Cappella 2002). In discussing the possible use of federal funding for character education or school vouchers, for instance, Electronic Dialogue groups tended to produce more opposing than supportive arguments and thus became on average less enthusiastic about such funding.

Do Discussions Affect the Quality of Opinions?
Assessing opinion quality is difficult (Price and Neijens 1997), but deliberation-induced changes in preferences did seem to reflect movement toward more informed and politically sophisticated positions. Statistical analyses of Price, Feldman, Freres, Zhang, and Cappella (2006) found that Healthcare Dialogue attendees were less likely than nonattendees to support tax-based reforms and were more supportive than nonattendees of government programming and regulations as a means to cut heath care costs. The differences between participants and nonparticipants parallel those between policy elites and general citizens prior to the discussions. Thus, deliberation appeared to move citizens in the direction of elite opinion (and because the shifts occurred to a greater degree in groups without elite members, they apparently were not simply the product of elite persuasion).

Another telling pattern is that the complexity of people's grasp of policy distinctions appeared to increase as a result of online discussion. Price, Arnold, Baek, and Cappella (2008) used latent-variable structural equation modeling to examine the interrelationships among fifteen separate policy-preference questions that reflected three distinct approaches to lowering the cost of prescription drugs. They found that attending the Healthcare Dialogue online deliberations resulted in weaker correlations among these three different, underlying approaches, suggesting that after discussing prescription-drug policy, people discriminated more finely among competing alternatives. By comparing the patterns found in health care policy elites to those of ordinary citizens, those among the most and least knowledgeable participants, those best and least well educated, and the like, Price et al. (2008) were able to show that this pattern of weaker correlations indeed reflected a more sophisticated grasp of the issues at stake.

Did Participation Foster Political Engagement?

Online discussion attendees, relative to nonattendees with comparable propensities to participate, score significantly higher in end-of-project social trust, community engagement, and political participation. Participants in the Electronic Dialogue discussion reported voting in the 2000 presidential election at significantly higher rates than their counterparts who did not attend, even after extensive controls (Price and Cappella 2002; Price, Goldthwaite, and Cappella 2002). People who attended the Healthcare Dialogue meetings reported increases in self-reported personal political efficacy and engagement in health policy-related activities such as working for advocacy groups, attending meetings, or donating money to a group pursing health care reform (Feldman and Freres 2006). Thus, the sorts of social and political capital that contribute to participation in online deliberations are themselves products of discussion as well, lending support to claims that social capital and deliberative behavior are mutually reinforcing. Although the estimated effects on civic engagement are small, results are consistent across a number of different indicators and across both projects.

We found almost no evidence that the observed gains in social trust or in electoral and community participation were mitigated by encountering disagreement (Price, Goldthwaite-Young, Cappella, and Romantan 2006). Estimated effects of Electronic Dialogue participation on postproject community engagement were slightly larger for those who encountered more supportive group members (based on coded discussion transcripts), but there were nonetheless significant positive effects of discussion even for those who met with substantial disagreement in their groups. Encountering disagreement did not moderate effects of discussion on either voting or postproject social trust.

Overall, How Do Citizens Fare in Online Discussions?
Results of both studies indicate robust and predictable differences between those who attend online discussions and those who were invited

but did not attend, with the former being significantly more knowledgeable, more politically engaged, and more active in their communities.
Nevertheless, most of the differences are small, leaving the group of
attendees broadly representative of the wider population. Extensive analyses of who contributes to the discussions reveal similar biases in participation, with the more advantaged segments of the population
contributing at higher rates than those who are less well educated,
members of racial minorities, and other traditionally disempowered
groups. Even so, the more striking pattern is of largely equitable distributions of words contributed across participants, and none of the studies
indicated any reticence on the part of people who held minority viewpoints on the issues. Indeed, those whose issue preferences were furthest
from other group members tend to contribute more words to the discussions than their peers. Careful analysis of interaction patterns between
elites and nonelites over time, on the other hand, did find subtle evidence
of the emergence of status differences as ordinary citizens learn to be
deferential to those with greater expertise (Baek and Price 2008).

In the discursive encounters examined, people freely and frankly
exchanged opinions, with nearly half of all expressed opinions being
backed up with what trained coders identified as a reason (although these
were not typically in the form of refutable evidence), and both opinion
expression and argumentation tended to be equitably distributed across
participants, regardless of status. Most participants found the discussions
to be engaging, interesting, and worthwhile, although elite participants
tended to have less enthusiasm for the experience than did lower-status
group members. Elites were more likely than others to cite the opportunity to hear others' views as a major attraction of participating, whereas
members of disempowered groups—females, less educated participants,
and members of racial minorities—were more likely than others to cite
the opportunity to express their own views as a major attraction. There
were few indications that people found that political disagreement was
off-putting or made them feel uncomfortable.

In balance, the findings indicate that randomly selected citizens adapted
well to the online environments, produced reasonably coherent discussions, willingly aired their disagreements, and responded favorably to
the experience. A series of statistical analyses point to generally positive
effects of participation in the discussions, including increased levels of
opinion holding, better understanding of arguments bearing the issues
discussed, and a more complex and differentiated understanding of

policy options. One of the field experiments, which involved the recruitment of a special sample of high-level health care policy elites, permitted comparisons of ordinary citizens with such high-status participants before and after engagement in deliberation over health care issues. These comparisons consistently show that the experience of deliberation brings ordinary citizens into closer alignment with elites, in terms of both their substantive policy choices and the way they perceive policy alternatives.

Design Decisions

The data summarized here bring with them many limitations because they reflect only two projects. Each was university-sponsored rather than government-run, drew from probability samples of the population rather than from self-selected pools of participants, and engaged citizens in a series of regulated, real-time, small-group discussions rather than the asynchronous message systems that might be more typical of online consultations. Lacking reasonable experimental comparisons to face-to-face deliberations, we cannot say which if any of our observations are the unique product of the online environment itself. Thus, although we might suspect that participants' openness and tolerance of disagreement resulted from the diminished social cues and relative anonymity afforded by text-based exchanges, such propositions must remain speculative. Similarly, in the absence of comparisons to other online deliberation programs or to typical Web-based discussions as they now occur naturally, we cannot say how much our findings stem from the particular manner in which these discussions were designed and undertaken.

Despite these limitations, however, these experiments in "online democracy" do take us some distance in addressing questions about the putative value deliberation and the capacities of ordinary citizens to engage in reasonable political discussions online. Our modest but important goal was to test whether, in principle, ordinary citizens would make good use of the opportunity to discuss public affairs and policy online. The picture emerging from these analyses shows them not meeting all the lofty ideals of deliberative theory but coming much closer than many would have expected. They adapted readily and well to the online environment. They engaged each other, displayed a willingness to disagree with and debate their opponents, learned arguments for and against their own views, responded on the whole favorably to their online experiences, and came away more trusting and civically engaged than comparable nonparticipants. Our findings consequently highlight the potential benefits of involving ordinary citizens in policy deliberations.

Although this research underscores citizens' capacities to offer productive online consultations, it offers little by way of directive guidance about how such consultations should be structured. In closing, more speculative ground is approached by considering the extent to which the largely laudable citizen behavior observed in these field experiments may have been context-dependent and also the differences that might be expected under varying communication systems and consultative designs. The conclusion draws attention to a few of the issues designers face.

• *Real-time interactions versus asynchronous postings*   For many practical reasons, online consultations may eschew the synchronous, real-time discussion formats examined here in favor of asynchronous exchanges, which permit greater flexibility and are far easier to manage. The logistical complication involved in arranging and conducting group meetings include scheduling and considerable expense. However, comments from participants in both projects suggest that the immediate, personal, and lively nature of the real-time group interactions had much, perhaps everything, to do with their success. Worth noting in this connection is the fact that the Healthcare Dialogue project constructed asynchronous bulletin boards for its participants to use between group discussions, but despite efforts to seed these asynchronous postings, only a few participants used this facility.

• *Citizen-driven versus designer-driven agendas*   When calling citizens together to discuss policy, there is a natural impulse to create a clear decision making structure to guide deliberations because of a fear of rambling and unproductive group discussions (see, for example, the choice frameworks and discussion guides prepared by the National Issues Forum). However, e-consultation designers need to permit citizens maximal flexibility in shaping their own agendas to prevent the foreclosure of unanticipated but valuable avenues of consideration and to maintain the legitimacy of the public consultation process. In the Healthcare Dialogue project, surveys of participants were conducted to determine which problems they thought were most pressing to address, and each round of discussions was designed to be responsive to the choices and interests of group members, as expressed in prediscussion surveys.

• *Light versus heavy group moderation*   Any use of group deliberation as part of an e-consultation will require consideration of group moderators and the roles they might play. Some practitioners of deliberative democracy heavily emphasize the training of facilitators who actively guide discussions, attempt to engage reticent participants, summarize progress, and otherwise lead and direct discussions. In contrast, both projects reported here used minimal moderation. Instead, they relied on scripts that determined exactly what comments were posted by moderators (and when), both to standardize the treatment of groups and to leave participants in control. The success of our discussions under these conditions calls into question the need for more elaborate and intrusive forms of group moderation.

• *Text-based versus audiovisual communication* Both the Electronic Dialogue project and the Healthcare Dialogue project used only simple, text-based interactions. Some aspects of public deliberation, particularly trust-building aspects, may be more effectively conveyed through aural or visual contact. On the other hand, the greater anonymity of the text-based discussions may have produced more open exchanges of viewpoints, and the use of writing seems to have enforced more thoughtful exchanges. We are unable to say at this point exactly what effect the particular online, text-based formats might have had on the strength of our results. However, there seemed to be little need to use either audio or video to accomplish group tasks, and when asked directly whether they would like to have incorporated images or audio, participants in the Electronic Dialogue project were cool to the idea, with most saying they preferred to exchange text only.

• *Single interactions versus meetings over time* Finally, it is worth noting that both projects relied on multiple, hour-long online meetings over a number of months. It is unclear whether single interactions or more superficial exchanges would have produced similar results. The projects also relied not just on the online group meetings but on periodic feedback delivered through surveys as well. This opportunity to provide feedback both individually (via the surveys) and in groups (via the discussions) may well have been central to the success of these ventures.

Careful studies of the implications of these sorts of design decisions remain to be conducted. Here we have marshaled evidence to suggest that citizens can indeed, at least under some conditions, prove reliable and engaging partners in sorting out even complicated issues like those surrounding health care reform. The major challenge of democracy-oriented policy research is not primarily one of establishing whether citizens are up to the task. Instead, the question is how we might, though systematic experimentation, formulate communication systems that best enable citizens to "play politics" fairly and well.

Notes

1. This review closely follows a similar compendium of findings presented in Price (2009).

2. These studies were supported by grants from the Pew Charitable Trusts, the Annenberg Public Policy Center of the University of Pennsylvania, and the National Science Foundation (Grant EIA-0306801) to Vincent Price and Joseph N. Cappella. Views expressed here are those of the author alone and do not necessarily reflect those of the sponsoring agencies.

References

Baek, Y. M., and V. Price. 2008. "Learning to Be Deferential: Effects of Group Composition and Social Status on Emerging Patterns of Online Discussion." Unpublished manuscript, Annenberg School for Communication, University of Pennsylvania.

Barber, B. 1984. *Strong Democracy: Participatory Politics for a New Age*. Berkeley: University of California Press.

Bargh, J. A., K. Y. A. McKenna, and G. M. Fitzsimmons. 2002. "Can You See the Real Me? Activation and Expression of the 'True Self' on the Internet." *Journal of Social Issues* 58, no. 1:33–48.

Becker, T., and C. D. Slaton. 2000. *The Future of Teledemocracy*. Westport, CT: Praeger.

Brown, R. 2000. *Group Processes: Dynamics within and between Groups*. Oxford: Blackwell.

Cappella, J. N., V. Price, and L. Nir. 2002. "Argument Repertoire as a Reliable and Valid Measure of Opinion Quality: Electronic Dialogue in Campaign 2000." *Political Communication* 19, no. 1:73–93.

Cohen, J. 1997. "Deliberation and Democratic Legitimacy." In *Deliberative Democracy: Essays on Reason and Politics*, edited by J. F. Bohman and W. Rehg, 67–91. Cambridge: MIT Press.

Converse, P. E. 1964. "The Nature of Belief Systems in Mass Publics." In *Ideology and Discontent*, edited by D. Apter, 206–261. New York: Free Press.

D'Agostino, R. B. 1998. "Tutorial in Biostatistics: Propensity Scoring Methods for Bias Reduction in the Comparison of a Treatment to a Non-randomized Control Group." *Statistics in Medicine* 17, no. 19:2265–2281.

Dahl, R. A. 1956. *A Preface to Democratic Theory*. Chicago: University of Chicago Press.

Dennis, A. R. 1996. "Information Exchange and Use in Group Decision Making: You Can Lead a Group to Information, But You Can't Make It Think." *Management Information Systems Quarterly* 20, no. 4:433–457.

Dryzek, J. S. 1990. *Discursive Democracy: Politics, Policy, and Political Science.* New York: Cambridge University Press.

Dubrovsky, V. J., S. Kiesler, and B. N. Sethna. 1991. "The Equalization Phenomenon: Status Effects in Computer-Mediated and Face-to-Face Decision Making Groups." *Human-Computer Interaction* 6, no. 2:119–146.

Eliasoph, N. 1998. *Avoiding Politics.* Cambridge: Cambridge University Press.

Feldman, L., and D. Freres. 2006. "Efficacy, Trust, and Engagement Analyses." Unpublished report of the Healthcare Dialogue project. Annenberg School, University of Pennsylvania.

Fishkin, J. S. 2000. "Virtual Democratic Possibilities: Prospects for Internet Democracy." Paper presented at the conference on Internet, Democracy and Public Goods, Belo Horizonte, Brazil, November 6-10.

Gallupe, R. B., G. DeSantis, and G. W. Dickson. 1988. "Computer-based Support for Problem Finding: An Experimental Investigation." *Management Information Systems Quarterly* 12, no. 2:277–296.

Gutmann, A., and D. Thompson. 1996. *Democracy and Disagreement.* Cambridge, Mass.: Harvard University Press.

Hibbing, J. R., and E. Theiss-Morse. 2002. *Stealth Democracy: America's Beliefs about How Government Should Work.* Cambridge: Cambridge University Press.

Hollingshead, A. B. 1996. "Information Suppression and Status Persistence in Group Decision Making: The Effects of Communication Media." *Human Communication Research* 23, no. 2:193–219.

Hollingshead, A. B. 1998. "Retrieval Processes in Transactive Memory Systems." *Journal of Personality and Social Psychology* 74, no. 3:659–671.

Hollingshead, A. B., and D. P. Brandon. 2003. "Potential Benefits of Communication in Transactive Memory Systems." *Human Communication Research* 29, no. 4:607–615.

Kiesler, S., J. Siegel, and T. McGuire. 1984. "Social Psychological Aspects of Computer-Mediated Communication." *American Psychologist* 39, no. 10:1123–1134.

Lippmann, W. 1922. *Public Opinion.* New York: Harcourt Brace Jovanovich.

Macpherson, C. B. 1977. *The Life and Times of Liberal Democracy.* Oxford: Oxford University Press.

Mansbridge, J. J. 1983. *Beyond Adversary Democracy.* Chicago: University of Chicago Press.

Mathews, D. 1994. *Politics for People: Finding a Responsible Public Voice.* Chicago: University of Chicago Press.

Mendelberg, T. 2002. "The Deliberative Citizen: Theory and Evidence." In *Political Decision Making, Deliberation and Participation: Research in*

Micropolitics, edited by Michael X. Delli Carpini, Leonie Huddy, and Robert Y. Shapiro, vol. 6, 151–193. Greenwich, CT: JAI Press.

Mutz, D. 2002. "The Consequences of Cross-Cutting Networks for Political Participation." *American Journal of Political Science* 46, no. 4:838–855.

Noelle-Neumann, E. 1984. *The Spiral of Silence: Public Opinion—Our Social Skin*. Chicago: University of Chicago Press.

Papacharissi, Z. 2004. "Democracy Online: Civility, Politeness, and the Democratic Potential of Online Political Discussion Groups." *New Media and Society* 6, no. 2:259–284.

Pateman, C. 1970. *Participation and Democratic Theory*. London: Cambridge University Press.

Pin, E. J. 1985. *Pleasure of Your Company: A Social-Psychological Analysis of Modern Sociability*. New York: Praeger.

Poster, M. 1999. "The Net as a Public Sphere." In *Communication in History: Technology, Culture, Society*, 3rd ed., edited by D. J. Crowley and P. Heyer, 335–337. New York: Longman.

Price, V. 1992. *Public Opinion*. Newbury Park, CA: Sage.

Price, V. 2009. "Citizens Deliberating Online: Theory and Some Evidence." In *Online Deliberation: Design, Research, and Practice*, edited by T. Davies and S. P. Gangadharan, 37–57. Stanford: CSLI.

Price, V., A. Arnold, Y. M. Baek, and J. N. Cappella. 2008. "Deliberation, Constraint and Complexity." Paper presented at the annual meeting of the International Communication Association, Montreal, Canada, May.

Price, V., and J. N. Cappella. 2002. "Online Deliberation and Its Influence: The Electronic Dialogue Project in Campaign 2000." *IT and Society* 1 (Summer):303–329. http://digilib.unsri.ac.id/download/v01i01a20.pdf.

Price, V., and J. N. Cappella. 2006. "Bringing an Informed Public into Policy Debates through Online Deliberation: The Case of Health Care Reform." Proceedings of the Seventh Annual International Conference on Digital Government Research, San Diego, CA, May 21–24, Digital Government Research Center.

Price, V., and C. David. 2005. "Talking about Elections: A Study of Patterns in Citizen Deliberation Online." Paper presented at the annual meeting of the International Communication Association, New York, May.

Price, V., L. Feldman, and J. N. Cappella. 2007. "Online Deliberation and Public Opinion about Health Care Policy." Paper presented at the annual conference of the American Association for Public Opinion Research, Anaheim, CA, May.

Price, V., and L. Feldman, D. Freres, W. Zhang, and J. N. Cappella. 2006. "Informing Public Opinion about Health Care Reform through Online Deliberation." Paper presented at the annual meeting of the International Communication Association, Dresden, Germany, June.

Price, V., D. Goldthwaite, and J. N. Cappella. 2002. "Civic Engagement, Social Trust, and Online Deliberation." Paper presented at the annual meeting of the American Association for Public Opinion Research, St. Petersburg, FL, May.

Price, V., D. Goldthwaite-Young, J. N. Cappella, and A. Romantan. 2006. "Online Political Discussion, Civic Engagement, and Social Trust." Unpublished manuscript, Annenberg School, University of Pennsylvania.

Price, V., and P. Neijens. 1997. "Opinion Quality in Public Opinion Research." *International Journal of Public Opinion Research* 9, no. 4:336–360.

Price, V., L. Nir, and J. Cappella. 2005. "Framing Public Discussion of Gay Civil Unions." *Public Opinion Quarterly* 69, no. 2:179–212.

Putnam, R. D. 2000. *Bowling Alone: The Collapse and Revival of American Community*. New York: Simon and Schuster.

Rains, S. A. 2005. "Leveling the Organizational Playing Field—Virtually: A Meta-Analysis of Experimental Research Assessing the Impact of Group Support System Use on Member Influence Behaviors." *Communication Research* 32, no. 2:193–234.

Rice, R. E. 1993. "Media Appropriateness: Using Social Presence Theory to Compare Traditional and New Organizational Media." *Human Communication Research* 19, no. 4:451–484.

Rosenbaum, P. R., and D. B. Rubin. 1983. "The Central Role of the Propensity Score in Observational Studies for Causal Effects." *Biometrika* 70, no. 1:41–55.

Sanders, L. M. 1997. "Against Deliberation." *Political Theory* 25, no. 3:347–376.

Schudson, M. 1997. "Why Conversation Is Not the Soul of Democracy." *Critical Studies in Mass Communication* 14, no. 4:297–309.

Schumpeter, J. A. 1942. *Capitalism, Socialism and Democracy*. New York: Harper.

Stromer-Galley, J. 2003. "Diversity of Political Conversation on the Internet: Users' Perspectives." *Journal of Computer-Mediated Communication* 8, no. 3.

Sunstein, C. 2001. *Republic.com*. Princeton: Princeton University Press.

Tidwell, L., and J. B. Walther. 2002. "Computer-Mediated Communication Effects on Disclosure, Impressions, and Interpersonal Evaluations: Getting to Know One Another a Bit at a Time." *Human Communication Research* 28, no. 3:317–348.

Undem, T. 2001. "Factors Affecting Discussion Quality: The Effects of Group Size, Gender, and Political Heterogeneity in Online Discussion Groups." Unpublished master's thesis, University of Pennsylvania, Philadelphia.

Walther, J. B. 1995. "Relational Aspects of Computer-Mediated Communication: Experimental Observations over Time." *Organization Science* 6, no. 2:186–203.

Warren, M. 1992. "Democratic Theory and Self-Transformation." *American Political Science Review* 86, no. 1:8–23.

Zhang, W. 2008. "Deliberation and the Disempowered: Access, Experience and Influence." Doctoral dissertation, Annenberg School for Communication, University of Pennsylvania.

7

The Participatory Journey in Online Consultations

Scott Wright

Introduction: Participation as a Journey

Ensuring that online consultation exercises are inclusive poses serious challenges for governments. E-inclusion activities typically focus on the digital divide, which persists as a core policy issue across Europe. The strategies deployed in an attempt to overcome the problems have changed over the years as our understanding of the digital divide has evolved. Although it is increasingly accepted that the problem is multifaceted and not just about having access to computers and the Internet, further work is necessary to understand the implications for inclusive consultations. Rather than focusing solely on the digital divide, this chapter takes a holistic approach to understanding barriers to participation in online consultations. This is necessary because, as Vincent Price (chapter 6 in this volume) demonstrates, many factors intermingle in shaping online participation. Focusing solely on the digital divide is likely to fail.

Research suggests that online political activity remains limited in the United Kingdom (Dutton and Helsper 2007), but findings do vary. According to the *Audit of Political Engagement* (Hansard Society 2007, 48), only 4 percent of respondents had participated in any kind of government or parliamentary consultation, and only 14 percent would be willing to participate in the future. The results stand in contrast to recent research by Stephen Coleman, Rachel Gibson, and Agnes Schneeberger (chapter 8 in this volume), which found that 92 percent of people are willing to take part in online consultations and that for many they appealed more than offline action. However, the perceived importance of the issue remains crucial (Lowndes, Pratchett, and Stoker 2001, 447–448), and actual participation remains low. Moreover, these data go only so far when we attempt to understand why a willingness to participate often does not translate into actual participation.[1]

This chapter brings together research from a range of academic and policy disciplines in an attempt to map out the potential barriers that can hinder a citizen's journey toward participation. If policy makers do not understand the various barriers, they cannot be expected to plan effective consultation strategies. But before beginning a detailed analysis of the barriers, it is necessary to outline and deconstruct in more detail the notion of a participatory journey. The metaphor of a participatory journey does not imply that there is a predetermined route or even beginning and end points for the journey. When developing online consultation initiatives, it must be acknowledged that there is a unique journey for each citizen. The backgrounds and experiences of citizens influence the journey that they take.[2] Thus, to continue the analogy, it would be more accurate to talk of journeys and variously skilled and experienced travelers using diverse modes of transport. To illustrate this point and the importance of considering users when designing institutional paths more generally, I have briefly outlined some hypothetical travelers and the journeys they face:

Journey 1: The expedition   This is the participatory challenge faced by most people. Those on an expedition face the most serious challenges: they have to travel far, often by slow routes and with significant barriers. These issues mean they are likely either not to start on their journey or to stop their journey along the way.

Journey 2: The long-haul flight   Citizens on the long-haul flight will likely have some previous (but limited) experience of political participation but will still face significant barriers, including disappointment with previous attempts to influence decisions.

Journey 3: The day trip   Citizens who fall into this category participate in politics but irregularly (once a year or so). They are typically civic-minded citizens with an interest in local issues and are aware of different routes to participation.

Journey 4: The commute   Commuters are individuals who participate so regularly that their journey is almost routinized. They are highly experienced with their chosen method of transport (for example, the Internet) and know shortcuts to make their journey more efficient and effective.

The agency of citizens is both constrained and facilitated by a range of institutional factors, which effectively lay out the topography of the land on which citizens travel. Governments may adopt heavily prescriptive paths, which limit choice; they may limit opportunities to participate between elections, following a Schumpeterian approach; they might (deliberately or otherwise) use language that puts people off participating; or they can fail to signpost participatory paths effectively. This list is not exhaustive. Put simply, if institutions construct mountainous terrain, then only the most committed, skilled, or organized groups will reach the summit. Research into barriers to participation has been conducted in the context of elections, and we know that the more barriers there are, the lower turnout becomes (Highton 2004; Brians and Grofman 1999; Leighley and Nagler 1992) and that people can suffer from fatigue when there are numerous voting options (Brockington 2003).

This study is conducted in the context of one particular form of participation—the consultation exercise, which some see as being an inherently limited route that falls seriously short of actual participatory democracy. Many of these shortcomings arise from how the consultation is designed and organized. My aim here is to tease out human agency and structural factors as well as how the ways in which they interplay contrive to inhibit participation. Given that much work has focused on the digital divide, the journey begins here.

The Digital Divide

The British government has spent millions of pounds on activities to close the digital divide among its citizens. One of the first initiatives, UKOnline, had its roots in the U.S. National Information Infrastructure (NII) and provided Internet access and training around the country—along with promises to provide Internet connections in every school and library. Decreasing the digital divide has grown in importance as a policy priority and is now, according to Jim Murphy, the e-inclusion minister, central to "social inclusion and in today's world this is therefore about social justice" (cited in British Educational Communications and Technology Agency [BECTA] 2008, 5). Moreover, the e-inclusion agenda is directly linked to strengthening representative democracy as one of six core benefits: "A digital "Big Bang" will transform how we participate in a modern democracy" (Department for Culture, Media, and Sport/Department for Business Innovation and Skills 2009, 28).

After many millions of pounds and numerous initiatives by both government and the third sector (the nonprofit, nongovernment sector), significant disparities persist. Age remains central: 90 percent of people under the age of eighteen use the Internet compared with 37 percent of those aged sixty-five to seventy-four and 24 percent of those seventy-five and over (Dutton, Helsper, and Gerberg 2009, 17). However, one in ten people under the age of eighteen are also digitally excluded in the United Kingdom, and this may affect them negatively in the future (in terms of employment, earnings, and education) (see Mossberger, Tolbert, and McNeal 2008).[3] Gender differences in Internet use continue to shrink with a slight bias toward men of 3 percent (ibid., 18). Income persists as a significant barrier: 97 percent of those earning over £40,000 use the Internet compared with 38 percent of those earning less that £12,500 (ibid., 16). Similarly, those who have (or are) attending a higher education institution are far more likely to have Internet access (93 percent) compared to those with a basic education (49 percent). Although there is a trend of increasing levels of Internet access over recent years among wealthier and better-educated groups, for those at the opposite end of the income and education spectrum the trend is one of mild decreases in access. Finally, people who report themselves as having a disability or health problem are significantly less likely to use the Internet (41 percent compared to 75 percent), a worrying (and surprising) finding given the hyping of new media as an empowering force for the disabled.

The government has recently announced a raft of new e-inclusion policy measures. Although individually they would be likely to fail given the complexity of the issue, collectively they stand a chance of increasing online uptake (even though the national plan lacks sufficient detail and is potentially the most important). The main policy measures include:

• Offering all low-income families (those with a combined income of under £15,500 per annum or those receiving certain benefits, such as Job Seekers Allowance) with children between the ages of seven and eighteen a free computer, three years free technical support, and free broadband Internet access for one year;
• Providing universal access to two megabits per second broadband by 2012, funded by a tax on phone lines; and
• Establishing a National Plan for Digital Participation, including a communications campaign, targeted outreach, and the digital switchover of public services.[4]

If policy makers are to deliver e-inclusion, they must recognize that different groups of digitally excluded people provide varying reasons for their exclusion and that therefore a multifaceted policy response is necessary. Although the national plan has some potential in this area, it is too early to say how the policy will be fleshed out in practice—and thus to assess its effectiveness.[5]

Measuring Internet penetration is the tip of a large iceberg. What is important is not the extent of Internet penetration but the reasons that underpin digital exclusion. The government has begun funding research into this subject, and the findings are a reminder of how complicated the situation is. The OFCOM/MORI report (2009) used both quantitative and qualitative methods to study home Internet access and found that 20 percent of people were planning to get Internet access in the next six months (often younger people with Internet access in another location), leading to a conclusion that experience of the Internet is an important demand stimulus. Encouraging demand is crucial because more people (42 percent) said the main reason they did not have the Internet at home was a lack of need or interest than those who lacked the necessary resources, such as skills (4 percent) or the finances to pay for a computer or the connection. Only 12 percent said they missed out, and 43 percent said they would not be interested in having Internet access, even if it was free.[6] The 2009 Oxford Internet Survey also looked at why people do not use the Internet and found "multiple and often interconnected reasons for their non-use. There is no one simple approach, but an array of individual and household circumstances that compound one another. In many ways, moving a significantly greater segment of Britons online will require work on a case-by-case basis, new ways to communicate the value of the Internet to non-users, and a major breakthrough in the accessibility of the Internet, such as advances in user interface designs, which would dramatically enhance the usability of the Internet for those non-users who presently do not see the benefits of inclusion" (Dutton et al. 2009, 6).

To summarize, the digital divide is not something that we will somehow "grow out of" as Internet penetration matures (Compaine 2001 argues that the digital divide is a myth but fails to note that the myth was an unnecessarily reductionist view of the digital divide). As technological developments continue, the danger is that many of today's relatively confident middle-aged users will be excluded from participating in the latest developments because they lack new skills. Even if there were universal Internet access, digital divides would still exist. For example, people have varying levels of online skill, and there will be an inevitable divide between those who create content and those who solely consume. It is unsurprising that the government's policy agenda has struggled to keep up given the rapid pace of change—highlighted by the sheer number of different proposals. But to what extent and how does the digital divide matter for the inclusiveness of consultations?

The Digital Divide and Political Participation

The digital divide clearly has implications for the inclusiveness of online consultations and political participation more generally. First, there is a debate about whether the Internet might balkanize political debate (Sunstein 2001), with several early empirical studies (Wilhelm 2000; Davis 1999) and some later ones (Hindman 2009) suggesting this is indeed the case. The concern is that the narrowcasting facilitated by the Internet will allow like-minded groups to talk among themselves, ignoring opposing views. In the consultative context, this might mean that deliberative experiments falter, that only certain groups (established organized stakeholders) get to hear about consultative opportunities, and only certain digitally literate voices will be heard, leaving others completely excluded. Linking these points together, this could result in the politically less interested completely ignoring politics, deliberately or otherwise.

Second, there is an ongoing concern over the extent to which the Internet harms or hinders the development of personal social capital, which is widely thought to affect the likelihood of someone participating in civic activity. Although several early studies suggested at best mixed findings or negative correlations between Internet use and social capital (Putnam 2000; Nie and Erbring 2000; Slouka 1995; Stoll 1995), subsequent empirical research has countered this (Hiltz and Turoff 1993; Wellman and Gulia 1999, 181). A growing literature suggests that it is not the Internet per se that matters but the extent to which it is used for collective, discursive actions (Norris 2003; Kobayashi, Ikeda, and Miyata 2006; Ellison, Steinfield, and Lampe 2007). This has important implications for how we analyze the digital divide—looking at not just who has access to what but also what they do with it.

In this vein, survey research by Mossberger et al. (2008) found that Internet use substantially increases civic engagement (controlling for other factors) but that a significant digital divide persists that was linked to age, wealth, education, and ethnicity. If this situation holds outside of the United States, then we can assume that using the Internet increases the likelihood that people will respond to consultations because they are more politically informed, more likely to discuss politics, and more likely to express an interest in politics (although this was not something that Mossberger et al. tested directly). Thus, the consequences of the digital divide are further compounded. There is a danger of unequal access to online consultations as well as a possible danger of inequality in wanting to participate in general. These findings have important implications for how we study the digital divide, but existing statistical research cannot always consider adequately the nuanced and diverse strategies that people employ to overcome their skills (and other) shortcomings.[7] Great care is necessary when developing such measures, which call for a mixture of quantitative and qualitative analysis.

Inclusive Consultations

Assessing the inclusiveness of citizen-government contact online is important because research suggests that it is one of the most frequent forms of contact people have with political institutions (Cohen 2006, 51). Some government departments have successfully delivered information about consultations and the chance to participate online—in some cases, with over 10 million respondents, according to a UK audit report (National Audit Office 2007, 6)—but this is far from the norm.

Before examining claims that governments are not inclusive enough in their consultations, we should first consider the nature of the consultation in question. Many consultations are not intended to be open to everyone. Their aim is to consult "relevant people" while avoiding "not helpful contributions."[8] Civil servants must balance competing demands among inclusiveness, cost, and efficiency. Consulting broadly creates costs for both government and respondents, and when and how to consult must be carefully balanced against those costs (Needham 2002, 705). In practice, this can lead to a focus on consulting with stakeholders, linked to an assumption that such groups are more likely to respond (although they can be equally overburdened and frustrated with the process; see chapter 10 in this volume) and are more likely to submit well-informed contributions (linked to the drive toward so-called evidence-based policy making). This may explain why the five principles of good regulation established by the Department for Business, Enterprise, and Regulatory Reform (BERR) do not directly cover representativeness. The British government's *Code of Practice on Consultation* is a little contradictory and may indicate a desire to balance the effectiveness of consultations with other criteria, such as being open. Initially, "effective consultation" is defined as a "[c]onsultation which is targeted at, and easily accessible to, those with a clear interest in the policy in question" (Department for Business, Enterprise, and Regulatory Reform 2008, 3). This is subsequently changed subtly to "those people the exercise is intended to reach" (4), with a further qualification that formal consultations "should be open to anyone."[9] Given these subtle differences, I settle here for a simple statement in the Code: "Any public sector organisation signing up to the Code needs to make its consultations easily accessible."[10]

Government departments increasingly prioritize online response channels (if only tacitly), and this is becoming the dominant route by which citizens travel. As the importance of the digital divide for inclusive consultations grows, it is likely to influence who replies and the overall message of public input. Although not directly about consultations, Bimber's analysis still holds: "Government officials who attempt to gauge public concerns by paying attention to citizens through e-mail will draw slightly different conclusions than they would from paying attention to traditional contacts through letters and phone. They are likely to conclude that older citizens are less concerned about public issues, and state and local governments might underestimate the size of their attentive constituencies" (Bimber 1999, 423–424).[11] Subsequent research seems to back up and strengthen this claim (Thomas and Streib 2003). But how does this tacit prioritization occur?

Governments typically argue that they attempt to mitigate the problem of the digital divide (and thus make documents easily accessible) by providing alternative forms of access to consultation documents. That is, if you are not online, you can get the consultation document by post. This approach is seriously deficient because all offline affected or interested parties probably would not be made aware that a consultation is happening and thus would not be in a position to ask for the printed consultation document. Civil servants themselves note that they often rely heavily on their Web site for advertising consultations and provide general information that might lead someone to partake in a consultation (National Audit Office 2007). The Code itself calls for "Making all the consultations run by a single organisation available in one place."[12] A heavily Web-oriented approach is suggested: "Such a service should be marketed and ideally accessible from a link on the organisations home page." Moreover, the Internet is an active, demand-led technology and thus it is unlikely that the average Web browser will happen to come across a government Web site, particularly its online consultation section (National Audit Office 2007). The digitally excluded may remain excluded. *Awareness* is the first key barrier to participation and affects both those with and without Internet access.

A systematic study of the participants and their routes to participation is beyond the scope of this study. An attempt was made to search archived consultations, but such information is rarely made public (often even basic information, requested in the guidelines, is not available). Interviewees have suggested that simply putting consultations online following a traditional format without making use of the interactive capacity of the Internet is unlikely to affect who responds or how many responses are made (see chapter 10 in this volume). Nevertheless, it is also widely agreed that "most respondents reply using electronic means." To emphasize the point, statistics from five consultations conducted by the Charity Commission show that e-mail is the most popular form of replying and that most responses come from organized groups rather than individuals:[13]

• *Public Benefit Consultations (Draft Subsector Guidance)*   78 percent of responses received via e-mail and 87 percent of all replies identified as from organizations (*n* = 684);

• *The Advancement of Education for the Public Benefit*   68 percent of responses received via email and 97 percent of all replies identified as from organizations (*n* = 166);

• *Public Benefit and Fee-Charging*   72 percent of responses received via email and 97 percent of all replies identified as from organizations (*n* = 189);

• *The Prevention or Relief of Poverty for the Public Benefit*   69 percent of responses received via email and 98 percent of all replies identified as from organizations (*n* = 58);

• *The Advancement of Religion for the Public Benefit*   90 percent of responses received via email and 72 percent of all replies identified as from organizations (*n* = 263);

• *The Advancement of Moral or Ethical Belief Systems for the Public Benefit*   100 percent of responses received via email and 100 percent of replies identified as from organizations (*n* = 8).[14]

We can surmise that the responses received offline were from stakeholder groups contacted directly at the consultation mapping stage. Groups might perceive that written responses are given more credence than online responses, although there is no direct evidence for this theory.

Broader Barriers to Inclusive Online Consultations

Exclusive Language
The use of language affects citizens' participatory journeys in several ways. Whether perception or reality, poor language skills undermine

confidence and discourage people from participating. Contributions that are poorly expressed or that do not follow established norms can be effectively sidelined within the decision process. An increasingly important manifestation of such concerns is where someone does not understand (or struggles with) the dominant language of a country. A brief review of British government consultation documents suggests that translations are not normally made available, even though the Welsh language has broad statutory parity, and a significant minority of people in the United Kingdom speak little or no English.[15] The government's consultation guidelines (Department for Business, Enterprise, and Regulatory Reform 2008, 10) merely state: "Thought should also be given to alternative versions of consultation documents which could be used to reach a wider audience, e.g. a young person's version, a Braille and audio version, Welsh and other language versions, an 'easy-read' version, etc."[16] This happens at the "consultation mapping" stage, where care must be taken to consider who the potential audience might be. If the mapping indicates a need to "consult specifically with people who have certain needs,"[17] then special arrangements should be made. However, it appears that, apart from special cases (such as consulting about children or consulting about Welsh language usage), the general rule is to assume a relatively narrow audience (given the general lack of alternative documents available online) and then to produce alternative formats when a "reasonable request" is made. It can, of course, be difficult to determine who the potential audience might be and this is likely linked to the perceptions of the civil servant responsible. Nevertheless, the process of having to ask for documents to be produced is a potentially serious barrier to participation.[18]

Another crucial linguistic factor is a concern that the language used in consultation documents is exclusionary. This might be a necessary evil in heavily technical matters, but it seems to belie claims of inclusivity. It also is a common complaint among third-sector groups along with the sheer volume of material sent out (English Heritage 2006). Moreover, as highlighted by the Plain English group, the language used in government consultations is problematic (Plain English 2008). For example, a recent consultation on expansion of Heathrow Airport was heavily criticized for its excessive jargon and assumptions about readers' knowledge, leading one member of Parliament to claim that "This document effectively takes away human rights. . . . No ordinary person with an interest in the plans to expand Heathrow could be expected to read and understand this." Another example from a government consultation document was cited by the 2006 English Heritage report: "Following the consultation period on the Scoping Report the Interim Sustainability Appraisal Report will be prepared to accompany the Issues and Options Paper. Subsequently the Final Sustainability Appraisal Report for Development Plan Document Number 2 will be prepared to accompany the Preferred Options Report for the Development Plan Document" (English Heritage 2006, 18). In spite of guidelines discouraging such practices, much evidence shows that the problem persists.

Exclusive Response Mechanisms

A consultation is a two-way process, and attention must be paid to the nature of the response mechanisms. The design of the feedback mechanism (that is, the participatory pathways marked by governments) affects the extent to which people will participate because people have different preferences and tolerances. The target audience and consultation goals must be carefully considered when determining response mechanisms. For example, the Digital Dialogues second-phase report (Ferguson, Griffiths, and Miller 2007) found that stakeholders were less willing to take part in public, open, online deliberative forums and preferred private channels.

There has been extensive experimentation with e-consultation platforms (Coleman 2004; Smith 2005; Wright 2006a, 2006b, 2007)—including simply providing information and documents online (such as the now closed consultations index), hosting deliberative discussion forums and polls, and establishing citizen panels (Miller and Williamson 2008). Although significant attention has rightly been paid to the benefits of deliberating online, given the context here, two warnings must be sounded. First, in spite of the potential for consultative experimentation, the vast majority of consultations follow a familiar format. Wright (2006a, 243) found that 95.8 percent of online consultations listed on the (now closed) consultations index featured only one-way communication, leading him to conclude that "Government departments were consulting, but the culture of consultation . . . had not changed."[19]

There is a hotly contested debate about the extent to which idealized models of deliberative democracy are exclusionary in nature because they can limit who and how people can legitimately participate (Saward 2000, especially chapters by Dryzek and Saward; Parkinson 2003, 36, 67–98). Deliberative structures can be an attempt to wrest power for the elite (Posner 2003). The danger is that when people are asked to participate in online deliberative processes, discussions can become dominated by those who have the time and resources to reply regularly, debates can degenerate into off-topic "flame wars," and the digital divide can exclude people (Wilhelm 2000; Davis 1999). Although these concerns are valid, a recent strand in the literature has sought to analyze whether e-consultation platforms can be designed to promote inclusion and deliberation.

Web Site Design and Moderation

Web site design and technological interfaces can positively affect political participation and online deliberation (Sack 2005; Wright 2005, Wright and Street 2007; Beierle 2004; Van der Heijden 2003) when they are intertwined with moderation practices (Edwards 2002; Wright 2006b).[20] Because Web sites can facilitate or obfuscate, liberate or stifle, it is neces-sary to understand the sociotechnical and political choices that inform Web site design and content. Multinational corporations, which often hold large government information technology contracts (such as the CitizenSpace deliberative platform), may simply not understand govern-ment practices (Horrocks 2009; Wright 2005). In an attempt to promote deliberation, several projects have brought together computer scientists and deliberative experts (political, social, and legal) to develop platforms (Noveck 2004; Muhlberger 2005; Price 2009).

There are more general debates about whether Web site design is inclusive—particularly for the elderly and disabled (Kennedy, Williams, and Bunning 2006; Kennedy, Thomas, and Evans 2009). This is one area where governments have intervened to promote inclusion. The U.S. federal government, for example, passed the Rehabilitation Act (section 508), and the Netherlands and Poland have chosen to "name and shame" Web sites that fail to comply with accessibility criteria. However, accord-ing to research conducted for the Riga initiative, only 3 percent of public Web sites met basic Web accessibility standards. Riga's target was 100 percent accessibility, yet progress is extremely slow, with only 5 percent currently meeting the targets (European Commission DG Information Society and Media 2007). There is a danger that significant minorities are being excluded from e-consultations, in explicit contravention of governments' own guidelines. This problem is compounded by the overall lack of usability and intuitiveness of government Web sites (Pratchett, Wingfield, and Karakaya-Polat 2006).

These studies must be seen in the context of another potential barrier. Arthur Lupia has suggested that the ephemeral nature of Internet brows-ing, which is often conducted with multiple windows open and alongside several other activities, may not be conducive to sustained attention and engagement and creates high barriers to engagement: "the structure of an online deliberation website must give participants an incentive to engage—an incentive strong enough to defeat participants' urges to attend to other stimuli when parts of the interaction are of less than immediate relevance to participants" (Lupia 2009, 64).

Personal and Political Will

Even if people theoretically have access to an online consultation and know that it is happening, a final barrier must be overcome: they must have sufficient will, desire, belief, engagement or motivation to participate. This less tangible, qualitative factor helps to put all the other pieces in the jigsaw together (Norris 2001; Katz, Rice, and Aspden 2001; Lenhart 2000). Without it, people are unlikely to become active.

Given the lack of trust in political institutions and citizens' concerns that government is a poor listener and might ignore any contributions they make (Coleman 2005), there is an onus on governments to persuade people to participate. The government has already started to incentivize various online activities (such as putting customers into prize drawings when they pay their bills online), and similar schemes could be adopted, as recommended by influential National Audit Office reports (2002, 14). Asking individuals to participate has also proved somewhat effective because people assume that general requests for participation do not refer to them. This is informed by low perceptions about their own political knowledge (55 percent of respondents to the government Audit of Participation categorized themselves as having little or no political knowledge) and the presentation of citizens as passive in the media (Lewis, Inthorn, and Wahl-Jorgensen 2005).

Given these circumstances, it might be better to think of the participatory journey as a circular walk. By this, I mean that consultations must be two-way: the journey does not end when a response is submitted. There is, arguably, a moral obligation to reply to consultation responses—to explain how people were listened to, why some people's demands were overlooked, and what effect contributions had on the policy developed. If this does not happen, the journey never reaches its conclusion, and participants can feel let down. Making the journey circular is something to be aspired to according to Thomas Gensemer, one of Barack Obama's Web gurus. He supports the notion that participatory devices must be designed to encourage a journey but notes that this (here, submitting a consultation response) should be the beginning of a process and not the end. People must at least perceive they are being listened to and institutions reactive (Lowndes, Pratchett, and Stoker 2006).

This can be taken further by encouraging a broader participatory culture—an ongoing (if intermittent) conversation (Coleman 2005).[21] Lowndes, Pratchett, and Stoker (2006, 283) have called this "the value of openness," which "does not require or assume large-scale and continuous direct participation" but "rests its case on the richness of democratic practice and the availability of options for extending participation." This, in turn, can be linked to a broader shift to move beyond formal consultations to a fuller (more informal) coproduction process: "whereas consultation tends to reassert traditional roles and divisions between users and officials by involving them in separate consultative exercises and generating wish-lists, effective co-production emphasizes the importance of dialogue, interaction and negotiation" (Needham 2007, 225). This is the ideal to which many participative democrats aspire. Using the language of the participatory journey, these can be seen as ongoing circular walks.

The barriers and opportunities presented so far have highlighted how the Internet, particularly e-consultations, are at the same time both inclusionary and exclusionary. A brief case study will help to map the interplay further.

The Domestic Violence Forum

The Home Affairs Committee of the British Parliament ran an anonymous online forum on domestic abuse in an attempt to consult with people who had experience with this issue.[22] Policy makers have found it difficult to hear directly from those affected by domestic violence, and MPs felt that online responses would be far different from those that would have been received via the standard procedure of giving evidence at select committee hearings. Of the 204 comments that were received, content analysis of the largest thread (104 messages) found that 53 percent of messages were from people giving often intimate details about their experiences of spousal abuse. A further 8 percent were from the friends or family of people who had been affected, and 18 percent were from professionals in the field. These were all presented as being from individuals; no third-sector organization responded directly—suggesting that this format of e-consultation did affect who participated.[23]

Analysis of a previous domestic abuse online consultation found that a community was formed that led to extensive interactions between participants (Coleman and Blumler 2009). Replies to this consultation were unusual: 66 percent of users made only one post, and 80 percent of messages were statements (30 percent were moderated to protect the identity of the poster).[24] The differences can probably be explained by the structure of the forum. There was no threading: messages were presented on top of each other, and there was only limited space for each message before a scrolling function took over (see Wright and Street 2007). Moreover, the decision to pose a question at the start of the thread led most people to reply directly to the question and not engage with each other.

The often traumatic responses, it is claimed, directly affected the policies put forward. Where the topic is sensitive, the ability to contribute anonymously online can influence both who contributes and what they contribute. Their contributions can be far more diverse and detailed than the presentations to a standard select committee. Although putting the consultation online opened up the process and arguably made it more inclusive, the digital divide issues outlined may still have affected the ability of some potential participants to participate (especially in these circumstances, where it might be difficult to get access by another means).[25]

Conclusion

Using the metaphor of a participatory journey, this chapter has attempted to map out some of the barriers that affect citizen participation in online consultations. Putting consultations online has the potential to increase the numbers of people who can respond, thereby altering the nature of the responses received. But the opportunities given with one hand may be taken away from some people with the other. This research has shown that careful consideration must be given to the selection, design, and advertising of the participatory route selected, particularly at the consultation mapping stage. The notion of mapping out consultations indicates how the choices made here can affect the terrain on which citizens must travel. Citizen bring their own baggage and face their own barriers to participation—suggesting that an open mind is necessary if consultations are to be inclusive. As Bill Dutton wrote ten years ago: "Digital government can erode or enhance democratic processes . . . [but] the outcome will be determined by the interaction of policy choices, management strategies and cultural responses—not by advanced technology alone. . . . The debate over appropriate policies for guiding the application of

ICTs in politics and governance needs to begin in earnest" (Dutton 1999, 193). This chapter shows that in the field of online consultations, progress has been made—but the journey is far from over.

Notes

1. Several reasons were given by respondents for this, including that they were not aware of opportunities to participate and that participation was for "other people" (Lowndes, Pratchett, and Stoker 2001, 451).

2. Citizens and authorities might have very different expectations about the point at which a journey ends and participation is deemed as successful.

3. Government intervention is necessary, although it is unclear how effective the UK government's free computer scheme will be as some (the ill-informed or digital luddites) are unlikely to want a computer unless they can be persuaded otherwise while others will choose (or be forced) not to keep up their Internet access (see below).

4. A recent report from the Department for Communities and Local Government (DLCG) (2008, 5) highlighted that there were "significant differences" in policy responses to the digital divide at the European level. One of the principal policy mechanisms for narrowing the digital divide in Europe is the i2010 Riga Targets on digital inclusion. Overall, 57 percent of Europeans did not use the Internet regularly in 2005, but this figure hides significant disparities. Riga constituted a series of targets, such as halving gaps in Internet usage and digital literacy between the EU average and older, female, disabled, and less educated people. Although the aims are ambitious, "progress towards the Riga targets is only happening at half the speed which is necessary to reach them by 2010" (9). There is an ongoing debate as to whether a more prescriptive approach should be adopted instead of the Open Method of Coordination (this allows each government to adopt its own policies and means that achieving the goals is effectively voluntary).

5. It is in this context that the third sector has a role to play. For example, Age Concern has run Silver Surfer schemes and an IT and Biscuits campaign to encourage older people to get online. Here the focus is not just on educating people how to use the Internet but also highlighting why the Internet might be of particular interest to an individual—on a case-by-case basis.

6. There was also evidence that some people accessed the Internet outside of the home occasionally (32 percent) and that others (36 percent) had proxy access such as through a friend (OFCOM/MORI 2009, 6).

7. Mossberger, Tolbert, and McNeal (2008) have rightly focused on the issue of skills and time spent online when analyzing the digital divide. However, Wright (2008) criticized the research for linking "digital citizenship" to daily Internet use as a proxy for skills because this measure may hide significant differences. Wright cites an example from his family. His brother is a sophisticated but infrequent Internet user, and his mother uses the Internet daily (to access eBay)

but uses family and friends to achieve even basic tasks, such as attaching files to email. Put simply, daily Internet use does not necessarily constitute either "skilled" or "effective" Internet use.

8. Interview with a senior civil servant.

9. The document covers only formal, written consultations and does not preclude other forms of consultation, such as informal discussion, which makes the emphasis on effectiveness all the more interesting.

10. http://www.bis.gov.uk/policies/better-regulation/consultation-guidance, accessed April 8, 2011.

11. Bimber goes on argue that age is likely to diminish as a factor as Internet penetration increases.

12. http://www.bis.gov.uk/policies/better-regulation/consultation-guidance, accessed April 8, 2011.

13. The archiving of consultations occurs haphazardly, and many government departments do not publish online summaries of who responded and how they did so.

14. Raw data provided by the Charity Commission.

15. At the European level, where multilingual online policy debates have been encouraged and multilingualism is more generally established within institutional structures, research suggests that English has become the dominant language, with over 90 percent of messages being written solely in English (Wodak and Wright 2006, 2007; Wright 2007). The English-as-lingua-franca model has been both welcomed (Seidlhofer 2003) and lambasted (Phillipson 2003), but the results show that the chances of being able to engage in a debate are much higher if you speak English, and therefore there is a significant linguistic divide.

16. http://www.bis.gov.uk/policies/better-regulation/consultation-guidance, accessed April 8, 2011.

17. http://www.bis.gov.uk/policies/better-regulation/consultation-guidance, accessed April 8, 2011.

18. Assuming that most people use search engines to find relevant information, there is also a danger that such facilities create language imbalances in search returns (Gerrand 2007; Paolillo 2005).

19. If the practice of consultations remains qualitatively similar, research suggests that the number of consultations being held has expanded significantly (Lowndes et al. 2001; Birch 2002; Needham 2002).

20. Some researchers maintain that textual communication lacks the richness needed to maintain deliberative exchanges and have instead opted to use audio technology akin to online conference calls (Iyengar, Luskin, and Fishkin 2003).

21. http://technology.timesonline.co.uk/tol/news/tech_and_web/article5761545.ece.

22. http://forums.parliament.uk/html/index.html, accessed 8 April, 2011.

23. A further 18 percent were uncodable; 3 percent were from politicians. The consultation report contains further analysis and is available at http://www

.publications.parliament.uk/pa/cm200708/cmselect/cmhaff/263/26318 .htm#a99, accessed April 8, 2011.

24. Overarching analysis is contained in the appendix to the consultation report and suggests a slightly higher overall level of replies, with just over half of participants making only one post. More details on the forum are available at http:// www.publications.parliament.uk/pa/cm200708/cmselect/cmhaff/263/26318 .htm#a99, accessed April 8, 2011.

25. An excellent offline example of an inclusive approach to response mechanisms was conducted by the National Health Service through its National Centre for Involvement. Issues were presented to people with learning difficulties in a variety of ways, including photographs, film, and music, and this was carried on into the feedback stage. People were allowed to choose from a range of feedback mechanisms the one that best suited them. These included a discussion group, a communication group (using signs and symbols), and a supported group where people could attend with a friend who could participate on their behalf.

References

Beierle, T. 2004. "Digital Deliberation: Engaging the Public through Online Policy Dialogues." In *Democracy Online: The Prospects for Political Renewal through the Internet*, edited by P. Shane, 155–166. London: Routledge.

Bimber, B. 1999. "The Internet and Citizen Communication with Government: Does the Medium Matter?" *Political Communication* 16, no. 4:409–428.

Birch, D. 2002. *Public Participation in Local Government: A Survey of Local Authorities*. London: ODPM.

Brians, C., and B. Grofman. 1999. "When Registration Barriers Fall, Who Votes? An Empirical Test of a Rational Choice Model." *Public Choice* 99, nos. 1–2:161–176.

British Educational Communications and Technology Agency (BECTA. 2008. *Extending Opportunity Final Report of the Minister's Taskforce on Home Access to Technology*. Coventry: BECTA.

Brockington, D. 2003. "A Low Information Theory of Ballot Position Effect." *Political Behavior* 25, no. 1:1–27.

Cohen, J. E. 2006. "Citizen Satisfaction with Contacting Government on the Internet." *Information Polity* 11, no. 1:51–65.

Coleman, S. 2004. "Connecting Parliament to the Public via the Internet: Two Case Studies of Online Consultations." *Information Communication and Society* 7, no. 1:1–22.

Coleman, S. 2005. *Direct Representation: Towards a Conversational Democracy*. London: IPPR.

Coleman, S., and J. Blumler. 2009. *The Internet and Democratic Citizenship*. Cambridge: Cambridge University Press.

Compaine, B., ed. 2001. *The Digital Divide*. Cambridge: MIT Press.

Davis, R. 1999. *The Web of Politics: The Internet's Impact on the American Political System*. Oxford: Oxford University Press.

Department for Business, Enterprise, and Regulatory Reform (BERR). 2008. *Code of Practice on Consultation*. London: BERR.

Department for Business Innovation and Skills. 2010. "Consultations Available in One Place." Accessed November 8, 2010. http://www.bis.gov.uk/policies/better-regulation/consultation-guidance.

Department for Communities and Local Government (DCLG). 2008. *An Analysis of International Digital Strategies: Why Develop a Digital Inclusion Strategy and What Should Be the Focus*. London: DCLG.

Department for Culture, Media, and Sport/Department for Business Innovation and Skills (DCMS/DBIS). 2009. *Digital Britain: Final Report*. London: HMSO.

Dutton, W. H. 1999. *Society on the Line: Information Politics in the Digital Age*. Oxford: Oxford University Press.

Dutton, W., E. J. Helsper, and M. Gerber. 2009. "The Internet in Britain: 2009." Oxford Internet Institute, University of Oxford, Oxford. Accessed November 29, 2010. http://microsites.oii.ox.ac.uk/oxis/publications.

Edwards, A. 2002. "The Moderator as an Emerging Democratic Intermediary: The Role of the Moderator in Internet Discussions about Public Issues." *Information Polity* 7, no. 1:3–20.

Ellison, N., C. Steinfield, and C. Lampe. 2007. "The Benefits of Facebook 'Friends': Social Capital and College Students' Use of Online Social Network Sites." *Journal of Computer-Mediated Communication* 12, no. 4. Accessed November 29, 2010. http://jcmc.indiana.edu/vol12/issue4/ellison.html.

English Heritage. 2006. *Making Consultations Matter*. Accessed November 29, 2010. http://hc.english-heritage.org.uk/content/pub/MCM_full.pdf.

European Commission DG Information Society and Media. 2007. "Measuring Progress in e-Inclusion: Riga Dashboard." Brussels: European Commission. Accessed April 8, 2011. http://ec.europa.eu/information_society/activities/einclusion/docs/i2010_initiative/rigadashboard.pdf.

Ferguson, R., B. Griffiths, and L. Miller. 2007. "Digital Dialogues Second Phase Report, August 2006–August 2007." London: Hansard Society. Accessed November 29, 2010. http://hansardsociety.org.uk/blogs/publications/archive/2007/11/06/digital-dialogues-second-phase-report-sept-2007.aspx.

Gerrand, P. 2007. "Estimating Linguistic Diversity on the Internet: A Taxonomy to Avoid Pitfalls and Paradoxes." *Journal of Computer-Mediated Communication* 12, no. 4, art. 8. http://jcmc.indiana.edu/vol12/issue4/gerrand.html.

Hansard Society. 2007. *Audit of Political Engagement*. London: Hansard Society.

Highton, B. 2004. "Voter Registration and Turnout in the United States." *Perspectives on Politics* 2, no. 3:507–515.

Hiltz, R., and M. Turoff. 1993. *The Network Nation: Human Communication via Computer*. 2nd ed. Cambridge: MIT Press.

Hindman, M. 2009. *The Myth of Digital Democracy*. Princeton, NJ: Princeton University Press.

Horrocks, I. 2009. "Experts and E-government: Power, Influence and the Capture of a Policy Domain." *Information Communication and Society* 12, no. 1:110–127.

Iyengar, S., R. Luskin, and J. Fishkin. (2003). "Facilitating Informed Public Opinion: Evidence from Face-to-Face and Online Deliberative Polls." Accessed November 29, 2010. http://pcl.stanford.edu/common/docs/research/iyengar/2003/facilitating.pdf.

Katz, J., R. E. Rice, and P. Aspden. 2001. "The Internet, 1995–2000: Access, Civic Involvement, and Social Interaction." *American Behavioral Scientist* 45, no. 3:405–420.

Kennedy, H., S. Thomas, and S. Evans. 2009. "Inclusive New Media Design: The Place of Accessibility Guidelines in the Work of Web Designers." In *Designing for the Twenty-first Century: Interdisciplinary Methods and Findings*, edited by T. Innis, 258–269. Farnham, UK: Gower.

Kennedy, H., P. Williams, and K. Bunning. 2006. "ICTs and Learning Disability: Multidisciplinary Perspectives on Project @pple." *Aslib Proceedings* 59, no. 1:97–112.

Kobayashi, T., K. Ikeda, and K. Miyata. 2006. "Social Capital Online: Collective Use of the Internet and Reciprocity as Lubricants of Democracy." *Information Communication and Society* 9, no. 5:582–611.

Leighley, J., and J. Nagler. 1992. "Individual and Systemic Influences on Turnout: Who Votes? 1984." *Journal of Politics* 54, no. 3:718–740.

Lewis, J., S. Inthorn, and K. Wahl-Jorgensen. 2005. *Citizens or Consumers: What the Media Tell Us about Political Participation*. Maidenhead: Open University Press.

Lowndes, V., L. Pratchett, and G. Stoker. 2001. "Trends in Public Participation: Part 2—Citizens' Perspectives." *Public Administration* 79, no. 2:445–455.

Lowndes, V., L. Pratchett, and G. Stoker. 2006. "Diagnosing and Remedying the Failings of Official Participation Schemes: The CLEAR Framework." *Social Policy and Society* 5, no. 2:281–291.

Lupia, A. 2009. "Can Online Deliberation Improve Politics? Scientific Foundations for Success." In *Online Deliberation: Design, Research and Practice*, edited by T. Davies and S. Gangadharan, 59–69. Stanford and Chicago: CSLI Publications and University of Chicago Press.

Miller, L., and A. Williamson. 2008. "Digital Dialogues Third Phase Report: August 2007–August 2008." London: Hansard Society. Accessed November 29, 2010. http://www.hansardsociety.org.uk/blogs/downloads/archive/2008/08/13/digital-dialogues-third-phase-report-august-2007-august-2008.aspx.

Mossberger, K., C. Tolbert, and R. McNeal. 2008. *Digital Citizenship*. Cambridge: MIT Press.

Muhlberger, P. 2005. "The Virtual Agora Project: A Research Design for Studying Democratic Deliberation." *Journal of Public Deliberation* 1, no. 1. Accessed November 29, 2010. http://services.bepress.com/cgi/viewcontent.cgi?article=100 1&context=jpd.

National Audit Office (NAO). 2002. *Government on the Web II*. London: HM Stationery Office.

National Audit Office (NAO). 2007. *Government on the Internet: Progress in Delivering Information and Services Online*. London: HM Stationery Office.

Needham, C. 2002. "Consultation: A Cure for Local Government?" *Parliamentary Affairs 55*, no. 4:699–714.

Needham, C. 2007. "Realising the Potential of Co-production: Negotiating Improvements in Public Services." *Social Policy and Society* 7, no. 2:221–231.

Nie, N. H., and L. Erbring. 2000. *Internet and Society: A Preliminary Report*. Accessed November 29, 2010. http://www.vermario.com/wiki/lib/exe/fetch.php/internet_society_report.pdf.

Norris, P. 2001. *Digital Divide: Civic Engagement, Information Poverty and the Internet Worldwide*. Cambridge: Cambridge University Press.

Norris, P. 2003. "Social Capital and ICTs: Widening or Reinforcing Social Networks?" Paper presented at the International Forum on Social Capital for Economic Revival, held by the Economic and Social Research Institute, Cabinet Office, Japan, Tokyo, March 24–25. Session 5, Social Capital and ICTs. Accessed November 29, 2010. http://www.esri.go.jp/en/workshop/030325/030325paper6 -e.pdf.

Noveck, B. S. 2004. "Unchat: Democratic Solution for a Wired World." In *Democracy Online: The Prospects for Democratic Renewal through the Internet*, edited by P. Shane, 21–34. London: Routledge.

OFCOM/MORI. 2009. *Accessing the Internet at Home: A Quantitative and Qualitative Study among People without the Internet at Home by Ipsos MORI*. London: OFCOM.

Paolillo, J. C. 2005. "Language Diversity on the Internet." In *Measuring Linguistic Diversity on the Internet*, edited by UNESCO Institute for Statistics, 43–89. Paris: UNESCO.

Parkinson, J. 2003. *Deliberating in the Real World*. Oxford: Oxford University Press.

Phillipson, R. 2003. *English-Only Europe? Challenging Language Policy*. London: Routledge.

Plain English. 2008. "Plain English: The Voice of Plain English Campaign." Issue 71. Accessed April 8, 2011. http://www.plainenglish.co.uk/press-office/press-releases/campaign-calls-for-withdrawal-of-heathrow-consultation -document-11-february-2008.html.

Posner, R. A. 2003. *Law, Pragmatism and Democracy*. Cambridge: Harvard University Press.

Pratchett, L., M. Wingfield, and R. Karakaya-Polat. 2006. "Local Democracy Online." *International Journal of Electronic Government Research* 2, no. 3:75–92.

Price, V. 2009. "Citizens Deliberating Online: Theory and Some Evidence." In *Online Deliberation: Design, Research and Practice*, edited by T. Davies and S. Gangadharan, 37–58. Stanford and Chicago: CSLI Publications and University of Chicago Press.

Putnam, R. 2000. *Bowling Alone: The Collapse and Revival of American Community*. New York: Simon and Schuster.

Sack, W. 2005. "Discourse Architecture and Very Large-Scale Conversations." In *Formations: IT and New Architectures in the Global Realm*, edited by R. Latham and S. Sassen, 242–282. Princeton, NJ: Princeton University Press.

Saward, M. 2000. *Democratic Innovation: Deliberation, Representation and Association*. London: Routledge.

Seidlhofer, B. 2003. "Brave New English? Zum bildungs/sprachenpolitischen Desiderat einer Konzeptualisierung von Englisch als Lingua franca." In *Die Kosten der Mehrsprachigkeit/ The Cost of Multilingualism*, edited by R. de Cillia, H. J. Krumm, and R. Wodak, 125–134. Vienna: Austrian Academy of Sciences.

Slouka, M. 1995. *War of the Worlds: Cyberspace and the High-Tech Assault on Reality*. New York: Basic Books.

Smith, G. 2005. *Power beyond the Ballot*. London: Power Inquiry.

Stoll, C. 1995. *Silicon Snake Oil: Second Thoughts on the Information Highway*. New York: Doubleday.

Sunstein, C. 2001. *Republic.com*. Princeton, NJ: Princeton University Press.

Thomas, J. C., and G. Streib. 2003. "The New Face of Government: Citizen-Initiated Contacts in the Era of E-Government." *Journal of Public Administration: Research and Theory* 13, no. 1:83–102.

Van der Heijden, H. 2003. "Factors Influencing the Usage of Websites: The Case of a Generic Portal in The Netherlands." *Information and Management* 40, no. 6:541–549.

Wellman, B., and M. Gulia. 1999. "Virtual Communities as Communities: Net Surfers Don't Ride Alone." In *Communities in Cyberspace*, edited by M. Smith and P. Kollock, 167–194. London: Routledge.

Wilhelm, A. G. 2000. *Democracy in the Digital Age: Challenges to Political Life in Cyberspace*. London: Routledge.

Wodak, R., and S. Wright. 2006. "The European Union in Cyberspace: Multilingual Democratic Participation in a Virtual Public Sphere." *Journal of Language and Politics* 5, no. 2:251–275.

Wodak, R., and S. Wright. 2007. "The European Union in Cyberspace: Democratic Participation via Online Multilingual Discussion Boards?" In *The Multilingual Internet: Language, Culture and Communication in Instant Messaging,*

Email and Chat, edited by B. Danet and S. Herring, 385–407. Oxford: Oxford University Press.

Wright, S. 2005. "Design Matters: The Political Efficacy of Government-Run Online Discussion Forums." In *The Internet and Politics: Citizens, Voters, and Activists*, edited S. Oates, D. Owen, and R. Gibson, 80–99. London: Routledge.

Wright, S. 2006a. "Electrifying Democracy: Ten Years of Policy and Practice." Special Issue on Politics and the Net: The First Ten Years. *Parliamentary Affairs* 59, no. 2:236–249.

Wright, S. 2006b. "Government-Run Online Discussion Fora: Moderation, Censorship and the Shadow of Control." *British Journal of Politics and International Relations* 8, no. 4:550–568.

Wright, S. 2007. "A Virtual European Public Sphere? The Futurum Discussion Forum." *Journal of European Public Policy* 14, no. 8:1167–1185.

Wright, S. 2008. Book Review of Digital Citizenship. *JITP* 5, no. 1:262–264.

Wright, S., and J. Street. 2007. "Democracy, Deliberation and Design: The Case of Online Discussion Forums." *New Media and Society* 9, no. 5:849–869.

8

Democratic Consultation and the E-Citizen

Stephen Coleman, Rachel Gibson, and Agnes I. Schneeberger

There are two ways of governing. One is to assume that a government that has been elected by a sufficient number of votes to legitimize political authority bears the job of deliberating and deciding on every matter of policy and legislation. The other way is for governments to assume that it is their job to represent the interests, preferences, and values of a diverse population, that elected representatives cannot hope to have all the answers to every policy challenge, and that citizens' experience and expertise are therefore necessary sources of both good sense and political legitimacy in policy making. Most governments veer between both approaches—sometimes insisting that their electoral mandate is legitimacy enough for deciding what is good for citizens and at other times (especially when faced with new problems, precarious risks, or genuine inexperience) turning to the public for input and guidance.

In the 1960s, the practice of consulting the public grew in significance as citizens became more educated, politically volatile, and less deferential and politicians became more attuned to notions of a "listening" government. In Britain, the 1969 Skeffington Report on *People and Planning* had a seminal influence. It argued that "one cannot leave all the problems to one's representatives. They need some help in reaching the right decision, and opportunity should be provided for discussions with all those involved" (Committee on Public Participation in Planning 1969, 3).

Most governments since then have relied increasingly on mechanisms of consultation, particularly in relation to planning decisions and policies affecting communities of interest. Various consultative techniques—including simple questionnaires, public hearings, citizens' juries, consensus conferences, deliberative polls, and visioning exercises—have been used. But the democratic effectiveness of these consultation methods has been questioned from at least three perspectives.

First, critics argue that consultative processes are too complex and time-consuming for most citizens. The higher the barriers to participation, the less representative the range of consultees will be. For example, if public hearings are dominated by legalistic and bureaucratic jargon, take place in official buildings at inconvenient times, and dismiss anecdotal, expressive, and symbolic forms of testimony, they are likely to attract participation from a relatively narrow social stratum of citizens who are richer, older, better educated, more confident, and more likely to be already organized in pressure groups. In contrast, socially excluded and marginalized groups, who are often the first to be affected by bad government policy decisions, are the least likely to be involved (see chapter 7 in this volume).

Second, there are some concerns about the narrowly consumerist nature of many consultations, which seem to address consultees as service consumers, home owners, or tax-paying residents rather than as rounded citizens. Related to these concerns are criticisms of the limited scope for reflection and deliberation within many consultative exercises, which seem to be confined to multiple-choice options rather than any kind of exchange of reasoned positions. Deliberative democrats have expressed disappointment at this failure to move beyond the counting of fixed preferences.

Third, there is a fear that consultations can be tokenistic exercises in which governments ask citizens for their views to legitimate already determined policy decisions. Evidence presented to the House of Commons Public Administration Select Committee (2001) inquiry into new forms of public participation, based on a survey of 332 UK local authorities, found that 20 percent considered that participatory consultation exercises strongly influenced final policy decisions, 16 percent thought that they led to better informed decisions, 20 percent considered that such exercises had very little effect on decisions, and 20 percent stated that they merely confirmed decisions that were already made. In her evidence to the inquiry, Sue Goss, director of public services development at the Office for Public Management, declared: "While organisations are learning to consult, they are failing to respond effectively to consultation and this harms potential relationships between citizens and government" (House of Commons Public Administration Select Committee 2001). The absence of a clearly visible feedback loop suggests that some consultations are one-way exercises. The result is a diminution of public confidence in the process and an increased sense that politicians are not prepared to listen.

Some scholars and policy makers have suggested that the Internet could open up a new space for more successful consultation practices. They argue that online consultations could be more convenient for busy people to access; that participants are less likely to be judged by one another on the basis of cultural or physical cues; that when sessions take place in shared, nonofficial space, citizens might feel less intimidated and forms of discursive intervention are less likely to be constrained; that asynchronous discussion allows people to join in and catch up in their own time; and that young people, who are most likely to spend time online, might be attracted to engage.

After over a decade of theoretical speculation, many online consultations have now taken place, and extensive empirical findings have been accumulated. Valuable scholarship has produced case studies of e-consultation exercises, the effectiveness of the software used, techniques of moderation and facilitation, the extent to which participants have adhered to norms of deliberation, attitudes of politicians and officials to these exercises, and to a limited extent, the effect of online consultations on the policy process itself. No empirical studies to date have explored in any depth the public's experience of and demand for being consulted online. This chapter presents an empirical analysis of support for online consultation among UK citizens who use the Internet.

Research Question and Robustness of Data

The research reported here is based on data collected from a survey of UK citizens between ages eighteen through seventy-five who had Internet access (n = 3,229).[1] The survey was conducted in March 2005 by YouGov. It was designed to examine the political views and activities of the online UK public, looking particularly at their levels of political engagement, trust, and interest and involvement in online consultation initiatives. Participants were drawn from the YouGov Panel, which comprises a collection of over 215,000 registered active respondents (as of September 2007). Survey respondents were selected through active sampling, which means that only specifically invited individuals participated in the survey to ensure correct proportions of basic demographics. The weighting procedures comprised a combination of different approaches derived from surveys such as the British census, the National Readership Survey, and YouGov's internal procedures (for further details, see Twyman 2008, 347). Two additional data sets were used to examine how closely the YouGov data set matched the wider population on selected demographic and political characteristics. These data sets were the British Election Study (BES)[2] conducted in 2005 and data from the UK National Census study from the year 2001.[3]

A comparison of demographics across the three data sets reveals that overall the weighted YouGov data are fairly representative of the wider UK population[4] (table 8.1). Beyond ascertaining the representativeness of the YouGov sample in demographic terms, we were interested in the extent to which it accurately captured the political outlook and interests of the wider UK population. For these purposes, we compared YouGov and BES respondents on a series of basic political traits, including the party they voted for in the national election from 2001, levels of political interest, and likelihood of voting in the upcoming general election. The results reveal a broad comparability across the two surveys in terms of political preferences, although the Conservative party receives slightly less support among YouGov respondents compared to the BES findings. Levels of political interest are considerably higher in the YouGov survey than those reported in the BES. YouGov survey participants were much more likely to agree that politics is interesting (10 percent point difference). Given these higher levels of interest, it is not surprising that the probability for voting in the next general election is also higher among YouGov respondents, with 9 percent more people saying they are certain or very likely to vote than in the BES sample (see table 8.2).

Attitudes toward Democracy

There was an almost equal split in the population of Internet users between those who are satisfied with the way that democracy works in the United Kingdom and those who are not. Over one in ten (13 percent) were very dissatisfied with democracy, with nonvoters in the 2005 general election twice as likely (22 percent) to be very dissatisfied as those who did vote (11 percent). Dissatisfaction with the current democratic process was strongly linked to party support: 19 percent of Conservative voters were very dissatisfied, compared with 13 percent of Liberal Democrats and 8 percent of Labor voters.

Over half (54 percent) of all respondents stated that they found politics interesting, but class and gender distinctions are striking in this regard. Sixty-two percent of people in the higher (more affluent, better educated) socioeconomic strata claimed to find politics interesting, compared with only 45 percent from the lower strata. About 63 percent

Table 8.1

Demographic representativeness of YouGov and BES samples

Variables	Census 2001	BES 2005	YouGov 2005
Sex:	(n = 52,041,916)	(n = 3,589)	(n = 3,229)
Female	51%	52%	52%
Male	49%	48%	48%
Age:	(n = 40,237,997)*	(n = 3,571)	(n = 3,227)
18 to 24	11%	11%	11%
25 to 34	18%	18%	19%
35 to 44	19%	20%	19%
45 to 59	25%	25%	29%
60+	27%	27%	22%
Education:[5]	(n = 61,676,955)	(n = 3,587)	(n = 3,116)
Degree or higher qualification, NVQ, and key skills 4 & 5	27%	34%	38%
A level, NVQ, and key skills 3	14%	13%	21%
O level, NVQ, and key skills 2	37%	19%	24%
Other qualification, key skills level 1, and entry level	2%	7%	5%
No qualifications	19%	27%	13%
Class:	(n = 40,666,546)	(n = 2,839)	(n = 3,229)
ABC1 (middle class)	52%	64%	54%
C2DE (working class)	48%	36%	46%

Notes: *Subset (excluding ages birth to seventeen years) of total population (n = 52,041,916). Figures may not add exactly due to rounding. *Sources:* Office for National Statistics, *Census 2001: First Results on Population in England and Wales*, http://www.statistics.gov.uk/census2001/pop2001/england_wales_ages.asp; *Census 2001: All Types of Qualification Held by People Aged 16–74*, http://www.statistics.gov.uk/StatBase/ssdataset.asp?vlnk=7553&Pos=&ColRank =2&Rank=240; *Census 2001: All People Aged 16 and Over in Households*, http://www.statistics.gov.uk/StatBase/ssdataset.asp?vlnk=7534&Pos=&ColRank =2&Rank=256; University of Essex/Economic and Social Research Council, *The British Election Study: Face to Face Survey Data: The 2005 BES Pre-Campaign Data*, http://www.essex.ac.uk/bes/2005/Face_to_face_survey_data.htm; YouGov, *What the World Thinks*, eDemocracy survey, March 10–16, 2005, http://today. yougov.co.uk/homepage.

Table 8.2
Comparing political outlooks of YouGov and BES respondents

Variables	BES 2005	YouGov 2005
Vote in 2001 general election	(n = 2,417)	(n = 2,575)
Labor	49%	51%
Conservative	31%	28%
Liberal Democrat	14%	16%
Nationalist (e.g., Scottish Nationalist Party or Plaid Cymru)	3%	2%
Green	1%	1%
Other	3%	3%
Politics is interesting:	(n = 3,580)	(n = 3,278)
Agree strongly	7%	18%
Agree somewhat	40%	39%
Neither agree nor disagree	16%	21%
Disagree somewhat	27%	14%
Disagree strongly	11%	8%
Likelihood of voting:	(n = 3,578)	(n = 3,078)
Certain	50%	61%
Very likely	19%	17%
Quite likely	12%	11%
Not very likely	9%	7%
Certain not to vote	10%	3%

Note: Figures may not add exactly due to rounding. *Sources:* University of Essex/ Economic and Social Research Council, *The British Election Study: Face to Face Survey Data: The 2005 BES Pre-Campaign Data*, http://www.essex.ac.uk/ bes/2005/Face_to_face_survey_data.htm; YouGov, *What the World Thinks*, eDemocracy survey, March 10–16, 2005, http://today.yougov.co.uk/homepage.

of men said that they find politics interesting, compared with 45 percent of women. Although over half of the respondents expressed, an interest in politics, most (58 percent) stated that they have no faith in politics to solve their problems. Women (62 percent) were significantly more likely to think this than men (54 percent), and those in lower socioeconomic strata (61 percent) had significantly less faith in politics than those in higher (55 percent). Eighteen- to twenty-four-year-olds (25 percent) were the least likely to express faith in politics, making them the most politically alienated group.

Asked about activities that they had engaged in within the past twelve months, 7 percent had participated in a demonstration, 8 percent had joined a pressure group, 11 percent had attended a political meeting, 15 percent had sent a letter to their member of Parliament, 16 percent had sent an email to their MP, and 57 percent had signed a petition. Contrary to the assumption that demonstrators are likely to be young, there were no significant age differences among the small group who had demonstrated; indeed, those twenty-five to twenty-nine years old and those sixty years and older were equally likely to have gone on a demonstration. Similarly, those joining pressure groups were more likely to be over age fifty than under age twenty-five.

There was no significant difference among people who reported sending letters to their MPs and those who sent emails. About 12 percent of respondents age fifty and over sent a letter to their MP within the previous year—the same percentage as those under age fifty. About 19 percent of of those age fifty and over had emailed their MP within the previous year, compared with 14 percent of those under age fifty.

Almost a third (32 percent) of respondents stated that they "leave politics and current affairs to other people." There was a significant gender difference here, with 24 percent of men and 39 percent of women distancing themselves from politics in this way. About 90 percent of respondents were not involved in the affairs of their local council, but most respondents (55 percent) said that they would like to be. Reasons for not participating fell into two categories: 56 percent of people stated that they lacked a personal interest in participating ("just not interested"; "too time-consuming"; "too inconvenient"), and around a third (34%) were put off by a belief that their council is not interested in their views and that participation would be inconsequential.

For the 90 percent of local nonparticipators—and particularly the 34 percent who might participate if they felt that they would be listened to and could exercise some influence—there are strong indications of low political efficacy acting as an obstacle to civic engagement. Political efficacy refers to people's belief in their capacity to influence the world around them (internal efficacy) and of political institutions to respond to them (external efficacy) (Lane 1959). About 78 percent of respondents said that they believed that what they think about political issues is unlikely to influence government, and 75 percent believe that governments do not care what ordinary people think. Asked how much influence they have on politics (with 0 lowest and 10 highest), only 5 percent of respondents fell into the 7 to 10 band, while 70 percent fell into the 0 to 3 band. Asked whether they would like more influence on the running of the country (with 0 lowest and 10 highest), only 2 percent fell into the 0 to 3 band, while 58 percent fell into the 7 to 10 band. In short, lack of political influence is not a direct consequence of a lack of desire to be influential.

Given these very low levels of political efficacy, a surprisingly large proportion of respondents (83 percent) believed that it is up to them to influence what happens in the area in which they live. About 88 percent of those in the higher socioeconomic strata believed this, as did 77 percent in the lower socioeconomic strata.

With political efficacy at such low levels, did respondents reject the current representative democratic system and favor a greater degree of direct democracy? We were somewhat surprised to find that a significant number of respondents were attracted to a greater degree of direct democracy. For example, 77 percent agreed that constituents should determine how their MP acts. Asked whether Parliament should be abolished altogether and replaced by direct plebiscites on all issues, most people were opposed, but almost one in four (23 percent) supported the idea. Almost a third of people who did not vote in the previous general election expressed support for direct voting on all issues.

Just over a third (35 percent) of respondents stated that they had a civic duty to discuss important political issues with friends and family—considerably fewer than the 82 percent who believe they have a duty to vote. About 34 percent were of the view that "political conversation is usually boring," and 37 percent believe that "talking about politics is too complicated for most people." Asked how often they actually speak to others about politics, there was a broad range of responses. About 38 percent of respondents claimed to talk about politics with people at work at least once a week, while almost half (46 percent) rarely or never discussed politics at work. Those in the higher socioeconomic strata were 12 percent more likely than those in the socioeconomic strata to discuss politics at work. About 42 percent of respondents claimed to talk about politics at least once a week with friends outside of work, while a third (33 percent) rarely or never do so. The main locus for political discussion was the family. Over half of all respondents (52 percent) discussed politics with other members of their family, with only one in four (25 percent) never or rarely doing so. We turn now to responses relating to communication with elected representatives and government.

Support for e-Government and e-Democracy

We turn now to the evidence from our survey on popular attitudes toward a range of e-government and e-democracy services and opportunities. Overall, the results show a significant degree of support for such services and for the wider rollout of measures. There is notably strong enthusiasm for the provision of more direct channels of input for citizens' views on local matters and for more opportunities to directly contact political bodies and representatives via the Internet. More specifically, a majority (73 percent) of Internet users have accessed the Web site of their local council Web site and would like to see such services expanded. Consultation on local issues as a direct form of participation is the most popular service that online citizens would like to make use of, ahead of a range of other services such as payment of council tax or the provision of grants and benefits. A majority of people would welcome the opportunity to vote online (77 percent). This illustrates the interest to make traditional forms of political participation available online.

Turning to the legislative branch of government, the survey results indicate that a vast majority of people (76 percent) would appreciate the presence and availability of their political representatives on the Internet. Similarly, a slightly larger majority of people (77 percent) agree or strongly agree that political representatives should use the Internet to find out the views of the public. In addition, a majority of people (42 percent) would like to be able to contribute to policy making via the Internet as an opportunity for an active form of participation by 2010. Finally, a large majority (86 percent) of people consider that the government should do more to promote e-democracy in general.

Although the strength of support for e-government and e-democracy services reported is clearly related to the overrepresentation of the politically active and interested within the YouGov sample discussed earlier, the data certainly reveal a strong degree of support among the online citizenry at least for a greater Web presence of their political representatives and for more chances to contribute to the policy making processes via the Internet.

Attitudes toward Online Consultation

Given the high levels of interest exhibited by our sample toward expanding the provision of e-government and e-democracy activities, particularly in terms of developing new channels for citizen feedback, it comes as little surprise to see that support for specific local- or national-government-sponsored online consultations is also strong. Just over nine out of ten respondents would be willing to be involved in such an event over the next year (92 percent), and a similar proportion believe that an online space should be available for citizens to debate policy issues. In addition, respondents were almost unanimous in wanting council Web sites to include opportunities for citizens to comment on policies by e-mail (98 percent). Respondents saw the main benefits of online consultation as being both instrumental—allowing them to share their experiences and expertise with policy makers (49 percent)—and expressive, giving them a sense of involvement in local affairs (45 percent).

When asked how much time they would be prepared to devote to an online consultation, a majority a majority of respondents stated that they would be willing to spend under ten minutes on consultations concerning key issues (51 percent). A significant minority (20 percent), however, claimed that they would be prepared to commit up to one hour.

When we turn to the extent to which this enthusiasm has translated into practical involvement with new consultative techniques, the topline findings make for somewhat less exciting reading. The vast majority of respondents (86 percent) had not actually participated in any local or national government online consultation over the past twelve months. Of course, e-consultative mechanisms, as noted earlier in the chapter, are still relatively new and rare events within Britain, and so the low participation does not necessarily reflect a resistance toward more active involvement by the public. Evidence in support of this point can be found if we probe the data a little further and examine the propensity of individuals to participate in more established modes of consultation. When offline techniques are considered, a much healthier picture of engagement is revealed, with 39 percent of respondents claiming to have taken part in a public meeting to discuss local issues. Furthermore, although a significant minority (20 percent) explained their nonparticipation as essentially stemming from their perception of it being a "wasted effort," the most commonly cited reason for not joining in was the lack of awareness that such events were happening (35 percent) followed by a lack of time. Given the high levels of enthusiasm that online consultative methods appear to stimulate and the fact that they would offer an effective solution to some of the major barriers facing their offline counterparts in terms of logistical and time concerns, one might expect engagement with online consultation to meet and even exceed levels experienced in the more traditional format.

Mobilizing the Potential of Online Consultation

To examine further the latent or untapped potential suggested by the data, we looked more deeply at supporters of online consultations and compared their response profiles with the wider pool of those who had engaged in some form of offline consultation. We wanted to identify those individuals who had declared an interest in participating in this type of forum but had not yet done so. Who were these latent enthusiasts for online consultation? Did most of them match the profile of those who were already active in offline consultation, making it likely to be just a matter of time before they graduated to the online environment? Or did they perhaps represent a wider group of less experienced or mobilized individuals who might be inclined to participate in online mode rather than offline?

To examine this proposition, we first sought to assess the extent of this latent interest in online consultation. We did so by cross-tabulating interest in being involved in an online consultation with actually having done so. This resulted in the findings reported in table 8.3. Here we can see that latent e-consultees (those who have not participated but would like to) form a majority within our sample (66 percent). There is also a smaller group of what we might call active enthusiasts (around one in ten of the sample) who have taken part in an e-consultation and would do so again. Sitting in opposition to these more positive orientations toward online consultations, we can also identify a very small group of "dismissives"—those who have not taken part in an online consultation

Table 8.3
Orientations toward online consultations

Have taken part in online consultation in past year	Would be willing to take part in e-consultation in next year			
	Yes	No	Don't know	Total
Yes	ACTIVE 13.5 (434)	REJECT 0.2 (6)	0.2 (6)	13.8 (446)
No	LATENT 66.3 (2,137)	DISMISS 6.9 (223)	8.5 (275)	81.8 (2,635)
Don't know	2.7 (88)	0.2 (6)	1.5 (47)	(141)
Total (row %)	82.5 (2,659)	7.3 (235)	10.2 (328)	100 (3,222)

Source: YouGov, *What the World Thinks*, eDemocracy survey, March 10–16, 2005, http://today.yougov.co.uk/homepage.

and would not want to do so in the future. Finally, the numbers of what could be termed "rejectors" (those who have taken part in an online consultation and would not want to again) are negligible.

Having empirically identified a sufficient number of individuals associated with three of these orientations toward online consultation (latent, active, and dismissive), we then examined who these individuals are and how they differ, if at all, from offline consultees. To do so, we ran a series of binary logistic regressions on our YouGov sample using a range of standard sociodemographic and political predictors of political activism. We examined the importance of age (measured in years), educational qualifications, sex, and class in predicting each of the three orientations toward online consultation, along with a number of measures of general political engagement (voting, contacting, levels of political knowledge, and interest in local politics) and two types of efficacy. The first efficacy measure focused on an individual's perception of his or her own ability to be heard by policy makers, and the second captured a broader understanding of how far people collectively were listened to by the government. In a final step, we ran a fourth regression analysis that examined the effect of these resources and outlooks on the propensity to engage in offline consultation. The results are reported in table 8.4.

The regression results reveal an interesting contrast in terms of the predictors of our three orientations toward online consultation and further between the types of individuals who are drawn toward offline and online modes of consultation. If we turn first to comparing the profiles of our active, latent, and dismissive online consultees (reported in the first three columns of table 8.4), it is clear that having a prior history of contacting a politician via traditional or offline methods is the major factor separating active supporters of online consultation from latent supporters. Although both groups exhibit high levels of interest in local politics and latents are also very politically knowledgeable, if one has already engaged in some form of contact with an elected representative, then one is significantly more likely to have participated in an online consultation. Conversely, among those who would like to engage in online consultation but have not as yet done so, there is a distinct lack of uptake for traditional methods of contact. Beyond these behavioral differences, however, it appears that the two groups do share concerns about the extent to which the government is listening to citizens' concerns. For latent supporters, the concerns center on their feeling that politicians are not interested in what they personally have to say (effic 1 approaches significance for this group), whereas for those who support

Table 8.4
Logistic regression analysis of sociodemographic and political correlates of engagement in online and offline consultation

	Model 1 (Active)		Model 2 (Latent)		Model 3 (Dismiss)		Model 4 (Offline)	
	Est	SE	Est	SE	Est	SE	Est	SE
Sociodemographic resources:								
Class (ABC1)	.23	.13	-.16	.09	.22	.17	.33**	.09
Age (Yrs)	-.003	.004	.001	.003	-.001	.005	.05**	.003
Sex (Male)	-.10	.11	.01	.08	.22	.16	.07	.08
Education:								
Youth training or apprentice	-.95*	.40	.29	.22	.30	.37	-.23	
Secondary	.24	.20	-.11	.14	.12	.26	.32*	
Postsecondary	.09	.21	.10	.15	-.22	.28	.75**	
University, diploma, or professional training	.11	.20	.02	.14	-.38	.27	.88**	
Political inclination:								
Voted	.10	.12	.14	.08	-.09	.16	.01	.08
Contact	.67**	.13	-.29**	.11	-.97**	.35	-.01	.11
Political interest	.90**	.09	.24**	.06	-.91**	.11	-.04	.06
Efficacy (1)	.01	.02	-0.3	.02	.05	.03	.04*	.02
Efficacy (2)	-.18**	.07	.07	.05	-.01	.10	.01	.05
Political knowledge	.03	.05	.21	.04	-.23**	.07	.04	.04
Constant	-4.33	.45	-.61	.30	.14	.54	-3.9	.32
Nagelkerke R-sq	0.13		.04		.13		.20	
(n)	2,924		2,924		2,924		2,924	

Notes: * $p < .05$, ** Statistically significant at $p < .01$. Excluded categories: Education—None/DK/NA; (C2DE). *Source*: YouGov, *What the World Thinks*, eDemocracy survey, March 10–16, 2005, http://today.yougov.co.uk/homepage.

online consultation and have engaged in it (actives), concerns focus more on their feelings that government is not interested in public opinion in general (effic 2). Taken together, these findings suggest a distinct mobilizing potential for the technology, in that interest in online consultation appears to be strongest among those who are engaged politically, who feel a considerable degree of disaffection with established elites, and who have actually eschewed or avoided use of more conventional offline methods of input.

Among those subscribing to our third orientation toward online consultation—the dismissives (those who have not participated in online consultations and do not want to do so)—we find evidence of a wider sense of political disaffection. Although (like the latent supporters of online consultation) such people are distinctly less likely to have engaged in offline contact with a politician, they are also significantly less interested in politics and less knowledgeable about the subject than the sample as a whole. Such findings indicate that outright dismissal of online consultation is likely to stem from a general detachment from politics in general rather than being a response to the technology itself.

When we turn to the results of the model predicting engagement in offline consultation (column 4), however, the full mobilizing potential of the Internet becomes most evident. Essentially, the findings present an entirely different and more conventional picture of participation, with the classic resources of age, class, and education driving individual involvement. In a nutshell, attendees at local public meetings are generally older, enjoy a high social status, and have a tertiary education. Levels of political interest, knowledge, and even engagement in other types of offline political activity do not appear to be relevant for predicting this type of participation when these factors are taken into account. The stark contrast in the findings for this model and those focusing on participation in online consultation is noteworthy. Rather than exacerbating the traditional participation gap between high- and low-status groups, online consultation appears to appeal to and draw in individuals from across the socioeconomic spectrum. Even more encouragingly, the vast majority of those who declare an interest in being consulted online do not appear to be particularly enthusiastic in their desire to engage in more conventional modes of input, such as writing to their representatives. Involvement in e-consultation therefore appears to be seen not simply as an alternative to existing channels but as a new and important opportunity in its own right.

Conclusions and Policy Implications

Three conclusions can be drawn from our findings. The first is that attitudes to democracy are nuanced and cannot be simply summed up in terms of "apathy," "disengagement," or "crisis." There are strong trends of civic disenchantment within the British population, but these are qualified by a continuing interest in politics and a desire to have more influence on policy formation and decision making. Our findings suggest that rather than wishing politics away, there is a widespread public feeling that governance and policy debate have become too distant from everyday life. This is reinforced by strong levels of support for a more direct relationship between elected representatives and citizens (and some support for direct democracy) as well as for using the interactive features of online communication to make consultation more meaningful. With support for local and national online consultations and e-democracy policies at such high levels, national, devolved, and local governments in the United Kingdom should be considering how rather than whether they should act on this demand. As suggested in the introduction to this volume, online consultations are best understood as "a kind of networked communication involving citizens (both participants and auditors), public decision makers (of both the legislative and administrative sort), bureaucrats, technicians, civil society organizations, and the media generally" rather than "simply as dialogues between citizen-participants and public decision makers" (chapter 1 in this volume). A more sophisticated approach to thinking about the ecology of public participation and consultation is called for.

Second, our more detailed analysis suggests that online consultations might engage more than "the usual suspects"—regular participators who fit the socioeconomic pattern of active citizenship. Although attitudes to democratic participation replicate standard patterns of socioeconomic inequality, this is not the case in relation to willingness to participate in online consultations. If this new method of consultation has a potential to activate many of those usually regarded as least likely to be engaged under any circumstances, then the Internet can be said to afford opportunities that are genuinely democratic. Our data tell us only about Internet users (now a majority of the UK population), but if by virtue of being online, this group can defy the seemingly fixed pattern of participation inequality, that surely points to an Internet affordance that calls for attention by policy makers who are interested in redressing social and political exclusion.

Third, it would make sense for the organizers of online consultations to reflect on the profile of the group we have labeled latent e-consultees. This substantial section of the population, added to those already committed to online consultation, could provide the critical mass necessary for e-consultative practices to gain democratic credibility and legitimacy. As we have indicated, whereas active e-consultees have a low level of external efficacy (stated simply, they doubt the willingness of politicians to listen to and learn from them), latent e-consultees are characterized by low internal efficacy, defined as "individuals' self-perception that they are capable of understanding politics and competent enough to participate in political acts" (Miller and Traugott 1980, 253). If their interest in communicating with government and representatives online is not to be squandered, then each of these two groups is in need of what we might call an "efficacy boost." But the nature of the stimulus needs to be different for each group, with "latents" offered strong encouragement to develop their confidence as civic actors, perhaps by combining lateral Citizen-to-Citizen with vertical Citizen-to-Government structures of online learning and discourse.

Our findings are open to the criticism that they are based on respondents' stated intentions. It is much easier to support a form of civic behavior in a survey than in everyday practice, and some respondents might have responded positively to some questions as a social desirability effect. Nonetheless, respondents differentiated between positive responses relating to online and offline options, so even accepting a gap between intentions and action, some intentions appealed more to some respondents and some to others. The lesson for policy makers is that they cannot take these intentions for granted. As advertisers well understand, an interest in doing something is an important step toward doing it (few people buy a product they had never intended to acquire), but there is broad scope for distraction between the expression of generally positive intentions and the consummation of specific actions. Online consultations need to be organized well, promoted vigorously, connected to meaningful institutional outcomes, and publicized as consequential. At present, few online consultations meet these conditions.

A final policy implication that flows from our analysis is that any new approach to consulting the public needs to start by addressing public attitudes to contemporary democracy and then move on to consider how communication technologies might play a role. Too often, it is the other way round, with e-solutions being driven by technocrats who have to make them be seen to work and have little sensitivity toward the problematics of democratic citizenship. By beginning with a nuanced profile of public attitudes, we have endeavored in our research to relate technological affordances to political needs. There is nothing inevitable about this linkage, and as is frequently implicit throughout this volume, in most states there is a significant tension between technological potentiality and institutional adaptation.

Notes

1. Responses were merged from two data files containing the same respondents. The split files resulted from the questionnaire's being fielded over two time periods—March 10–15, 2005 ($n = 3,360$) and March 10–16, 2005 ($n = 3,229$).

2. The BES 2005 sample, drawn from the Post Office's official Postcode Address File, is representative of the British population ages eighteen to ninety-seven (excluding Northern Ireland). The face-to-face computer-assisted personal interviews (CAPI), conducted by the National Center for Social Research (NATCEN) from February 2005 to April 2005, comprise a random sample of the adult population of Britain living in private households ($n = 3,589$). The weighting procedure was designed to correct for unequal selection probabilities (e.g., caused by oversampling of Scotland and Wales and marginal constituencies in England and the selection of one person per address for interview) and calibration weighting to fit the profile of the sample to population estimates for Britain.

3. The Census, last conducted on April 29, 2001, is an obligatory nationwide self-completion survey covering every UK household or communal homes at the same time, asking the same core questions everywhere in the country. The data used for this research are representative of the population in England and Wales ($n = 52,041,916$). Although the Census in England and Wales is planned and carried out by the Office for National Statistics, the General Register Office for Scotland and the Northern Ireland Statistics and Research Agency are responsible for the rest of the United Kingdom.

4. In terms of sex, the identical YouGov and BES data match almost exactly the census figures. On age, there appears to be a slight skew toward the older age groups among YouGov respondents, particularly those ages forty-five to fifty-nine, while the age group of sixty and over is slightly underrepresented compared to the BES and census data. With regard to education, there appears to be an overrepresentation of university-educated respondents and those with basic education within both BES and YouGov data and a lack of those with O-level education. People with no qualifications are overrepresented in the BES data and are underrepresented in the YouGov data. Finally, although we have only a relatively crude two-category measure of class—upper and middle, and lower-middle and working—the distributions reveal a skew in the BES sample toward those of higher social grade (see table 8.1).

5. The education categories are defined as follows: "Degree or higher qualification/NVQ and key skills 4 and 5" comprises university or CNAA higher degrees (e.g., MS, PhD); university or CNAA first degrees (e.g., BA, BS); university/poly diploma; other technical, professional, or higher qualification; teaching qualification (not degree); nursing qualification (e.g., SEN, SRN, SCM, RGN); HNC/

HND; BTEC higher; NVQ levels 4 and 5; and City and Guilds level 4. "A level/ NVQ and key skills 3" comprises A levels typically gained at age 18, required for university entrance; AS level; GCE A level; Higher School Certificate; Scottish Higher/Ordinary/Lower Certificate; advanced craft certificates; NVQ level 3; Advanced GNVQ; NVQ/SVQ 3; ONC/OND; and City and Guilds level 3. "O level/NVQ and key skills 2" comprises O levels, GCSE grades A–C, typically gained at age 16 at the end of compulsory schooling; O levels (any grades); GCSE (any grades); CSE (any grades); GCE O level; GCSE; School Certificate; Scottish Standard grades; Ordinary bands; NVQ/SVQ level 2; City and Guilds level 2; and GNVQ intermediate. "Other qualifications/key skills level 1 and entry level" comprises CSE below grade 1, NVQ 1, GNVQ/GSVQ foundation level; City & Guilds level 1; Clerical and commercial qualifications; Recognized trade apprenticeship; Youth training certificate/skill seeker; and other qualifications including overseas qualifications. "No qualifications" indicates no formal qualifications.

References

Committee on Public Participation in Planning. 1969. *People and Planning: Report of the Committee on Public Participation in Planning.* London: Her Majesty's Stationery Office.

House of Commons Public Administration Select Committee. 2001. *Sixth Report: Public Participation: Issues and Innovations.* London: Her Majesty's Stationery Office.

Lane, R. E. 1959. *Political Life: Why People Get Involved with Politics.* Glencoe, IL: Free Press.

Miller, W. E., and S. Traugott. 1980. *American National Election Studies Data Sourcebook, 1952–1978.* Cambridge: Harvard University Press.

Office for National Statistics. 2001a. *Census 2001: All People Aged 16 and Over in Households.* http://www.statistics.gov.uk/StatBase/ssdataset.asp?vlnk=7534& Pos=&ColRank=2&Rank=256.

Office for National Statistics. 2001b. *Census 2001: All Types of Qualification Held by People Aged 16–74.* http://www.statistics.gov.uk/StatBase/ssdataset.asp ?vlnk=7553&Pos=&ColRank=2&Rank=240.

Office for National Statistics. 2001c. *Census 2001: First Results on Population in England and Wales.* http://www.statistics.gov.uk/census2001/pop2001/ england_wales_ages.asp.

Twyman, J. 2008. "Getting It Right: YouGov and Online Survey Research in Britain." *Journal of Elections, Public Opinion and Parties* 18, no. 4:343–354.

University of Essex/Economic and Social Research Council. 2005. *The British Election Study: Face to Face Survey Data: The 2005 BES Pre-Campaign Data.* http://www.essex.ac.uk/bes/2005/Face_to_face_survey_data.htm.

YouGov. 2005. *What the World Thinks.* eDemocracy survey. March 10–16. http://today.yougov.co.uk/homepage.

9

The Technological Dimension of Deliberation: A Comparison between Online and Offline Participation

Laurence Monnoyer-Smith

This chapter explores how publics divide up between online and offline discussions and why they choose one modality or the other for debating. In the context of a controversial academic literature on the topic of inclusion and deliberation (Monnoyer-Smith 2009), the focus here is on the close relationship between the technological setup of a deliberative space and the form of participation through which citizens choose to engage with it. In line with the call in the introduction to this volume to "see how the [consultative] experience is constructed by social, political, and legal forces, including the design of the online consultation experience itself," this chapter draws on field data from a public debate held in 2007 by the French National Public Debate Commission (CNDP) to discuss the upgrading of a wastewater treatment facility located in the northwestern Paris suburb of Achères with a view to discussing actors' positioning in a public debate when mediated by a technological device—who is affected by the device and how it affects the various forms of participation.

All deliberative devices have a technological dimension. In the simplest and oldest form of deliberation, the technology consists of spaces that are set up and allocated for public discourse. Their layout, their architecture, and the distribution of speech they suppose comprise the technological dimension of the public deliberative space that various democratic constitutional traditions helped to construct (Abélès 2000). However, a deeper understanding of technology requires analysis of both the infrastructure that supports deliberation as well as the particular ways in which humans relate to technological objects. From this standpoint, analyzing the ways in which legal discourse is shaped by administrative judges' use of pen and ink to annotate hard-copy drafts of proposed legal opinions may be as revealing as an analysis of online discussion forums packed with an array of multimedia applications (Lessig 1999; Latour 2004).

Deliberation theorists have only recently taken into account the substantial layer of technology in their analyses of political discussion and deliberation. Their examinations of the deliberative paradigm have tended to concentrate either on the normative dimension of deliberation, its limitations, and its grounding in language (Schudson 1997; Manin 2005; Bächtiger and Pedrini 2008) or on the quality of debating itself (Steiner, Bächtiger, Spörndli, and Steenberge 2004; Stromer-Galley 2007; Kies 2009; Black, Burkhalter, Gastil, and Stromer-Gallery 2009). Consequently, online deliberation and consultation devices have been envisioned and assessed primarily as new tools for potentially deepening democracy within the scope of a deliberative paradigm laid down by philosophy and political science (Macpherson 1977; Barber 1984, Cohen 1989; Fraser 1992; Dryzek 2000). This framework has supported a variety of research efforts that compare deliberation in online and face-to-face venues to assess which venue better approximates a normative model of deliberation (Witschge 2002):

Initial research into virtual political debate in the 1990s often exploited Habermas' notions of public sphere and deliberation. Generally, researchers compared its characteristics against those of the ideal public space, only to end up with the disappointing conclusion that information and communication technology (ICT) cannot attain the deliberative ideal. (Greffet and Wojcik 2008, 25)

As Greffet and Wojcik show, the basic question at the heart of these early studies has been how technology affects the criteria demanded by deliberative theory—inclusion, sincerity, dissent, and transparency. The type and number of criteria have varied over time and by author (Dahlberg 2001; Stromer-Galley 2005, 2007; Kies 2010).

This chapter, however, explores technology from a somewhat different frame. Technology can be seen as more than a set of neutral tools that more or less assist people in the satisfaction of preexisting normative criteria. Any technology can be seen as a specific political setup that allocates power resources to participants in public discussion. The issue is not a matter of measuring the gap between a given device and the satisfaction of normative criteria. Instead, the question posed is how technological change reallocates power as compared to preexisting technologies of discussion (Wright and Street 2007; Bennett 2008; Coleman 2008). This approach is triggering renewed interest among scholars from a variety of disciplines in the technological dimension of democratic discourse. It targets the effects of new technological frameworks on relations among political actors.

For scholars working within this frame, the object of analysis is no longer the online discussion as mere text: it is the entire process of producing online discussions as an exercise in the negotiation of power (Witschge 2008). We concern ourselves with the apparent discussants in an online forum but also with, for example, the Web site designers and the officials who make topics available for public debate. We seek to explore any shifts in power relations induced by deliberative devices: either they compete against preexisting real-world devices and discussion formats and casts of actors, or they are filling in a mediation deficit between political leaders and the citizenry (Coleman 2005a, b). As Witschge (2008, 79) notes: "Online texts are part of broader social practices and reflect, negotiate or resist, and feed back into existing social power relations like any other discourse and thus this aspect of the discourse needs to be examined."

In this chapter, the generic hypothesis is that citizens participate online or offline because they feel the technological arrangement provided is best suited to their ability to express themselves, considering the distribution of power within the deliberative space. Three main factors of power distortion are therefore studied—gender, social status, and knowledge.

Public Debate on the Seine Aval Wastewater Treatment Facility

The Seine Aval unit is the largest wastewater treatment facility in Europe and comes second only to that of Chicago, Illinois (United States) for throughput. It lies west of Paris, straddling the municipalities of Achères and Saint-Germain-en-Laye along the Oise and Seine rivers. Intake is from Paris proper and a fraction of Greater Paris, and the wastewater of these two municipalities is treated elsewhere. It has undergone periodic upgrades since opening in 1940 to cope with rising intake due to demographic growth and to growing volumes of rainwater. Initial throughput of 200,000 cubic meters per day in 1940 rose to 2.1 million m^3 per day in 1990, and now averages 1.7 million m^3 per day to cover the needs of 6 million inhabitants.[1]

Because of new European regulations[2] and resentment from the local population, the facility operator, SIAPP,[3] is reviewing all its options. Outdated and in breach of regulations, the facility faces issues of efficiency, safety, public health standards, environmental requirements, and other regulations. Exasperated by the facility's noise and foul odors, the local population and their elected officials have been challenging further expansion of the facility and arguing for smaller facilities closer to waste-water sources across Greater Paris. Given the scope of this public works upgrade (estimated at 800 million or U.S. $1.1 billion), owner/operator SIAAP is required by law to submit the project to public scrutiny, and as an independent government agency, CNDP organized the public debate. To that end, it set up an ad hoc CPDP commission chaired by CNDP representatives, a general secretary, technical experts, and an ICT researcher. Six months later, fifteen local public meetings were held from September to December 2007. Hearings of all actors were held in September and October, followed by meetings on specific issues in November and summaries of discussions in December.

In addition, a dedicated Web site was put up for local residents and members of the public who were unable to attend the meetings, all held from 8 p.m. to 11 p.m. As well as providing information, the Web site also hosted an innovative interactive section with postings of meeting minutes, a question-and-answer section for quick responses to questions (asked by email, by letter, or at meetings),[4] meeting digests and slide-shows, plus any supporting documentation, local and national press digests, and a blog.

Although CNDP had previously set up discussion forums and even instant messaging on its Web sites before, it had never allowed direct posting of comments. As it happened, no posting ever required deletion. A blogfeed published summaries of meeting discussions that participants could edit prior to validation and archiving, and videos by CPDP staff and ancillary discussion information were posted.

Forms of Participation, Methodological Considerations, and Statistics

To analyze participation formats in relation to the function of technical devices, I pursued three types of observation—ethnomethodological fieldwork with colleagues as participating observers,[5] two quantitative questionnaires administered at the start and close of the debate, and qualitative analysis of the public meetings and of blog content.

The questionnaires looked at civic engagement in the context of per-sonal sociological profiles—participants' levels of knowledge about the subject, their form of expression, and the technical devices they used. Of the 163 responses, 34 questionnaires were completed online, and 129 in face-to-face interviews; 66.3 percent of respondents attended debates in person, and the remainder participated mainly online. This last figure is high because most questionnaires were administered during public meetings and related events. Given the imbalance between the on- and offline samples, the results presented here are only those that are statistically validated by chi square testing. This chapter looks at participation by age, gender, income bracket, and knowledge levels and shows that backdoor channels arose on the Web site that enabled participants to work around the structuring effects of face-to-face debate.[6]

Some fifteen hundred persons attended 15 public debate meetings. Whether representing associations, government agencies, or simply themselves, numerous actors attended several meetings, especially thematic meetings devoted to individual nuisances generated by the facility.[7] The Web site and blog scored 14,000 hits and 3,800 hits, respectively (IP addresses were counted only once per day). There were 126 postings from twenty-five individuals; twelve dominated the discussion, and thirteen submitted only one message each.

Comparing several questionnaires produces a fairly good sociological profile of the participants. The first questionnaire was a popup that asked visitors their geographical location ($n = 152$), and the second, containing two parts, was handed out to the audience at meetings ($n = 258$). The first part of the questionnaire was handed out at the start of debating and sought to determine where the audience came from and how they had learned of the meeting. In November, a second part was added to map out the forms and formats of involvement in the debates, levels of participants' knowledge and personal interest in environmental issues, and the standard sociological variables. Our mapping demonstrated that most meeting participants were local inhabitants, while the Web site attracted a far wider population with hits from all over the country.

Gender Participation

One interesting result of the survey is the gender breakdown of participants: although males dominated in meetings and in online debates, a higher proportion of women contributed to the Web site and the blog. Public speaking remains a male activity. At meetings, males accounted for 83.9 percent of all questions and comments and constituted 63.9 percent of the audience. Online, they accounted for 66.7 percent of blog questions and comments. As shown in table 9.1, males dominate across the entire spectrum of available modes of involvement.

Table 9.1
Breakdown of participation by gender (dependent variable) (percentage)

Form of participation	No answer	Male	Female	Total
No reply	8.3	58.3	33.3	100
I attended one or more public meetings	3.7	**63.9**	32.4	
I attended other meetings about the public meetings	10.3	69.0	20.7	
I posted to the CPDP blog	11.1	**66.7**	22.2	
I asked a question on the DPDP Web site	7.7	84.6	7.7	
I asked a question by letter or prepaid postcard	22.2	55.6	22.2	
I asked a question or commented at a public meeting	10.0	83.9	16.1	
I looked for more information by mail or in documents	12.2	69.4	18.4	
I visited the CPDP Web site	6.5	71.4	22.1	
Other	14.3	71.4	14.3	
Total	**7.4**	**62.6**	**30.1**	

Note: Boldface indicates noteworthy figures that are generally discussed in the text.

Gender is the dependent variable in table 9.1. However, finer analysis is obtained when gender is applied as an independent variable. Although women speak less and listen more in public (10 percent spoke, compared with about 25 percent of males)[8] and fewer asked questions (6.1 percent asked versus 15.7 percent of males), they contributed in writing. There was greater gender balance in blog comments, where participation is 4.1 percent female and 5.9 percent male.

It thus appears that blogging attenuated the effects of offline gender imbalance: online writing apparently suited women more than meetings, where males overwhelmed participation (table 9.2). Women seemed also more comfortable with giving their opinion than asking questions, and when they did so, women used snailmail (4.1 percent) more than the Web site (2.0 percent). Men exhibited the opposite behavior: they favored asking questions (10.8 percent of males asked online versus 4.9 percent used snailmail) over giving their opinions online.

Table 9.2
Breakdown of participation by gender (independent variable) (percentage)

Form of participation	No answer	Male	Female	Total
No reply	8.3	6.9	8.2	7.4
Attended one or more public meetings	33.3	19.6	12.2	66.3
Attended other meetings about the public meetings	25.0	19.6	12.2	17.8
Posted to the CPDP blog	8.3	**5.9**	**4.1**	5.5
Asked a question on the DPDP Web site	8.3	**10.8**	**2.0**	8.0
Asked a question by letter or prepaid postcard	16.7	**4.9**	**4.1**	5.5
Asked a question or commented at a public meeting	0.0	**25.5**	**10.2**	19.0
Looked for more information by mail or in documentation	50.0	33.3	18.4	30.1
Visited the CPDP Web site	41.7	53.9	34.7	47.2
Other	8.3	4.9	2.0	4.3
Total	100.0	100.0	100.0	100.0

Note: Boldface indicates noteworthy figures that are generally discussed in the text.

Participation by Social Status

Meeting audiences were 73.1 percent homeowners and 22.2 percent tenants (table 9.3). This is consistent with the assumption that homeowners' substantial capital investment gives them a stronger interest in sanitation than other populations have. Homeowners accounted for 93.5 percent of oral interventions at meetings against 3.2 percent for tenants. This divide carries over to Web site visits, where they account for 14.3 percent of visits against 22 percent of meeting participants. However, the trend improves when it comes to participation. Tenants accounted for 8 percent of Web site questions and over 11 percent of blog postings against 3.2 percent of oral interventions. Nonetheless, the statistical relevance of this data are meager, showing that age, gender, and knowledge levels correlate better with participation than social status does. In summary, the institutional weight of oral contributions by homeowners

Table 9.3
Breakdown of participation by social status (percentage)

Form of participation	No answer	Homeowner	Tenant	Total
No reply	0.0	6.0	13.5	**7.4**
Attended one or more public meetings	50.0	68.1	64.9	**66.3**
Attended other meetings about the public meetings	10.0	20.7	10.8	**17.8**
Posted to the CPDP blog	0.0	6.9	2.7	**5.5**
Asked a question on the DPDP Web site	0.0	10.2	2.7	**8.0**
Asked a question by letter or prepaid postcard	10.0	5.2	5.4	**5.5**
Asked a question or commented at a public meeting	10.0	25.0	2.7	**19.0**
Looked for more information by mail or in documentation	20.0	29.3	35.1	**30.1**
Visited the CPDP Web site	50.0	52.6	29.7	**47.2**
Other	10.0	3.4	5.4	**4.3**
Total	**100.0**	**100.0**	**100.0**	**100.0**

Note: Boldface indicates noteworthy figures that are generally discussed in the text.

and other real estate holders at meetings upstaged the words of tenants, who thus chose to express themselves online.

Participation by Knowledge Levels

The correlation of knowledge to participation was among the most surprising. Foreknowledge of the issues, notably through meeting attendance, was a strong indicator of the form that participation took. Some two thirds of meeting audience members and 90 percent of speakers reported having a "fairly clear idea" of the issues under discussion. For unassociated and therefore less informed individuals, the CPDP Web site became the prime source of information and interaction, and their level of participation (44.4 percent) closely trailed that of informed participants (55.6 percent). Likewise, although failing to speak at meetings, the less informed accounted for almost a quarter of online questions asked

Table 9.4

Breakdown of participation by knowledge levels (independent variable) (percentage)

Form of participation	No answer	With knowledge	Without knowledge	Total
No reply	0.0	75.0	25.0	100.0
Attended one or more public meetings	3.7	**68.5**	**27.8**	
Attended other meetings about the public meetings	0.0	96.6	3.4	
Posted to the CPDP blog	0.0	**55.6**	**44.4**	
Asked a question on the DPDP Web site	0.0	76.9	23.1	
Asked a question by letter or prepaid postcard	0.0	88.9	11.1	
Asked a question or commented at a public meeting	6.5	**90.3**	**3.2**	
Sought more information by mail or in documents	0.0	61.2	32.5	
Visited the CPDP Web site	3.9	63.6	32.5	
Other	0.0	71.4	28.6	

Note: Boldface indicates noteworthy figures that are generally discussed in the text.

(table 9.4). It therefore appears that the blog is a forum that is suited to novice participants.

The CPDP Web site was a critical information source for anyone whose personal network was too limited to help muster a full range of arguments. The research strategies of the less informed relied essentially on the Web site, whereas the more knowledgeable consulted the Web site but could also draw on the information resources of their civic associations. Over a quarter attended wastewater-related meetings other than those held by the CPDP (table 9.5).

Discussion

The gender divide was a strong characteristic of public-meeting attendance. The figures support previous findings that stress the

Table 9.5
Breakdown of participation by knowledge levels (dependent variable) (percentage)

Form of participation	No answer	With knowledge	Without knowledge
No reply	0.0	8.3	6.0
Attended one or more public meetings	100.0	67.9	60.0
Attended other meetings about the public meetings	0.0	**25.7**	2.0
Posted to the CPDP blog	0.0	**4.6**	**8.0**
Asked a question on the DPDP Web site	0.0	9.2	6.0
Asked a question by letter or prepaid postcard	0.0	7.3	2.0
Asked a question or commented at a public meeting	50.0	**25.7**	**2.0**
Sought more information by mail or in documents	0.0	27.5	38.0
Visited the CPDP Web site	75.0	**45.0**	**50.0**
Other	0.0	4.6	4.0
Total	**100.0**	**100.0**	**100.0**

Note: Boldface indicates noteworthy figures that are generally discussed in the text.

preponderance of male participation in public debate and a traditional male monopoly on speaking because of the type of discussion formats used in face-to-face exchanges (Young 2000; Dahlberg 2001; Seyle et al. 2008). Women also show more dissatisfaction with deliberative procedures than men do: as Seyle et al. report, they feel that men do not listen and that women do not receive opportunities to speak. Reviewing the numerous other studies confirming the difficulties that women face when they try to take the floor, some linguists highlight deep differences between how men and women approach argumentation in public debates (Farrell 1979). Women prefer walking "the listener or reader through a set of experiences and/or along a line of reasoning, holding off the conclusion until they have made it almost impossible to reject the validity— emotional or logical—of what they say" (Farrell 1979, 909), while men start off with their conclusions before explaining the supporting reasons.

Perceived as "more effective," the male strategy of rhetoric is the one taught in schools and universities, and this gender divide erodes as level of education rises (Calla Carrillo and De la Mata 2004). This may explain why women are uncomfortable about speaking in public and why our figures show that women preferred blogging. Further qualitative studies are needed for a better grasp of women's reluctance to speak in public, despite their high attendance rates at thematic meetings, especially those concerning health and children.

Disparities do not disappear online, however. Other studies report a strong presence online of people from those social categories that already dominate offline activity—that is, educated, politically concerned, male Caucasians: "Not only are there many more men than women posting on the list but also a masculine, agonistic style of discourse pre-dominates despite the high level of respect fostered" (Dahlberg 2001, 626), and this is particularly true in the case of politically oriented Web sites (Hill and Hughes 1998; Davis 1999; Wilhelm 2000a, 200b). Beyond the inequality of online presence and access, we see gender differences in usage (for example, women are less likely than men to share creative input online) (Hargittai and Walejko 2008). This point corroborates the thesis that online expression spaces come with built-in language formats that may use standard argumentative formats but go on to differ in semantic and rhetorical formatting (Monnoyer-Smith 2006a, 2006b).

The dominance effect that is inherent in deliberative devices (through language and other means) does not disappear online, and the gender divide in the forms of access provided to citizens persists online. In this sense, one advantage of online deliberation over face-to-face participation is the potential to diversify access formats into discussion forums, blogs, mailing lists, and chats to open up expression space to a wider range of populations. Nonetheless, online debate is a real alternative to speaking in public. In this study, CPDP realized the dominance effect inscribed into the procedure and therefore aimed to give participants alternate channels of self-expression.

Participation in face-to-face discussion significantly correlated with home ownership. Not only do the people in this subpopulation have a vested interest in the quality of life in their local area, but any change in that quality may threaten the value of their real estate holdings. Although noise and foul odors affect homeowner and tenant alike, homeowners are more strongly motivated to improve the quality of their lives, if only because they cannot move out as cheaply as tenants can. Indeed, some tenants told interviewers that they had already decided to move else-where because of wastewater facility emissions. Unsurprisingly, the study shows that homeowners participated more actively across the board because their home location motivated them to engage in activities that affected their quality of life.

Nevertheless, a salient finding of the study is that tenants are far likelier to participate in online meetings than in face-to-face meetings. It confirms current research that has found stronger e-participation by those socioprofessional categories with the least access to institutional arenas. In his own studies, Muhlberger (2004, 235) has found that

The educated and home owners discuss politics about as much as anyone else online, but much less than would be expected from their level of Internet access. . . . It may be that the educated and homeowners . . . have more discussions offline and so do not use online forums; and that they do not find Internet political discussion sufficiently high in quality or sufficiently pertinent to their concern.

This partially validates the hypothesis that tenants, who are often younger and more financially vulnerable than homeowners, prefer online delib-erative tools.

Finally, the 66.9 percent of face-to-face meeting participants who reported having a clear idea of the subject at hand were usually very knowledgeable about the issues under discussion. Over two thirds had already prepared a set of arguments developed through their involvement in local political and civic associations. A substantial share of partici-pants at public meetings had also attended meetings elsewhere on the same issue.

These results concur particularly well with work by Vincent Price showing that there is higher participation in public debates by members of a population who have a wide "argument repertoire" in the subject at hand (Cappella, Price, and Nir 2002; Price 2009). This explains why over 90 percent of speakers at meetings already had a clear idea of the issues.

High knowledge levels are seen online, but we found an exception in the blog, which seem to attract the less informed. Internet usage is notable as an information space offering opportunities to interact with persons less concerned or informed about a given subject. Very little research has looked at the special role played by online discussion spaces in reaching the less informed. Face-to-face public debate appears to support the acquisition and exchange of information. The Internet enables navigation between areas of information content and induces discrimination between them, so the effects of symbolic dominance in face-to-face debate probably explain why the less informed participate in online discussions.

Conclusion

Deliberative devices empower citizens to redraw the frontiers of grass-roots participation and restructure the distribution of opportunities for citizens to speak up about public policy issues. For Foucault, deliberative machines are tools that impose the rules of power and form part of a global setup for deliberation. Therefore, they provide a unique platform of argumentation and rhetoric that lacks an offline equivalent and that welcomes women, the less informed, and the socioculturally deprived. Citizens with an established presence in other discussion spaces will exploit technology differently. One hypothesis arising from our study is that the setup of these discussion spaces is a reflexive act by the actors who design and promote them because they realize the intrinsic limitations of face-to-face participation. In this context, Bruno Latour's research suggests that new forms of mediation constituted by digital technologies reflect a search for reconnection between the citizenry and politics. Technological artifacts thus cannot be reduced to their purely mechanical dimension and must be perceived in all their sociological substance. Although we might be tempted to situate their instrumentalization in the context of a deliberative setup that would reinforce the traditional powers of representation, field observations report that they can also attract actors who rework the traditional forms of political mediation. From that perspective, any analysis of the appropriation of technological devices should take account of the gap they generate in the distribution of power among various categories of the population. The contributions of online deliberations can be evaluated in terms of the aptitude of people in these new categories to produce new normative references that differ from those that usually result from traditional offline deliberations.

Notes

1. Plans to boost throughput capacity to 2.7 million cubic meters per day have been shelved.
2. The EU Court of Justice fined France 380 million (U.S. $500 million) for failure to implement the 1991 EU wastewater directive. The fine falls due in 2011 unless Seine Aval and other facilities meet the required standards before then.

3. Syndicat Interdépartemental pour l'Assainissement de l'Agglomération Parisienne (established in 1970).

4. Debate generated a total of 193 questions and answers, of which eighty-five were sourced in public meetings, fifty-six in prepaid postcards, thirty-nine in Web site postings, and three in the mails by associations, government agencies, and individuals.

5. The author was a CPDP member; students performed the fieldwork.

6. We did not focus here on backdoor channels initiated by participants to divert from controlling effects from public authority. For such an approach, see Monnoyer-Smith (2007).

7. Some actors (such as representatives of local associations and of Seine Normandie waterworks, which was financing expansion of the Seine Aval facility) attended all meetings.

8. However, 90 percent of women tracking the issue also attended face-to-face meetings, as did 69.8 percent of men.

References

Abélès, Marc. 2000. *Un ethnologue à l'Assemblée*. Paris: Odile Jacob.

Bächtiger, André, and Seraina Pedrini. 2008. "Dissecting Deliberative Democracy: A Review of Theoretical Concepts and Empirical Findings." Paper presented at the Elections Public Opinion and Parties Annual Conference, Manchester, UK, September 12–14.

Barber, Benjamin. 1984. *Strong Democracy: Participatory Politics for a New Age*. Berkeley: University of California Press.

Bennett, Lance W. 2008. "Youth and Digital Democracy: Intersections of Practice, Policy and the Marketplace." In *Civic Life Online: Learning How Digital Media Can Engage Youth*, edited by Lance W. Bennett, 25–50. Cambridge: MIT Press.

Black, Laura W., Stephanie Burkhalter, John Gastil, and Jennifer Stromer-Galley. 2009. "Methods for Analyzing and Measuring Group Deliberation." In *Sourcebook for Political Communication Research: Methods, Measures, and Analytical Techniques*, edited by Erik Page Bucy and R. Lance Holbert, 323–345. Mahwah, NJ: Routledge.

Cala Carrillo, Jesus, and Manuel De la Mata. 2004. "Educational Background, Modes of Discourses and Argumentation: Comparing Women and Men." *Argumentation* 18:403–426.

Cappella, Joseph N., Vincent Price, and Lilach Nir. 2002. "Argument Repertoire as a Reliable and Valid Measure of Opinion Quality: Electronic Dialogue during Campaign 2000." *Political Communication* 19:73–93.

Cohen, Joshua. 1989. "Deliberation and Democratic Legitimacy." In *The Good Polity: Normative Analysis of the State*, edited by Alan Hamlin and Philip Pettit, 127–142. Oxford: Basil Blackwell.

Coleman, Stephen. 2005a. *Direct Representation: Towards a Conversational Democracy.* London: IPPR.

Coleman, Stephen. 2005b. "New Mediation and Direct Representation: Reconceptualizing Representation in the Digital Age." *New Media and Society* 7, no. 2:177–198.

Coleman, Stephen. 2008. "Doing IT for Themselves: Management versus Autonomy in Youth E-Citizenship." In *Civic Life Online: Learning How Digital Media Can Engage Youth*, edited by Lance W. Bennett, 189–206. Cambridge: MIT Press.

Dahlberg, Lincoln. 2001. "The Internet and Democratic Discourse: Exploring the Prospects of Online Deliberative Forums Extending the Public Sphere." *Information Communication and Society* 4, no. 4:615–633.

Davis, Richard. 1999. *The Web of Politics: The Internet's Impact on the American Political System.* New York: Oxford University Press.

Dryzek, John S. 2000. *Deliberative Democracy and Beyond: Liberals, Critics, Contestations.* Oxford: Oxford University Press.

Farrell, Thomas J. 1979. "The Female and Male Modes of Rhetoric." *College English* 40, no. 8:909–921.

Foucault, Michel. 1975. *Surveiller et punir.* Paris: Gallimard.

Fraser, Nancy. 1992. "Rethinking the Public Sphere: A Contribution to the Critique of Actually Existing Democracy." In *Habermas and the Public Sphere*, edited by Craig Calhoun, 109–142. Cambridge: MIT Press.

Greffet, Fabienne, and Stéphanie Wojcik. 2008. "Parler politique en ligne. Une revue des travaux français et anglo-saxons." *Reseaux* 150:19–50.

Hargittai, Eszter, and Gina Walejko. 2008. "The Participation Divide: Content Creation and Sharing in the Digital Age." *Information Communication and Society* 11, no. 2:239–256.

Hill, Kevin A., and John E. Hughes. 1998. *Cyberpolitics: Citizen Activism in the Age of the Internet.* Lanham, MD: Rowman & Littlefield.

Kies, Raphaël. 2009. "Variations in Deliberativeness of Web-Debates: Analysis of the External Impact Hypothesis." Paper presented at the Twenty-first International Political Science Association World Congress, Santiago, Chile, July 11–16.

Kies, Raphaël. 2010. Promises and Limits of Web-deliberation. London: Palgrave Macmillan.

Latour, Bruno. 2004. *La fabrique du droit. Une ethnographie du Conseil d'Etat.* Paris: La découverte.

Lessig, Lawrence. 1999. *Codes and Other Laws of Cyberspace.* New York: Basic Books.

Macpherson, Crawford Brough. 1977. *The Life and Times of Liberal Democracy.* Oxford: Oxford University Press.

Manin, Bernard. 2005. "Délibération et discussion." *Swiss Political Science Review* 10, no. 4:34–46.

Monnoyer-Smith, Laurence. 2006a. "Citizen's Deliberation on the Internet: An Exploratory Study." *International Journal of Electronic Government Research* 2, no. 3:58–74.

Monnoyer-Smith, Laurence. 2006b. "Etre créatif sous la contrainte. Une analyse des formes nouvelles de la délibération politique." *Politix* 75:75–101.

Monnoyer-Smith, Laurence. 2007. "Citizens' Deliberation on the Internet: A French Case. In *E-Government Research: Policy and Management*, edited by Donald Norris, 230–253. New York: IGI.

Monnoyer-Smith, Laurence, 2009. "Deliberation and Inclusion: Framing Online Public Debate to Enlarge Participation. A Theoretical Proposal." *I/S: A Journal for Law and Policy for the Information Society* 5, no. 1: 87–115.

Muhlberger, Peter. 2004. "Access, Skill, and Motivation in Online Political Discussion: Testing Cyber-Realism." In *Democracy Online: The Prospects for Political Renewal through the Internet*, edited by Peter M. Shane, 225–237. New York: Routledge.

Price, Vincent. 2009. "Citizens Deliberating Online: Theory and Some Evidence." In *Online Deliberation: Design, Research, and Practice*, edited by Todd Davies and Seeta Peña Gangadharan, 37–58. Chicago: CSLI/University of Chicago Press.

Schudson, Michael. 1997. "Why Conversation Is Not the Soul of Democracy." *Critical Studies in Mass Communication* 14, no. 4:297–309.

Seyle, Conor D., Meghan McGlohen, Pam Ryan, Sarah Cotton, Ann Parker, Toula Skaidas, and Jennifer Durham-Fowler. 2008. "Deliberative Quality across Time and Gender: An Introduction to the Effectiveness of Deliberation Scale (Poster)." Poster presented at the Annual Scientific Meeting of the International Society of Political Psychology, Paris, France, July 8. Accessed November 29, 2010. http://www.allacademic.com//meta/p_mla_apa_research_citation/2/4/5/8/8/pages245886/p245886-1.php.

Steiner, Jürg, André Bächtiger, Markus Spörndli, and Marco R. Steenberge. 2004. *Deliberative Politics in Action: Analysing Parliamentary Discourse*. Cambridge: Cambridge University Press.

Stromer-Galley, Jennifer. 2005. "Decoding Deliberation." Paper presented at the Second Conference on Online Deliberation, Stanford, CA, May 20–22.

Stromer-Galley, Jennifer. 2007. "Measuring Deliberation's Content: A Coding Scheme." *Journal of Public Deliberation* 3, no. 1. Accessed November 29, 2010. http://services.bepress.com/jpd/vol3/iss1/art12.

Wilhelm, Anthony G. 2000a. *Democracy in the Digital Age: Challenges to Political Life in Cyberspace*. London: Routledge.

Wilhelm, Anthony G. 2000b. "Virtual Sounding Boards: How Deliberative Is Online Political Discussion?" In *Digital Democracy: Discourse and Decision Making in the Information Age*, edited by Brian N. Hague and Brian Loader, 154–178. London: Routledge.

Witschge, Tamara. 2002. "Online Deliberation: Possibilities of the Internet for Deliberative Democracy." Paper presented at the INSITES conference, Pittsburgh, PA, September 20–21.

Witschge, Tamara. 2008. "Examining Online Public Discourse in Context: A Mixed Method Approach." *Javnost: The Public* 15, no. 2: 75–92.

Wright, Scott, and John Street. 2007. "Democracy, Deliberation and Design: The Case of Online Discussion Forum." *New Media and Society* 9, no. 5:849–869.

Young, Marion I. 2000. *Inclusion and Democracy*. Oxford: Oxford University Press.

10

The Third Sector as E-Democratic Intermediaries

Scott Wright and Stephen Coleman[1]

A main focus of the literature on online policy consultation has been on direct relationships between government and individual citizens, but in reality, most attempts by governments to gather policy evidence and seek the views of grassroots experts are mediated via the third sector—nonprofit, nongovernmental organizations. Democracy requires intermediaries. Both political parties and mainstream media institutions (the press and broadcasting) have long performed important intermediary roles, opening up connective spaces between disparate communities, social interests, and ideological perspectives to the opaque web of governance. In an increasingly fragmented, decentralized, and networked society, can third-sector organizations (TSOs) serve as communicative intermediaries, thereby reshaping the geography of democratic representation?

Although definitions of *third sector* vary from one country to the next (Defourny and Nyssens 2006), the UK government's Office of the Third Sector[2] suggests that it has certain basic characteristics, such as being independent from government, being driven by values, and reinvesting any financial surpluses to further social, environmental, or cultural objectives. The term *third sector* derives from its position as being neither of the public nor the private sector. It encompasses voluntary and community organizations, charities, social enterprises, cooperatives, and mutual aid societies both large and small (Fennell, Gavelin, and Wilson 2008, 17). Although governments have come to recognize that the third sector has a unique "reach, size and range of experience" and is "ideally placed to help public bodies better understand society's needs and comment on how a policy is likely to work in practice" (ibid., 23), there has also been a candid acknowledgment that the "framework for consultation has been too rigid to engage the broad composition and varied nature of third sector organizations" (ibid., 13).

We argue in this chapter that involving third-sector organizations in the development and delivery of policy offers clear democratic advantages insofar as they can help to ensure more accountable, legitimate, and socially relevant governance. But for these benefits to be realized in practice, third-sector communication must be based on two key principles:

• If third-sector organizations are to be regarded as speaking for their memberships and wider interest communities, then they have to engage in ongoing and meaningful communication with the people they claim to represent. This involves using technologies of communication that enable "speaking for" to be legitimized by "speaking with."

• If third-sector organizations are to devote energy and resources to becoming democratic intermediaries, then they must engage at timely moments in the policy process (not after essential decisions have been made) and are entitled to expect meaningful feedback from policy makers in response to their inputs. Consulting them should not be a merely token or checkbox exercise.

With these two principles in mind, we set out to explore three research questions:

• Why are new technologies being used by the third sector to engage in the policy-development process?

• How are new media used by the third sector to gain input from their members and supporters on matters of policy?

• How effective are government consultation procedures in enabling TSOs to perform as democratic intermediaries?

We explored these issues through semistructured interviews. Given the breadth of the third sector, we decided to focus on a range of large and small environmental and human rights groups. Interviews were conducted in two phases in mid-2009 and early 2010, with a mixture of face-to-face and telephone interviews. Representatives from sixteen third-sector organizations were interviewed. Our main interest was in these organizations' policy-related actors rather than their Web strategists or operators, so our interviewees included directors of campaigns, directors of policy, and leading organizational strategists.

The Growing Role of Technology[3]

One of the clearest findings from our research is that all the groups now use information and communication technologies (ICTs) and that many had seen a significant growth in ICTs in the last two years. Email was still considered to be the most important tool, but groups experimented with an array of tools, including blogs, social networks, and viral videos. Examples of how new media are used to enhance consultation are discussed in the next section. Here we summarize why third-sector organizations are now adopting digital information and communication technologies. Interviewees outlined a complex picture, intertwining benefits with defensive or protective strategies:

• Digital ICTs allow greater "horizontal communication between members" (personal interviews with Ann Doherty, Friends of the Earth Campaign; Tim Hancock, Amnesty International; Ray Mitchell, Age Concern; Neil Sinden, Campaign to Protect Rural England).

• Digital ICTs can facilitate the authentic voices of members, which has a greater effect on policy makers.[4]

• Although digital ICTs are not inexpensive, they can be resource effective.

Many tasks are difficult, if not impossible, to do without digital ICTs.

• Potential supporters and targets are now comfortable with and often expect digital communication. If third-sector organizations failed to adopt digital ICTs, they might lose relevance.

• ICTs allow significant sharing of knowledge, and positive experiences encourage greater and more experimental use.

The Downsides of New Media

Despite this clear movement in the direction of more digitized and interactive communication with members and supporters, interviewees also expressed misgivings. First, some perceived a threat that competitors may steal a lead on them through the use of new media. Many third-sector organizations that share similar values and aims have complex working relationships: "A lot of the bigger, more traditional NGOs have political issues amongst themselves and quite often find it quite hard to work together" (Ian Keith, Avaaz, personal interview). Tim Hancock stated:

Amnesty has always lived in a complex relationship with other NGOs. We need people to join us and we need financial support which means that, you know, we want them to give their money to Amnesty rather than Oxfam. So, in a sense, other NGOs are competitors, but in another sense they are collaborators and partners and we campaign with them.

All the groups interviewed observed and learned from their competitors, and many cited success stories (such as Moveon.org) that inspired their own use of social media.[5] The growing recognition that new media use can have positive effects appears to have stoked this pressure to keep up. Ray Mitchell (Age Concern) neatly summarizes the concern:

You can get left behind, your voice can be drowned out if you don't get involved. . . . Greenpeace go off and start creating their own electronic news releases and everyone goes, "Ah, I wish I'd thought of that." Suddenly everyone is producing them. Works for a while and then, "OK, let's forget it now," so you have to come up with something else. . . . So innovation—it drives the innovation.

A broader concern for established third-sector organizations is that they could have their claim to speak for specific constituencies challenged by the growth of virtual networks (such as Avaaz) that can quickly mobilize vast numbers of people and might be fracturing their voice. For Hancock:

We have to be almost as good as they are in their online presence, and it also means that we have to be very aware of what we can do and can't do, in comparison, and also concentrate on what's unique about us. So we are—Amnesty is unlikely to be as quick and dynamic as somebody like Avaaz or . . . Moveon. org. We put a lot of institutional weight behind a lot of our campaigns. Changing direction on a weekly or monthly basis is something that we find quite difficult. Now, we've got to get better at that, I believe, so we've got to be a bit more dynamic, but I don't think we're ever going to get to the point where some others are.[6]

A second concern was that third-sector organizations might be challenged online by groups that disagree with their stances, giving rise to third-sector cyberbattles. Ray Mitchell, who previously worked at Amnesty International, cited an interesting example from his time there. Amnesty attempted to mobilize people to use social networks with a view to blocking an imminent execution in the United States, but this backfired when a counter campaign was launched online and was used by the governor to justify the execution. Brian Fitzgerald pointed out that Greenpeace's members would like to put more information on their Web site, but this could put them "at odds with our lawyers, who don't like courts producing evidence from our own Web site of premeditation and possible conspiracy to commit a crime." Many groups seemed acutely aware that so-called smart mobs (Rheingold 2002)—fluid, fast, issue-based network formations—could work both for and against their interests.

A third concern was that online interaction could expose fractures within a third-sector organization. The Stop the War Coalition faced challenges resulting from the need to build diverse coalitions around controversial and potentially divisive issues (Tansy Haskins, Stop the War, personal interview). Stop the War has its roots in the established Socialist Workers Party, and certain party stances (such as criticism of religion) were suppressed to ensure a broad base, including people from a range of not otherwise harmonious political, ethnic, and religious perspectives.[7] As our interviewee from the coalition put it: "I think the decision was taken quite early on that the Stop the War coalition wanted to be—you know, wanted to be sort of as united as possible and if we had a discussion part of the Web site, it would probably lead more to disunity than unity." Ann Doherty (Friends of the Earth International) and Brian Fitzgerald (Greenpeace) talked about how green ideology (see Dobson 2000, 84–87) has influenced its uptake of new media, as there remain conflicts of perspective about how far greens should rely on technology. Fitzgerald (2005) has stated elsewhere that "Greenpeace's love affair with technology is an uneasy one. E-waste is piling up in Asia—full of toxic materials. The phones and computers we use to organize mass protest are consuming resources and energy at alarming rates." However, the "trend has been steadily toward wider acceptance" (Brian Fitzgerald, Greenpeace, personal interview).[8]

A widely raised fourth concern about use of new media was the digital divide, broadly defined (chapter 7 in this volume). Third-sector organizations were concerned about not excluding supporters, and many kept offline channels open wherever possible. But even where supporters had Internet access, trials with online forums and social networking did not always work. Conor O'Gorman from the British Association of Shooting and Conservation (BASC) explained how an advisory committee

set up a specific closed internet forum for discussion by the majority of the committee, and that started off really well but then fizzled out. So, you know, it sounded like a good idea—let's interact outside the meetings, let's develop things—but you start the thing and it doesn't work. . . . Probably because the type of people who you want information from tend to be over forty. You know, they are the people with developed expertise but aren't maybe so comfortable with some of the newer media. E-mail, for them, is probably what Internet forums are for people in their twenties. So while people in their twenties and thirties will interact on forums, to get your experts interacting—they're more comfortable with email.

The rapid pace of technological change has created challenges. Neil Sinden, for example, stated that the Campaign to Protect Rural England

(CPRE) had not always "been very strategic about how we've gone about developing our use of online media." Tim Hancock from Amnesty stated:

You have to understand the resources and time that it takes to do stuff well, and you can be in danger of the tail wagging the dog. All the communication and the benefits that it yields can start to become the thing you think about, rather than the actual purpose for communicating in the first place.

Although all of these concerns were widely cited, all interviewees felt that, on balance, the benefits of new media use outweighed the costs. Our feeling is that perhaps researchers in this area should pay more attention to these often understated costs rather than focusing overwhelmingly on the well-known opportunities.

Legitimacy and Internal Consultation

Third-sector organizations typically justify the legitimacy of their demands and actions on the democratic grounds that they speak for particular groups of people or sets of interests.[9] The extent to which unelected representatives can speak for others is open to question (Street 2004; Rehfeld 2005; Saward 2009). Edwards (1999, 258) has provided a useful definition of *democratic legitimacy* as "having the right to be and do something in society—a sense that an organization is lawful, proper, admissible and justified in doing what it does, and saying what it says, and that it continues to enjoy the support of an identifiable community." The crux of this definition is that representation, even at the informal level, can be justified only if it receives ongoing support from a represented constituency. This implies that some form of interactive communication must occur with those being represented. The extent to which this happens when third-sector organizations contribute to policy consultations is hotly debated. Collingwood and Logister (2005, 176) note that transnational third-sector organizations criticize international organizations for their opacity and undemocratic behavior but are themselves open to the criticism that they are "unaccountable, insufficiently transparent and unrepresentative." To speak for a particular constituency (whether geographical, issue-based, or ideological) requires that you speak *to* that group or at least hear from them in some meaningful form. Furthermore, just because a group can speak loudly does not mean that its position has been well considered. Ian Johnson, head of democratic engagement in the UK Department for Justice, emphasized that many

TSOs "aren't very democratic really," and this must be considered when conducting consultations: "You need to be a little bit wary about, you know, 'We speak as the voice of X number of members.'" The danger, for Johnson, is that by "just engaging with the bigger [third-sector organizations], you don't really get the authentic voice of the people who you want to contact because you've got these big organizational issues" (personal interview with Ian Johnson, UK Ministry of Justice).[10]

Third-sector organizations are aware of these perceived limitations. Interviewees suggested that a range of strategies, often involving new media, were being used to gain input from members on policy positions. The extent to which these organizations consult internally and the ways that such input affects their responses to government consultations vary greatly due to different institutional structures, different operating cultures, and the complexity of the issues under consideration. Our evidence from interviews suggests that new media were being used to facilitate several approaches to internal consultation.

Online Surveys

All groups undertook (largely online) surveys of one kind or another. Frequencies varied from weekly (Avaaz) to yearly (Stonewall), reflecting the different structures, resources, operating cultures, and perceptions of fluidity of membership views within organizations. Groups such as the British Heart Foundation use online expert surveys (from doctors) to develop their evidence base, while others use them to ensure they understand what their members think are the key issues. The annual Stonewall survey, for example, highlighted asylum and aging as being prominent issues for members, and this led to further research to develop their evidence base and subsequent policy recommendations. Similarly, Netmums' first national survey found that the often hidden issue of postnatal depression was prevalent, and they used "survey results to . . . push the debate at government level."

Email Lists

All groups maintain email lists in one form or another. Some groups (such as the CPRE) may use relatively small lists of experts with whom they engage regularly on an informal basis. In the context of consultations, the broader email lists are used to advertise consultations and surveys, invite feedback on specific issues, and drive people to relevant parts of a third-sector organization's Web site. They are used largely to help keep the machine running.

Closed-Access Internal Online Forums

Several groups have tried member-only forums to discuss policy development, particularly where decisions are difficult. The CPRE, for example, explained how a difficult policy choice on whether to support onshore wind farms has led to a new, online approach:

We're broadly pro-renewable energy. We're broadly supportive of the need to . . . mitigate climate change, *but* there are landscape impacts of new infrastructure of things like wind farms in the countryside. . . . It was a *huge* struggle really to gather together fairly divergent views and come to a clear position on what our overall position should be. . . . For the first time for some years, we had to have a couple of discussions at board level about elements of that policy, . . . which we wouldn't normally expect to do. We would normally have expected to have dealt with that largely at the level of the policy committee and at staff level. . . . Now, that's partly because of the complex nature of the issue itself. . . . But also, I would say, due to the, you know, the growing ease with which people have been able to raise issues and raise concerns and express doubts about, you know, our likely position. (Neil Sinden, personal interview)

In an attempt to overcome these problems, the CPRE is "trialing a new method" that combines the "traditional approach" of sending out "a circular to invite members to nominate themselves or to nominate people to sit on a task group to deliberate policy and to come up with a draft proposal," with the extra step of placing the draft on the members-only online forum, where members can discuss this at length. This will then lead to a revised draft, which will be sent to the board.[11]

Open-Access Forums "Owned" by the Organization

Open-access forums are used to help share information and advice and build a sense of community among members and supporters. They sometimes have an informal policy role. Policy officers at Age Concern, for example, ask questions (about campaign issues or language used, for example) in their online community but also sit back and just listen to what people are saying—effectively using the forum as an informal public space that can be tapped into. The Netmums forum is central to that organization, which tends to use surveys to consult members but also spends time "watching our forums and seeing what is happening on those, pull up ideas that we recognize need some work on" (Sally Russell, personal interview).

Broader Online Forums

Several groups, either formally or informally, listened to or posted messages in external online forums. Rationales were diverse. According to Derek Munn (of Stonewall):

We make sure that different people keep an eye on that stuff [such as Queer Youth Network and Ginger Beer] and intervene as appropriate. So in the same way that Dale, as well as the sort of official Stonewall posts, will come in on debates and go, "Hold on, I'm not sure that's quite accurate," Ruth, our head of policy . . . has the Ginger Beer message board just scrolling along, but every so often she'll come in.

Conor O'Gorman (BASC) noted that a variety of external forums were used: "Some of the forums are public, and some aren't. The better ones are closed—where people have to register. People feel more secure in that environment."[12] O'Gorman suggested that such forums played a positive role in ad hoc policy development:

With regard to actually developing feedback from people in the interactive way, Internet forums are where it really happens. So BASC staff have memberships of various shooting forums on the Internet and various discussion threads get started up—not necessarily by us but by other people—and, you know, that provides information that does inform how we develop things.

Social Media and Web 2.0

All the groups had experimented with applications such as Facebook, Twitter, and YouTube. Most felt that these were becoming increasingly important for them, with some suggesting that they were beginning to challenge email as their most important tool. Julia Toft (British Heart Foundation) believes:

It's at a tipping point now or very soon after the [2010 British General] Election. . . . There will be—I won't say young, but there will a lot of new MPs. It's going to be the biggest turnover . . . definitely since '97, anyway—the biggest turnover of MPs. So I think that increasingly there will be an opportunity to use those kinds of channels.

The potential to generate horizontal communication among supporters and thus to facilitate organic grassroots movements was considered particularly important (see chapter 3 in this volume). As Ray Mitchell (Age Concern) put it: "We're not prescribing. We're just giving people the space and the matter, the information, and some ideas that they can spark off, really." Similarly, Amnesty was redesigning its online content to make it

a tool for our groups so that they can see what each other are doing, share resources, download resources which are provided centrally, share experiences. And we think that by doing that, it will also be able to demonstrate to visitors to the Web site—Amnesty as a kind of popular movement . . . to project our values and to be seen to be living those values. (Tim Hancock, personal interview)

For the virtual group, Avaaz, generating offline meetings through social media was particularly important:

This is about a community. It's not about a bunch of staff sending emails to a big group of people. It's about a community talking together and moving together and taking action together. [Members] are basically Avaaz staff. They are part of the community. They help to shape the decisions that we make. (Ian Keith, personal interview)

Most groups were very happy with the amount of "friends," hits, and what might be called soft support that Web 2.0 activities generated. But Web 2.0 created several challenges.

First, running effective Web 2.0 tools is resource intensive:

It's very time-consuming to keep these things updated, and we—we're very lucky in that actually we have a volunteer who gives us a couple of hours a day to look after Facebook for us, and she's very good at doing that. But . . . in terms of the blog and Twitter and things, I actually do those myself. . . . We don't have any extra resources to do it. (Steve Taylor, The League, personal interview)

Second, several groups noted problems encountered in moderating comments, in terms of both the volume received and the technical limitations. Steve Taylor (The League) observed:

The problem on Facebook is that . . . the comments field is free and people can just comment and . . . there's no way of moderating that other than reactive deletion when it's out of order. So for example, when we've published stories on Facebook about the threat of repeal of the hunting act . . . , we quite often get very anti-Conservative diatribes appearing which we are technically responsible for, and as a charity we can't be party political, so we have to delete them.

Third, Web 2.0 is exacerbating a trend of managing the relationship between what might be called soft supporters and strong activists. It was widely felt that the sheer volume of new, often softer support generated by Web 2.0 was a significant benefit but needed careful handling to ensure broader goals were met. As Steve Taylor said,

One of the issues we have with Facebook is that a lot of people who support us on there . . . they *can* actually go beyond Facebook, and so they will follow links from Facebook to our blog or to other things that we ask them to do. But in terms of really engaging them as campaigners and campaign supporters outside the Facebook world, that has proved quite difficult.

This concern was also reflected by Tim Hancock of Amnesty:

The thing we want to really do is to make sure that we've got really good union between online and offline. We really want to avoid compartmentalizing people and viewing somebody as being just an online person when the reality is that they will write an email, go to a meeting, join a demo, write a letter, and blog about it.

Direct Contact with Government

Rather than consulting internally and producing an official response, several groups have "trialed" asking their members to reply directly to government consultations using both new and old media. Interviewees' opinions about the effectiveness and legitimacy of mass responses to consultations were strongly divided. The CPRE, for example, coordinated a mass response to a planning consultation that generated thousands of responses, but it felt that these responses were effectively bundled together and disregarded by government. This experience "did drive it home to me that it's not enough just to generate quantity. We need to find ways of actually ensuring that the quality of our engagement is understood and respected and taken into account perhaps more than it otherwise might be" (Neil Sinden, CPRE, personal interview). The e-rule-making approach, which has been adopted in the United States (see chapters 11 and 13 in this volume), utilizes software to count generic responses and separate them from those that have been crafted individually (Shulman 2009). Sally Russell, cofounder of Netmums, felt that asking people to respond directly in their own words to a consultation (as opposed to providing a standard response) raised a number of issues:

A lot of it [consultation jargon] is impenetrable. And to be honest, as well, I think they often don't ask the right questions. . . . They [usually] are directed at practitioners who work in the field. And so, you know, trying to find a way to allow people easily to understand what's being asked and how to construct their answers can be quite difficult.

She also noted that problems might arise from directing people to government Web sites (see chapter 7 in this volume):

I think people feel quite at ease about giving us answers which we can then pass on. And, you know, if you take them through to another official Web site and then encourage them to do something then—. . . to be honest, it's quite unlikely to work. You're not going to get the same level of response.

Overall, she felt that consulting internally

gives a much richer information base. . . . We will get thousands of comments, and . . . we are able to sift and sort those into groups, so people can actually really get a picture of the . . . sort of issues portrayed by people and their individual voices. But when you sort of cross them together, it becomes very, very powerful. . . . And that just wouldn't happen with government consultation and the analysis that they do.

A related concern was whether governments can determine who has a legitimate right to participate in a consultation, given the interdependent context of a globalized world. Examples cited by interviewees included environmental legislation and seal culling. More generally, there was a concern on the part of some third-sector organizations that mass-membership responses might lead to populism: "Government has to recognize that sometimes they have to be the— kind of guardians of common sense and not necessarily reflect what public opinion is" (Steve Taylor, personal interview).[13] Derek Munn, from Stonewall, expressed this concern: "We don't encourage people to sign petitions or write to their MP. . . . We don't see the 50,000 [supporters] as, you know, people we can use for online activism. That's not the style we use." Instead, their approach is

based on not bothering people unnecessarily. So ministers . . . know that we're not going to be constantly bombarding them. They know that if the call comes, it's serious. And they also know that we're not going to be condemning them in a knee-jerk way in the press. We're going to hold off that and speak to them privately.

In the context of a high volume of online noise, it was felt that a more traditional offline lobbying approach would be more effective: "We cultivate direct, personal links with relevant ministers and obviously opposition spokespeople in case there is a change. . . . Personal contact remains key for relations with Parliament and government." This suggests that there are distinct limits to the potential of new media and that the sheer volume of information and feedback might actually help to strengthen the influence of larger, well-resourced third-sector organizations.

The Democratic Limitations of Online Government Consultations

Although most interviewees expressed the view that government consultation procedures have improved significantly, most felt that a lot of work remains to be done before they can be considered democratic and consequential. A number of interviewees were critical about when and how governments choose to consult. Sally Russell (Netmums) reflected a general concern that many government departments failed to tell stakeholders about consultations that might be relevant to them: "We're often not aware of what consultations are going on unless we go out looking for them." She felt that consultations were often conducted too late in the policy cycle:

There tends to be a lot of work done reading around policy areas and doing . . . reviews of literature and so on. But behind closed doors, [there is] a lot of discussion about the evidence and all the rest of it, and then they come out with a policy and say, "This is what we want to do. What does everybody think?"

A second concern was that it was widely felt that consultation input is ignored. Tim Hancock from Amnesty stated:

I think it is very difficult to say that every consultation exercise is genuine. Some undoubtedly are, though, so it's not something that is always an attempt to be seen to be consulting. I think there have been changes when ministers have heard the opinions of consultees. I think that often happens not just on the basis of the written submission that you provide but any kind of follow up meetings. I think that often is a signal that the government is taking the consultation seriously—kind of going beyond, going beyond the paper exercise.[14]

Sally Russell gave two examples of where Netmums were directly involved in the consultation process but felt ignored in the final result:

We were invited to have an input [on the consultation about alcohol and young people policy]. We were seen as a stakeholder in the process, [but] we couldn't see that the input that we made had really made a difference to the way in which they then took the campaign forward. . . . It has been quite depressing recently. They have been using their engagement as a PR stunt as far as I can see.

Conor O'Gorman (the BASC) was worried that people were "coming to a decision themselves and then asking for opinions on that draft position, which is more or less final." Neil Sinden (the CPRE) provided some positive examples of online interaction with ministers (such as a Web chat with David Miliband), but he was more doubtful about the general picture: "I have a healthy dose of skepticism about how far the online avenues are being taken seriously by ministers." This view was supported by Ray Mitchell (Age Concern), who took part in "Ask the PM a Question" on YouTube:

I asked a very serious question about Guantanamo Bay. . . . The response from Gordon Brown was, "You're wrong" (laughs). And I watched the reply, and it was basically, you know, "Thank you very much for your reply. Anyway, you're wrong." It was just like that, and that is, like, . . . still monologue, isn't it? That's where we're at. What we mean by consultation is "We'll listen" or "We'll accept your submission." . . . They're called submissions, aren't they? They're not called conversations or discussions or anything. "Join our discussion": no. "Submit": yes. Which is an interesting word in itself.[15]

Finally, there were specific concerns about the structure of online consultations, which can be "really annoying" because:

[Y]ou can't go back from a page to a previous page and you end up . . . . —I'll end up—giving up and ringing up the person and going, "I'm not going through this. I'll send you a note about our concerns." So these things where you have to go through lots of pages, . . . I personally find that it makes it much less likely that I will respond to that consultation. (Derek Munn, Stonewall, personal interview)

Conor O'Gorman noted that a recent consultation initiated by the government agency Natural England invited third-sector organizations to comment on different sections of a 250-page consultation document. Although this could have been an interesting exercise, it was felt that the 3,000-character limit for responses was not adequate, and so email was used instead. He expressed further concerns about the number of consultations taking place at any one time and the limited period allowed for reply: "There seem to be more and more of them every year," and you have to "put less time into each one because there are so many happening." One interviewee recalled a consultation that would affect at least a million people but that received only thirty-five responses. It is hard to attribute such a response to uninterest, however, because of the perceived lack of publicity given to consultations. To help cope with the lack of publicity, many organizations had systems in place for identifying and responding to consultations, including intranets and extranets with tables of all active relevant consultations, as well as a record of which departments were dealing with the responses and how far along they were. Where such schemes were in use, they were considered very helpful in managing the process and ensuring effective and timely responses.

Conclusion: Intermediary Spaces

In trying to understand the current practices and potentialities of third-sector organizations as democratic intermediaries, we have been stimulated by the seminal and highly insightful analysis of Bach and Stark (2004). In their account of the coevolution of third-sector organizations (which they referred to as *NGOs*, meaning "nongovernmental organizations") and interactive technologies, Bach and Stark argue that new knowledge spaces are emerging within which the third sector is shifting its emphasis "from brokering information to facilitating knowledge" (ibid., 109). Rather than contribute to a discussion in which the form of these organizations is assumed to be fixed and known "and only their effect remains to be worked out," Bach and Stark argue that the very rationale and nature of third-sector organizations are being redefined by the recombinant logic of linking, searching, and interactive technologies:

[W]e can think of NGOs themselves as participating in a high-stakes, large-scale version of searching for something but not knowing what it is (and only possibly recognizing it when they see it!). The impetus for search here is the normative mission of NGOs to work for social justice, ameliorate economic inequalities, empower individuals, and prevent excessive suffering and death. Information itself is of little use here—NGOs that imitate statistical offices will remain information brokers. Those looking for solutions, however, will use search to link and to interact; these NGOs become a social technology where the logic of one is refracted through the other. (Bach and Stark 2002, 11)

Although they dismiss the "superficial isomorphism" of a deterministic relationship between third-sector organization roles and digital technologies, Bach and Stark argue for the creation of new knowledge spaces characterized by the affordances of technologies of intermediation.

Our research provides valuable although clearly limited, empirical support for Bach and Stark's hypotheses, pointing to a widespread sense that the rules of the traditional game are no longer stable. Our findings suggest that the organizations we have examined are caught in an ambivalent position between transformed effects and defensive form. Most of them still think of their remits in terms of information-brokerage, maintaining old organizational strategies that protect them from the hyperporosity of unbounded connectivity, while at the same time sensing that the tools of their trade as well as their trade itself are undergoing radical changes. At this relatively early stage in the coevolution of third-sector organizations and e-technologies, this ambivalence takes the form of anxiety more often than transformative strategic vision.

Returning to our two key principles of effective third-sector intermediation, we observe that efforts to strengthen the representative legitimacy of the third sector and feelings of political efficacy related to its integral role within governance are currently hesitant, unconfident, and unsystematic. Democratic intermediation depends on trusted spaces in which government-citizen links can take place, but our interviewees seemed unsure how far such spaces could be constituted by an online replication of their offline organizational structures and how far notions such as organization, membership, and public translate meaningfully into networked communication contexts. Coleman and Kaposi (2009, 320) have argued, in relation to new democracies, that "to move beyond vertical-elitist democracy, they need to establish and nurture spaces within which the public can speak for themselves in spontaneous and unregulated ways." This is clearly no less the case for established democracies in which spaces of democratic intermediation, such as political parties and public-service broadcasters, have faced identity crises and contraction in recent years. To the extent that the widespread assumption that the civic energies once attached to these declining spaces are migrating to dispersed networks of online interaction turns out to be empirically valid, the cultivation of new democratic spaces in which the third sector—rather than a conglomeration of competing third-sector organizations—can re-present discrete publics could be one of the best hopes for consultative democracy. On the basis of the exploratory research reported in this chapter, the third sector is some way from acknowledging or acting on this potential, although there are clear signs that the notion of coevolution between organizations and digital communication technologies is being felt if not fully comprehended.

Organizations Interviewed

Age Concern (Ray Mitchell, director of campaigns)

Amnesty International (Tim Hancock, UK campaigns director)

Avaaz (Ian Keith, global campaigner)

British Association of Shooting and Conservation (BASC) (Conor O'Gorman, policy development manager)

British Heart Foundation (BHF) (Mubeen Bhutta, policy manager, and Julia Toft, advocacy manager)

Campaign to Protect Rural England (CPRE) (Neil Sinden, director of policy and campaigns)

Friends of the Earth International (Ann Doherty, communications coordinator)

Greenpeace (Brian Fitzgerald, head of digital communications)

The League (Steve Taylor, head of campaigns and communications)

Netmums (Sally Russell, cofounder and director)

Network Norwich (Keith Morris, manager)

Stonewall (Derek Munn, director of public affairs)

Stop the War (Tansy Hoskins, campaign coordinator)

UK Ministry of Justice (Ian Johnson, director of democratic engagement)

Notes

1. This research was supported by a grant from the British Academy. We thank them and all our interviewees for their help.

2. Under the Conservative-Liberal Democrat Coalition government, this has now become the Office of Civil Society and is charged with leading the so-called Big Society agenda.

3. We used a broad definition of new media—including email, Web sites, and social networking—because we wanted to assess the breadth of online activities and the importance accorded by third-sector organizations to different technologies.

4. Age Concern, for example, gives out video and audio-recording devices to allow older people to create video diaries, which can be circulated to policy makers and community and local groups: "That's the next step in this. And we're not prescribing. We're just giving people the space and the matter, the information, and some ideas that they can spark off really."

5. Many of the interviewees expressed insecurities about their use of new technology and were worried that they were not doing enough when compared to other groups.

6. Similarly, Fitzgerald noted that they lose "a lot of potential traffic" to "groups like Treehugger, Avaaz, Grist, and many small, nimble groups that arise around single issues. But to be honest, I think the competition to be more effective and engaging is a great thing and has led to a greater diversity of environmental groups with a wider set of tactical and strategic tools."

7. Pickerill (2008, 3) quotes a former Stop the War press officer who said that there was a feeling that "nothing should be allowed to confuse anybody about what was the absolute priority, which meant that the arguments, complex arguments about secularism and religion were not heard. . . . So, for example, pretty early on, those people who questioned the link with MAB [Muslim Association of Britain] were castigated as Islamophobes."

8. The public nature of the Internet has also forced some third-sector organizations to moderate their online activities. Although a group may want to publicize its activities and allow people to feel directly engaged, the use of global positioning systems and other tags so people can follow, for example, antiwhaling ships or the location of rare animals raises security issues. Similarly, publicizing direct action online can raise legal issues.

9. But governments may often value third-sector organizations for the technical expertise they bring to issues (see Taylor and Warburton 2003).

10. In a similar vein, Simon Jenkins of the National Trust argued that it "is run from London like a nationwide dukedom" and that it was dominated by land agents at the expense of members, wardens and tenants who were "slightly below the salt" (McSmith 2008). This concern is also reflected in the UK government's consultation guidance (Department for Business, Enterprise, and

Regulatory Reform 2008, 12): "It is important to understand who different bodies represent, and how the response has been pulled together, e.g. whether the views of members of a representative body were sought prior to drafting the response."

11. Sinden did express significant concern: "with the online discussion, potentially all hell will break loose. You know, you put this draft policy out, and however much you explain that this has been the result of a deliberative process, you know, with a group of people that have been selected on the basis of a range of different skills and areas of expertise, . . . that isn't necessarily going to mean much to people who engage in the online discussion [who might] feel that it is basically fair game for them just to brain dump anything they think about the issues that they're being consulted on."

12. O'Gorman noted that security was a concern because of the nature of the topic.

13. Steve Taylor continued: "You know, personally, for me, it's a problem because I—the basis of our campaign against hunting is to say that the public don't want it back, but the public actually do support the restoration of the death penalty, which I think is a shocking idea. So you can't constantly rely on public opinion."

14. Tim Hancock from Amnesty noted that you have to question: "'Are we going out here and consulting on this policy because we think there is likely to be a change?,' or are we having an interesting discussion about an interesting issue? And I think you've always got to be clear about that so that you don't start raising expectations."

15. The detailed, qualitative findings have been supported by a recent quantitative survey of the third sector that had 43,939 respondents. Asked whether local statutory bodies "consult your organization on issues which affect you or are of interest to you," only 4 percent strongly agreed, and 18 percent tended to agree; 3 percent strongly agreed, and 13 percent tended to agree that they "involve your organization appropriately in developing and carrying out policy on issues which affect you"; and 2 percent strongly agreed, and 11 percent tended to agree that they "act upon your organization's opinions and/or responses to consultation."

References

Bach, Jonathan, and David Stark. 2002. "Link, Search, Interact: The Co-Evolution of NGOs and Interactive Technology." Working Paper, Center on Organizational Innovation, Columbia University. Presented at the Workshop on Information Technology and Global Security, Social Science Research Council, New York City, February 28. http://www.coi.columbia.edu/.stage/pdf/bach_stark_lsi.pdf.

Bach, Jonathan, and David Stark. 2004. "Link, Search, Interact: The Co-Evolution of NGOs and Interactive Technology." *Theory, Culture and Society* 21, no. 3:101–117.

Coleman, S., and I. Kaposi. 2009. "A Study of E-Participation Projects in Third-Wave Democracies." *International Journal of Electronic Governance* 2, no. 4:302–327.

Collingwood, V., and L. Logister. 2005. "State of the Art: Addressing the INGO 'Legitimacy Deficit.'" *Political Studies Review* 3, no. 2:175–192.

Defourny, J., and M. Nyssens. 2006. "Defining Social Enterprise." In *Social Enterprises at the Crossroads of Market, Public Policies and Civil Society*, edited by M. Nyssens, 3–26. London: Routledge.

Department for Business, Enterprise, and Regulatory Reform (BERR). 2004. *Code of Practice on Consultation*. London: BERR.

Dobson, A. 2000. *Green Political Thought*. London: Routledge.

Edwards, M. 1999. "Legitimacy and Values in NGOs and International Organisations: Some Sceptical Thoughts." In *International Perspectives on Voluntary Action: Reshaping the Third Sector*, edited by D. Lewis, 258–267. London: Earthscan.

Fennell, Emily, Karin Gavelin, and Richard Wilson. 2008. *Better Together: Improving Consultation with the Third Sector*. London: Cabinet Office of the Third Sector. Accessed December 1, 2010. http://www.involve.org.uk/better-together.

Fitzgerald, B. 2005. "Technology Then and Now." Accessed November 29, 2010. http://www.greenpeace.org/international/rainbow-warrior-bombing/messages-and-mediums-1985-2005.

McSmith, Andy. 2008. "Sir Simon Jenkins: History Man." The Independent, July 8. Accessed May 12, 2011. http://www.independent.co.uk/news/people/profiles/sir-simon-jenkins-history-man-860553.html.

Pickerill, J. 2008. "Finding Unity across Difference? The Alliances and Fractures of the Anti-war Movement in Britain." Paper presented to Political Studies Association Annual Conference. Accessed November 29, 2010. http://www.antiwarresearch.info/docs/Pickerill-PSA2008.pdf.

Rehfeld, Andrew. 2005. *The Concept of Constituency: Political Representation, Democratic Legitimacy, and Institutional Design*. Cambridge: Cambridge University Press.

Rheingold, Howard. 2002. *Smart Mobs: The Next Social Revolution*. Cambridge: Perseus.

Saward, Michael. 2009. "Authorisation and Authenticity: Representation and the Unelected." *Journal of Political Philosophy* 17, no. 1:1–22.

Shulman, Stuart W. 2009. "The Case against Mass E-mails: Perverse Incentives and Low-Quality Public Participation in U.S. Federal Rulemaking." *Policy and Internet* 1, no. 1: art. 2.

Street, John. 2004. "Celebrity Politicians: Popular Culture and Political Representation." *British Journal of Politics and International Relations* 6, no. 4:435–452.

Taylor, M., and D. Warburton. 2003. "Legitimacy and the Role of UK Third Sector Organizations in the Policy Process." *Voluntas* 14, no. 3:321–338.

11

A Survey of Federal Agency Rulemakers' Attitudes about E-Rulemaking

Jeffrey S. Lubbers

Background on Rulemaking in the United States

In the United States, the 1946 Administrative Procedure Act (APA) contains the general requirements for the promulgation of regulations by federal agencies. This procedure is often called "notice-and-comment" rulemaking, based on the requirements of the operative APA section—(1) publication of a notice of proposed rulemaking, (2) opportunity for public participation in the rulemaking by submission of written comments, and (3) publication of a final rule and accompanying statement of basis and purpose not less than thirty days before the rule's effective date (see chapter 13 in this volume).

These requirements may be exceeded by agencies voluntarily or pursuant to other programmatic statutes that provide more elaborate public procedures. However, even this procedural floor does not apply to all rulemaking. Certain types of rules are exempted from some of these requirements, and entire classes of rules are totally exempted from APA notice-and-comment requirements. These exemptions reflect the APA drafters' cautious approach to imposing procedural requirements on a myriad of agency functions, as well as their willingness, in some situations, to permit agencies a measure of discretion in fashioning procedures that are appropriate to the particular rulemaking involved. This basic APA model has proved successful and is being emulated around the world.[1]

Electronic Rulemaking (E-Rulemaking)

The technological revolution introduced by the Internet is changing the character of rulemaking. What once was an all-paper process—with paper notices published in a paper *Federal Register*, paper comments submitted by hand or by post to the agency, and paper comments filed in a filing cabinet in a room in the bowels of an agency—has been largely replaced by an electronic process with electronic notices, comments, and dockets available for anyone around the world to access with a click of a computer mouse. The U.S. government has established a government Web portal (http://www.regulations.gov) that allows the public to file comments on any pending rule.[2] Much has been written about this "rulemaking revolution," even though it is in its early stages.[3] The main touted benefits from e-rulemaking are increased opportunities for information dissemination, public participation, and governmental transparency, along with better outcomes and greater trust in government. Commenters can now email their comments to the agency with a keystroke, and agencies can post all comments on their Web sites for everyone in cyberspace to read and react to. The days of having to travel to Washington to physically visit a dusty records repository are over. Possibilities abound for enhancing the entire notice-and-comment process.[4]

In e-rulemaking, notices can be improved and more widely disseminated.[5] Automatic notices can be generated by request to individuals who have requested them. Notices can be made word-searchable, and alternative or revised drafts can be posted with the changes clearly designated. Moreover, related studies, required draft regulatory analyses, and other information can be linked to the notices to provide easier public access. The comment process can also be made much more user-friendly and responsive to agency needs through the use of request-for-comments forms, the segmentation of proposed rules for comments, and opportunities to file reply comments[6]—even producing threads of comments on particular issues. And the final stage of rulemaking can be enhanced though new publication techniques, such as linking all other related regulatory documents and final regulatory analyses and then grouping comments and the agency's response.

Others have focused on the possibilities of using these electronic tools for more interactive rulemaking (e.g., Beierle 2003). Suggestions for "deliberative dialogues" (Noveck 2004, 499), "online chat rooms" (Johnson 1998),[7] or "electronic negotiated rulemaking" concerning proposed regulation, (Beierle 2003) have proliferated, but so far their potential is untapped. It remains to be seen whether e-rulemaking will revolutionize public participation. As one leading commentator has concluded, "Electronic rulemaking may transform the process fundamentally or it may simply digitize established paper-based processes" (Shulman 2004, 35). The route that e-rulemaking takes in the future may depend on how well a series of legal and technical questions[8] can be answered.

But if the process is to be transformative, this transformation of the rulemaking (and docketing) process should be viewed as having two main purposes—an informational one (of providing a global, seamless view of each rulemaking) and a participatory one. Achieving the informational goal means providing access to every meaningful step in the generation of a rule—from the statute enacted by Congress that authorizes the rule and the earliest agency action (perhaps an "advance notice of proposed rulemaking") to the last step in the process—whether it is the final rule, a decision in a court challenge, or later agency amendments, interpretations, guidelines, or enforcement actions.[9] It also means that the public should be provided a vertical view of pending or final rules (a drilling down into the meaningful agency and outside studies and analyses that are now found in the docket, along with the public comments, for any significant proposed and final rule)—and, where possible through links, into those secondary studies and analyses referenced in the primary studies.

The participatory goal of the transformation of rulemaking is ultimately to make it possible for participants to participate in real time with other stakeholders in a rulemaking process (an idealized chat room) that will allow a more rational, more interactive, and less adversarial path to an optimum final rule. And as information-filtering technologies (à la Google) become more sophisticated and allow more tailoring for individualized needs, commenters will also be able to zero in on their particular interests and contribute more targeted comments.[10]

Both the informational and the participatory goals raise issues that require further research and experimentation. Informational issues include ways to integrate existing sources of information and docketing concerns (such as those related to scanning, archiving, the handling of attachments, copyright, authentication, security, and privacy). Participatory issues include ways to produce better, more targeted notices; ways to provide easier, more convenient comment opportunities; the choice of rules to govern rulemaking chat rooms; and the broad question of electronic negotiated rulemaking.[11]

The Effect of E-Rulemaking on the Agencies

One outcome of increased public participation is an increased number of comments that agencies have to digest and react to. Blizzards of comments have become increasingly common in controversial rulemakings, and e-rulemaking will further this trend. Peter Strauss has warned of some of the problems this might cause:

I think we're going to see an enormous explosion in the volume of rulemaking comments, and some of them will be quite manipulative. And it will be a challenge for the agencies receiving these comments to tell the one from the other, the valid from the invalid. And then, once they have received hundreds of thousands, tens of thousands of comments, the impulse to treat them as a reflection of e-democracy—we're hearing from the people, and what we do ought to reflect the people, rather than we are collecting information and what we ought to do ought to reflect the outcome of that information—is going to be quite strong. (American University Center for Rulemaking 2004, 28)

Michael Herz (2004, 148–149) concurs that this enormous volume of comments may be a problem:

What can realistically be expected of an agency dealing with a million comments, thousands of which duplicate one another? The old model of careful individual consideration is inapplicable. Unavoidably, the agency will start to do what, for example, Members of Congress do: avoid the subtleties and keep a running tally with the grossest sort of division—basically "for" or "against."[12]

This, he cautions, may lead to two significant problems. One is "information overload" (Herz 2004, 149; see also May 2003, 44; Rossi 1997, 224–228)—although, as Stuart Shulman has pointed out, technology may also simplify the task of sorting and categorizing voluminous comments (American University Center for Rulemaking 2005, panel 4, 18).[13] The other is a general politicization of the rulemaking process—moving away from the technocratic model of rulemaking (where the substance of the comment is more important than who submitted it or how many times it was repeated) to a type of referendum. "In short," Herz notes, rather disquietingly, "the new technology is forcing agencies toward a particular model of the process and function of rulemaking, as opposed to enabling agencies better to function under the model chosen independent of that technology" (Herz 2004, 150–151).[14] Other researchers have found a proliferation of "form comments" (Schlosberg, Zavetoski and Shulman 2005),[15] making Noveck's concern about the use of robot programs to generate "notice and spam" all the more disquieting (Noveck 2004, 441).

The Survey

To find out how the advent of e-rulemaking is perceived among federal rulemakers, I designed and distributed a survey of rulemakers, using an electronic survey program.[16] After designing the questions with helpful constructive criticism from Peter Strauss and Neil Eisner, an experienced rulemaking supervisor from the Department of Transportation, I circulated the survey to Eisner and other supervisors and asked that they encourage their rulemaking staffers to take this survey.

The survey is intended to be exploratory, not definitive. I used a combination of convenience and snowball sampling because the desired sample characteristics (in this case, federal rulemakers who use e-rulemaking) are not numerous or identifiable and not easy to access. I relied primarily on referrals from the federal rulemaking supervisors.[17] Thus, the sample is small, and results may not be completely representative of the e-rulemaking population. Moreover, the voluntary nature of the survey makes the respondents a nonrandom, self-selected group. Nonetheless, the survey of federal rulemakers is the first of its kind on this topic and provides some insights and early indications of the attitudes and perceptions of those on the firing line of this new technology.

After a little more than a month of collecting responses, I had seventy-four responses from a wide variety of agencies. The breakdown was as follows:[18]

Department of Transportation (DOT)	17
Department of Homeland Security (DHS)	12
Department of Labor (DOL)	8
Environmental Protection Agency (EPA)	8
Department of the Treasury (Treasury)	7
Department of Energy (DOE)	5
Department of Veterans Affairs (DVA)	4
Department of Commerce (DOC)	2
Department of the Interior (DOI)	2
Department of Health and Human Services (HHS)	1
Department of Housing and Urban Development (HUD)	1
Federal Communications Commission (FCC)	1
Federal Election Commission (FEC)	1
Unidentified	4

A large majority of the respondents spent most of their work time on rulemaking activities:

Percentage	Number
100%	20
90–99	17
75–89	14
50–74	9
25–49	7
10–24	5
5	1
No answer	1

About three fifths of the respondents described themselves as "more of a line employee" ($n = 45$), and two fifths as more of a "supervisor" ($n = 29$).

Most were attorneys:

Attorney	47
Policy expert in the field	8
Technical expert in the field	5
Economist	2
Political scientist	1
Other	11

The "other" category included four "regulations analysts," including one with a JD degree; two "writer-editors"; two "IT"; one "project manager"; and one with a "varied" background.

The age of the respondents skewed rather high:

Age	Number
Below 30	7
30–39	14
40–49	21
50–59	22
60 and above	10

Rulemaking experience was also correspondingly high but was well distributed:

Years of experience	Number
0–2	12
3–5	11
6–10	18
11–20	16
Over 20	17

Most of the respondents had worked with rulemaking both before and after the advent of e-rulemaking (47), 11 had worked only with the new system, 15 skipped this question, and one had not worked at all with e-rulemaking. Some of the questions discussed below were asked only of those who had worked before and after.

Positive Effects of E-Rulemaking (from the Rulemakers' Perspective)
I asked a series of sixteen questions to see whether e-rulemaking has made it more or less easy to undertake some positive rulemaking activities. They were framed as follows: "When compared to the old system of paper comments, has the advent of e-rulemaking made it more difficult or easier for your agency to do the following?"

I used a seven-point range: (1) Much more difficult under the new system; (2) More difficult . . . ; (3) A little more difficult . . . ; (4) The same as under the old system; (5) A little easier under the new system; (6) Easier . . . ; (7) Much easier. . . . I also allowed an "N/A" answer ("Insufficient experience with this issue").

Sixty-four of the seventy-four respondents answered this long question, although some of those (including presumably those who had not worked with both systems) answered N/A for many of them. But all but two of the sixteen questions elicited at least thirty-six ranked answers.

Question 1.   When compared to the old system of paper comments, has the advent of e-rulemaking made it more difficult or easier for your agency to do the following?
a. Conduct proactive notification and outreach to the public by maintaining target mailing lists (or listservs) of people who are interested in selected aspects of your rulemaking agendas?

	Number	Percentage
(1) Much more difficult under the new system	0	0%
(2) More difficult . . .	0	0
(3) A little more difficult . . .	1	3
(4) The same	11	30
(5) A little easier	3	8
(6) Easier . . .	12	32
(7) Much easier	10	27
N/A (Insufficient experience with this issue)	27	
Total	64	

Average score 5.51 ($n = 37$)

Only one respondent answered that it was harder to undertake targeted outreach under the e-rulemaking system, and twenty-five said it was easier to some degree. The average score on this question was a high 5.51.

The full results for the remaining subparts of question 1 are contained in the appendix to this chapter. The summary results appear in table 11.1. Significantly, after tabulating an average of the ranked answers for each of the sixteen questions, all of them exceeded 4 ("same as under the old system") and twelve of them exceeded 5. This means that the advent of e-rulemaking has been positive for each activity. The three activities with the highest average scores were "Coordinate the rulemaking internally by allowing many people to look at the same rulemaking docket without getting in each other's way" (5.70), information dissemination (5.67), and "proactive notification and outreach" (5.51). The four questions that led to only mildly positive responses were those relating to negotiated rulemaking (4.19), obtaining comments on segments of the rule (4.64), sorting such comments (4.70), and presenting alternatives to the proposed rule to the public (4.73).

Worrisome Effects of E-Rulemaking (from the Rulemakers' Perspective)
Using a similar seven-point scale, I then asked a series of ten questions to see whether e-rulemaking has increased the level of concern about some of the worries mentioned above. All but one of the ten questions elicited at least thirty-six ranked answers.

Question 2. "When compared to the old system of paper comments, has the advent of e-rulemaking caused your agency to worry more or less about the following?"
a. Outside intervention ("hacking") into your rulemaking proceedings?

	Number	Percentage
(1) Worry much more under the new system	3	8%
(2) Worry more	9	24
(3) Worry a little more	12	32
(4) The same as under the old system	7	19
(5) Worry a little less	1	3
(6) Worry less	2	5
(7) Worry much less	3	8

Table 11.1
Summary results of the positive effects of e-rulemaking

Question	Average score	Number
a. Conduct proactive notification and outreach?	5.51	37
b. Identify and find appropriate stakeholders?	4.81	42
c. Disseminate information relevant to the agency's proposed rulemaking (e.g., studies, economic analyses, legal analyses), so as to generate more informed commenters?	5.67	46
d. Present to the public competing or multiple alternatives to the proposed rules?	4.73	37
e. Stimulate public comments generally?	5.33	51
f. Sort and analyze public comments generally?	5.02	51
g. Obtain public comments specifically addressed to particular portions or segments of the proposed rule?	4.64	47
h. Sort and analyze public comments specifically addressed to particular portions or segments of the proposed rule?	4.70	46
i. Use the concept of "reply comments"?	5.44	25
j. Place summaries of ex parte communications in the record more quickly.	5.16	38
k. Coordinate the rulemaking internally by allowing many people to look at the same rulemaking docket without getting in each other's way?	5.70	43
l. Coordinate the rulemaking externally with OMB [Office of Management and Budget] or other interested government entities?	5.23	40
m. Conduct interactive proceedings in rulemaking, such as "negotiated rulemaking?"	4.19	16
n. Craft a preamble to the final rule that responds to comments and includes all relevant studies and analyses?	5.05	44
o. Develop and implement appropriate archival practices relating to rulemakings (such as retiring records, etc.)?	5.25	36
p. Periodically evaluate and review the rule (and related rules), once promulgated?	5.19	37

	Number	Percentage
N/A (Insufficient experience with this issue):	25	
Total	62	

Average score 3.32 ($n = 37$)

Only six respondents answered that they were less worried about hacking in the new system, and twenty-four worried more to some degree. The average score on this question was a low 3.32.

Again, for brevity's sake, the full results for the remaining subparts of question 2 are contained in the appendix to this chapter. The summary results are presented in table 11.2. After tabulating an average of the ranked answers for each of the ten questions, eight of them were below 4 ("same as under the old system"), meaning that the advent of e-rule-making has produced some heightened worries. The greatest worries (lowest average scores) concerned "Inappropriate exposure of materials in the rulemaking docket that might contain confidential business information" (3.11), "Ensuring the protection of the privacy of commenters" (3.13), "Inappropriate exposure of materials in the rulemaking docket that might contain copyrighted materials" (3.20), and "Inappropriate exposure of materials in the rulemaking docket that might contain indecent or obscene language or materials" (3.30). Attorney respondents were even more worried about these last four categories (3.00, 2.90, 3.03, 3.25). Only two of the hypothesized concerns were less worrisome under the e-rulemaking system: "Integrating (scanned) paper comments with e-mailed or electronically submitted comments" (4.14) and "Risk of information-destruction or other irretrievable loss of rulemaking information" (4.09).

Other Effects of E-Rulemaking (from the Rulemakers' Perspective)

The following questions were to be answered only by those forty-seven respondents who had indicated that they had worked with rulemaking both before and after the advent of e-rulemaking. (Those who had not were directed to skip these questions.) As the number of respondents for these answers varied only from forty-nine to fifty, it appears that respondents complied with this direction.[19] The survey advised respondents: "This and questions 3–11 may be difficult to answer with great certainty. Please provide your impressions as one who has been involved in rulemaking both before and after e-rulemaking."

An important issue is whether e-rulemaking has led to an increase in public comments. Only one respondent reported fewer comments,

Table 11.2
Summary results of the worrisome effects of e-rulemaking

Question	Average score	Number
a. *Outside intervention ("hacking")?*	3.32	37
b. *Acquiring viruses via attachments submitted in comments?*	3.31	36
c. *Inappropriate exposure of materials in the rulemaking docket that might contain confidential business information?*	3.11	45
d. *Inappropriate exposure of materials in the rulemaking docket that might contain copyrighted materials?*	3.20	46
e. *Inappropriate exposure of materials in the rulemaking docket that might contain indecent or obscene language or materials?*	3.30	44
f. *Inappropriate exposure of information in the rulemaking docket that might lead to national security problems?*	3.82	28
g. *Risk of information-destruction or other irretrievable loss of rulemaking information?*	4.09	43
h. *Integrating (scanned) paper comments with e-mailed or electronically submitted comments?*	4.14	49
i. *The authenticity of comments?*	3.81	47
j. *Ensuring the protection of the privacy of commenters?*	3.13	46

thirteen reported the same, and thirty-one reported some level of increase. The average score among those who provided a ranking was a high 5.36 out of 7.

2. Number of comments?

	Number	Percentage
(1) Many fewer	0	0%
(2) Fewer	1	2
(3) Slightly fewer	0	0
(4) The same	13	26
(5) Slightly more	9	18

	Number	Percentage
(6) More	12	24
(7) Many more	10	20
Don't know	5	10
Response count	50	

Average score 5.36 ($n = 45$)

What about the usefulness of the comments? The responses on whether the advent of e-rulemaking has led to more or fewer comments "that provide new useful information or arguments" led to a split decision. The average of the rankings here was 3.8 (or close to "the same"). Three fifths of the respondents indicated no difference in this respect.

3. *Comments with new useful information or arguments?*

	Number	Percentage
(1) Many fewer	2	4%
(2) Fewer	5	10
(3) Slightly fewer	1	2
(4) The same	30	60
(5) Slightly more	4	8
(6) More	2	4
(7) Many more	0	0
Don't know	6	12
Response count	50	

Average score 3.80 ($n = 44$)

E-rulemaking was perceived by many as not generating more useful comments. It was also strongly perceived to generate more comments "that provide only opinions without supporting facts or arguments." No one reported fewer such comments, but twenty-five respondents reported an increase.

4. *Comments that only provide opinions without supporting facts or arguments?*

	Number	Percentage
(1) Many more	10	20%
(2) More	5	10
(3) Slightly more	10	20
(4) The same	17	34
(5) Slightly fewer	0	0
(6) Fewer	0	0

	Number	Percentage
(7) Many fewer	0	0
Don't know	8	16
Response count	50	

Average score 2.81 (*n* = 42)

Even more telling is the high number of people who reported an increase in the number of comments that "are identical or nearly identical": twenty reported an increase, with thirteen of these answering "many more." Only one respondent reported fewer such comments.

5. *Comments that are identical or nearly identical?*

	Number	Percentage
(1) Many more	13	26%
(2) More	7	14
(3) Slightly more	4	8
(4) The same	14	29
(5) Slightly fewer	0	0
(6) Fewer	1	2
(7) Many fewer	0	0
Don't know	10	20
Response count	49	

Average score 2.59 (*n* = 39)

Despite this tendency toward more opinionated and more similar comments, most rulemakers nonetheless reported that e-rulemaking has not caused them to place less "value on the comments by the average citizen." Three fourths of the respondents answered "the same" for this question.

6. *Value of the comments of average citizens?*

	Number	Percentage
(1) Much less	1	2%
(2) Less	3	6
(3) Slightly less	3	6
(4) The same	38	76
(5) Slightly higher	0	0
(6) Higher	2	4
(7) Much higher	3	6
Response count	50	

Average score 4.02 (*n* = 50)

Does e-rulemaking perhaps lead to more commenters responding to others' comments or to economic analyses in the docket? One might hypothesize that this would be the case since such comments and analyses are easier to access online by potential commenters. There is at least some indication that this is occurring, especially with respect to reacting to others' comments.

7. In your experience, with the advent of e-rulemaking, have you seen more commenters responding to comments already in the docket?

	Number
Yes	20
No	16
Don't know	14

8. In your experience, with the advent of e-rulemaking, have commenters made more references to economic analyses and other supporting documents in the docket?

	Number
Yes	7
No	22
Don't know	20

E-rulemaking has also led to a slight increase in the number of questions to the agencies about ongoing rulemakings:

9. Number of questions to your office about ongoing rulemakings

	Number	**Percentage**
(1) Many fewer	0	0%
(2) Fewer	4	8
(3) Slightly fewer	2	4
(4) The same	22	44
(5) Slightly more	5	10
(6) More	5	10
(7) Many more	1	2
Don't know	11	22
Response count	50	

Average score 4.21 ($n = 39$)

Most agency rulemakers reported some opportunity to consult with and learn from their counterparts in other agencies about e-rulemaking issues, but more than half reported that this opportunity was less than adequate.

10. As an agency rulemaker, how much opportunity have you had to consult with and learn from your counterparts in other agencies about e-rulemaking issues?

	Number	Percentage
None	8	14%
Minimal opportunity	25	42
Adequate opportunity	18	31
Great opportunity	8	14

A few narrative responses were received to this question. Several commenters lauded the efforts of some agencies (such as EPA and Treasury) to conduct workshops and share information, but others wished for more: "Simply not enough"; "I hope there will be many more opportunities in the future"; "I believe that in general we do a terrible job of facilitating the exchange of knowledge, best practices, and lessons learned"; "It would be great to have a more advanced training on the use of e-rulemaking dealing less with the mechanics."

The survey also sought to elicit information about how agencies deal with the e-comments. One question simply asked if agency rulemakers tended to make hard (paper) copies of e-comments. Of the fifty-nine responses, only eight said "never"; most (twenty-four) said "occasionally," nine said "usually," and eighteen said "always."

This question stimulated a number of narrative responses. One (from the Department of Labor) reported: "We still legally have to keep a paper copy of all comments; once a docket closes and we post electronic comments we print them all out." Another (no agency identified) explained: "When a rulemaking results in litigation, hard copies of the administrative record (including comments) need to be made for the parties and the court. Also, if a rule is complex, requests for hard copies from within the agency are inevitable." A third had another pragmatic explanation: "It is virtually impossible to review complex or lengthy electronic comments without making a hard copy. The same goes for sharing comments with colleagues for review and consideration, particularly if those colleagues do not have access to the e-comments." Several others said something like this: "I will make copies of significant comments that will be used to change analysis or be responded to in [the] preamble."

Another question asked whether the respondent's agency used "computer-based 'sorting' technology to help categorize (or identify duplicate) e-comments." Of the fifty-nine respondents, twenty did not know; of those who did know, seventeen said yes, and twenty-two said no. Of the twelve who expressed an opinion on this, three said this technology was "very helpful," six said "helpful," two said "a little helpful," and only one said "not at all." Two respondents (from the Labor and Homeland Security Departments) reported that their agency had hired a contractor to do this.

As to the question of whether e-rulemaking helped agencies promulgate rules more efficiently or promulgate higher-quality rules, the responses were encouraging: twenty-three of forty-four respondents reported an increase in efficiency as opposed to only eight who reported a decline.

11. In toto, and as a general matter, has the advent of e-rulemaking allowed your agency to promulgate rules less or more efficiently?

	Number	Percentage
(1) Much less	1	2%
(2) Less	6	12
(3) Slightly less	1	2
(4) The same	13	26
(5) Slightly more	7	14
(6) More	13	26
(7) Much more	3	6
Don't know/no opinion	6	12
Response count	50	

Average score 4.61 ($n = 44$)

The responses about higher-quality rules were also positive, although somewhat less so, with twelve of forty-four respondents reporting an increase in quality and five reporting a decrease. The main difference with the efficiency question is that twice as many respondents answered "the same" as to quality.

12. In toto, and as a general matter, in your opinion, has the advent of e-rulemaking made it less or more easier for your agency to promulgate higher quality rules?

	Number	Percentage
(1) Much less	0	0%
(2) Less	2	4
(3) Slightly less	3	6
(4) The same	27	54
(5) Slightly more	3	6
(6) More	7	14
(7) Much more	2	4
Don't know/no opinion	6	12
Response count	50	

Average score 4.36 ($n = 44$)

One factor to keep in mind concerning agency staff attitudes toward e-rulemaking is the increasing use of electronic dockets for other agency actions. Of the fifty-nine respondents, thirty-six answered reported that their agency uses e-dockets for actions other than rulemaking, and twenty-three said they did not. According to the narrative answers, agencies were using e-dockets for adjudication, guidances, notices, Paperwork Reduction Act notices, draft legislation, peer-reviewed matters, and certain correspondence.

One commenter waxed enthusiastic about e-dockets:

E-dockets are fantastic. Currently the Federal Transit Administration (FTA) is using an e-docket to formulate an agency policy statement. Also, FTA uses e-dockets as forms of electronic filing systems . . . for various administrative adjudications, such as charter service adjudications. Complainants may file complaints electronically on an e-docket. Once a complainant files a complaint on an e-docket, the respondent may respond electronically via the e-docket. FTA posts its decisions on the e-docket. Ultimately, this process increases transparency in government, and we have not received as many FOIA requests for these documents because the documents are easily accessible.

For the last question on the survey, which was open ended and asked "for any other comments," twenty-six respondents answered. The following are the most significant comments. They tend to divide equally between favorable and unfavorable, although those with a complaint may be more likely to respond to such a question.

Rulemakers' General Comments on E-Rulemaking
1. Generally positive comments
- "E-rulemaking is the obvious choice for encouraging public comment and allowing easy access to records from anywhere and without risking

the loss of original hard copies. My only complaint is that the process is not completely electronic: we still generate many paper copies of each rule or proposal."

• "Having an electronic docket has enabled me to manage comments to my rulemaking projects much more easily. I now can just tell people on my rulemaking project how to go to regulations.gov instead of having to make hard copies of the comments and distributing them to the team members on a regular basis."

• "E-rulemaking has improved public access and internal efficiency, but we are not yet using all the potential tools that it makes available."

• "It is a very powerful tool. We need to continue to inform the public on how best to use the tool. We need to continue to add the next phase to the Federal Docket Management System (FDMS)—namely, more rule-making development tools for the rule writer."

• "With more people using the Internet, it seems the right way to conduct rulemaking and promises to reach more folks who don't read the *Federal Register*. In addition to reaching older members of society, making the process available online makes it more likely we will reach members of Generation X and the Millennium Generation. I was informed by an IT person in a regs development workshop, however, that an online rulemaking docket did not constitute a blog because you have to open the NPRM (or other documents published in the *Federal Register*) to get to the core subject. But you could set up a blog with a link to the docket, webcast live public meetings, and record them as podcast files for downloading from the docket."

• "Interesting topic where many questions are yet unanswered. I think at this point the benefits to the agency are not fully evident since much time is spent on learning the new systems, but hopefully in the near future it will prove more efficient than the previous paper-based system."

• "E-rulemaking is better at letting the public know what the agencies are doing than it is at providing thoughtful input into the decisions themselves."

• "I support it. . . . In addition to making agency rulemaking more accessible to the public, it makes it easy for me to check DOL and other agency rulemakings and comments. It's a great research tool."

• "Good start but they need to further refine the process for better functionality."

- "Makes it much easier for the public to see the comments, less work for the agency to respond to requests for copies of comments. Less likelihood that important comments will go missing due to mistake or design."
- "E-rulemaking hasn't changed the process of rulemaking. What it has done is provide easier access to already public documents. That is, interested parties can get documents at their desktop rather than having to go to a docket room."

2. Generally negative comments

- "Many of the initial fears (e.g., authenticity of comments, transmissions of viruses, etc.) have not yet come to pass, but they are a constant concern."
- "Because of intermittent FDMS and regulations.gov system outages, we continue to maintain an in-house paper-based parallel process for managing comments. Unless the reliability of e-rulemaking-related systems increases to the point where we are comfortable enough to move away from paper, we will not fully realize the potential efficiencies that can be gained by moving to the electronic platform."
- "We have been 'live' with FDMS less than a year, and have had only two or three rules in the system. One rule had only one (supportive) comment, and another has had well over a thousand so far, but mostly an industry-generated paper letter-writing campaign from individuals whose names and addresses we must type and load into FDMS, a royal pain in the neck for our tiny staff."
- "If you work at an agency or bureau that doesn't do many regulations, it's difficult to remember all the technology steps that are required to post a regulation. I find myself having to relearn the process each time. That is frustrating."
- "It's difficult to isolate the effect of e-rulemaking on the rulewriting process because as more tools become available, the pressure grows to delay decisions and rulewriting until closer to the deadline."
- "The system is very user friendly for public commenters and very user unfriendly for government regulators. Indeed, the system design seems to thwart at every stage the efficient assembly and review of public comments. It is difficult to access the comments, print them out, sort them by topic, match up attachments with cover documents, etc. Each comment has to be downloaded or printed separately before it can be skimmed for content. When there are thousands of comments, that takes an

unreasonably long time. It was much faster to take a stack of hard-copy comments and page through them to sort out the duplicates and hone in on the helpful, substantive letters. Plus, they could be easily sorted, flagged, and tabbed with notes and comments. In addition, it now takes much longer for comments to work their way from the technical folks that manage the e-rulemaking system to the regulatory folks that actually write the regulations (which could be many people on a complex regulation). I used to get the comments within a day or two of the close of the comment period; now it can take weeks."

• "As my agency's FDMS administrator, I have found FDMS/regulations.gov hard to use, confusing, and not intuitive at all. I also believe that what is now regulations.gov should be integrated into the *Federal Register* so that the *Federal Register's* online version of a rulemaking document contains a hotlink directly to the regulations.gov docket and comment form for that rulemaking document."

• "It was much easier under the former USDOT e-docket system than under the regulations.gov system. More features and ability to analyze comments better."

• "We have had quite a few technical glitches that I guess, over time, will be ironed out. For example, I cannot directly upload documents to the docket in one of my rules."

• "E-rulemaking, including drafting and review of rulemaking documents, has resulted in reduction in the quality of the reviews and rise in inclination of reviewer to revise text to meet personal style. Overall, this affects the timing and quality of rules."

• "I believe it is more costly to my agency because we have had to maintain two systems—our old electronic system and the FDMS."

• "We view it as a benefit for the public, not necessarily as providing a great advantage for the agency."

Conclusion

It is fair to conclude, based on this relatively small sample, that agency rulemakers are generally receptive to e-rulemaking, although a common theme of their early evaluations was that the new system is a boon for the public but a bane for the agency. A large majority of respondents reported a general increase in rulemaking efficiency, and a smaller majority reported a general increase in rulemaking quality. They said this even though they were also generally dubious about the usefulness of the resulting additional comments. In addition, a series of questions asked whether e-rulemaking has made it more or less easy to undertake some positive rulemaking activities, and in each case the answer was that it was easier.

On the other hand, another series of questions asked whether e-rulemaking has increased the level of concern about some of the worries hypothetically associated with e-rulemaking, and for eight questions the answer was that worries had increased. The issues that were most worrisome included protection of commenters' privacy, exposure of confidential business information, exposure of copyrighted materials, and indecent or obscene language. These are essentially legal questions that policy makers will have to wrestle with and solve before e-rulemaking can reach its full potential.

Thus, the early picture is mixed. The new system is better at engendering more public participation, although most agency rulemakers did not report receiving a concomitant increase in useful information or arguments among the additional comments. Moreover, although rulemakers are impressed with the internal administrative and coordination benefits provided by the new technology, they also have heightened concerns about the potential problems of inappropriate worldwide exposure of certain information in their electronic dockets.

This survey is a preliminary one, but it can provide a baseline for future surveys as e-rulemaking develops and can also help provide a research agenda for studying the legal, technical, and practical questions that are arising as technology transforms the rulemaking process into a more transparent and global participatory process. It also highlights the degree to which professional staff members who bear critical responsibility for an agency's processing and analysis of public input are a key constituency for online consultation between citizens and policy makers.

Appendix

Question 1. When compared to the old system of paper comments, has the advent of e-rulemaking made it more difficult or easier for your agency to do the following?

a. Conduct proactive notification and outreach to the public by maintaining target mailing lists (or listservs) of people who are interested in selected aspects of your rulemaking agendas?

	Number	Percentage
(1) Much more difficult under the new system	0	0%
(2) More difficult	0	0
(3) A little more difficult	1	3
(4) The same	11	30
(5) A little easier	3	8
(6) Easier	12	32
(7) Much easier	10	27
N/A (Insufficient experience with this issue)	27	
Total	64	

Average score 5.51 (n = 37)

b. Identify and find appropriate stakeholders?

	Number	Percentage
(1) Much more difficult under the new system	0	0%
(2) More difficult	1	2
(3) A little more difficult	3	7
(4) The same	16	38
(5) A little easier	9	21
(6) Easier	9	21
(7) Much easier	4	10
N/A	22	
Total	64	

Average score 4.81 (n = 42)

c. Disseminate information relevant to the agency's proposed rulemaking (e.g., studies, economic analyses, legal analyses), so as to generate more informed commenters?

	Number	Percentage
(1) Much more difficult under the new system	0	0%
(2) More difficult	0	0
(3) A little more difficult	2	4
(4) The same	10	22

	Number	Percentage
(5) A little easier	5	11
(6) Easier	13	28
(7) Much easier	16	35
N/A	18	
Total	64	

Average score 5.67 (*n* = 46)

d. Present to the public competing or multiple alternatives to the proposed rules?

	Number	Percentage
(1) Much more difficult under the new system	0	0%
(2) More difficult	0	0
(3) A little more difficult	1	3
(4) The same	22	59
(5) A little easier	5	14
(6) Easier	3	8
(7) Much easier	6	16
N/A	26	
Total	63	

Average score 4.73 (*n* = 37)

e. Stimulate public comments generally?

	Number	Percentage
(1) Much more difficult under the new system	0	0%
(2) More difficult	2	4
(3) A little more difficult	0	0
(4) The same	17	33
(5) A little easier	5	10
(6) Easier	14	27
(7) Much easier	13	25
N/A	13	
Total	64	

Average score 5.33 (*n* = 51)

f. Sort and analyze public comments generally?

	Number	Percentage
(1) Much more difficult under the new system	4	8%
(2) More difficult	2	4
(3) A little more difficult	2	4
(4) The same	12	24
(5) A little easier	5	10
(6) Easier	13	25
(7) Much easier	13	25
N/A	13	
Total	64	

Average score 5.02 ($n = 51$)

g. Obtain public comments specifically addressed to particular portions or segments of the proposed rule?

	Number	Percentage
(1) Much more difficult under the new system	0	0%
(2) More difficult	0	0
(3) A little more difficult	7	15
(4) The same	21	45
(5) A little easier	4	8
(6) Easier	12	26
(7) Much easier	3	6
N/A	17	
Total	64	

Average score 4.64 ($n = 47$)

h. Sort and analyze public comments specifically addressed to particular portions or segments of the proposed rule?

	Number	Percentage
(1) Much more difficult under the new system	4	9%
(2) More difficult	1	2
(3) A little more difficult	4	9
(4) The same	15	33
(5) A little easier	4	9

	Number	Percentage
(6) Easier	10	22
(7) Much easier	8	17
N/A	18	
Total	64	

Average score: 4.70 ($n = 46$)

i. Use the concept of "reply comments"?

	Number	Percentage
(1) Much more difficult under the new system	1	4%
(2) More difficult	1	4
(3) A little more difficult	1	4
(4) The same	3	12
(5) A little easier	3	12
(6) Easier	9	36
(7) Much easier	7	28
N/A	34	
Total	59	

Average score 5.44 ($n = 25$)

j. Place summaries of ex parte communications in the record more quickly?

	Number	Percentage
(1) Much more difficult under the new system	0	0%
(2) More difficult	1	3
(3) A little more difficult	1	3
(4) The same	16	42
(5) A little easier	5	13
(6) Easier	5	13
(7) Much easier	10	26
N/A	20	
Total	58	

Average score: 5.16 ($n = 38$)

k. Coordinate the rulemaking internally by allowing many people to look at the same rulemaking docket without getting in each other's way?

	Number	Percentage
(1) Much more difficult under the new system	1	2%
(2) More difficult	1	2
(3) A little more difficult	0	0
(4) The same	9	21
(5) A little easier	4	9
(6) Easier	10	23
(7) Much easier	18	42
N/A	16	
Total	59	

Average score 5.70 ($n = 43$)

l. Coordinate the rulemaking externally with OMB or other interested government entities?

	Number	Percentage
(1) Much more difficult under the new system	1	2%
(2) More difficult	0	0
(3) A little more difficult	0	0
(4) The same	13	32
(5) A little easier	6	15
(6) Easier	14	35
(7) Much easier	6	15
N/A	22	
Total	62	

Average score 5.23 ($n = 40$)

m. Conduct interactive proceedings in rulemaking, such as "negotiated rulemaking"?

	Number	Percentage
(1) Much more difficult under the new system	2	12%
(2) More difficult	0	0
(3) A little more difficult	1	6

	Number	Percentage
(4) The same	7	44
(5) A little easier	2	12
(6) Easier	2	12
(7) Much easier	2	12
N/A	43	
Total	59	

Average score 4.19 (*n* = 16)

n. Craft a preamble to the final rule that responds to comments and includes all relevant studies and analyses?

	Number	Percentage
(1) Much more difficult under the new system	0	0%
(2) More difficult	1	2
(3) A little more difficult	1	2
(4) The same	17	39
(5) A little easier	7	16
(6) Easier	12	27
(7) Much easier	6	14
N/A	16	
Total	60	

Average score 5.05 (*n* = 44)

o. Develop and implement appropriate archival practices relating to rulemakings (such as retiring records, etc.)?

	Number	Percentage
(1) Much more difficult under the new system	1	3%
(2) More difficult	0	0
(3) A little more difficult	1	3
(4) The same	11	31
(5) A little easier	5	14
(6) Easier	10	28
(7) Much easier	8	22
N/A	22	
Total	58	

Average score 5.25 (*n* = 36)

p. Periodically evaluate and review the rule (and related rules), once promulgated?

	Number	Percentage
(1) Much more difficult under the new system	0	0%
(2) More difficult	1	3
(3) A little more difficult	0	0
(4) The same	15	41
(5) A little easier	4	11
(6) Easier	9	24
(7) Much easier	8	22
N/A	25	
Total	62	

Average score 5.19 (n = 37)

Question 2. "When compared to the old system of paper comments, has the advent of e-rulemaking caused your agency to worry more or less about the following?"

a. Outside intervention ("hacking") into your rulemaking proceedings?

	Number	Percentage
(1) Worry much more under the new system	3	8%
(2) Worry more	9	24
(3) Worry a little more	12	32
(4) The same as under the old system	7	19
(5) Worry a little less	1	3
(6) Worry less	2	5
(7) Worry much less	3	8
N/A (Insufficient experience with this issue)	25	
Total	62	

Average score 3.32 (n = 37)

b. Acquiring viruses via attachments submitted in comments?

	Number	Percentage
(1) Worry much more under the new system	5	14%

	Number	Percentage
(2) Worry more	8	22
(3) Worry a little more	11	31
(4) The same as under the old system	7	19
(5) Worry a little less	1	3
(6) Worry less	4	11
(7) Worry much less	0	0
N/A (Insufficient experience with this issue)	26	
Total	62	

Average score 3.31 ($n = 36$)

c. Inappropriate exposure of materials in the rulemaking docket that might contain confidential business information?

	Number	Percentage
(1) Worry much more under the new system	5	11%
(2) Worry more	11	24
(3) Worry a little more	14	31
(4) The same as under the old system	10	22
(5) Worry a little less	1	2
(6) Worry less	2	4
(7) Worry much less	2	4
N/A (Insufficient experience with this issue)	17	
Total	62	

Average score 3.11 ($n = 45$)

d. Inappropriate exposure of materials in the rulemaking docket that might contain copyrighted materials?

	Number	Percentage
(1) Worry much more under the new system	4	9%
(2) Worry more	9	20
(3) Worry a little more	19	41
(4) The same as under the old system	9	20
(5) Worry a little less	1	2
(6) Worry less	1	2

	Number	Percentage
(7) Worry much less	3	7
N/A (Insufficient experience with this issue)	16	
Total	62	

Average score 3.20 ($n = 46$)

e. Inappropriate exposure of materials in the rulemaking docket that might contain indecent or obscene language or materials?

	Number	Percentage
(1) Worry much more under the new system	3	7%
(2) Worry more	8	18
(3) Worry a little more	16	36
(4) The same as under the old system	13	30
(5) Worry a little less	0	0
(6) Worry less	2	5
(7) Worry much less	2	5
N/A (Insufficient experience with this issue)	18	
Total	62	

Average score 3.30 ($n = 44$)

f. Inappropriate exposure of information in the rulemaking docket that might lead to national security problems?

	Number	Percentage
(1) Worry much more under the new system	2	7%
(2) Worry more	0	0
(3) Worry a little more	7	25
(4) The same as under the old system	15	54
(5) Worry a little less	1	4
(6) Worry less	2	7
(7) Worry much less	1	4
N/A (Insufficient experience with this issue)	34	
Total	62	

Average score 3.82 ($n = 28$)

g. Risk of information-destruction or other irretrievable loss of rulemaking information?

	Number	Percentage
(1) Worry much more under the new system	2	5%
(2) Worry more	4	9
(3) Worry a little more	8	19
(4) The same as under the old system	17	40
(5) Worry a little less	5	12
(6) Worry less	0	0
(7) Worry much less	7	16
N/A (Insufficient experience with this issue)	19	
Total	62	

Average score 4.09 (*n* = 43)

h. Integrating (scanned) paper comments with e-mailed or electronically submitted comments?

	Number	Percentage
(1) Worry much more under the new system	4	8%
(2) Worry more	5	10
(3) Worry a little more	10	20
(4) The same as under the old system	13	27
(5) Worry a little less	4	8
(6) Worry less	4	8
(7) Worry much less	9	18
N/A (Insufficient experience with this issue)	13	
Total	62	

Average score 4.14 (*n* = 49)

i. The authenticity of comments?

	Number	Percentage
(1) Worry much more under the new system	3	6%
(2) Worry more	6	13
(3) Worry a little more	5	11

	Number	Percentage
(4) The same as under the old system	25	53
(5) Worry a little less	2	4
(6) Worry less	3	6
(7) Worry much less	3	6
N/A (Insufficient experience with this issue)	15	
Total	62	

Average score 3.81 ($n = 47$)

j. Ensuring the protection of the privacy of commenters?

	Number	Percentage
(1) Worry much more under the new system	7	15%
(2) Worry more	6	13
(3) Worry a little more	15	33
(4) The same as under the old system	14	30
(5) Worry a little less	1	2
(6) Worry less	2	4
(7) Worry much less	1	2
N/A (Insufficient experience with this issue)	16	
Total	62	

Average score 3.13 ($n = 46$)

Notes

1. See Lubbers (2006b, 5–6) and Uga (2004, 36–38) (describing the public comment procedures in Japan). However, for a lamentation about how the basic model has become overly laden with other review and analysis requirements in the United States, see Lubbers (2008).

2. For a comprehensive discussion of the history, goals, and remaining challenges of this effort, see Committee on the Status and Future of Federal E-Rulemaking (2008).

3. Much of the following discussion is derived from Lubbers (2006a). For a succinct history of the rise of e-rulemaking, see Coglianese (2004). See also Shulman (2005), Noveck (2004), Brandon and Carlitz (2002), and Zavestoski and Shulman (2002). Links to some of these and many other related papers and studies are available on the Web site of the Harvard University's John F. Kennedy School's Regulatory Policy Program, available at http://www.hks.harvard.edu/m-rcbg/rpp/erulemaking/papers&reports.htm.

4. Note, however, that the APA's notice requirement is not met when an agency gives notice of a proposed rule only on the Internet instead of in the *Federal Register*. Utilities Solid Waste Activities Group v. EPA, 236 F.3d 749, 754 (D.C. Cir. 2001).

5. Many of the ideas in this paragraph for enhanced citizen participation through e-rulemaking are discussed more fully in Noveck (2004, 471–494).

6. As one agency expert described it, "[W]e can say the comment period ends on November 1st. From November 1st, for example, to December 1st, we're going to allow anybody to come back and reply to what someone else has said. Not say something new, but reply to what others said. It will help the agency, at least theoretically, [to] more efficiently address the comments that they've received." American University Center for Rulemaking (2004, 77) (comments by Neil Eisner, Department of Transportation).

7. Johnson discusses early experiments by the Nuclear Regulatory Commission.

8. The following discussion is adapted from Lubbers (2002).

9. I am indebted to Cary Coglianese for this insight.

10. Stuart Shulman persuasively illustrated this last point in a presentation to the fall 2005 meeting of the ABA Section of Administrative Law and Regulatory Practice.

11. For more on these issues, see Lubbers (2006a, 227–236).

12. Herz also points out that "There is one important caveat, however. To the extent that the comments are duplicative, the burden of responding is not increased" (2004, 149 n. 78).

13. Shulman states: "Part of what we're doing with the computer scientists is developing tools for dealing with this information flood, and we're making some progress on developing the computer science side where we'll be able to deliver a tool to agency personnel who want to identify quickly as possible those clusters of duplicate and near-duplicate e-mails" (quoted in Lubbers 2006a, 238 n. 144). For a technical paper describing these promising techniques for sorting comments, see Yang and Callen (2005).

14. Herz points to the example of the "roadless rule," a heavily litigated rule that was issued in the waning days of the Clinton administration and that attempted to restrict road construction in large parts of Forest Service land:

The rule has generated a number of legal challenges, with several district judges finding defects in the process, and the Bush administration is considering diluting its protections in Alaska. Comments on the proposed rule and/or the Draft EIS, and on the current Alaska proposals, numbered in the millions and have been overwhelmingly in favor of stringent protections. Press coverage has overwhelmingly treated the comment process as a sort of vote. This conception can also be seen in an amicus brief submitted to the 9th Circuit in Kootenai Tribe by the Montana Attorney General. The brief's basic point had nothing to do with legality, but came down to this: "hey, Montanans overwhelmingly support this rule, as shown by tabulating our comments during the process." Emphasizing that 67 percent of commenters in Montana (and 96 percent nationwide) favored stronger protections than were anticipated in the Draft EIS, and that the Forest Service responded by strengthening protections, the brief concludes that the rule is "the product of public rulemaking at its most effective." What's more, the Ninth Circuit placed some weight on this argument. (Herz 2004, 150–151)

15. They found significant differences between respondents who submitted original comments and those who submitted form letters. For more such research, see generally the Web site of the e-rulemaking group at the University of Pittsburgh, http://erulemaking.ucsur.pitt.edu.

16. I used Survey Monkey (professional subscription), available at www.surveymonkey.com.

17. Neil Eisner periodically convenes a brown bag lunch group of his peers from other agencies. I circulated an email to each of them with the survey link and asked for their help in circulating it to their staffs. I also used the Federal Yellow Book to look for other such supervisors and sent emails to those that I found. Finally, I attended a conference of agency rulemakers and solicited their cooperation.

18. Some respondents also mentioned their subagencies. For example, five of the DOT respondents were from the Federal Aviation Administration (FAA), and five were from other different subagencies. Five of DHS's were from the Coast Guard (USCG), and three from the Transportation Safety Administration (TSA). The overrepresentation of the DOT may have stemmed from the circulation of the notice of the survey by Eisner. On the other hand, DOT is also a very active rulemaking department.

19. Note that it is possible that a few of those who skipped the indicator question might have nonetheless answered some of the follow-up questions. On the other hand, a number answered "Don't know" for each question.

References

American University Center for Rulemaking. 2004. "E-rulemaking Conference Transcript." Accessed December 1, 2010. http://www1.american.edu/academics/provost/rulemaking/transcripts.pdf.

American University Center for Rulemaking. 2005. "Conference on the State of Rulemaking in the Federal Government Transcript." On file with author.

Beierle, Thomas C. 2003. "Discussing the Rules: Electronic Rulemaking and Democratic Deliberation" Resources for the Future Discussion Paper 03-22. Accessed December 1, 2010. http://www.rff.org/rff/Documents/RFF-DP-03–2.pdf.

Brandon, Barbara H., and Robert D. Carlitz. 2002. "Online Rulemaking and Other Tools for Strengthening Our Civil Infrastructure." *Administrative Law Review* 54, no. 4:1421–1478.

Coglianese, Cary. 2004. "E-Rulemaking: Information Technology and the Regulatory Process." *Administrative Law Review* 56, no. 2:353–402.

Committee on the Status and Future of Federal E-Rulemaking. 2008. *Achieving the Potential: The Future of Federal E-rulemaking, A Report to Congress and the President*, American Bar Association. Accessed December 1, 2010. http://resource.org/change.gov/ceri-report-web-version.fixed.pdf.

Herz, Michael. 2004. "Rulemaking." In *Developments in Administrative Law and Regulatory Practice 2002–2003*, edited by J. Lubbers, 129–157. Chicago: American Bar Association.

Johnson, Stephen M. 1998. "The Internet Changes Everything: Revolutionizing Public Participation and Access to Government Information Through the Internet." *Administrative Law Review* 50, no. 2:277–337.

Lubbers, Jeffrey S. 2002. "The Future of Electronic Rulemaking: A Research Agenda." *Administrative and Regulatory Law News* 27, no. 4:6.

Lubbers, Jeffrey S. 2006a. *A Guide to Federal Agency Rulemaking*. 4th ed. Chicago: American Bar Association.

Lubbers, Jeffrey S. 2006b. "Notice-and-Comment Rulemaking Comes to China." *Administrative & Regulatory Law News* 32, no. 1:5–6.

Lubbers, Jeffrey S. 2008. "The Transformation of the U.S. Rulemaking Process— For Better or Worse." *Ohio Northern University Law Review* 34, no. 2:469–482.

May, Randolph J. 2003. "Under Pressure: Campaign-Style Tactics Are the Wrong Way to Influence Agency Decisions." *Legal Times* 26, no. 27 (July 7):44.

Noveck, Beth Simone. 2004. "The Electronic Revolution in Rulemaking." *Emory Law Journal* 53, no. 2:433–522.

Rossi, Jim. 1997. "Participation Run Amok: The Costs of Mass Participation for Deliberative Agency Decisionmaking." *Northwestern University Law Review* 92, no. 1:173–250.

Schlosberg, David, Stephen Zavetoski, and Stuart Shulman. 2005. "To Submit a Form or Not to Submit a Form, That Is the (Real) Question: Deliberation and Mass Participation in U.S. Regulatory Rulemaking." Accessed December 1, 2010. http://erulemaking.ucsur.pitt.edu/doc/papers/SDEST_stanford_precon.pdf.

Shulman, Stuart W. 2004. *The Internet Still Might (but Probably Won't) Change Everything: Stakeholder Views on the Future of Electronic Rulemaking*. Accessed December 1, 2010. http://erulemaking.ucsur.pitt.edu/doc/reports/e-rulemaking_final.pdf.

Shulman, Stuart W. 2005. "E-Rulemaking: Issues in Current Research and Practice." *International Journal of Public Administration* 28, no. 7–8:621–641.

Uga, Katsuya. 2004. "Development of the Concepts of 'Transparency' and 'Accountability' in Japanese Administrative Law." *University of Tokyo Journal of Law and Politics* 1, no. 1:25–44.

Yang, Hui, and Jamie Callen. 2005. "Near Duplicate Detection for eRulemaking." In *Proceedings of the Fifth National Conference on Digital Government Research*. Accessed December 1, 2010. http://erulemaking.ucsur.pitt.edu/doc/papers/dgo05-huiyang.pdf.

Zavestoski, Stephen, and Stuart W. Shulman. 2002. "The Internet and Environmental Decision Making: An Introduction." *Organization and Environment* 15, no. 3:323–327.

12

The Internet and the Madisonian Cycle: Possibilities and Prospects for Consultative Representation

David Lazer, Michael Neblo, and Kevin Esterling[1]

The Internet has the potential to transform our democracy—a potential that has received substantial scholarly attention (e.g., DiMaggio, Hargittai, Neuman, and Robinson 2001; Hindman 2009; Bimber 2003; Mayer-Schönberger and Lazer 2007). This attention has focused on the potential transformational effects of the technology on civil society and, in the political realm, on the ways that the Internet might transform political discourse. Researchers have devoted less attention, however, to how the Internet might transform existing institutions for connecting citizens to elected officials. This relationship is the fundamental building block of a representative democracy, and it has come under increasing strain as our country has grown from a few million to a few hundred million, as congressional districts have swelled from a few tens of thousands to well over 600,000, as the number of matters that the state is involved in has multiplied, and as policy problems have grown more complex. Contemporary Washington politics is now almost exclusively the domain of entrepreneurial legislators, highly trained committee staff, legal counsel, agency heads, lobbyists, and expert policy analysts. Today, it is difficult for interested citizens to understand the policy process or have their voices heard in it (Heclo 1974; Lupia and McCubbins 1998). Because of this and other trends, citizens have become increasingly disengaged from the work of Congress.

The Internet offers tools that might help to arrest this trend, to rewire the informational flows undergirding our democracy (Mayer-Schönberger and Lazer 2007), and thus to increase the participation of citizens in the consultative process with their representatives. A well-designed Internet strategy by members of Congress can provide citizens with information that is useful for understanding a policy as it develops and with a way to interact more symmetrically with both their member of

Congress and with each other. Wisely used, the Internet can reconnect citizens and Congress.

This potential for change has been largely unrealized and unstudied. Although there has been a considerable amount of scholarship on the effects of the Internet on government, governance, and society (e.g., Mayer-Schönberger and Lazer 2007; Bellamy and Taylor 1998; DiMaggio, Hargittai, Neuman, and Robinson 2001; Fountain 2001; Yates, Orlikowski, and Okamura 1999), we have identified little systematic research on how members of Congress use or should use the Internet to provide information to their constituents. This lack of scholarship is matched by a lack of progress by members in using their Web sites.

This lag is unsurprising and significant. Members of Congress are accustomed to and tend to be very good at interacting face to face with constituents. Digital interaction, however, is inherently new terrain for many members, and any new activity entails uncertainty and risk. Implementing innovations and making effective use of them require new knowledge and new operating procedures. As a consequence, adoption of Web technologies is neither automatic nor effortless. As Dawes and her colleagues (1999, 21) write, "Throughout our history, developments in technology have emerged much faster than the evolution of organizational forms."

This lag is significant because the widespread adoption and use of Web-based technologies among citizens creates the potential for greater citizen participation in and knowledge and trust of their government. Web technologies allow citizens a kind of access to the government irrespective of their geographic proximity to the seat of government and increasingly irrespective of their wealth and educational level. When citizens have better knowledge of the hard choices Congress often has to make and the rationale that legislators have for making them, many citizens may reinvest their trust in government (Bianco 1994). Wisely used, the Internet can reconnect citizens and Congress in meaningful ways. The lack of the use of the Internet by members is thus potentially a serious missed opportunity for our democracy.

In this chapter, we summarize the results of extensive research we have conducted on the use of the Internet by members of Congress. We begin by discussing a republican deliberative ideal, which we label the Madisonian cycle—a deliberative process that encompasses the representative and the represented. We then turn to a discussion of what members of Congress are actually doing with the Internet, finding that often they are not taking advantage of many of the features of the Internet with their official Web sites. This leads to a question: how do members conceive of the potential of the Internet? Our answer is that their conception is predictably narrower and more instrumental than the normative ideal. Because the official Web sites do not allow members to convey different messages to different constituencies, it is often politically counterproductive to put much policy information on the Web site. We then turn to a set of experimental studies we conducted on the potential use of the Internet by members. We conducted randomized experiments with twelve U.S. representatives and one U.S. senator who interacted with constituents in online town hall meetings. Our findings were encouraging: these sessions reached a diverse set of constituents and substantially affect the participation rates, policy knowledge, and support for the member.

The Madisonian Cycle

The second charge against the House of Representatives is, that it will be too small to possess a due knowledge of the interests of its constituents. It is a sound and important principle that the representative ought to be acquainted with the interests and circumstances of his constituents.

—James Madison, No. 56, *The Federalist Papers*

I would want to know with the specific issues how they voted, for or against, and why they voted for or against. That's what I want to know, because sometimes when you just hear how the vote went and you see that your representative voted one way or the other, you may get angry or whatever, but if you see why they voted that way, you may be pleased that they would rationalize it out.

—Richmond participant in focus group on Congressional Web sites (Congressional Management Foundation 2001, 4)

Members of Congress have a general duty (and a strong incentive) to enact policies that will be popular in their districts. However, they typically have better information with which to make policy judgments than most citizens do, so they do not simply vote for whatever an uninformed public thinks that it wants at the moment. Members of Congress generally do not and should not assume either the role of a paternalistic "trustee" or a rubber-stamp "delegate" (Pitkin 1967). An alternative model envisions a cycle of deliberation that allows citizens to formulate and communicate their general interests, legislators to debate and craft policies to advance those interests and persuade their constituents of the (sometimes nonobvious) connection between the two, after which the process repeats itself in a cycle of feedback. This picture portrays a more

Madisonian or "republican" model of deliberative representation (Held 1996).

The Madisonian feedback cycle is implicit in many models of the public-policy process. Citizen engagement is one of the core principles of constitutional democratic government (Bohman and Rehg 1997; Gutmann and Thompson 1997; Habermas 1996, Neblo 2000). However, empirical research on deliberation to date has focused almost exclusively on either deliberation among elites, such as members of Congress (Bessette 1994), or among citizens (Fishkin 1997) rather than between citizens and their representatives. The relative neglect afforded citizen-representative deliberation is due to a narrow definition of the term *deliberation*—that is, one that confines it to cooperative, symmetric communication in real time among a discrete set of people who are trying to solve a common problem. However, the original theorists of deliberative democracy also had something broader in mind—a kind of deliberative culture that includes, in addition to deliberation in the narrow sense, locally asymmetric communication between elements of civil society and government in the service of a larger, ongoing public dialog (Habermas 1996). For example, a policy address or letters to a representative or senator could be understood as contributing to the deliberative cycle in this broader sense.

How Do Members of Congress Conceive of the Internet?

An examination of official member Web sites indicates that they are not heavily used to enable public discourse. A majority of Web sites do not offer any indication of the member's voting record (Congressional Management Foundation 2001) and do not make their party affiliation obvious on their homepage. In the appendix to this chapter, we offer two case studies of member Web sites. One obstacle is the inertia of senior members (Esterling, Lazer, and Neblo 2011). One communications director we interviewed said that the very senior member she worked for asked to see his Web site (for the first time) because a few constituents complimented it: "He came to me one day. He says, 'I need to see my Web site'—and turns on his TV (laugh)." In this first generation of members, there is a powerful generational effect that will fade as turnover occurs. However, the key question is whether in the long run the strategic interests of members will align with the use of the Internet to enable a discursive process with constituents. We now turn to an examination of those strategic interests.

Structuring the Discourse: Channeling Social Control over Deliberation

Any discursive setting requires a medium that provides and constrains opportunities for communication. Key dimensions to any medium for communication relevant to our discussion below is its publicness and its permanence. In the Habermasian ideal—the Parisian cafés—discussion is necessarily semipublic, semiprivate, and ephemeral. Alternative media and forums available in the past include published works (public and potentially permanent), discussions in salons (private and ephemeral), and letters (private and potentially permanent).

Putting aside the normative issues, these two dimensions of communication are important for strategic reasons. The public/private dimension is important because the public aspect of a discussion subjects its participants to social control. Participants in that discussion must necessarily think of the reactions of third parties. In some cases, third parties will be far more important than the immediate parties to a discussion. Will a particular statement be subject to social approval or opprobrium?

The permanent/ephemeral dimension potentially constrains speakers in another fashion—increased intertemporal accountability. This accountability comes from statements that are contradicted by future facts (such as George Bush's "mission accomplished") and that are inconsistent across time (also known as the flip flop).

This analysis highlights that the choice of forum for deliberation is a strategic one. Assuming that actors have a choice of forums that differ in their publicness and permanence, what would they choose? It is not clear that actors necessarily wish to avoid social control because approval may be highly beneficial. For example, Barack Obama's early public and recorded statement in opposition to the war in Iraq was indisputably beneficial to his political career.

To explore how members of Congress conceived of the potential of the Internet, we conducted interviews with people from ninety-nine separate congressional offices that lasted roughly forty-five minutes each. Although we attempted to recruit a sample reflective of the body, the offices tilted somewhat in the direction of being Democratic and urban; when splitting the sample along these strata, we did not note any significant differences (for details, see Lazer, Mergel, Ziniel, Esterling, and Neblo 2011). These interviews were conducted during the spring and summer of 2006 with congressional staffers who had primary responsibility for the member's official Web site. The interviewee was most commonly the member's press secretary or communications director but also included legislative directors and systems administrators. These interviews were transcribed and coded with NVivo.

Conception of the Point of the Web Site

How do offices conceive of their Web sites? Do they see the Web sites as a means for fostering ongoing discussions with constituents about policy? In fact, few of the people that we interviewed conceived of the Web sites in that fashion. Most offices see the Web sites as a means for (1) delivering services and (2) presenting a sense of who the member is (which does not necessarily involve reference to policy). As one communications director stated, "It's all about making the congresswoman look good." Another communications director, in explaining why the member's Web site did not make clear the party affiliation of the member:

[Y]ou want people to feel comfortable going to it. . . . If they're a Democrat and you're a Republican, you don't want it in their face because then they don't want to take the time to learn about you. And . . . that's kind of a hospitality question. You don't want people to feel alienated from the moment they open up the Web page.

So from the perspective of many offices, the informational efficiency of party affiliation as a shortcut to understanding a member's positions is a drawback. The worry is that party information will discourage constituents of the other party from viewing the site's content. Thus, for example, an important function of the Web site is to facilitate delivery of constituent services, but some constituents may not feel comfortable approaching an office if they are of the opposite political persuasion. As another interviewee stated, "[W]e want people to know that it doesn't matter what party you are, it doesn't matter what party we are."

In fact, if a Web site spurs a dialog on the political issues of constituents, it is a sign of failure, not success:

[Y]ou can put a lot a information on there, but sometimes you may put something on there that really shouldn't be on there—like . . . his stance on abortion. If we put it on there, it's going to cause a bunch of work. It's going to cause a bunch of phone calls and letters that we're going to have to respond to. And . . . after the fact, it's like—well, . . . shouldn't of put it up there. So we try to stay away from the controversial issues on the Web site.

In short, most interviewees indicated that conveying policy information on the Web site was exclusively in service of the goal of making the member "look good," as one press secretary states: "I guess the biggest goal is to communicate to the constituents that we're doing a good job.

Our goal is not to necessarily give the congresswoman's opinion on every issue."

Concern over Opposition Research

The key mechanism of social control in electoral politics is the ballot. And the vessel of that control is the opposition candidate, who has the incentive to thoroughly examine every statement and political act of a member and to communicate them to voters in as unflattering a light as possible. It is therefore not surprising that many interviewees expressed concern about the potential for the use of content on the Web site for opposition research. One press secretary from an office with a particular paucity of policy-relevant material on its Web site offered a summary of lessons learned from the preceding election:

A concern is that it [the Web site] is so good that it's going to help out opposition research. I don't think ours is that way, but I know our opponent last campaign had a wonderful campaign Web site. And anytime he said anything, he put it on there, and he had a blog, and it was updated daily. And I don't know how much traffic he got, but boy, any time we needed to find something he said, we'd type in what we thought he said in the search engine, and it would pop up. So I don't ever want us to have that happen to our Web site. I mean obviously anything we put on there, we're comfortable defending. . . . But we need to be kind of cognizant that we don't want to just hand over a bunch of opposition research to the other side.

So transparency is potentially damaging for a member because information that is favorable with some constituencies in some circumstances can be recycled by opponents as unfavorable for other audiences. As another interviewee stated, "If you're putting information out to everyone, . . . your political opponents get that information too and can try to use that in their own ways." With a controversial issue like abortion, as one interviewee stated, "Unless you're out there taking a lead on it, you're not going to put controversial stuff on your Web site—because it's going to show up in your opponent's ads two years from now." There is also an important temporal dimension. As one individual stated, there is a "fear of being pinned down on an issue" because of earlier statements.

Thus, although the key objective of the Web site is to make a member "look good," there is a significant concern about the possibility that issue-relevant material will be used to make the member look bad by a future opponent.

Of Media and Message

The Web site strategy used by various congressional offices is contingent on the circumstances of the particular member in their district. For example, in revealing party affiliation, the partisan leanings of the district are important. The two interviewees below offer opposing cases of congruence between the party affiliations of the member and the district:

We've got a very Democratic district, so . . . it makes sense to, you know, have some [party] credentials on there [on the Web site].

Well, in [state X,] being a Democrat doesn't do anything for us politically. In fact, having a D by your name—it's a challenge to get elected. So that's not something that we're ashamed of, by any means, but it's not something we're going to broadcast if we don't need to. . . . I mean, we are a little bit off to the left. So that's not something we put up front.

The second quote above hints at one of the distinctive qualities of the Internet as a means for communication: it does not discriminate among recipients of the message.

The issue of the targeting of communications becomes especially important with controversial issues, where significant numbers of constituents might be alienated by a position but others might approve, as the following interviewees highlight:

The congresswoman may have to take a very tough position on an issue because she feels that is the right position to take on that particular issue. But we may not actively publicize it and promote it outside of certain constituencies.

[Do you have all of your press releases that you have ever done up here?] Not all of them. . . . Some controversial things we won't put on there. We'll just send them to people who want to know.

That is, certain types of messages should go only to particular individuals.

The wholesale nature of the official Web site is therefore seen as a significant drawback for certain types of messages. As discussed above, other media allow customization of messages, with email and letters being at the opposite end of the spectrum. As this one informant suggests, policy information is conveyed differently in emails and on the Web site:

[Question: How's the content (that people get from e-mails) different, if at all, from the content that's up on the Web site?] Very different. We'll answer individual emails with strong policy statements.

The Web site is seen by many offices as limited by its wholesale nature. IT does not allow them to target different constituencies or individuals with different messages.

An Alternative Model of Online Deliberation

Although official Web sites may not offer representatives a means for deliberating with constituents about issues of the day, the Internet and other technologies offer other ways for them to connect. To explore one means, we conducted a series of online town hall meetings between constituents and members of Congress and were encouraged about the possibilities of an Internet-enabled democracy. Space does not allow a full exposition of our analyses, which were published in several papers, but here we provide a summary of the methodology and our key results, referencing the relevant papers.

Research Design

Our research objective was to assess the effect of participation in online town hall meetings on participating constituents. To evaluate the potential effect, we recruited twelve U.S. representatives and one U.S. senator to participate in twenty-one online sessions.[2] The topic for discussion in the session with the representatives was immigration and with the senator detainee policy. The twenty sessions with representatives were conducted in the summer of 2006 and had about twenty participants each; the one session with the senator was conducted in the summer of 2008 and had 193 participants.

A town hall meeting was structured so that the member of Congress could speak via "voice over Internet protocol" and their constituents could hear their comments over their computers (their statements were also transcribed in real time for participants to read in case audio problems were encountered). Participants submitted statements or questions for the member. These were managed by someone on the research team, who posted them in order to the member, removing redundant or off-topic questions.

To evaluate the effects of participation in a session, we needed to construct a counterfactual. After recruiting potential participants and administering a background survey, we randomly assigned individuals to one of two control conditions or to an online town hall meeting with their member. Individuals who participated in the meeting were given two-page background materials before the meeting and later participated in an online town hall meeting with their member. The two control conditions were meant to distinguish between the effects of the background materials and actual town hall meeting. In control condition 1, participants were given the background materials, and in control condition 2, they were given nothing. One week after the session, all subjects were given another survey, and immediately after the election, a final survey.

The mode of inference was based on a comparison of the treatment group to the two control groups. Inference was complicated by the fact that we could not control whether individuals who were invited to a session actually showed up. We discuss the statistical methodology we developed to deal with this endogeneity in Esterling, Neblo, and Lazer (2011a). Below we summarize our key findings.

Key Findings

The online townhalls drew diverse participants.

As noted above, not all individuals who were invited to participate actually showed up for the town hall meeting. Who chooses to deliberate (Neblo, Esterling, Kennedy, Lazer, and Sokhey, 2010)? There is a twofold concern. The first is that online participation, generally, will reflect the digital divide, amplifying existing participation rates along various socioeconomic strata. The second is that deliberative opportunities naturally tend to select an unrepresentative array of people, again magnifying existing participation inequalities. The intersection of online with deliberation thus has a double potential for increasing existing political inequalities.

Our findings were generally reassuring that this is not the case. We found that of seven demographic predictors of lower participation rates—youth, belonging to a racial minority, being female, lower rates of attendance at religious services, weak partisan identification, low income levels, and low education levels—only education has the predicted association with choosing to participate in one of these sessions. The other six factors actually had the opposite sign than that predicted (although not significantly in all cases). Further, we found that individuals who expressed frustration with the political status quo—"stealth democrats" (see Hibbing and Theiss-Morse 2002)—were far more likely to choose to participate.

This finding does not eliminate the concern that online town hall meetings will amplify existing political inequalities because that inequality may be driven by dimensions of the process. For example, if online town hall meetings were to become standard practice for members of Congress, how would they recruit participants? Many of these mechanisms of recruitment would naturally create certain inequalities in participation. However, our findings suggest that is not inherent in the medium and that it offers the potential of reaching individuals who are currently not deeply engaged in our democracy.

Participation in the online town hall meetings increased other forms of political participation.

What effect did the sessions have on political participation after the town hall meetings? Several measures could be examined, and all suggest that participation levels increased. Voting rates increased—from 77 percent for controls to 82 percent for treatment subjects. And although 41 percent of the control subjects reported not closely following the election, this was the case for only 23 percent of the treatment subjects (see Lazer, Neblo, Esterling, and Goldschmidt 2009). We also found dramatic increases in the probability of talking about the policy in question. For the sessions with the senator, we included a series of questions about the individuals with whom the survey participant talks to about politics, and we found that the probability of talking about the senator and about detainee policy nearly doubled (see Lazer, Sokhey, Neblo, and Esterling 2010). An important secondary implication of this finding is that the sessions affected quite a few people indirectly—perhaps significantly more than participated directly.

Participation in the town hall meetings increased policy knowledge.

One of the key outcomes of participation in a deliberative session is whether it increases policy knowledge. To that end, we asked six questions about immigration policy (example: "Under current law, is it a felony to reside illegally in the United States?"). We found that participants had a 10 to 20 percent increased probability of giving a right answer relative to (full) controls (Esterling, Neblo, and Lazer 2011b). We did not find that this effect was mediated by whether the member mentioned the particular fact in the session. Improvement seemed to be driven by the motivation generated by the prospect of participating, combined with providing background materials that contained the relevant information.

Participants were more likely to vote for their member and to take his or her position on the issues discussed.

A key issue is whether the use of a particular modality of communication with constituents is consistent with the strategic communication needs of a member. Our results suggest this is the case. The probability that a control subject would vote for the member was 49 percent and that town hall meeting participants would vote for the member was 56 percent. The effect on swing voters was particularly dramatic. An individual predicted to have a 50 percent chance of voting for the member in the control condition (based on presession survey questions, such as party affiliation), had a 73 percent chance of voting for the member after having participated in the town hall meeting. Similarly, there were increased positive sentiments about the member across the board—big increases in approval rating (from 46 percent to 62 percent) and in trust that the member would "do what is right" all or most of the time (from 38 percent to 52 percent). There were also big increases in the fraction of participants describing the member as trustworthy, accessible, compassionate, fair, hardworking, understands people like me, knowledgeable, and qualified (with percentage increases ranging from 16 percent to 32 percent). We observed similar increases in the large session with the senator, suggesting that these effects scale with larger session size, which should make them a practical communication tool for members.

In short, these findings suggest that online town hall meetings are powerfully consistent with the strategic imperative of the particular members to communicate with constituents. They were also very popular with the constituents who participated, where 95 percent of participants in the session with the representative and a remarkable 99 percent of participants in the session with the U.S. senator indicated interest in participating in similar sessions in the future. The qualitative comments that people offered were similarly positive. As one participant wrote, "I believe we are experiencing the one way our elected representatives can hear our voice and do what we want."

Conclusion

Deliberation in a republic needs to encompass the relationship between the representative and the represented. The Internet, as a technology, offers the potential for deliberation and consultation to scale up to the magnitude and complexity of the modern world. The above analysis offers a mixture of pessimism and optimism in the reality and potential of the Internet in enabling the Madisonian cycle. The current reality of how members of Congress use their Web sites is not encouraging. There is relatively little policy content on Web sites, even to the point that many members do not even make their party affiliation clear on their Web sites. Our data suggest that this is an unsurprising consequence of the strategic use of the Internet as a communication medium by members. The official Web sites do not allow members to customize their message to particular individuals—a conservative Republican sees the same Web site as a liberal Democrat. As a result, there is a significant danger that the Web site will alienate constituents if it offers clear information on where the member stands on an issue. The permanence of the medium also means that the likelihood that statements could be used for opposition research at some undetermined point in the future is high. Thus, although recent election cycles have highlighted the importance of the Internet in the electoral process, it is less clear what the potential is with respect to enabling a consultative process between representatives and citizens in the United States.

Our optimism comes from the model of deliberation that online town hall meetings represent. Our experiments suggest that these online meetings can reach a diverse set of people and can be especially effective at recruiting individuals who are alienated from politics. These sessions increased policy knowledge, mobilized participation more generally, and could fit with the strategic communication objectives of members. The model we offer is not meant to be limited to the technical details of the sessions that we hosted. Rather, the sessions demonstrate that current communication technology allows members of Congress to reach into the living rooms of their constituents to facilitate a genuinely deliberative dialog. There is room for improvement from a normative point of view. For practical reasons, these town hall meetings did not allow easy follow-up questions to the member by the questioner, so a discursive back and forth between a member and a particular constituent was not possible. Closely related to this was the fact that the bandwidth from constituent to member was limited to text, engineering an unnecessary asymmetry between the member and his or her constituents. These were design choices that were based on constraints that existed when we conducted these experiments, but they are not inherent to the medium. More research needs to be done to make these kinds of sessions effective.

It is also not clear what design choices are in the interest of members to make. For example, one of the essential features of the online sessions was the control of the sessions by a neutral party. The audience was not preselected to be sympathetic to the member, and the questions were not picked to make the member look good. However, the Internet does enable an invisible, potentially insidious control of the deliberative process. We suspect that this would be counterproductive. The authenticity of these sessions enhanced their effect on constituents in a way that was productive for the member (even if it occasionally left them confronting uncomfortable questions in the actual session). Much like official Web sites, members have a set of choices about whether and how to use the Internet for authentic deliberation. Our findings suggest that there is a pathway that will both enhance our democracy and be consistent with the reelection objectives of members.

Further, and critically from the perspective of the preceding analysis, participants almost universally approved of the sessions and generally emerged with higher approval of their member of Congress. The members who participated also reported that the town hall meeting was a valuable way to hear about the concerns of their constituents. In short, this may be a type of online forum in which both representatives and citizens are motivated to participate in. This is not to say that online town hall meetings offer the complete answer to creating a consultative process to the legislature, but our results indicate that they offer a fruitful path forward.

Appendix

A Case Study of an Official Member Website

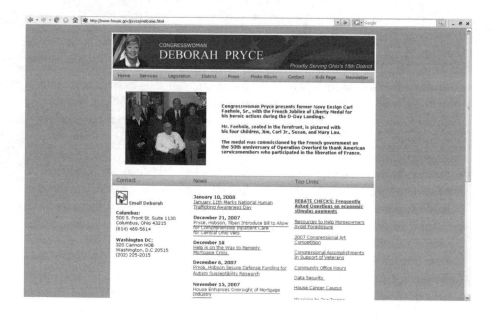

This is the home page of Congresswoman Deborah Pryce. The home page contains the most current press releases but lacks a search tool for users to find specific issue content within the press releases. Congresswoman Pryce's political party is not immediately clear. There is no link to an issues page, but clicking the legislation link brings the reader to the page below.

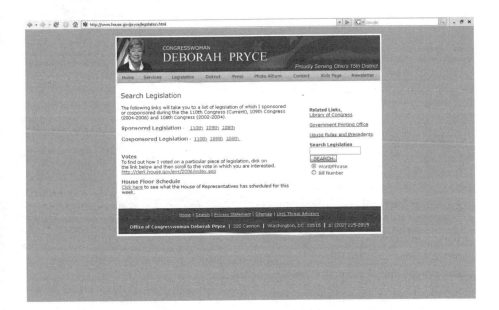

The Legislation page contains links to Congresswoman Pryce's sponsored and cosponsored bills and voting record through the Thomas system and the Clerk of the House Web sites. Although the link to Thomas provides collections of the congresswoman's sponsored bills and the link to the clerk can collect her voting records, no additional information is provided by the congresswoman's own Web site about her legislative priorities, rationales for the legislation she sponsors, or explanations of her vote choice.

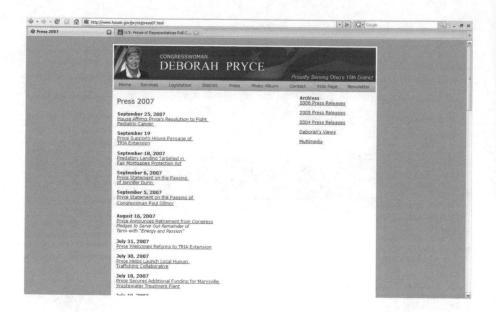

Clicking on the Press link brings the reader to a page of press releases. Press releases are provided for the past four years, but there is no tool for searching through the press releases by issue content. On the right side of the page, there is a link to a page called Deborah's Views. Clicking on the link brings the reader to the page below.

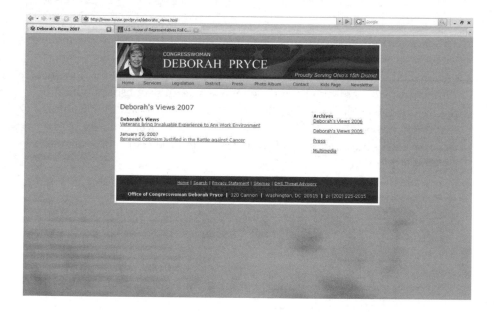

This is the Deborah's Views page provided in early 2008. The only two views listed ("Veterans Bring Invaluable Experience to Any Work Environment" and "Renewed Optimism Justified in the Battle against Cancer") are politically uncontroversial. The lack of views and press releases after September 2007 may be explained by the congresswoman's decision not to seek reelection, but there is no evidence that she ever had a page explaining her issue positions or justifying her vote choices. This lack of policy information may reflect the competitive nature of her Columbus district. Congresswoman Pryce's district was extremely competitive in 2006, she won by less than 1 percent of the vote, and the district also split its 2004 presidential vote between George W. Bush and John F. Kerry, 50 percent to 49 percent.

Notes

1. The authors gratefully acknowledge support from NSF grant # 0429452. Any opinions, findings, and conclusions or recommendations expressed in this material are those of the authors and do not necessarily reflect the views of the National Science Foundation.
2. The Senator was Carl Levin. The twelve representatives were Earl Blumenauer, Michael Capuano, James Clyburn, Mike Conaway, Anna Eshoo, Jack Kingston, Zoe Lofgren, Don Manzullo, Jim Matheson, David Price, George Radanovich, and Dave Weldon.

References

Bellamy, C., and J. Taylor. 1998. *Governing in the Information Age*. Buckingham: Open University Press.

Bessette, J. M. 1994. *The Mild Voice of Reason: Deliberative Democracy and American National Government*. Chicago: University of Chicago Press.

Bianco, W. T. 1994. *Trust: Representatives and Constituents*. Ann Arbor: University of Michigan Press.

Bimber, B. A. 2003. *Information and American Democracy: Technology in the Evolution of Political Power*. Cambridge: Cambridge University Press.

Bohman, J., and W. Rehg, eds. 1997. *Deliberative Democracy: Essays on Reason and Politics*. Cambridge: MIT Press.

Congressional Management Foundation (CMF). 2001. "Constituents and Your Website: What Citizens Want to See on Congressional Websites." Accessed December 1, 2010. http://www.cmfweb.org/storage/cmfweb/documents/CMF _Pubs/constituentsandwebsites.pdf.

Dawes, Sharon S., Peter A. Bloniarz, and Kristine L. Kelly. 1999. *Some Assembly Required: Building a Digital Government for the 21st Century*. Albany, N.Y.: Center for Technology in Government.

DiMaggio, P. J., E. Hargittai, W. R. Neuman, and J. P. Robinson. 2001. "Social Implications of the Internet." *Annual Review of Sociology* 27:307–336.

Esterling, Kevin M., David M.J. Lazer, and Michael A. Neblo. 2011. "Representative Communication: Website Interactivity and 'Distributional Path Dependence' in the U.S. Congress." *Political Communication* 19 (Spring):205–226.

Esterling, Kevin M., Michael A. Neblo, and David M.J. Lazer. . 2011a. "Estimating Treatment Effects in the Presence of Noncompliance and Nonresponse: The Generalized Endogenous Treatment Model." *Political Analysis,* forthcoming.

Esterling, Kevin M., Michael A. Neblo, and David M.J. Lazer.2011b. "Means, Motive, and Opportunity in Becoming Informed about Politics: A Deliberative Field Experiment with Members of Congress and Their Constituents." *Public Opinion Quarterly,* forthcoming. [advance access published May 16, 2011, doi:10.1093/poq/nfr001].

Fishkin, J. 1997. *The Voice of the People: Public Opinion and Democracy.* New Haven: Yale University Press.

Folk, Nicole, and Kathy Goldschmidt. 2003. "Congress Online 2003: Turning the Corner on the Information Age." Congress Online Project. Accessed December 1, 2010. http://www.cmfweb.org/storage/cmfweb/documents/CMF _Pubs/congressonline2003.pdf.

Fountain, J. E. 2001. *Building the Virtual State: Information Technology and Institutional Change.* Washington, DC: Brookings.

Gutmann, A., and D. Thompson. 1997. *Democracy and Disagreement.* Cambridge: Harvard University Press.

Habermas, J. 1996. *Between Facts and Norms: Contributions to a Discourse Theory of Law and Democracy.* Cambridge: MIT Press.

Heclo, H. 1974. *Modern Social Politics in Britain and Sweden: From Relief to Income Maintenance.* New Haven: Yale University Press.

Held, D. 1996. *Models of Democracy.* Oxford: Polity Press.

Hibbing, J., and E. Theiss-Morse. 2002. *Stealth Democracy: Americans' Beliefs about How Government Should Work.* Cambridge: Cambridge University Press.

Hindman, M. S. 2009. *The Myth of Digital Democracy.* Princeton, NJ: Princeton University Press.

Lazer, David, Ines A. Mergel, Curtis E. Ziniel, Kevin M. Esterling, and Michael A. Neblo. 2011. "The Multiple Institutional Logics of Innovation." *International Public Management Journal,* forthcoming.

Lazer, D., M. Neblo, K. Esterling, and K. Goldschmidt. 2009. "Online Townhalls: Exploring Democracy in the Twenty-first Century." Congressional Management Foundation. Accessed December 1, 2010. http://www.cmfweb.org/ storage/cmfweb/documents/CMF_Pubs/online-town-hall-meetings.pdf.

Lazer, David, Anand E. Sokhey, Michael A. Neblo, and Kevin M. Esterling. 2010. "Deliberative Ripples: The Network Effects of Political Events." Social Science Research Network. Accessed December 1, 2010. http://ssrn.com/ abstract=1656553.

Lupia, A., and M. D. McCubbins. 1998. *The Democratic Dilemma: Can Citizens Learn What They Need to Know?* New York: Cambridge University Press.

Madison, James. 2003. In Alexander Hamilton, James Madison, and John Jay, *The Federalist Papers*. No. 56. New York: New American Library.

Mayer-Schönberger, V., and D. Lazer. 2007. *Governance and Information Technology: From Electronic Government to Information Government*. Cambridge: MIT Press.

Neblo, M. A. 2000. "Thinking through Democracy: Deliberative Politics in Theory and Practice." Unpublished dissertation, University of Chicago.

Neblo, Michael A., Kevin M. Esterling, Ryan Kennedy, David Lazer, and Anand E. Sokhey. 2010. "Who Wants to Deliberate—and Why?" *American Political Science Review* 104:566–583.

Pitkin, H. F. 1967. *The Concept of Representation*. Berkeley: University of California Press.

Yates, J., W. J. Orlikowski, and K. Okamura. 1999. "Explicit and Implicit Structuring of Genres in Electronic Communication: Reinforcement and Change of Social Interaction." *Organization Science* 10, no. 1:83–103.

III

The Legal Architecture of Online Consultation

13

Legal Frameworks and Institutional Contexts for Public Consultation Regarding Administrative Action: The United States

Peter L. Strauss

The electronic democracy to which this volume is addressed finds reflection at all levels of American government (federal, state, and local), and its tools can be employed by any political actor—legislature, executive, or administrative bureaucracy. This chapter addresses online practices in the national government of the United States and only in relation to essentially bureaucratic (administrative) actors. The U.S. Congress maintains a remarkable database giving the public near simultaneous access to all records of its actions,[1] but it has yet to develop regular electronic means for consultation with the public about its legislative agenda—contrasting sharply, in this respect, with the European Union (see chapter 14 in this volume). Individual members of Congress may have Web presences that allow them to consult with their constituencies, but these are idiosyncratic and at an early stage of development (see chapter 12 in this volume). More is happening in presidential offices. Within days of President Barack Obama's inauguration, the Office of Management and Budget (OMB) published a memorandum entitled "Citizen-Centered E-Government: Developing the Action Plan," promising that "Electronic government is one of the five key elements in the President's Management and Performance Plan."[2] An Office of E-Government and Information Technology is a part of OMB, although at this writing its Web site is inactive.[3] The Office of Science and Technology Policy,[4] a separate White House office, also addresses e-government issues. In May to July 2009, under the leadership of Beth Simone Noveck, a noted American legal scholar of e-government, the Office of Science of Technology Policy conducted a Web-based discussion of e-governance issues intended to inform the initiative, and at this writing, its results can still be viewed on the Web (see chapter 1 in this volume).[5]

All this activity, however, began too recently to be assessed in this chapter, which was principally written before President Obama's inauguration. Instead, the focus here is on a context in which electronic consultation by executive branch policy makers has been developing for over a decade and has reached a point of considerable, although not final maturity. This is the American practice of developing administrative regulations (subsidiary legislation). Initially developed haphazardly, agency by agency, it is now (albeit with friction in the gears) moving toward a centralized regime.[6] The practice is rarely consultative in the full sense that Peter Shane hypothesizes in the imaginary nation of Agora (see chapter 1 in this volume). Although the public is given opportunities for input and the input processes are transparent in varying degrees, there are no online exchanges in the nature of a conversation or round table.

The Organization of the Federal Executive for Rulemaking in the United States

The General Procedure

It seems useful first to describe briefly the procedures by which regulations (subsidiary legislation) are developed by the federal bureaucracy, without reference to the developing electronic components of the process. Rulemaking requires statutory authorization and occurs subject to more exacting judicial review for regularity than statutes receive, but it is strictly an executive branch activity. American law sharply distinguishes between rulemaking and legislation. Congress legislates, but it does not participate directly in rulemaking. It has the possibility of disapproving its result only by enacting a new statute.[7]

Although exceptions exist, virtually any regulation purporting to govern private conduct must be adopted by procedures at least as rigorous as those described in section 553 of the federal Administrative Procedure Act.[8] Section 553 establishes the ordinary procedures to be used by any agency statutorily authorized to adopt regulations.[9] Other than a subsection enabling any person to petition an agency to undertake a rulemaking—a petition must be responded to, and its denial is reviewable under permissive standards—it imagines rulemaking usually to begin with a notice of a proposal for rulemaking[10] published in the daily *Federal Register* of government public notices. Although the section itself is permissive respecting the necessary content of the notice, it is now understood that notice for any significant rule should contain the text of the proposed regulation and an explanation of its purpose and that the agency should simultaneously make available the data or studies on which it may be relying in making the proposal.

As its second step, the section ordinarily requires the agency to give the public an opportunity to submit views and data—to comment on the proposal. The requirement is for an opportunity to submit written materials by a date certain specified in the notice. Agencies are free—but ordinarily not statutorily required—to introduce elements of orality into this comment process.[11] The Administrative Procedure Act imagines only one round of comments, so its text does not contemplate an opportunity to respond to the comments of others. With paper comments, perhaps simultaneously mailed to a single distant location, timely access to the comments of others was not expected, and any access would be difficult. Agencies remained free, however, to consider late-filed comments, and for important rulemakings there may occasionally have been efforts to reply to the timely posted and possibly significant submissions of others.

Section 553's third requirement is that the agency, after considering this commentary, publish a "concise general statement of . . . basis and purpose" as the preface of any regulation it finally adopts. Again, the language is modest, but courts have insisted on relatively detailed explanations, including a response to any adverse commentary that the reviewing court is persuaded to regard as having been "significant." Given the retrospective, litigation-driven character of this evaluation, statements of basis and purpose for important rulemakings have long and defensively exceeded the dimensions suggested by "concise general." Adopted regulations, with their statements of basis and purpose, are also published in the *Federal Register*. The regulatory text, but not the statements of basis and purpose, are collected in the Code of Federal Regulations.

Agency soft law—guidance documents, interpretations, general statements of policy, staff manuals, and the like—is excepted from the procedures of section 553. Section 552(a), however, which is part of the federal Freedom of Information Act, anticipates that such documents can significantly affect private conduct and indeed are intended to be followed by agency staff. Thus, it twice provides that soft law documents may be used in a manner prejudicial to private interests only if published—either in the *Federal Register* or in an indexed compendium maintained by the agency.

Presidential Involvement in Rulemaking

If rulemaking is an executive branch activity, what is the role of the U.S. President? Recently, a majority of the U.S. Supreme Court treated an important rulemaking as executive action and ruled on the constitutional challenge to it—whether the authority conferred on an executive agency (the Environmental Protection Agency, in this instance) was sufficiently bounded by statute to permit a court to assure its legality.[12] Yet a majority of the Court has also said, in a proposition not called into question in any later opinion, that "the President's power to see that the laws are faithfully executed refutes the idea that he is to be a lawmaker."[13] These two propositions, looking in quite opposite directions, are not easily reconciled.

The legislation authorizing rulemaking almost invariably makes it an agency activity, empowering a particular element of government (such as the Environmental Protection Agency or the Federal Communications Commission) to act within a limited frame of reference. These organizations are headed by persons appointed by the President. They are unmistakably executive branch officials, and yet they are not the President. In recent decades, however, both the President and Congress have adopted measures that create significant roles for centralized oversight of rulemaking processes, and these roles that have tended to blur the lines between politics and administration.

On Congress's side, these include the National Environmental Policy Act,[14] the Paperwork Reduction Act,[15] the Regulatory Flexibility Act of 1980[16] (subsequently amended and extended by the Small Business Regulatory Enforcement Fairness Act),[17] the Unfunded Mandates Reform Act of 1995,[18] the Electronic Freedom of Information Act of 1996,[19] and E-Government Act of 2002.[20] The last two, which have significant implications for cyberdemocracy, are discussed below.

On the executive side, several presidential documents also speak to agency procedures in rulemaking. Of particular salience has been a series of Executive Orders, now described as Executive Order 12,866, providing for centralized review in the Office of Information and Regulatory Analysis (OIRA), another element of the OMB.[21] Although other White House offices, and the President and Vice President themselves, may significantly influence rulemaking from time to time,[22] these are influences that tend to stay out of public view. Responding to concerns about OIRA's transparency and possibly inappropriate political influences on rulemaking's ostensibly open policy making processes, President Obama quickly directed a thoroughgoing review of Executive Order 12,866 and procedures under it—a review that voluntarily included a notice-and-comment process like that required of agency rulemaking, with comments that at this writing remain posted on the Web.[23] Changes presumably will have occurred between this writing and its publication, and the Office of Information and Regulatory Analysis Web site will help the reader find her way.

Information Technology Resources for the Stages of Rulemaking

As remarked above, the federal government's information technology (IT) presence began as an agency-by-agency process. Even government-wide resources, such as the *Federal Register* or the Code of Federal Regulations, were available online and searchable only if and to the extent that a responsible agency—in this case, the Government Printing Office—provided. For years, the best free Internet source for the United States Code and the Code of Federal Regulations was a private site maintained by Cornell University's Legal Information Institute.

Agency initiatives were highly variable. A few agency initiatives approached the concept of consultation. Thus, the Department of Transportation's Research and Special Programs Administration (now its Pipeline and Hazardous Materials Safety Administration) has occasionally used chat rooms in connection with proposed rulemakings, incorporating the back and forth into its docket. At one point, the Nuclear Regulatory Commission opened an experimental interactive dialog with members of its regulatory community on some technical issues of interest. The experiment, however, failed to generate significant participation. When a Department of Agriculture rulemaking setting standards for organic produce attracted a large and strongly committed audience, the Department provided an unusually full exposure of available data online and invited more interactive commentary. What virtually all agencies ordinarily provided, however, was an opportunity to comment and some access to materials already filed in electronic form.

Perhaps the most expansive early development of Web-based resources for rulemaking occurred in the Department of Transportation—a cabinet department that has responsibilities for assuring the safety, among other things, of all forms of transport and has become one of the government's major rulemakers. At an early stage in government's development of a Web presence, it made a wide range of documents available and searchable on its Web site, accepted electronically filed comments, and developed listserv capacities permitting citizens to be informed of some filings of interest to them. Particularly significant was its development of a data-management system for all public documents held by the department. It was ultimately brought to the point of replacing DOT's paper records. Materials submitted or generated in paper form were promptly[24] scanned into the docket, since that was DOT's only comprehensive record. This meant that all material that might be associated with a rulemaking docket could be found on the system, providing ready access from any computer to all associated scientific reports or comments already filed. Thus conceived as an efficiency measure for DOT employees, the data-management system also greatly enlarged public access to the materials of rulemaking.

Today, all government rulemaking (except that conducted by some independent regulatory commissions) must be conducted through Regulations.gov, a Web site presenting a uniform face for all, with materials presented (to the extent they are presented) via a single Federal Docket Management System (FDMS) that the public accesses through that site. Regrettably, it would take a major effort to reproduce the Department of Transportation's data-management system's capacities in the FDMS, and thus the latter system is and appears likely to remain considerably more limited in content and usability. For example, agencies are neither required nor necessarily afforded the resources to convert into electronic form materials that they receive in paper. Even for materials available to the agency in electronic form, the agency controls if and when they are posted to the FDMS and whether, if posted, they will be available to other agencies and to the public. As a result, the system cannot be regarded as a complete or contemporaneous record of a rulemaking.

In 2008, anticipating the presidential election, a committee of the Administrative Law and Regulatory Practice Section of the American Bar Association published a report to Congress and the President on the status and future of federal e-rulemaking—*Achieving the Potential: The Future of Federal e-Rulemaking* (Committee on the Status and Future of Federal E-Rulemaking 2008)—that substantially informs this essay. *Achieving the Potential* provides a detailed account of the federal government's development of electronic rulemaking activities, ultimately leading to Regulations.gov and the federal data-management system (facilities still being created) and makes many recommendations for their improvement. The following paragraphs largely reorganize the American Bar Association account, with reference as well to additional materials, to create a picture of the significance of Regulations.gov and the FDMS throughout the chronology of an ordinary rulemaking. As will become apparent, these two entities, in addition to engaging the public, also arm the White House's oversight and control over rulemaking.

The Decision to Undertake a Rulemaking

Public Petitions
Regulations.gov is structured to present rulemakings that have been proposed and to permit commentary on them. Hence, petitions to begin a rulemaking must still be filed in paper form, not electronically. Unless an agency chooses to invite comment on a petition for rulemaking, a petition is unlikely to become an element of the FDMS.[25]

The Rulemaking Plan and Regulatory Agenda
The brief discussion of rulemaking under the Administrative Procedure Act began with the agency's publication of a notice of proposed rulemaking because (unless there has been a petition) that is where the statute first takes hold. Much occurs before this stage is reached, however. Bureaucratically, there must be a decision to make a rulemaking effort—to begin analysis and drafting. For years now, both statute and executive orders (now Executive Order 12,866) have addressed this decision.

Since 1980, the Regulatory Flexibility Act[26] has required agencies to publish brief descriptions of these decisions, including contact information for interested persons, in Regulatory Agendas published each April and October in the *Federal Register*. Hard to search and incomplete, the agendas could be found electronically only on a site maintained by the University of Massachusetts. The regulatory agenda is an element of the FDMS, searchable via Regulations.gov, but agenda items are not directly linked to the relevant e-rulemaking docket, and the Agenda is not yet fully searchable. Regulations.gov provides no opportunity for a person finding a matter of interest on the regulatory agenda to enroll for notice of further developments. A Regulation Identification Number (RIN) that can be found in the agenda provides a limited basis for integration of the regulatory agenda entry with the corresponding proposal for rulemaking, should one eventuate.

Since the mid-1980s, executive orders have required agencies to submit to the President an annual regulatory plan—a requirement that for publication purposes is well integrated with the Regulatory Flexibility Act's Unified Regulatory Agenda. Regulatory plans are obligations of every agency, including independent regulatory commissions, as well as the single-headed agencies like the Environmental Protection Agency and the Occupational Safety and Health Administration, albeit the enforcement of this obligation against the independent regulatory commissions is unclear. The regulatory plan and its processes are opaque to the Internet. The current version of Executive Order 12,866 makes a variety of commitments to transparency respecting both its processes for overseeing individual rulemakings and the detailed impact analyses that it requires for the more important of these rulemakings. As developed below, this has resulted in Web availability of a range of information. No such commitments are made in relation to the regulatory plan, and no electronic materials about it (beyond what may result from the inclusion of plan events in a regulatory agenda publication) are available on the Web.

Development of a Draft Regulation

Required Preliminary Analyses
Under Executive Order 12,866, agencies need to submit to the Office of Information and Regulatory Affairs summary analyses of each projected individual rulemaking, which includes information that may be required by other measures, such as the Regulatory Flexibility Act. If the agency or OIRA concludes that the significance of the regulation under consideration requires extensive analysis under the terms of the order—a process that may involve informal consultations that will go unnoticed in electronic records—a formal draft analysis will be prepared and submitted.

Under the transparency commitments of EO 12,866, the fact of formal submission of a draft to OIRA, the pendency of its review, and a summary outcome are all noted and publicly available on the OIRA Web site. Should there be meetings at OIRA on the matter, the fact and subject of each meeting, together with a list of its attendees, will also be posted there. The draft itself, however, and any communications that may pass back and forth about it are not posted by OIRA. OIRA undertakes in the executive order both to limit the extent to which its consultations can be used by persons outside government for backdoor commentary and to assure that written materials it sends to the agency will become a part of the agency docket, including an indication of changes made in the agency's formal submission during OIRA review. It is a matter of individual agency practice whether the content of meetings is memorialized in any way. Although the draft analysis will be supplied to OIRA in electronic form, whether and within what time frame these records find their way onto the FDMS is agency-dependent.

Since the Department of Transportation committed itself to complete electronic dockets under its own docket-management system before the decision was taken to have a single FDMS, DOT's prompt posting of all materials is ensured by the need for internal availability. That need puts into the rulemaking docket reasonably full accounts of meetings at OIRA, written materials coming from OIRA, and the like. The only question will be the fact and timing of their availability to the public—an issue that the FDMS has thus far left to agency decision; DOT has thus far continued its practice of liberal exposure. The result is to bring these materials within the comment process.

Because the commitment to the FDMS is not a commitment to its use as a substitute for paper dockets, there is little certainty for agencies generally that materials like these will appear in it. That would require a commitment to translating hard-copy documents into electronic form, entailing funds and personnel not readily available. Indeed, because an agency's decision to place its materials on FDMS is binary—they may either be restricted to the agency alone or opened to outside access by both other agencies and the public—FDMS's utility within government as well as without it, even as to materials that have been placed there, is significantly less than might be hoped for. *Achieving the Potential* reports that the "agency only" choice is often made for reasons including concerns about possible pornographic content, the confidentiality of private business information, and the integrity of the internal deliberative process. These issues are compounded by significant limitations on searchability within FDMS and its general inaccessibility to external search engines such as Google.

Data Assembly and Availability

What is true for OIRA's interventions is also true for the internal agency documents that may underlie eventual rulemaking. Scientific studies and other materials that courts may require to be available for public comment (and that agencies would find themselves compelled to release in response to a generalized Freedom of Information Act request) need not be received in electronic form. If received in paper form, they need not be scanned into the FDMS and thus will not be found there. This will include even draft economic impact statements made in compliance with Executive Order 12,866, which requires them to be made available for public comment in association with a proposed rule. There is no requirement that the statement be made an element of the FDMS accessible to the public and other government agencies when the proposal itself is posted on Regulations.gov.

The Notice of Proposed Rulemaking and Opportunity to Comment

Receiving Notice

The formal place for publication of notices of proposed rulemaking remains the printed *Federal Register*. Nonetheless, agencies are obliged to make every notice of proposed rulemaking accessible through Regulations.gov and to accept comments submitted by that portal. One might suppose that Regulations.gov would offer some form of registration to make it possible to receive notice electronically when matters of likely interest are posted or (as was possible on the Department of Transportation's data-management system) whenever changes occur to a docket of known interest. At the moment, however, Regulations.gov affords more limited possibilities for automatic notice. One may register only for an RSS feed for all of a chosen agency's notices appearing in the *Federal Register*. Once a docket number is known, one may register in connection with that—but docket numbers are known only after notice has been published. For any more pointed registration for rulemaking notices, one must rely on individual agencies—and the current approach to centralized e-government has tended to dampen agency initiatives in such matters.

A One-Way or Two-Way Street? The Chance to See and Respond

Consistent with the general current permissiveness of the FDMS system, agencies are obliged to accept comments filed via Regulations.gov, but they are not required to make that portal exclusive. Comments may be filed directly with the agency, either in paper or electronic form. Indeed, some limitations on the Regulations.gov interface (one can directly submit a comment of up to 2,000 characters and attach a single larger file) make it likely that direct submission of comments to the agency will continue to be the dominant form. Moreover, even if a comment is filed via Regulations.gov, agency personnel must affirmatively decide to post that comment before it can find its way into the publicly searchable areas of the FDMS. These decisions are inhibited by concerns about privacy and confidentiality, as already noted, and in any event need not be timely. Comments filed directly with the agency require additional steps, and if the comments are filed on paper, these steps are expensive and time-consuming. *Achieving the Potential* reports many reasons to believe that, at present, this process is slow when it happens and incomplete.

The conventional view of rulemaking—that it is a process by which agencies inform themselves—is not compromised by these lacunae. The existence of a single deadline for the filing of all commentary suggests that responsive comment is not an expected rulemaking element. Indeed, the governing U.S. Supreme Court interpretation of section 553 emphatically rejects the idea that rulemaking entails a back-and-forth process, consultative in the fullest sense.[27] Nonetheless, the remarkably expanded availability of materials promised by the information age carries with it the possibility of reading the comments of others much more readily than when doing so required a visit to a Washington office. In fact, many comments are filed before the stated deadline, permitting response. Most important, the deadline for commentary is highly artificial. It signals only that there is an end to the agency's obligation to pay attention to what one might say. As would not be the case for a deadline in adjudication, it is not improper to submit a late-filed comment. Nothing prevents an agency from reading such a comment if it wishes to. It would not be surprising, in this respect, to see a gradual replacement of the "expert judgment" model currently underlying rulemaking by one that understood it in a more plebescitary, politically consultative light.

Decision Processes within the Administration

Internally, the availability of rulemaking materials in electronic form can considerably aid decision processes. Important materials can be on as many desks simultaneously as need be. Software has been developed, *Achieving the Potential* notes, that permits amalgamating what may be a very large number of comments and quickly distinguishing elements that are unique from those that may have been supplied to members by an interested nongovernmental organization in the form of an electronic postcard—a considerable work savings over manual processing. To the extent that Regulations.gov becomes a portal used for such postcards— and they are more easily entered there than would be more detailed commentary—this may be an important benefit. Grassroots comment campaigns of this character of course predated it.

This is also the time when, for significant rulemaking, Executive Order 12,866 requires submission and clearance of a final economic impact statement—a process thought often to entail a fair amount of pressure from the White House as to how contested elements should be resolved.[28] Similar mechanisms and issues respecting transparency are present here as for draft statements at the prenotice stage of the process.

Adoption

With adoption, regulations enter electronic databases associated with the *Federal Register* and the Code of Federal Regulations. Additionally, the Electronic Freedom of Information Act requires agencies to maintain an electronic library in which they can be found.

"Soft Law": Guidance, the Web, and Consultation

The Electronic Freedom of Information Act (E-FOIA)

With the adoption of the Electronic Freedom of Information Act (E-FOIA), federal agencies came under the legal obligation to make soft law instruments available in Web-based libraries, a practice that many agencies had already adopted voluntarily. This obligation has since been reinforced by OMB directives and advice.[29] Although not consultations, these postings expand the transparency of government and arm oversight, industry, and citizen petitions and other responses pointing in a consultative direction. Particularly for science and technology-based regulators, such as the Federal Aviation Administration, the Nuclear Regulatory Commission, or the Food and Drug Administration, the volume of guidance materials issued by the agency may be an order of magnitude greater than its body of regulations.

The current preference for standards (regulations that define results to be achieved) rather than rules (regulations that specify the precise means to be employed) arms this phenomenon. When an agency has defined by regulation the results that must be shown, the regulated will value advice from the agency about any (nonexclusive) means by which it has determined those results can be assured. But regulations generally, like statutes, invariably leave issues of detail and application unresolved, and one common kind of consultative practice is the advice letter, in which inquiring citizens or organizations are informed of an agency's interpretation of their legal obligations in relation to defined particular circumstances. This kind of soft law is hardly limited to technological regulation; the administration of tax, customs, and labor laws, among others, readily invite it.

The transformative effect of having this volume of materials available and readily searchable on the Internet can be easily appreciated. The author's favorite example, one of long standing, is the body of advice letters issued by the General Counsel of the National Highway Traffic Safety Administration (NHTSA) of the Department of Transportation in response to inquiries about the meaning and application of its regulations concerning motor vehicle safety.[30] These letters have always been public documents in the sense that any citizen could go to the office of the General Counsel and ask to inspect them. Previously, that would require searching perhaps imperfectly indexed physical files in Washington, D.C., likely a job for a hired agent (such as a lawyer) and one that would consume expensive hours. For several years, however, the letters have been posted on the NHTSA Web site, and it is possible to perform a nearly instantaneous search from a personal computer, a search that is more accurate than a physical search could possibly have been. The value of this asset was so obvious that private organizations that had created their own electronic files of earlier letters donated their records to NHTSA as soon as this utility was created. Transparency and regularity were tremendously enhanced.

Informal and Encouraged Practices

The importance of guidance documents has resulted in increasing statutory and presidential attention to them. Congress has made the Food and Drug Administration's Good Guidance Practices, initially an agency initiative to promote consultation with those likely to be influenced by its soft law pronouncements, into legally required procedures.[31] (Since guidance, by definition, cannot be legally binding even if influential, this is itself a somewhat soft requirement. A search of Lexis on August 2, 2008, returned no federal cases and only six law review articles that referred to this statutory guidance obligation.) In amendments adopted in 2007, President George W. Bush added "significant" guidance documents to Executive Order 12,866, requiring advance notification of them to OIRA, with the possibility that OIRA could require submission of a draft and brief explanation, and "notify the agency when additional consultation [with OIRA] will be required before [its] issuance."[32] Within a week, OMB had issued a "Final Bulletin for Agency Good Guidance Practices,"[33] (itself the product of a public notice-and-comment process), which required agencies to maintain a separate listing on its Web site of all guidance documents meeting the executive order definition, to "establish and clearly advertise on its Web site a means for the public to submit comments electronically . . . and to submit a request electronically" for change, and to establish an office to receive and address complaints

about guidance practices.[34] The bulletin made clear that these requirements were not judicially enforceable and that agency response to comments was not ordinarily required.[35] However, for "economically
significant guidance documents"—a subset of "significant guidance documents" defined as any that "may reasonably be anticipated to lead to
an annual effect on the economy of $100 million or more or adversely
affect in a material way the economy or a sector of the economy"
(excluding budgetary measures)[36]—the bulletin instructed agencies to use
procedures somewhat resembling notice-and-comment procedures but
apparently not requiring use of Regulations.gov for electronic consultation.[37] It appears that agencies are to use their own Web sites for
receiving comments (if electronically filed) and providing a responsive
discussion of its conclusions after comments have been received. Even
though President Obama rescinded the amendment that President
Bush had made to Executive Order 12,866 extending its terms to guidance documents, this element was met with considerable approbation in
regulated communities, and practices like these have continued in
response to a less formal directive from the Office of Management and
Budget.

Less formal, more immediate, and more intimate than the process for
adopting regulations, it seems at least possible that these measures, for
some agencies at least, will result in processes more genuinely consultative (in a public sense) than notice-and-comment rulemaking. The way
in which Regulations.gov and the FDMS have been constructed—
limitations that will take much effort to overcome and quite possibly will
not be forthcoming—tend to reinforce the preexisting reality that "consultation" in rulemaking was often a better description of agency relations with the White House than with the general public. Those
consultations occur behind essentially closed doors that the Internet
world does not seem poised to open. Over a decade and a half ago, an
administrative law scholar who had served as general counsel to the
Environmental Protection Agency (one of the federal government's most
important rulemakers and the managing partner thus far in the development of Regulations.gov and the FDMS) wrote:

What was once (perhaps) a means for securing public input into agency decisions
has become today primarily a method for compiling a record for judicial review.
No administrator in Washington turns to full-scale notice-and-comment rulemaking when she is genuinely interested in obtaining input from interested
parties. Notice-and-comment rulemaking is to public participation as Japanese
Kabuki theater is to human passions—a highly stylized process for displaying in

a formal way the essence of something which in real life takes place in other venues. To secure the genuine reality, rather than a formal show, of public participation, a variety of techniques is available—from informal meetings with trade associations and other constituency groups, to roundtables, to floating "trial balloons" in speeches or leaks to the trade press, to the more formal techniques of advisory committees and negotiated rulemaking. (Elliott 1992, 1492–1493)

"Notice" of proposed rulemaking appears in Regulations.gov only after all these processes—which are not on the Web and likely not captured in any electronic record—have occurred, and the compromises resulting from them have been secured. To expect much movement often to occur at such a late stage in the development of a proposal is irrational. To attribute it to electronic processes that are not universal—that need not (probably will not) reflect even the totality of public inputs the agency has received—compounds the problem.

Conclusion

This chapter has attempted to provide a descriptive, not a normative, account of the consultation situation respecting policy making in the United States. One may see increasing commitments to transparency and interactivity as the Internet makes possible both the ready dispersion of knowledge and broad opportunities for contribution. Whether these developments will effectively enhance the experience and actuality of democracy in the affected communities is open to question. The model of Athens was unworkable even at the level of our small eighteenth-century nation-state and is much less so in the large United States of today. Electronic communication opens avenues for participation but hardly solves the problem of dealing with number and may indeed complicate it—both in an ordinary way (for example, the technology gap between rich and poor) and in vulnerability to manipulations. We may confidently expect these developments to continue and significant problems to be revealed and require attention as they do.

Notes

1. http://thomas.loc.gov.
2. Memorandum from Mitchell E. Daniels Jr., Director, Office of Management and Budget, to the Heads of Executive Departments and Agencies, re: Citizen-Centered E-Government: Developing the Action Plan (July 18, 2001), available at http://www.whitehouse.gov/omb/memoranda_m01-28.

3. http://www.whitehouse.gov/omb/e-gov.

4. http://www.whitehouse.gov/administration/eop/ostp.

5. Available at http://mixedink.com/#/opengov. The Office of Science and Technology Policy maintains an online blog, http://www.whitehouse.gov/administration/eop/ostp, where further developments on these and other e-government issues may be followed.

6. See the discussion in the text following note 23 below. The Administrative Law and Regulatory Practice Section of the American Bar Association published a 2008 report to Congress and the President on the status and future of federal e-rulemaking (Committee on the Status and the Future of Federal E-Rulemaking 2008).

7. The Congressional Review Act, U.S.C. tit. 5, sec. 801 et seq., creates a short-form legislative process for such disapprovals, but as they must take the form of legislative action, they require presidential agreement (or supermajorities in both houses to override a presidential veto). This makes likely (as thus far has proved to be the case) that such legislation will be successfully enacted only in very particular circumstances—as when a regulation is adopted in the waning days of one administration but remains open to the statutory process at the beginning of the next administration, in which both houses of Congress and the presidency are in the control of the other political party (Cohen and Strauss 1997, 101).

8. U.S.C. tit. 5, sec. 553.

9. Statutes governing the procedures required of individual agencies occasionally require more elaborate, so-called hybrid procedures—for example, requirements of oral elements—or may invoke a more formal procedure described in the APA itself for "on-the-record" rulemaking. As these do not significantly affect electronic usages, they are not further discussed here.

10. A little-used chapter of the statute, more recently enacted, provides for "negotiated rulemaking"—the development of the proposal in a public procedure through the negotiations of a small committee of public and private persons selected for their interest in the matter (U.S.C. tit. 5, sec. 561–570). Although the processes for identifying the occasions for negotiated rulemaking and constituting its committee may involve electronic communication (in the manner of all government notices), negotiated rulemaking as such will not be further discussed here (see Harter 1982, 2000).

11. The exception would be for hybrid procedures requiring such an opportunity. Where "on the record" rulemaking is required, the APA gives the agency some discretion to use written procedures only.

12. Whitman v. American Trucking Association, 531 U.S. 457, 471 (2001).

13. Youngstown Sheet and Tube Co. v. Sawyer, 343 U.S. 579, 587 (1952).

14. U.S.C. tit. 42, sec. 4321 et seq.

15. U.S.C. tit. 44, sec. 3501 et seq.

16. U.S.C. tit. 5, sec. 601–612.

17. Ibid., sec. 801–808.

18. U.S.C. tit. 2, sec. 1531 et seq.

19. Electronic Freedom of Information Act Amendments of 1996, Pub. L. No. 104-231, 110 Stat. 3048 (1996).

20. U.S.C. tit. 44, sec. 3601 et seq.

21. Available at http://www.whitehouse.gov/omb/inforeg_regmatters.

22. See an article by now-Justice Elena Kagan recounting her experience of presidential direction of agency rulemaking during Clinton administration (Kagan 2001), as well as a journalistic report that Vice President Dick Cheney attempted to control decisions as slight as the amount of water having to be released from a federal dam to protect threatened fish populations (Becker and Gelman 2007). See also Letter from Henry A Waxman, Chair, House Committee on Oversight and Government Reform, to Susan A. Dudley, Administrator, Office of Information and Regulatory Affairs (April 30, 2008), visited September 9, 2009 at http://oversight.house.gov/documents/20080430103958.pdf ("For over a year, the Office of Information and Regulatory Affairs has blocked the National Marine Fisheries Service from issuing a rule to protect [right] whales from being killed by ships. According to documents obtained by the Committee, the rule's delay appears to be due to baseless objections by White House officials"). The text of the letter was no longer available on the Web at publication, but a trace of it could still be found at http://waxman.house.gov/News/DocumentPrint.aspx?DocumentID=113402 (visited March 31, 2011). The rule was finally issued in mid-October 2008.

23. http://www.reginfo.gov/public/jsp/EO/fedRegReview/publicComments.jsp.

24. The Department of Transportation's standard, generally met, was to post everything within eight working hours of receipt. The transition to FDMS, for which posting is more complicated, has slowed posting a bit.

25. The Department of Transportation, consistent with effective maintenance of complete electronic records on the FDMS and now that its data-management system has been shut down, has created for itself a procedure within FDMS to permit electronic submissions, as of petitions for rulemaking, before a docket has been created (see docketsinfo.dot.gov).

26. U.S.C. tit. 5, sec. 601–612.

27. Vermont Yankee Nuclear Power Corporation v. Natural Resources Defense Council, 435 U.S. 519, 547–548 (1978). Readers are entitled to know that the author, then general counsel to the United States Nuclear Regulatory Commission, was an author of the government's brief in the case.

28. See "Waxman Threatens to Cite Johnson with Contempt over Documents" (2008), reporting on an investigation into the refusal of the Environmental Protection Agency's administrator, Stephen Johnson, to turn over documents related to the agency's ozone rulemaking, which President Bush appears to have directed to be amended hours before it was due for release.

29. See Memorandum from Office of Management and Budget to the Heads of Executive Departments and Agencies (January 18, 2007), available at http://

www.whitehouse.gov/omb/memoranda/fy2007/m07-07.pdf (including the attachment "Final Bulletin for Agency Good Guidance Practices").

30. Available at http://isearch.nhtsa.gov.

31. Food and Drug Modernization Act of 1997, U.S.C. tit. 21, sec. 371(h).

32. Executive Order 12,866, as amended by Executive Order 13,422 (72 FR 2763, January 18, 2007), sec. 9.

33. Office of Management and Budget. 2007. "Final Bulletin for Agency Good Guidance Practices," *Federal Register,* vol. 72, pp. 3,432-3,440, available at http://www.whitehouse.gov/omb/memoranda/fy2007/m07-07.pdf (January 25, 2007).. The authors of the document, Paul Noe and John Graham, have written discursively about it at (Noe and Graham 2008).

34. "Final Bulletin for Agency Good Guidance Practices," at III (Office of Management and Budget 2007, 3440).

35. Ibid., at VI (Office of Management and Budget 2007, 3440).

36. Ibid., at I(5) (Office of Management and Budget 2007, 3439).

37. In addition to publishing notice in the *Federal Register* that a draft document is available, the agency was to "[p]ost the draft document on the Internet and make it publicly available in hard copy (or notify the public how they can review the guidance document if it is not in a format that permits such electronic posting with reasonable efforts)" ibid., at. IV(1)(b) (Office of Management and Budget 2007, 3440). As of August 2, 2008, Regulations.gov lists no "economically significant guidance" for comment.

References

Becker, Jo, and Barton Gelman. 2007. "Leaving No Tracks on Environmental Policy." *Washington Post*, June 27.

Cohen, Daniel, and Peter L. Strauss. 1997. "Congressional Review of Agency Regulations." *Administrative Law Review* 49:101–110.

Committee on the Status and the Future of Federal E-Rulemaking. 2008. *Achieving the Potential: The Future of Federal e-Rulemaking*. Washington, DC: American Bar Association. Accessed December 1, 2010. http://ceri.law.cornell.edu/documents/report-web-version.pdf.

Elliott, E. Donald. 1992. "Re-Inventing Rulemaking." *Duke Law Journal* 41:1490–1496.

Harter, Philip J. 1982. "Negotiating Regulations: A Cure for Malaise." *Georgetown Law Journal* 71:1–118.

Harter, Philip J. 2000. "Assessing the Assessors: The Actual Performance of Negotiated Rulemaking." *New York University Environmental Law Journal* 9:32–59.

Kagan, Elena. 2001. "Presidential Administration." *Harvard Law Review* 114:2245–2385.

Noe, Paul, and John Graham. 2008. "Due Process and Management for Guidance Documents: Good Governance Long Overdue." *Yale Journal on Regulation* 25:103–112.

Office of Management and Budget. 2007. "Final Bulletin for Agency Good Guidance Practices." *Federal Register,* vol. 72, p. 3,432-3,440, January 27. Accessed May 12, 2011. http://www.whitehouse.gov/omb/memoranda/fy2007/m07-07.pdf.

"Waxman Threatens to Cite Johnson with Contempt over Documents." 2008. *Inside the EPA,* June 20.

14

Legal Frameworks and Institutional Contexts for Public Policy Consultation Regarding Administrative Action: The European Union

Polona Pičman Štefančič

The European Union's use of electronic consultation by executive branch actors engaged in policy making differs considerably from United States practice. In the EU, the most prominent use of information communication technologies (ICTs) to support public consultations occurs through the EU's executive body, the European Commission.[1] The Commission has provided central coordination for the use of electronic consultation venues from the outset. Its Your Voice in Europe Web site and other resources began as centralized resources, so there is less variation across the various directorates general (DGs) than is commonly observed among federal agencies in the United States, although some differences among the directorates general may be observed. The Commission's uses are most prominent in developing proposals for legislation, which must subsequently win approvals by the Council of the EU and the European Parliament, the EU's directly political bodies. As in the United States, consultation tends to be a request for inputs rather than a staged conversation. For the development of subsidiary legislation, where the practice of comitology prevails, transparency and public consultation are much less evident. As in American settings, the tension between objective or expert processes and political ones is observable and the source of considerable difficulties (see chapter 13 in this volume).

The Institutional Context for Norm Creation in the EU

Established relations between governing European institutions greatly affect the position of public consultation in the EU norm-creation processes: opportunities for meaningful public consultation depend on the system-specific structures and processes through which government decisions are made. In addition, the two prevailing models of representative and participatory democracy[2] further shape the specifics of the EU public consultation practices. To understand how the complexity of the EU institutional setting affects public consultations, it might be useful to imagine EU governance as a triangular interplay between the Commission, the Parliament, and the Council. The rules of their interactions are guided by the following cycle of EU norm creation. The Parliament and the Council are vested with legislative powers, but the Commission is exclusively empowered with the right to draft legislation that member states, relying on the Commission's implementation measures and guidelines, are required to apply.

In this norm-creation cycle, the separation of executive and legislative powers is often blurred. The Commission (the EU executive, which is often referred to as the European administrative authority)[3] has, in accordance with the EU and EC treaties,[4] a virtual monopoly over the right to initiate legislation within areas of Community competence.[5] This positions the Commission in the spotlight of our research. Due to its right of initiative, the Commission is particularly interested in inputs from all stakeholders, including citizens as individuals, firms, organized interest groups, representative organizations, and nongovernmental organizations in general. This directly stems from the EU legal framework, which states that "The Commission should . . . consult widely before proposing legislation and, wherever appropriate, publish consultation documents."[6] When developing and implementing EU policies, therefore, the Commission is committed to an inclusive consultation approach. Public consultations are the Commission's preferred method of involving the general public in policy shaping as well as in testing its policy proposals. As expressed by the Commission:

By fulfilling its duty to consult, the Commission ensures that its proposals are technically viable, practically workable and based on a bottom-up approach. In other words, good consultation serves a double purpose by helping to improve the quality of the policy outcome and at the same time enhancing the involvement of interested parties and the public at large.[7]

To ensure that EU policies are thoroughly balanced and in sync with all relevant EU interests, the Commission conducts public consultations in all stages of its policy development.[8] In this policy making cycle, two main consultation models can be identified—public consultations conducted (1) in the process of drafting legislation[9] to be proposed for adoption to the Council of the European Union and to the European Parliament and (2) in the process of developing subsidiary legislation (implementing measures) under the Commission's practice of comitology. Although both consultation models were designed to support the Commission's legitimacy, they differ considerably regarding the rules of public engagement and consultation procedures.

The Commission's Role in Drafting Legislative Proposals

To identify the features that most affect public consultations in these two consultation models, we must first explore how the Commission treats public consultations in its norm-creation processes.[10] Imagine that the EU is presented with a question about whether, in the name of public health, the transfat content of commercially prepared food should be regulated.[11] In accordance with the EU and the EC treaties, the Commission first addresses this issue by drafting a legislative proposal and presenting this proposal to the Parliament and the Council for adoption.

The impulse to legislate the transfat content of commercially prepared food could come from a number of various actors in addition to the Commission itself. Other European institutions,[12] the member states, stakeholders, lobbyists, and even civil society in general[13] could all play initiative roles in this process.[14] As made clear by the Commission's White Paper on European Governance: "[The] quality of . . . EU policy depends on ensuring wide participation throughout the policy chain—from conception to implementation."[15] Because the adoption of a proposal depends on how well the Commission balances competing EU interests, the Commission needs to undertake several steps to ensure wide consultations with all relevant stakeholders.

To start the drafting, the Commission prepares a preliminary policy analysis in the form of a white paper. In preparing such a preliminary policy analysis, the directorate general (DG) responsible might begin an introductory and informal consultation with selected experts and the member states. To gather additional information, the Commission also conducts various meetings with stakeholders from both public and private sectors, including representatives from the European institutions.

Wider public consultations begin as soon as the intention to legislate the issue in question would appear on the Commission agenda as part of either an annual policy strategy or the work program.[16] Accompanying the work program, a brief account of the matter under development is presented in the Commission roadmap, and a preliminary policy and impact analysis of potential economic, social, and environmental impacts can be conducted at this time.[17] In the roadmap, the Commission presents and circulates its plan for the impact assessment required for the proposal,[18] including a framework for the planned consultations and the necessary involvement of experts. The responsible directorate general presents the likely effects of each policy option and indicates which effects may warrant further analysis, including who is likely to be affected by the new policy. At this point, the Commission might also set up an interservice steering group, which is compulsory for all issues of a cross-cutting nature.

Next, interested parties are consulted, and expertise is collected. To launch a well-balanced consultation plan, the responsible directorate general identifies the objective of the consultation, the elements of the impact assessment for which consultation is necessary, the target groups, the appropriate consultation tools, and the appropriate time for consultations. Broader public consultations are conducted through the Commission's centrally managed Web portal, called Your Voice in Europe. This offers the public an opportunity to participate in the consultations through a series of structured inquiries, posing questions about their preferences on the transfat regulation. In addition, for those who desire to participate in a more discursive manner, access to a free-form posting system is provided. These online consultations are open for a minimum period of six weeks.

In accordance with well-established practice, the Commission also can approach those deemed to be stakeholders. In this case, ad hoc consultation is conducted with selected European and national-level participants. Furthermore, to support a more systematic dialog with representatives of regional and local authorities, the Commission can elicit an opinion from the responsible advisory group, standing committee, or established European authority. In the case of regulating the transfat content of commercially prepared foods, for example, the Commission could elicit an opinion from its Advisory Group on the Food Chain and Animal and Plant Health and its Standing Committee on the Food Chain and Animal Health. Because transfat content in food addresses public health and consumer safety, the Directorate General for Health and Safety (DG SANCO) might further request a scientific opinion from the European Food Safety Authority (EFSA).[19] To ensure the accountability, plurality, and integrity of the expertise used, the directorate general throughout this process sets the scope and objectives of the experts' involvement, and all documents related to the gathered data are made public.

Afterwards, the directorates general for legal service and for the budget are consulted. Pending their approval, the impact analysis is carried out, and its results are submitted into an interservice consultation. Then, an explanatory memorandum for the proposal is prepared presenting the reasons for the proposed legislation, including the extended impact assessment report. The public is informed of the influence that consultations had in the process of drafting the proposal. At this point, the responsible directorate general also justifies the proposal's relevance with regard to the EU principles of subsidiarity and proportionality.[20] In addition, the financial and budgetary implications affecting the EU, its member states, business sector, and citizens are presented and explained at this time.

Only after all these requirements are met and the explanatory memorandum is made public can the proposal finally be submitted to the College of Commissioners for approval and proposed to the Council and the Parliament for adoption.[21]

Although public consultations are officially regarded as a vital part of EU norm-creation, the Parliament and the Council remain responsible for deciding the fate of legislative proposals. In this process, consultations of interested parties can only "supplement and never replace the procedures and decisions of legislative bodies which possess democratic legitimacy; only the Council and Parliament, as co-legislators, can take responsible decisions on the context of legislative procedures."[22] The guiding principle for the consultations conducted by the Commission is therefore "to give interested parties a voice, but not a vote."[23]

Creating Administrative Measures under the Delegated Implementing Powers

To enable their correct application, adopted legal instruments often require further detailing. This often is left to member states. At the level of the EU, however, the means of achieving compliance may be left for specification through Commission "implementing measures." For example, the Commission Regulation can lay down detailed rules for the application of the regulation of the European Parliament and of the Council. In this process, the Commission has a prerogative to design appropriate measures for smooth implementation of the general principles set by the underlying legislation itself. To make things somewhat confusing, many legislative acts in the European Union are formally called regulations, and implementing measures undertaken by the Commission also are generally referred to as regulations.[24]

Usually, the adopted regulations delegate the authority to regulate relevant topics to the Commission with provisions that stipulate the essential elements of the powers thus conferred. In such cases, the

Commission's authority to implement new policy is normally carried out through the so-called comitology process in which decisions are made through a formal process of consulting member states.[25] In this process, the Commission exercises its delegated legislative powers through its various comitology committees.

In comparison to the process of drafting legislative proposals for directives and regulations, the comitology process is characterized by a significantly lower degree of consultative openness. Here, the general public has limited opportunities to influence the process of drafting implementing measures. The decisions subjected to comitology usually do not appear in the Commission annual policy strategies or work programs, and there is no formal requirement for the consultations to be launched via the Internet. Although the comitology committee meetings may be preceded by public notice, in practice the attendance is usually limited to the committee members and the invited experts. In this process, an impact assessment of the implementing measures is often not even required. Consequently, the decision on how to draft implementing measures rests not on the public but rather on the preferences laid down by the invited experts, member states, and preselected stakeholders.

To illustrate this considerable lack of consultative openness, we should return to our imaginary case of regulating the transfat content of commercially prepared food. Let us presume that the underlying regulation governing transfat issues would, for example, require a system of prior authorization for all related substances, products, or processes, providing that "the implementing rules for the application of this article shall be established by the Commission." In this case, when the request for authorization of a product containing transfat is submitted (either at the member-state level or to the Commission directly), the Commission would first have to request the European Food Safety Authority (EFSA) to provide its scientific opinion. At this stage, a risk assessment would be prepared, and scientific and technical evaluation would be undertaken. The EFSA scientific opinion would then serve as the scientific basis for the drafting and adoption of the community implementing measures.

After obtaining the scientific opinion and risk assessment, the Commission's internal services would have to submit the drafted implementing measures to the comitology committee. This committee would comprise a number of member state representatives qualified in this particular field and would be chaired by a nonvoting representative of the Commission. Under this Committee, the implementing measures would then be prepared in accordance with the regulatory procedure. After a draft was placed before it, the comitology committee would deliberate on it and deliver its opinion by majority voting. If the envisioned measures would be in compliance with the opinion of the comitology committee, the Commission would adopt them, and they would come into force routinely.[26] In accordance with established Commission practice, wider public consultations would not be a part of this process.

ICT Resources for the Commission's Norm-Creation Processes

Guided by both internal and external forces, the European Commission has developed a rich tradition of public consultations. Until recently, these consultations varied substantially across different directorates general. Each of the Commission departments essentially developed its own internal method for consulting its respective interested parties and stakeholders, making the Commission's consultation practices inconsistent, nontransparent, and complex.

To enable more efficient consultations with outside interest parties, the Commission acknowledged the need to make public consultations more open and transparent. Information and communication technology (ICT) was quickly recognized as a vital mechanism for supporting these endeavors. Its potential promised "to improve governance by using the Internet for collecting and analyzing reactions in the marketplace for use in the European Union's policy making process."[27] Accordingly, ICT would be employed "to evaluate existing EU policies and assess their impacts," "for open consultations on new initiatives," and "to respond more quickly and accurately to the demands of citizens, consumers and business," all with the objective to make EU policy making "more transparent, comprehensive and effective."[28]

The Interactive Policy Making Initiative

The first clear indication that the Commission was considering employing ICT to facilitate its consultation practices came with the Interactive Policy Making Initiative. In 2001, the Commission launched this initiative to widen opportunities for stakeholders to actively participate in the EU policy shaping. With the aim "to use modern technologies, particularly the Internet, to allow both Member State administrations and EU institutions to understand the needs of citizens and enterprises better"

(European Commission 2007), the initiative opened a new area for wide public consultation.

In employing digital ICT, the Commission envisioned wider, more consistent, and more structured consultations with stakeholders. Its goal was to increase transparency of European policy making and—by making consultations more open, transparent, and effective—to provide greater accountability to the people. Following these principles, the Commission expressed the need to build a framework for consultation that would be "coherent, yet flexible enough to take account of the specific requirements of all the diverse interests, and of the need to design appropriate consultation strategies for each policy proposal."[29] In using ICT to collect and analyze impulses from the marketplace, the goal was to make the EU more quickly and accurately responsive to the needs of citizens, consumers, and business.

The Interactive Policy Making Initiative sprouted two Web-based mechanisms that were designed to facilitate public consultation. To allow "more rapid and targeted responses to emerging issues and problems" (IDABC 2007), a special feedback mechanism was first launched in 2000. This Web-based project was to collect inputs from a group of three hundred preselected participants or contact points, such as Info Centers, the European Consumer Centers, and the Citizens Signpost Service. In 2001, another Web-based project, called Your Voice in Europe, was launched.[30] Designed as a single access point to Commission consultations, Your Voice in Europe was developed to facilitate much wider consultations to provide a structured and predictable consultation interface, support and promote wider consultation with all stakeholders and interested parties, and improve the assessment of the effects of policies. These aims would be accomplished through easy-to-use and straightforward online questionnaires, providing respondents with easier participation models and the Commission with more tangible inputs to analyze.

To facilitate well-structured and efficient public consultations that allow all interested parties to voice their opinion, the Commission adopted its Communication on General Principles and Minimum Standards for Consultation.[31] Themselves a product of public consultation, these principles and standards, in force since 2003, provide a general framework for public consultations, unifying consultation practices across different directorates general. Participation, openness, accountability, effectiveness, and coherence of consultation were recognized as the Commission's guiding principles[32] and applied in public consultation practices.

Online Consultation Practices and Open Issues

The European Commission is committed to applying the General Principles and Minimum Standards to all consultations on its major policy proposals and green papers.[33] Public consultations are launched on the Your Voice in Europe portal, usually providing the public with questionnaires divided into sections that ask general questions on, for example, strategic approach, key enablers for the proposed policy, and critical success factors. More detailed questions might also be included. From the outset, a summary of the context, scope, and objectives of consultation is presented, including a description of specific issues open for discussion or questions with particular importance for the Commission. The respondents are usually offered the choice of multiple answers that they select by ticking. Apart from offering multiple-choice answers, the consultations are usually structured in a way that allows users to give additional comments in the form of free text. The available space for free text might be limited, but participants are encouraged to give further extensive comments via e-mail.

For each consultation, a special public consultation paper is prepared. Such papers are used as tools to explore the views of interested parties on a preliminary proposal. Generally, they state that "the suggestions contained in this document do not prejudge the form and content of any future proposal by the European Commission." Their objective is to explain the basics of the ongoing consultation—the purpose of consultation, the people who are consulted, and the ways that the public can participate.

In 2008, the Commission announced its commitment to reinforce its endeavors to unify consultation practices with the European Transparency Initiative. In it, the Commission communicated its decision to develop a standardized consultation template for all consultations with directorates general. A model template is to be used for all public consultations launched via the Web pages of the competent directorates general and linked to the Your Voice in Europe portal. In addition, a systematic link between the recently launched Register of Representative Interests and the ongoing public consultation is to be opened. This will automatically inform all unregistered entities about the registration requirements and allow them to register when they make their submission to the consultation. The need for registration is well aligned with the Commission's need to identify the roles of respondents (for example, citizens or organizations, public authorities or private sector) and assess their submissions.

Although the Your Voice in Europe portal provides access to consultations by particular policy areas (such as agriculture, customs, or the environment) and specific target groups (such as stakeholders, general public, competent authorities, or any combination of those), a subscription to electronic notice (either for specific policy areas or specific target-group categories) is not provided. Your Voice in Europe provides remarkably limited possibilities for automatic notifications. Although it is reasonable to assume that such a service could contribute considerably to the Commission's objective of including a wide range of EU stakeholders in its policy-shaping activities,[34] no service to receive a notice when matters of interests are posted is offered, nor is it possible to register for a rich site summary (RSS) feed via Your Voice in Europe. This lack of notification services is surprising considering the otherwise well-established practice of subscribing to RSS feeds in the work of the directorates general and the Commission administration. For example, subscribing to the Commission's portal on the information society[35] enables users to receive newsroom e-mail updates as well as RSS feeds on all Commission policies and activities related to the information society, irrespective of the internal Commission department or directorate general that is responsible for them. What is more, the information society portal allows its users to specify the categories of RSS feeds they want to receive according to the type of news, themes, or information society policies or activities in which they are interested. These practices make the lack of Your Voice in Europe notification services even more conspicuous.

Online Access to Documents

The Your Voice in Europe portal provides direct access to the documents under consultation as well as access to the accompanying information material, including reports, studies, and general information documents on Community objectives and policies. The underlying legal framework for public access to documents is provided by article 255 of the Treat Establishing the European Community (TEC)[36] and implemented through Regulation (EC) No. 1049/2001.[37] Following this regulation, the Commission made available online access to all official texts of its COM documents[38] (since 1999) and official journals (since 1998).

In addition, the Commission is required to provide access to its unpublished documents, either through a register of documents or following individual requests.[39] Under these provisions, the Commission must make available a reference to related documentation (including, where applicable, the Commission's supporting documents) and also to other information relevant to public consultation (such as the details of any pertinent hearings, meetings, or conferences, all in electronic form).

In spring 2008, the Commission proposed some amendments to the Regulation on Public Access to European Parliament, Council, and Commission Documents.[40] Stemming from six years of experiences with Regulation (EC) No. 1049/2001, the Commission determined that the implementation of the right of public access to documents was in need of revision. Regarding online public consultations, the revised article 12 is of special interest. Its provisions were redrafted to propose a legal basis for direct public access to all preparatory documents relating to legal acts, addressing the need for active online dissemination.[41] With this, registers and Web sites could be made more comprehensive and easier to access from the outset, providing public consultations with even more transparency.

Until such active dissemination is put into action, another ICT-facilitated database can be of use to those interested in gathering information relevant to the ongoing public consultation. A database on interinstitutional procedures called PreLex was designed by the Commission to allow its users to monitor and follow the Commission's official documents (including proposals, recommendations, and communications) throughout the different stages of the EU decision making process. On this Web site, people can gather information on the stage that any legislative act currently occupies, decisions of the institutions and services responsible, and references to relevant documents. The PreLex Web site can be easily searched and has links to electronic texts that are undergoing decision making processes. As in the case of the Your Voice in Europe portal, one cannot register to receive automatic updates about preselected subjects of interest.

Transparency

According to its official policy, the Commission is committed to openness and transparency in public consultations, and there are imperatives for both the legitimacy and accountability of the EU. The need to ensure transparency stems from numerous sources: "The Union must be open to public scrutiny and accountable for its work. This requires a high level of openness and transparency. It should [always] be clear how the Union has reached a decision."[42]

Two kinds of information are of particular interest when it comes to the transparency of public consultations—who is consulted and how the submitted inputs from either citizens or experts affect the decision making. To address these issues, the Commission in 2000 first launched Consultation, the European Commission and Civil Society (CONECCS), a voluntary database providing information on structured consultative bodies and expert groups advising the Commission. This database was used as a source of information for both the Commission and the general public. It includes trade unions, employers' federations, NGOs, consumer groups, organizations representing social and economic players, charities, and community-based organizations.

In June 2008, CONECCS was replaced with the Voluntary Register of Interest Representatives.[43] With the objective "to increase transparency through reinforced application of the Commission's consultation standards based, in particular, on a standard website for internet consultations,"[44] this register provides a more structured framework for the activities of interest representatives. A user-friendly Web interface allows online registration, and all interest representatives engaged in influencing the EU decision making are invited to register. The public has open access to the register, which essentially contributes to a high level of transparency, effectively opening the Commission's work to public scrutiny.[45]

In addition to interest representatives, engaged experts may also significantly shape the final outcome of consultation.[46] The Commission openly admits that "the interplay between policy-makers, experts, interested parties and the public at large is a crucial part of policy making."[47] It is clear that decisions regarding the stakeholders to be consulted and the experts to be engaged may significantly shape the results of a policy making process. The ways in which issues are framed, experts selected, and evidence is handled all play their part. Even with the empirical sciences, the interpretation of results may notably vary from one consulted expert to another.[48]

The independence of expert advice is increasingly put into question. To support the transparency of its consultations with experts, the Commission adopted guidelines for the collection and use of expertise.[49] In effect since 2002, these guidelines were set up "to establish a sound knowledge base for better policies" and "to uphold the Commission's determination that the process of collecting and using expert advice should be credible."[50] To ensure plurality, integrity, and credibility of the expertise used (and therefore also the legitimacy of its work), the Commission is committed to an open approach when seeking and acting on advice from experts. To give a transparent overview of the advisory bodies, an online Register of Expert Groups[51] was established.

To ensure transparency of decision making, all directorates general are required to publish collected expert advice online at a single access point.[52] An explanatory note on the policy issue and the use of expert advice must be published, including criteria for selecting the experts, the names of experts consulted,[53] their declarations of interest, and a summary record of any meetings held and advice given, including dissenting views. Furthermore, the directorates general must indicate if and how the collected advice was used in decision making. They are required to maintain a record of the whole process, including terms of reference and the main contributions of different experts.

In the process of public consultation, other contributions must also be made public and published on the Internet. Contributions received are published on the Your Voice in Europe portal in the language in which they are submitted, including the authors' names, unless respondents indicate a wish to remain anonymous or request that their entire contribution be treated as confidential. The Commission is further required to acknowledge the receipt of the submissions, either by collective or individual acknowledgment (either by e-mail or on the Your Voice in Europe portal). In practice, both methods are exercised, depending on the number of comments received and the resources available.[54]

The Commission is also required to provide adequate feedback to responding parties and to the public at large. The Commission must analyze the results of consultation and prepare a summary report. The Commission's main mechanism for providing feedback to participants is through an official Commission document approved by the College of Commissioners; this is the explanatory memorandum accompanying each legislative proposal. Additional feedback may be provided in communications following the consultation process and in the impact assessment reports.[55] In general, for reasons of incompatibility with the principle of effectiveness in decision making, the Commission decided to avoid the idea of providing feedback on an individual basis. Instead, general results of public consultations are published on the directorates general Web sites linked to the Your Voice in Europe portal, including explanations of how consultations were conducted and how the results were taken into account.

In this comment-assessment process, no provisions address the question of how mass-campaign submissions (such as mass mailings or preformulated letters) are to be assessed as compared with more substantive and individualized inputs. However, it is implied that the Commission is capable of proportional and just evaluation of the inputs. This is supported by the requirement for identification from all those wishing to participate and further reinforced by the Commission's requirement to publish contributions and to produce explanations of how different views are taken into account. Nevertheless, not all contributions have been published on the Internet, and the Commission admitted to "cases of insufficient feedback on how comments received via consultations were or were not taken into account in the final policy proposal from the Commission."[56] Accordingly, clear rules on how these questions are tackled could promote the transparency of the whole consultation process.

The Your Voice in Europe portal does not support public consultations as a two-way process. The provisions on publishing public contributions and required feedback indicate that Commission consultations, as conducted via the portal, are designed to support only a one-way stream of input. This may also be evident from the Commission's definition of consultation, which refers to, according to the minimum standards, "those processes through which the Commission wishes to trigger input from outside interested parties for the shaping of policy prior to a decision by the Commission." Additional public deliberation on the comments submitted is therefore not envisioned as an integral part of the consultation process.

Anonymity versus Identification

For consultation to be meaningful and credible, it is "essential to spell out who participated."[57] On the Your Voice in Europe portal, the Commission introduced different mechanisms for identifying individual respondents and those representing organized interests. In each consultation, the specific role of the participant is identified. Generally, the respondents may choose to answer the consultation questions in the role of a citizen as individual or, for example, on behalf of an organization or public authority. A privacy statement explains which personal information will be collected (for example, name, company or organization, email address, telephone number, and country of participant), for what purpose, and through which technical means.[58] This information helps to identify the respondents, particularly in case of multiple replies, and to allow them to be recontacted if clarification on the information supplied is needed. With such data, the Commission can also get an idea of the profiles of stakeholders interested in a specific policy field, and the information gathered may aid interpretation of the results of the consultation, allowing those results to be considering in light of various respondents' attributes (such as by country of residence). In general, the contact data may also be used for inviting the relevant organizations and individuals to a future experts meeting or public hearing. Nevertheless, the respondents are entitled to decline future contact.

To identify a respondent, the Your Voice in Europe system uses session "cookies." These cookies are put in place to ensure communication between the client and the server, and they are not intended to collect any personal or confidential information or any user's Internet protocol address. They are configured in a way that allows them to expire after the session has been terminated.

As a rule, collected personal data remain in the database until the results of a consultation have been completely analyzed. After they have been usefully exploited, the submissions are rendered anonymous, usually no later than three to five years from the end of the consultation, as indicated by the privacy statement in each case.

The Timeframe for Consultation and Its Limits

When setting time limits for consultation, the objective is to strike a reasonable balance between providing adequate opportunities for the participants to offer their inputs and facilitating effective and timely decision making. According to the minimum standards, the Commission is required "to provide sufficient time for planning and responses to invitations and written contributions." As a guideline, the Commission must strive to allow at least eight weeks for the reception of responses to written public consultations.[59] This minimum consultation period was set in response to many interest organizations arguing that European and transnational associations could require more time to consult their membership and submit consolidated viewpoints for consideration. Furthermore, when dealing with issues that are cross-disciplinary and cross-national, even more time might be required.

To offer a reasonable compromise, the minimum standards have the possibility that the minimum of eight weeks may be prolonged to take into account requirements related either to the content of a proposal or the nature of the participants.[60] On the other hand, the consultation period may also be shortened. This applies to cases deemed urgent and cases in which participants have already had ample opportunities to consolidate and express their preferences.

The Legal Nature of the Minimum Standards for Consultation

Although they set important guidelines for public consultation, neither the general principles nor the minimum standards are legally binding. Instead, these guidelines were adopted in the form of a Commission communication, a policy document that does not permit judicial review. Although confronted with the risk of not being able to ensure consistency in consultations due to a lack of legal enforceability, the Commission decided that this approach was nonetheless more appropriate to avoid "a situation in which a Commission proposal could be challenged in the Court on the grounds of alleged lack of consultation with interested parties."[61] With this reasoning, the Commission declined requests to adopt legally binding rules, arguing that such an approach would be "overlegalistic" and "incompatible with the need for timely delivery of policy." In addition, the Commission was of the opinion "that improvement of its consultation practice should not be based on a 'command and control' approach but rather on providing the appropriate guidance and assistance to Commission officials in charge of running the consultation processes."[62]

Even so, to ensure consistency in its consultation processes, many believe that a legally binding instrument would provide more predictability and coherence to the Commission's consultative practices. Although, under the current regime, all directorates general are required to follow guidelines set by the Commission, the participants in fact have little leverage to ensure their right to participate and the right to be consulted.

The Multilingual Challenge

The European multilingual challenge is undoubtedly complex. In the EU, there are currently twenty-three official languages, yet, as of 2009, the Your Voice in Europe portal offers access in only eleven different languages. Although the Commission is required to provide translations of all official documents to all EU languages,[63] public consultations do not fall under these requirements.

This situation puts considerable constraints on the consultation process, and it is easy to imagine the difficulties that citizens have when participating in a foreign language. The first challenge is therefore the question of translation. Preparing translations presents a practical constraint, inevitably delaying the process of making available relevant information and documents online.

Here the dilemma is whether no material should be published until it is available in all EU languages or whether the original version be published immediately and translations provided later on. From the beginning, the handling of this dilemma has been guided by the desire to balance between the need for swift publication and the availability of translation resources. To support timely publication, a special approach to multilingualism allowing limited language mixing on the EU Web sites was adopted.[64] All top-level pages are available in all EU languages, and subsites may continue to be available only in a limited number. When deciding whether to publish documents in different languages, speed of publication is prioritized. The directorates general must immediately publish all required documents in their source language and add translations when available.[65] In addition, to provide citizens with efficient and easy-to-use access to information, directorates general are required to provide translations of all main documents, at least in their summary form, as quickly as possible.

The Your Voice in Europe Discussions

The Your Voice in Europe portal also facilitates public discussions. Yet these have to be distinguished from public consultations as conducted in the Commission's process of norm creation. They are broader and less specific in nature. Online forums focus mainly on general issues (such as the future of the EU or multilingualism) and offer citizens the opportunity to discuss issues directly with leading figures and to exchange views with other citizens interested in the same topics. These online discussions are not fully consultative in their nature. Although they may advance the democratic flow of information, they do not fall within the category of public consultation as it is most strictly understood.

Conclusion

This chapter has attempted to elucidate both the institutional and normative context in which public-policy consultations occur in the European Union. Delving into the EU institutional and legal framework, we see a host of objectives set out for supporting public consultations. The European Commission is increasingly committed to an all-inclusive consultation approach. Indeed, the Commission was among the first to recognize the Internet as an efficient facilitator of more open and transparent consultation. Today, online consultations are being viewed as the Commission's preferred method for involving the general public in both norm creation and the testing of policy proposals.

At the same time, the Commission's goal to increase its transparency and accountability by making consultations more open, transparent, and effective has yet to be achieved fully. The current trend of staging online consultations as predominately one-way communication streams for gathering inputs still has a long way to go before it can be regarded as a two-way structured dialog. In moving toward a genuinely deliberative process, problems of dealing with the volume of public contributions will become even more prominent, and a balanced evaluation of inputs yet more complicated. The question of multilingualism also looms large and awaits its solution. So far, these issues have remained largely untested in the EU. Yet addressing these concerns is likely to be of vital importance for the future of the European democracy.

Notes

1. For an analysis of consultations within the EU at the local level, see chapter 4 in this volume.

2. Although the representative model best describes the European Parliament (the elected representative of the citizens of Europe), the participative model presumably supports the legitimacy of the European Commission.

3. See Weiler (1999).

4. See consolidated versions of the Treaty on European Union and of the Treaty Establishing the European Community, December 29, 2006, 2006 O.J. (C321) 1.

5. According to the Treaty Establishing the European Community—see Consolidated Version of the Treaty Establishing the European Community, December 24, 2002, 2002 O.J. (C 325) 33 (hereinafter TEC)—the Commission has a near monopoly to propose legislation. For all matters in the first pillar (that is, European Communities), the Commission is the only one entitled to propose legislation. The exemptions to this monopoly rule are rather small in proportion. They refer mainly to the third pillar (that is, police and judicial cooperation in criminal matters), where both the Commission and the member states have the right of initiative.

6. Protocol No. 30 to the Amsterdam Treaty on the Application of the Principles of Subsidiarity and Proportionality, October 2, 1997, 1997 O.J. (C340) 105.

7. Commission Communication Toward a Reinforced Culture of Consultation and Dialogue: Proposal for General Principles and Minimum Standards for

Consultation of Interested Parties by the Commission, at 5, COM (2002) 277 final (June 5, 2002).

8. Public consultations are a vital element of EU policy making that supplements the EU's need for an efficient balancing of diverse national preferences where questions of comparison, harmonization, validation, and interoperability often play a key role.

9. Although it may be argued that legislative drafting does not constitute administrative policy making in the ordinary sense, the way in which the European Commission develops legislative proposals makes its legislative drafting activity an especially important vehicle for the administration to engage Europeans in a wide-ranging policy making process. For example, such a drafting process may start when the Commission publishes a green paper, a policy document designed to stimulate consultation on given topics at European level. Such consultations often give rise to actual legislative drafting. In such cases, the Commission then outlines the developments in another form of policy document, the white paper, thus creating yet another preparatory instrument in its legislative cycle. The fact that all the above processes are conducted under the Commission, the EU chief executive body, makes the EU legislative drafting process unusual.

10. See Strauss, Smith, and Bergkamp (2006).

11. For practical examples of various consultation practices, see Dabrowska (2007). To convey the complexity of EU practices, I have created what in 2009 is a hypothetical policy making episode and synthesized the relevant aspects of law and administration as they also appear in 2009. At least some of these details will surely have changed by 2011, when this chapter appears in print.

12. Although they do not have the right to propose legislation, both Parliament and Council may influence the initiation of a legislative proposal. For example, according to TEC article192, the Parliament may, acting by a majority of its members, ask the Commission to submit any appropriate proposal on matters on which it considers that a Community act is required for the purpose of implementing the treaty. Similar provisions, TEC article 208, refer to the role of the Council. The Council may ask the Commission to undertake any studies the Council considers desirable for the attainment of common objectives and to submit to it any appropriate proposals.

13. Were the Treaty of Lisbon—Treaty of Lisbon amending the Treaty on European Union and the Treaty establishing the European Community, December 13, 2007, 2007 O.J. (C 306) 1—to come into force, citizens would be given the right to directly invite the Commission to propose certain legislation. In this manner, for example, the Treaty Establishing Constitution for Europe—December 16, 2004, 2004 O.J. (C 310) 47 (hereinafter Constitution for Europe)—suggested that a million or more citizens, nationals of "significant number of Member States," may "take the initiative of inviting the Commission . . . to submit any appropriate proposal on matters where citizens consider that a legal act of the Union is required."

14. See House of Lords, EU Committee 2008, 9–10: "The Treaties set out the general competences of the institutions and govern only the basic principles of

the operation of the specific legislative procedures," whereas "the actual process is ad hoc, unconstrained by formal rules, and characterized by informal institutional practice and various channels of consultation and cooperation."

15. Commission White Paper on European Governance, COM (2001) 428 final (July 25, 2001) (hereinafter Commission White Paper on European Governance).

16. According to the Commission Rules of Procedure—2000 O.J. (L 308) 26, as last amended by Commission Decision (EC) No. 65/2007 of June 2, 2007, 2007 O.J. (L 32) 144—each term the Commission has to establish, after entering into office, its five-year strategic plan. To realize the plan's objectives, each year the Commission adopts an annual policy strategy (APS) that defines political priorities and key initiatives for the following year. To reach institutional agreement, the Commission then presents the APS to the Council and the European Parliament. Based on the results of such interinstitutional dialog, the Commission determines its plan of decision by adopting a work program, setting out major political priorities, and identifying the legislative initiatives, executive acts, and other acts that it intends to adopt for the realization of the APS priorities. For more, see http://ec.europa.eu/atwork/index_en.htm.

17. Although the usual practice of the directorates general indicates that the preliminary impact assessment would most likely be carried out through an internal interdepartmental consultation, the directorate general might also, on its own initiative, decide to start wider preliminary consultations. Should a directorate general deem that its proposal would require an in-depth assessment, such preliminary consultation might precede even the APS announcement.

18. The impact assessment, now required for every proposal, was first introduced to identify and assess the problem at stake; to recognize likely effects of the proposed policy in the economic, environmental and social fields; and to outline the advantages and disadvantages of each solution. It was designed primarily to assist political decision making. Thus, it is easy enough to imagine its considerable effects on the consultation process. See also European Commission (2010).

19. The Economic and Social Committee might also provide an opinion. For example, see Opinion of the European Economic and Social Committee on Animal Welfare: Labeling, 2007 O.J. (C 161) 17.

20. According to these principles, the Commission may propose legislation only if it is more effective to do so on the EU level and would regulate only with the intensity necessary to achieve the desired objectives.

21. Draft European legislative acts sent to the European Parliament and to the Council are also forwarded to national Parliaments for scrutiny. See Protocol on the Role of the National Parliaments in the European Union, December 16, 2004, 2004 O.J. (C 310) 204. Nevertheless, established practice suggests national parliaments would not play significant role in this process.

22. European Parliament Resolution on the Commission White Paper on European Governance, European Parliament Document A5 399 (2001).

23. Commission Communication, Toward a Reinforced Culture of Consultation and Dialogue: General Principles and Minimum Standards for Consultation of Interested Parties by the Commission, COM (2002) 704 final (December 11, 2002) (hereafter General Principles and Minimum Standards for Consultation).

24. A Commission regulation is to be distinguished from a regulation adopted by the European Parliament and the Council and from a Council regulation. Although a regulation adopted by the European Parliament and the Council (adopted through the codecisional legislative procedure that has become by far the most important procedure in legislative practice—hence, the name) is a general legal instrument of a binding nature, the Commission regulation is an administrative act prepared and adopted solely by the Commission. Its regulative power depends entirely on the authority of the relevant regulation adopted by the European Parliament and the Council or the relevant Council regulation on which it is based. For example, see Commission Regulation (EC) No. 498/2007 of March 26, 2007, laying down detailed rules for the implementation of Council Regulation (EC) No. 1198/2006 on the European Fisheries Fund.

25. See Council Decision and Standard Rules of Procedure (EC) No. 468/1999 of February 6, 2001, 2001 O.J. (C 38) 3.

26. In the event that the Commission's proposal would fail to gain support from the Comitology Committee, the Commission could no longer adopt the proposal on its own. In this case, the Commission would have to, without delay, submit the proposal to the Council and inform the Parliament of the existing situation.

27. Commission Communication on Interactive Policy Making, April 3, 2001, 2001 O.J. (C 1014).

28. Ibid.

29. General Principles and Minimum Standards for Consultation, note 23 above.

30. The creation of the Your Voice in Europe Web site reflects the Commission's clear recognition of the benefits of openness to outside inputs. The Commission's need to establish its own credibility adds to the Commission's incentives to offer considerable opportunities for public contribution. Being an unelected institution, its legitimacy cannot be considered as given. Conducting wide-range consultations with the peoples of the EU can provide the Commission with a desirable (as well as necessary) democratic character. Conducting wide public consultation therefore serves a dual purpose: it helps to improve the quality of the policy outcome and enhances the Commission's credibility and legitimacy.

31. See note 23 above.

32. To ensure that interested parties are properly heard in the Commission's policy making, the Commission adopted the following standards for conducting public consultations:

1. All communications relating to consultation should be clear and concise, and should include all necessary information to facilitate responses.

2. When defining the target group(s) in a consultation process, the Commission should ensure that relevant parties have an opportunity to express their opinions.

3. The Commission should ensure adequate awareness-raising publicity and adapt its communication channels to meet the needs of all target audiences. Without excluding other communication tools, open public consultations should be published on the Internet and announced at the "single access point."

4. The Commission should provide sufficient time for planning and responses to invitations and written contributions. The Commission should strive to allow at least 8 weeks for reception of responses to written public consultations and 20 working days notice for meetings.

5. Receipt of contributions should be acknowledged. Results of open public consultation should be displayed on Web sites linked to the single access point on the Internet. . . . Contributions to open public consultations will be made public on the single access point. Results of other forms of consultation should, as far as possible, also be subject to public scrutiny on the single access point on the Internet. The Commission will provide adequate feedback to responding parties and to the public at large.

33. Minimum standards for consultation do not apply to the formal consultation of the member states, consultation under the social dialog (TEC articles 137–139) and consultations required under international agreements.

34. Such an objective could also be reached by notifying those stakeholders registered via the Register of Interest Organization, yet citizens (as individuals) are not included in this register.

35. http://ec.europa.eu/information_society/newsroom/cf/rss-list.cfm.

36. TEC article 255:

1. Any citizen of the Union, and any natural or legal person residing or having its registered office in a Member State, shall have a right of access to European Parliament, Council and Commission documents, subject to the principles and the conditions to be defined in accordance with paragraphs 2 and 3.

2. General principles and limits on grounds of public or private interest governing this right of access to documents shall be determined by the Council, acting in accordance with the procedure referred to in Article 251 within two years of the entry into force of the Treaty of Amsterdam.

3. Each institution referred to above shall elaborate in its own Rules of Procedure specific provisions regarding access to its documents.

37. Regulation of the European Parliament and of the Council regarding public access to European Parliament, Council and Commission Documents (EC) No. 1049/2001 of May 30, 2001, 2001 O.J. (L 145) 43 (hereinafter Regulation (EC) No. 1049/2001).

38. The European Commission Register of Commission Documents defines "COM documents" as comprising "Proposed legislation and other Commission

communications to the Council and/or the other institutions, and their preparatory papers," and "Commission documents for the other institutions (legislative
proposals, communications, reports, etc.)." http://ec.europa.eu/transparency/
regdoc/aidetypesdoc.cfm?CL=en&&&.

39. The Commission has already created a register of documents plus a special
register of documents related to the work of its comitology committees.

40. Commission Proposal for a Regulation of the European Parliament and of
the Council Regarding Public Access to European Parliament, Council and Commission Documents, COM (2008) 229 final (April 30, 2008).

41. TEC article 12:

> 1. Documents drawn up or received in the course of procedures for the adop-
> tion of EU legislative acts or non-legislative acts of general application shall,
> subject to arts. 4 and 9, be made directly accessible to the public.
>
> 2. Where possible, other documents, notably documents relating to the devel-
> opment of policy or strategy, shall be made directly accessible in electronic
> form.

42. Commission Communication on Strategic Objectives 2005–2009, Europe
2010: A Partnership for European Renewal—Prosperity, Solidarity and Security,
COM (2005) 12 final (January 26, 2005).

43. https://webgate.ec.europa.eu/transparency/regrin/welcome.do?locale=en.

44. Commission Communication on European Transparency Initiative: A
Framework for Relations with Interest Representatives (Register and Code of
Conduct), COM (2008) 323 final (May 27, 2008).

45. After more than a year since its launch, there are currently more than two
thousand interest representatives in the register (data from October 2009), yet
there is still a long way to go before the majority of organizations participating
in the Commission's consultations will actually be registered. For more, see
European Commission Register for Interest Representatives (2010).

46. The Commission requires strong expertise to ensure that EU policies have a
sound knowledge base. With this objective, the Commission maintains a high
level of in-house expertise. When required, the Commission may additionally
call on external specialists in different fields to provide advice.

47. Commission Communication on the Collection and Use of Expertise by the
Commission: Principles and Guidelines, "Improving the Knowledge Base for
Better Policies," COM (2002) 713 final (December 11, 2002). These issues were
further addressed by the Commission White Paper on European Governance (see
note 21 above).

48. This is especially notorious when addressing controversial issues. For
example, when regulating BSE, or mad-cow disease, the Commission was confronted "by a panoply of conflicting expert opinions coming variously from
within the academic world, from those with practical knowledge, and from those
with direct stakes in the policy issue." Ibid.

49. Ibid.

50. Ibid.

51. Available at http://ec.europa.eu/transparency/regexpert.

52. General Principles and Minimum Standards for Consultation, note 23 above, at 20.

53. According to the Commission: "It may be appropriate, in some circumstances, to withhold the identity of experts, for example, to protect them against undue external pressures or to protect the legitimate interests of those concerned with the process. Any embargo on the identity of experts should normally be limited in time, and duly justified." Commission Communication on the Collection and Use of Expertise by the Commission: Principles and Guidelines—Improving the Knowledge Base for Better Policies, at 18, COM (2002) 713 final (December 11, 2002), accessed December 7, 2010, http://eur-lex.europa.eu/LexUriServ/site/en/com/2002/com2002_0713en01.pdf.

54. If comments are posted on the Your Voice in Europe portal within fifteen working days, this is considered as the acknowledgment of receipt.

55. See European Commission (2010).

56. See Commission Green Paper on European Transparency Initiative, COM (2006) 194 final (May 3, 2006).

57. General Principles and Minimum Standards for Consultation, note 23 above, at 12.

58. In addition, as indicated above, organized parties are required to provide information on interests they represent as well as on inclusiveness of their representation before they participate in consultation. To support this objective, the Your Voice in Europe portal was upgraded to ask interest groups to register and fill in an electronic questionnaire about their objectives, financial situation, and the interests they represent.

59. General Principles and Minimum Standards for Consultation, note 23 above, at 21.

60. According to Standard D, a consultation period longer than eight weeks is allowed to take account of (1) the need for European or national organizations to consult their members to produce a consolidated viewpoint, (2) certain existing binding instruments (this applies, in particular, to notification requirements under the World Trade Organization agreement), (3) the specificity of a given proposal (for example, because of the diversity of the interested parties or the complexity of the issue at stake), or (4) main holiday periods.

61. General Principles and Minimum Standards for Consultation, note 23 above, at 10.

62. Ibid.

63. See Regulation (EC) No. 1049/2001, note 37 above.

64. A special internal network has already been set up to ensure consistency in linguistic practice.

65. See Commission Communication on Multilingualism: An Asset for Europe and a Shared Commitment, COM (2008) 566 final (September 18, 2008).

References

Dabrowska, Patrycja. 2007. "Civil Society Involvement in the EU Regulations on GMOs." *Journal of Civil Society* 3, no. 3:287–304.

European Commission. 2007. "What Is IPM (Interactive Policy Making)?" Accessed December 7, 2010. http://ec.europa.eu/yourvoice/ipm/index_en.htm.

European Commission. 2010. "Impact Assessment." Accessed December 7, 2010. http://ec.europa.eu/governance/impact/index_en.htm.

European Commission Register for Interest Representatives. 2010. "Statistics for Register." Accessed December 7, 2010. https://webgate.ec.europa.eu/transparency/regrin/consultation/statistics.do.

House of Lords, EU Committee. 2008. *Initiation of EU Legislation, Twenty-second Report of Session 2007–08*. London: Authority of the House of Lords.

Interoperable Delivery of European eGovernment Services to Public Administrations, Businesses, and Citizens (IDABC). 2007. "IPM: Interactive Policy Making." Accessed December 7, 2010. http://ec.europa.eu/idabc/en/document/6541/5927 .html.

Strauss, Peter, Turner T. Smith, and Lucas Bergkamp. 2006. *Norm Creation in the European Union*. Washington, DC: American Bar Association. http://www .abanet.org/adminlaw/eu/Reports_Rulemaking_06-30-06.pdf.

Weiler, Joseph H. H. 1999. *The Constitution of Europe*. Cambridge: Cambridge University Press.

15

The Legal Environment for Electronic Democracy

Peter M. Shane and Polona Pičman Štefančič

When government officials sit down to plan the possibilities for online consultation, they are likely to find that law significantly shapes their prospects for moving forward. Some of that effect will stem from relatively esoteric features of the relevant law of public administration. In the United States, for example, federal agencies are ordinarily required to get approval from the Office of Management and Budget (OMB) before they engage in the "collection of information," defined as "obtaining, . . . facts or opinions . . . for an agency . . . calling for . . . answers to identical questions posed to . . . ten or more persons, other than agencies, instrumentalities, or employees of the United States."[1] If an online consultation—even a blog—falls within this definition, then the agency is unable to move forward without an additional level of bureaucratic clearance. Fortunately—but only after considerable deliberation—OMB has concluded that blogs and similar online discussion forms do not constitute "information collections" requiring OMB preclearance, as long as they do not take the form of actual surveys comprising "specific questions or a series of specific prompts."[2]

Similarly, U.S. law imposes a series of notice, record keeping, and other administrative requirements for anything that amounts to a federal "advisory committee." Such a committee is defined as "any committee, . . . conference, panel, . . . or other similar group, . . . which is— established or utilized by one or more agencies . . . in the interest of obtaining advice and recommendations."[3] Given the administrative burdens involved, agencies may well be discouraged from designing online consultations that arguably organize members of the public in a way that resembles this definition.

Numerous other examples can be found regarding government procurement regulations. To the extent that governments use private vendors to provide the technology support for online consultations, terms of service agreements between the public and private partner may present niggling issues on topics like indemnification, the use and security of data, commercialization of the online site, and choice of law for the resolution of disputes (Shane, 2011).

The focus of this chapter, however, is on what are arguably more bedrock elements in any legal system as it shapes the nature of the relevant society's public communication environment. These elements— what people are free to say, the discretion that government has to set and enforce ground rules for communication with government, the quality of public information that is available, and the willingness of government officials to experiment with online discussion—all depend, in part, on a background patchwork of constitutional, statutory, and regulatory provisions that delineate the rights and duties of forum sponsors and participants. Together, these form an information and communication law regime that directly affects the design of government-supported online consultations and advances or reduces their capacity to transform any country's democratic discourse.

It is impossible, in the space of a chapter, to describe more than one legal regime in any detail. Yet some degree of comparative analysis is invaluable in highlighting the points on which legal regimes are likely to differ and in suggesting the multiple resolutions that are plausible with regard to contentious issues. Consequently, although our analysis focuses on the legal regime of the United States, we use brief comparisons to the European Union and its member states to bring several key issues into sharper relief. In this chapter, we survey some of the most fundamental categories of legal rules that are likely to shape e-democracy initiatives. We show how the design possibilities available for e-democracy initiatives within any jurisdiction can be shaped by the public's information and communication rights and by rules affecting the duties and liabilities of government forum sponsors and managers.

Communication Rights

The "right to take part in the government of one's country" is embedded in the Universal Declaration of Human Rights[4] and is manifested in a variety of ways in the U.S. Constitution, which guarantees rights of free speech and assembly, as well as the right to petition the government for a redress of grievances.[5] Although the European Union (EU) Charter of Fundamental Rights does not explicitly address citizens' right to participate, popular engagement in governance stands as one of the EU's major political objectives. For example, the EU i2010 eGovernment Action Plan addresses the strengthening of citizens' participation as one of its primary goals.[6]

Central to the right of participation is the right of free expression. The right of any person in the United States to speak in an online forum depends on whether government agencies—"state actors," as they are called in U.S. constitutional law—are effectively in charge of the forum. Managers of private forums may manage the information shared through their forums as they wish (e.g., Jesdanun 2008). On the other hand, government agencies at all levels—national, state, and local—are bound by the First Amendment to the United States Constitution, which generally stands as a stringent bar to government censorship in public forums.[7] On the international level, freedom of expression was embedded in the United Nations (UN) Universal Declaration of Human Rights—the "common standard of achievement for all peoples and all nations"—over sixty years ago.[8] The UN further reinforced this principle in the International Covenant on Civil and Political Rights,[9] which entered into force in 1976.

The Council of Europe has addressed freedom of expression in its European context. In 1950, the Convention for the Protection of Human Rights and Fundamental Freedoms established that "everyone has the right to freedom of expression." Fifty years later, the EU itself took this wording when adopting its Charter of Fundamental Rights of the European Union. In addition to these international obligations common to all EU member states, European constitutional traditions also play a part. For example, in Slovenia—home to one of the authors of this chapter— the constitution guarantees the freedom of expression of thought and of speech,[10] and similar provisions can also be found in other European national constitutions.

Presumably, any nation that purports to protect free expression will require government agencies that sponsor online consultations to refrain from censoring or editing comments in a way that discriminates according to the speaker's point of view. In the United States, so-called viewpoint discrimination is strongly disfavored under the First Amendment.[11] Any government practice that treats the creation, organization, or dissemination of public comments differently according to the point of view expressed is unlawful unless the relevant agency can show that the practice is narrowly tailored to achieve what American courts call a "compelling" government interest.[12] Except in special contexts, such as prisons, this is essentially impossible to show. A government agency that opens an online consultation will thus have to welcome all points of view without discrimination.

Other possible implications of the right to free expression may well differ from system to system. One point of difference may be the degree to which the right of free expression is deemed to imply a right to have one's view actually taken into account.

For example, with its Act on the Freedom of Electronic Information, Hungary has adopted provisions requiring all organizations preparing legislation to ensure "that anybody can comment on and make proposals concerning the drafts of legal regulations."[13] Such drafting authorities are legally obligated to consider the submitted comments and then to produce and publish "a summary of the comments along with an explanation for the rejection of the comments not accepted."[14]

The connection between rights of expression or participation and an obligation of government response may also affect EU states through international law, particularly in the area of environmental protection. For example, the United Nations Economic Commission for Europe (UNECE) Convention on access to information, public participation, and access to justice in environmental matters (Århus Convention),[15] approved also by the EU,[16] requires decision makers to take into account the outcome of public participation in environmental decisions.[17] This convention has provided all persons who feel their participation rights might have been impaired with the right, in the appropriate circumstances, to a review procedure under national legislation. Thus, for example, the Slovenian Constitutional Court recently annulled a decree on free-range species simply because the public participation procedure had not been appropriately addressed. The court ruled that "the legislator should, when delegating power to the executive for adopting administrative regulations . . . , also make provisions on procedural rules for efficient public participation in the process of developing these regulations."[18]

Under U.S. law, there is only an attenuated requirement for federal agencies to consider public input, even when the law otherwise commands that an agency allow public comment on an instance of proposed policy making. An opportunity for public input is a necessary feature of most significant administrative rule making that occurs pursuant to the procedural dictates of the federal Administrative Procedure Act (APA) (Strauss, chapter 13, this volume).[19] The APA is silent, however, on any requirement that those comments be considered. Whatever requirement exists has been inferred from the authority that courts enjoy, under the APA, to set aside agency action that is "arbitrary or capricious."[20] Courts have long interpreted this standard as invalidating administrative rules that agencies promulgate without responding to trenchant objections brought to the agency's attention through public comment.[21]

Although European courts may thus go further than U.S. courts in connecting the public's rights of expression with an agency's obligation to consider, the actual breadth of the noncensorship right is broader in the United States. Within narrow exceptions, U.S. agencies may not censor comments—even in a viewpoint-neutral way—on generalized grounds of social harmfulness. The United States Supreme Court, for example, has held that speech that is legally obscene is not protected under the First Amendment,[22] so comments that are obscene may be excluded from an online forum. The range of speech that falls within the definition of obscenity is very limited, however. It includes only that speech that (1) "the average person, applying contemporary community standards," would find appealing to the "prurient interest" when the speech is taken as whole; (2) depicts or describes sexual conduct in a patently offensive way that is also defined in state or federal law; and (3) lacks serious literary, artistic, political, or social value.[23] Speech that is merely indecent is constitutionally protected, whether in print or online. Thus, constitutionally protected speech, including indecent speech, can typically be regulated based on its content only to achieve a compelling governmental interest and only if the regulation is narrowly tailored to that objective. For example, even speech that seems to endorse unlawful behavior may be regulated only where the advocacy in question is "directed to inciting or producing imminent lawless action," and is likely to do so.[24]

Where European law may be more tolerant of regulation based on the social harm of individual expression is with regard to hate speech. Any limitation of speech, no matter how ostensibly justified on grounds of morality, inevitably collides with the freedom of expression, and different legal regimes tend to attach different priorities to these principles. For example, in evaluating the online sale of Nazi memorabilia, a French court ruled that such an act violates the French Criminal Code.[25] When the same case was first presented to a U.S. court, it was initially ruled that "enforcement of the French order by a United States court would be inconsistent with the First Amendment."[26]

In the EU, these issues are complicated by the fact that even the member states have not established a unified principle that suggests the legitimate balance between morality or civility and the freedom of expression. Although dissemination of racist or xenophobic material is prohibited by international law[27] and, at least in some member states, also by constitutional law, [28] such restrictions of the freedom of expression are by no means universally accepted. For example, the recently adopted EU framework decision on combating racism and xenophobia stopped short of outlawing holocaust denial because the EU member states could not reach a consensus on justified limits of the freedom of expression. Contrary to Germany, France, and others that have already criminalized such conduct, countries like Great Britain, Ireland, Denmark, and Sweden have resisted unified legislation as a violation of civil liberties (Goldirova 2007).[29] When confronted with the need to condone racist statements, they favored freedom of expression, which effectively stopped the EU from criminalizing these acts.

Nevertheless, the EU decision did set the framework for criminalizing certain acts of racism and xenophobia. EU member states are now required to adopt national legislation that will introduce criminal penalties for any "public incitement to discrimination, violence or racial hatred in respect of a group of persons or a member of such a group defined by reference to color, race, religion or national or ethnic origin."[30] All acts "publicly condoning, denying or grossly trivializing crimes of genocide, crimes against humanity and war crimes" will be punishable by imprisonment.[31] Such criminalization could well affect the tolerability of certain forms of expressions in online consultations.

It does not follow from these starting points, however, that even the U.S. government lacks all authority to shape communicative norms in an online forum. To begin with, the U.S. Supreme Court interprets the First Amendment to allow substantial government authority to regulate the "time, place, and manner" of expression even in a public forum. Time, place, and manner regulations cannot be pretextual attempts to suppress or control message content. But a regulation that is viewpoint neutral may be upheld if it is reasonable in the sense of furthering a significant government interest and not intruding unnecessarily on freedom of expression.[32] Under "time, place, and manner" doctrine, it is legally uncontroversial for government agencies in the United States to sponsor online deliberative forums that limit the length of individual messages and allow participants only a specified numbers of posts per day. Such regulations would apply equally to all messages, regardless of content, thus satisfying the requirement of viewpoint neutrality. They would uphold a significant government interest in maintaining the inclusiveness and usability of the forum. They would not limit the channels of communication, since participants could presumably include links within their posts that could take interested readers to lengthier expositions of their views.

A potentially broader legal ground on which government agencies could propose to set norms for online consultation involves the so-called public forum doctrine. The U.S. Constitution is deemed by courts to accord maximum free speech protection to places that "by long tradition or by government fiat have been devoted to assembly or debate."[33] Such places are deemed public forums in American law. Streets and parks are the paradigm examples, but nearly the same protection applies to other forums on public property that the government opens by design as places of free expressive activity.

Governments are also allowed, however, to run what are confusingly called nonpublic forums. These include new kinds of forums that are not linked by tradition or principle to the standards of maximum free speech. In such forums, despite government ownership or control, the government "may reserve the forum for its intended purposes, communicative or otherwise, as long as the regulation on speech is reasonable and not an effort to suppress expression merely because public officials oppose the speaker's view."[34] On this ground, the Supreme Court has upheld restrictions on the use of a public school's internal mailing system,[35] the solicitation of charitable contributions through a government-run charity drive,[36] and the solicitation of funds at public airports.[37] The nonpublic forum doctrine would enable governments to restrict online consultations to designated subject matter. For example, comments regarding troop deployments to Afghanistan could be excluded from an online consultation on wetlands preservation on the ground that comments on the war were irrelevant to the purpose of the forum.[38]

The more interesting and more difficult questions pertain to the government's authority to impose on online consultations a variety of viewpoint-neutral regulations aimed at creating the most constructive and inclusive deliberative forums. A government agency might well take the position that citizens are less likely to partake in an online consultation if they are worried about personally abusive or otherwise obnoxious responses. An imposition of some sort of civility norm could be enforced in a variety of ways. One mechanism—the least problematic—is a filtering system that operates through participant ratings. That is, when a message is submitted, other participants are allowed to score the message for its contribution to the conversation. Low-scoring messages are demoted automatically to the end of the thread, essentially pushing them into obscurity. In addition, site visitors are allowed to filter the messages they read according to the messages' average scores, essentially ignoring those messages that participants rate as poor (Froomkin 2004). On the expectation that uncivil comments will score badly, such measures should simultaneously create an incentive for civil expression and a penalty for breaches of deliberative norms. Because neither measure would actually prevent any communicative act by the public or involve government officials in subjective judgments of what is or is not appropriate, both seem immune to constitutional challenge.

Government agencies might be tempted to screen messages on grounds of civility.[39] An online forum rule could state that "The portions of any message that subject identifiable individuals to insult or abuse shall be deleted." An equivalent regulation of this breadth would be unconstitutional if applied to public speakers in a city park. On the other hand, similar rules are imposed routinely in a variety of government settings, such as face-to-face judicial proceedings and legislative and administrative hearings.[40] Because online consultations represent a new form of public interaction with the government, judicial application of the non-public forum doctrine to such consultations is likely to depend on the courts' contextual understanding of the nature of these interactions: is posting in an online consultation like addressing a public park or a hearing room?

In favor of its authority to regulate online discussions, a government agency could cite the Supreme Court's decision in *Perry Education Association v. Perry Local Educators Association*,[41] which upheld the right of a public school system to permit the schools' internal mail system to be used by the union that had been elected to represent the district's teachers but not by a rival union. The Court based its decision, in part, on the school district's interest in preserving "labor peace"[42] within the schools. This might be read to suggest a government authority to head off conflict within a nonpublic forum to preserve the peaceful use of that forum for its intended purposes. In a similar vein, the Court held that the federal government could preclude legal defense and political advocacy groups from participating in the government's annual fund-raising campaign on behalf of charitable agencies that provide health and welfare services directly to individuals.[43] A plurality determined that the order was reasonable in light of the government's desire "to avoid interruptions to the performance of the duties of its employees."[44]

On the other hand, direct government screening of individual posts to a deliberative forum might be regarded as an unreasonable imposition on speech. In *International Society for Krishna Consciousness v. Lee*[45] and *Lee v. International Society for Krishna Consciousness*,[46] the Court upheld the right of metropolitan airport authorities to limit the places in public airports where individuals could solicit money but overturned a ban on the sale or distribution of literature. A plurality of Justices did not think the hazards posed to "weary, harried, or hurried" travelers by potentially aggressive distributors of literature were sufficiently weighty to justify a broad suppression of communicative activity that did not itself involve inherent threats of fraud or coercion.[47] The decision upholding the restriction on solicitation was upheld narrowly based in part on the fact that governments have not created airports primarily as areas for expressive activity but rather to facilitate commercial, for-profit enterprises. But the commercial nature of airports could not justify a complete ban on literature distribution—and it is likely that courts would be yet more solicitous of expressive freedom in an online consultation space in which communication is intended to be the primary activity.

Prediction in this context is difficult not only because the relevant analogies are uncertain but because the issues posed trigger conflicting policy considerations of significant weight. On one hand, courts may appreciate online consultations as important new efforts by government to make citizen communication with the government both more accessible and more meaningful. Policing too stringently the rules that government may impose to maintain the decorum of the consultations will likely discourage government agencies from sponsoring such forums altogether. Few government sponsors are likely to welcome the risk that communications made available through government Web sites will alienate the public and discourage widespread engagement. Government officials already have some authority to limit disruptive speech as a means of preserving good order in face-to-face proceedings.[48] Perhaps an online consultation is best understood as the virtual equivalent of a real-space hearing room in which the officials in charge are empowered to cut off speakers who fail to respect viewpoint-neutral rules of decorum.

On the other hand, courts may be persuaded that preserving order in an online space to which no one is physically confined and in which one speaker's voice cannot literally drown out another's is an entirely different proposition from keeping order in a face-to-face conversation. Non-censorial alternatives like voluntary rating and filtering exist. If applicable norms are stated generally (such as a ban on inflammatory or insulting remarks) rather than specifically, they might seem to entail a degree of subjectivity in implementation that risks creating opportunities for viewpoint-based suppression. In the American legal context, these issues are likely to be sorted out only incrementally as governments experiment with interactive online discourse and challenges reach the courts. Because of the U.S. common law approach to constitutional adjudication, resolving these questions definitively through laws or regulations is not possible.

Perhaps the most important of these rather difficult issues involves the question of online identity management. Online forums generally handle identity management in one of four ways. In some privately managed forums, such as those organized by E-democracy.org, people may participate only if their posts are personally identified to them (E-democracy.org 2009). Other forums allow entirely anonymous participation. Between these poles, a forum could allow people not to disclose their offline identity but would require their chosen online identity to be stable—or at least require them to maintain more than one email account to support multiple online voices. In any such forum, someone could participate as "conlawboy1952" but would need to have all contributions identically tagged. Another approach would combine the prospect for public anonymity—actual names never appear onscreen—with private registration. To participate in the forum, an individual would have to register at least certain verifiable attributes of his or her offline identity.

It is unobjectionable legally for governments to run online forums in which people have the choice of participating anonymously or can volunteer as much or as little demographic data as possible. It likewise is unobjectionable to take measures to ensure that participants are at least authentic individuals—not "bots"—and are participating through verifiable email accounts. A typical step would be to require a would-be participant to register by typing the letters or numbers appearing in a non-machine-readable image randomly generated on the page. If alternatives exist to support access for persons with disabilities, such measures do not place any burden on freedom of expression that raises First Amendment concern. It also seems unobjectionable for the government to seek to elicit some voluntary disclosure of identity, even for participants using online pseudonyms, by offering some kind of modest premium, such as a discount coupon for the Government Printing Office.

It is widely believed, however, that people behave more constructively in online environments if they are compelled to participate through a stable online identity (Egenfeldt-Nielsen 2006).[49] It seems plausible that disclosing one's actual identity to the forum manager would reinforce this accountability effect. Requirements for providing personal data to participate do not appear to be unlawful in the European context. For example, the EU Your Voice in Europe portal[50] requires participants to provide detailed profiles. To be able to participate, users must provide a name, contact details (such as email), and country of residence. In addition, information about the organization for which the comments are made and the nature of the organization for which participants work are standard compulsory elements of registering for consultation.

Whether government agencies can insist on such conditions is more problematic under U.S. law. A rule prohibiting anonymous participation in a government-sponsored forum is almost surely unconstitutional. The U.S. Supreme Court has repeatedly overturned state laws seeking to prevent anonymous pamphleteering,[51] and anonymous political expression bears a proud tradition in American culture. America's most honored political tracts—*The Federalist Papers*—were published under the pseudonym Publius by Alexander Hamilton, James Madison, and John Jay. The government might argue that a ban on anonymous online participation in a particular forum does not significantly burden speech, given that citizens may freely submit their anonymous thoughts to government decision makers using other channels. If the forum presents an opportunity to influence both government decision makers and other citizen-participants in the deliberation, however, then the exclusion of anonymous participants may be problematic.

Measures to ensure a stable online identity, even if pseudonymous, could fare better. Such measures appear reasonably calculated to facilitate orderly discussion, and it is difficult to see how such a constraint burdens any freedom of expression—except the freedom to appear fraudulently as if one person's views are the views of more than just one individual.

Participants, anonymous or not, are still be constrained by laws limiting certain kinds of speech. They are not immune, for example, from libel laws—although U.S. libel law provides significant room for the criticism of public officials. The Supreme Court has famously held that individuals may not be held liable in damages in the United States for criticism of a public official unless a defamatory falsehood is published with "actual malice"—that is, with knowledge that the statement is false or "reckless" (not merely "negligent") in its disregard for the truth.[52] The category of public official includes "at the very least . . . those among the hierarchy of government employees who have, or appear to the public to have, substantial responsibility for or control over the conduct of governmental affairs."[53] Thus, people participating in an online government forum would be legally free to speak critically of government officials, so long as their comments did not include assertions of facts they knew to be false or assertions of fact so plainly doubtful that their repetition without any investigation would amount to recklessness.

The publication through an online forum of classified national security information, trade secrets, or material protected by copyright could also result in legal liability for the speaker. Even if the speaker is anonymous and his or her identity unknown to the government, the First Amendment does not bar efforts by the government or by injured private parties to subpoena identifying information about the participant from his or her Internet service provider.[54] In this sense, the right of anonymous participation remains subject to the limitation that apparently unlawful speech can still trigger rights of discovery aimed at unearthing the identity of the person committing the unlawful speech act.

A perspective on the regulation of open forums that focuses on the role of the First Amendment stresses the role of government in supporting free speech through restraints on the exercise of government authority. Authorities in the United States, however, may go yet further to support free expression. So-called Strategic Lawsuits against Public Participation, or SLAPP suits, have become a common tool, typically of business interests, for seeking to deter participation in government forums by individuals who might speak critically of the SLAPP suit plaintiffs. Although typically without merit, these suits can impose significant costs on public speakers who have to shoulder costs in time and money to defend their right to speak freely. Nearly half the states have adopted some form of anti-SLAPP suit legislation designed to bring an early halt to such litigation (Daerr-Bannon 2008). The most protective statute is California's, which provides as follows:

A cause of action against a person arising from any act of that person in furtherance of the person's right of petition or free speech under the United States or California Constitution in connection with a public issue shall be subject to a special motion to strike, unless the court determines that the plaintiff has established that there is a probability that the plaintiff will prevail on the claim.[55]

If the defendant in such a California lawsuit—that is, the person seeking to participate freely in the government forum at issue—should prevail, the party who brought the SLAPP suit to chill that participation is liable to pay the defendant's costs and attorney's fees.[56] Anti-SLAPP suit statutes thus go beyond the First Amendment in seeking to protect the right to speak freely against even private abuse of the machinery of government.

Yet another way in which governments may provide affirmative support for free expression is by guaranteeing a right of participation in any language that the speaker prefers. In the multinational context of the EU, the question of language is of key concern. The multilingual challenge is substantial in the EU, with its twenty-three official European languages; a vast number of documents need to be translated on a daily basis. As a rule, all legislative acts must be translated in all European languages. In addition, white and green papers adopted by the Commission must be made available in all of the EU official languages, and other documents produced by the EU institutions are typically translated into as many official languages as possible, taking into account available resources.

In both the United States and the European Union, however, there is no enforceable obligation of the government to conduct online consultations in multiple languages. The European Charter states only that "every person may write to the institutions of the Union in one of the languages of the Treaties and must have an answer in the same language,"[57] and similar rights are frequently expressed within EU member states' constitutions, as well. For example, the Slovenian Constitution states that "everyone has the right to use his language . . . in the exercise of his rights" and in "procedures before state and other bodies performing a public function."[58]

This general right, however, has not been regarded as implying a universal right to translation. The Your Voice in Europe portal,[59] which was set up before the EU enlargements of 2004 and 2007, offered only eleven of twenty-three official languages as of 2009, although all twenty-three are now represented. In addition, there is no legal ground that would require the Commission to produce consultation documents in all of the EU official languages. In practice, documents of a legally nonbinding nature are commonly published only in English, French, and German. According to one of the Commission's officers, the Commission did not think it efficient to translate Your Voice in Europe into new languages while plans are pending to overhaul the Web site entirely.[60]

Information Rights

In addition to the direct regulation or protection of free speech rights, governments may augment or impede the quality of online consultations in other ways. Such consultations may also be shaped by public rights to government information and even by the intersection of government records laws and the messages exchanged in an online consultation. For example, a typical feature of government consultations is the provision, by a relevant agency, of some background information that implicitly or explicitly frames the request for public input. The most highly developed form of online consultation in the United States is federal e-rulemaking, the online solicitation of public comment with regard to proposed administrative regulations.[61] In the typical case, the agency provides a text of the proposed regulation, a statement that explains the nature and rationale of the proposal, and a citation to the agency's legal authority to propound the regulation. Although the agency is required by law to provide only "a concise general statement" of the proposed rule's basis and purpose,[62] the information provided on an important federal rule is likely to be detailed and lengthy. Moreover, U.S. courts have inferred from the public's entitlement to participate in rulemaking that federal agencies are required to submit to public review all data that the agency regards as constituting critical support for its proposed policy.[63]

The public may well perceive, however, that one measure of the genuineness of an online consultation is the government's willingness to share more information than simply its own description of the relevant problem and the documents that support a particular view of the most promising resolution. In this sense, the scope of the public's legal right to know can significantly shape the tenor of an online consultation. Citizens of the European Union have rights, of various scope, to public information, and those rights are guaranteed at both the national and transnational levels.[64] In the United States, the right to know is embodied principally in a national Freedom of Information Act,[65] which treats all government records as falling within one of three categories. The most basic government information—for example, descriptions of agency organization and the text of all legally binding rules—must be published by the agency.[66] A second tier of information, including statements of agency policy and the final opinions in all administrative adjudications, must be made "available for public inspection and copying."[67] Now that agencies make a lot of this material available online, the distinction between mandatory publication and making materials available for inspection is frequently of little significance. For agency records that do not fall within these foundational categories, members of the public are entitled to see anything on request so long as the record is reasonably described and does not fall within one of nine categories of statutory exemption from mandatory disclosure, which cover, for example, national security and certain law enforcement information, as well as personnel and medical files.[68] Every state has a similar law, although they vary in their details and the ease with which citizens may enforce their rights under them.[69] Governments may embrace even more vigorous proactive efforts to make policy-relevant information available for public analysis. It has been suggested that the federal government should be legally obliged to make data available online in universally accessible formats to allow citizens to make use of the data to take action not only on the federal level but also in their own communities.

Agencies may have something of the reverse concern. Once a member of the public contributes a post to an online consultation, an agency may worry that such a contribution becomes an agency record that is itself susceptible to cumbersome management requirements. For example, to the extent that federal agencies hold public comments in a form that makes them retrievable by the name of the contributor or some identifying link, those comments would form records covered by the requirements of the Privacy Act.[70] Records maintained under the Privacy Act are ordinarily subject to certain limitations on subsequent disclosure, requirements that accounts be kept of further disclosures, and mandatory opportunities for citizens to inspect and, where appropriate, correct their records. With regard to comments posted in online forums, three implications follow under federal privacy law. First, posted responses to consultations are exempt from Privacy Act requirements if they are, either anonymous or stored in a way that they are not retrievable by the agency according to the identity of the contributor. Second, even if they are retrievable, agencies can relieve themselves of any limits on subsequent publication by declaring the public availability of all public comments to be a "routine use" of such records.[71] Finally, the agency may well be obligated to account to any participant in an online consultation if a third party later requests to see anything he or she contributed to an electronic deliberation.[72]

Federal agencies in the United States have another, arguably more subtle concern for the management of public comments as a form of public record. When federal agencies promulgate regulations, the new regulations are typically subject to judicial review. The federal administrative procedure act contemplates that the review will be based on a "record"[73] but does not define what that record consists of. Case law, however, has established the proposition that the record proffered by an agency should be sufficient to enable the court to perceive the issues that the agency was required to consider in promulgating the rule and the reasoning the agency followed in addressing those issues. If it appears that the agency neglected or treated unreasonably a serious issue that the public brought to its attention during the public comment period, then the agency runs the risk that its rule will be voided by the court as "arbitrary" and "capricious."

This framework poses a management question for agencies: should each comment that is submitted in an online consultation be considered part of the record that agency personnel regard themselves as obligated to compile and consider in promulgating a final rule? If so, then depending on the volume of comments received, the burden of analysis for agency staff could easily become considerable. If not, then it is not clear how the public is to understand the significance of the input it is being asked to provide. This conundrum has spurred agency interest in text-analysis tools that allow agency staff to sort, analyze, and disseminate large volumes of textual input. Unless there is a public expectation that online input receives serious consideration, it is difficult to see the motivation for providing thoughtful, well-substantiated analysis. A duty of serious consideration, however, in the face of what may prove to be many tens of thousands of online comments could overwhelm an agency that lacks efficient workflow processes to deal with such input (Shane 2011).

Potential Liabilities of Government Forum Sponsors and Managers

The potential complications that administrative law poses for administrative agencies that run online consultations suggest that the law affects the prospects for successful online consultation both by shaping the larger discursive context in which they take place and also by making such consultations more or less burdensome for the sponsoring agencies. Staging a consultation inevitably entails some cost in time and budget. Whether there may be additional costs in terms of legal requirements or even potential liabilities imposed is also a matter of law.

For example, a government agency might be deterred from staging an online consultation if it is worried about potential liability for the unlawful posting on its Web sites of copyrighted material. In the United States, however, two factors mitigate against such concern. First, government agencies are not suable in damages except to the extent they waive their so-called sovereign immunity to suit. (A general principle of sovereign immunity does not generally protect executive authorities from suit in Europe.) In the United States, legislatures may thus choose not to expose administrative agencies within their control to damage claims for infringements of intellectual property.[74] Perhaps more important, however, there is no liability to a Web site sponsor under U.S. copyright law when third parties improperly upload to the Web site any material that is protected by copyright, so long as on notification of the claimed infringement, the Web site operator "responds expeditiously to remove" the material in question.[75] Hence, if citizens infringe on third parties' intellectual property rights in an online consultation, the agency is not at risk of financial liability but merely has the burden of taking down any copyrighted material after a dispute is brought to the agency's attention. Indeed, if the government stages its consultation through a third-party Web site, the obligation will presumably be shouldered by the Web site provider, not the government agency.

Similar concerns may arise for agencies worried that material posted online might incur liability if it is defamatory against a third party or somehow invades a third party's privacy in violation of state tort law. As with the copyright scenario, however, there are two lines of defense. First, federal and state laws are likely to immunize both the government and its employees from liability for tort violations of this sort. The U.S. Supreme Court, for example, has held that federal officers are absolutely immune to state tort liability for acts committed within their official authority.[76] Federal agencies themselves cannot be held liable in damages for defamation because the federal government, pursuant to the Federal Torts Claims Act, has preserved its immunity from damage suits based on libel or slander.[77]

Second, to the extent that tort liability depends, in this context, on finding that a government agency or employee acted as the online "publisher" of defamatory or otherwise tortious material, federal law protects Web site operators from liability in precisely this situation. The Communications Decency Act provides: "No provider or user of an interactive computer service shall be treated as the publisher or speaker of any information provided by another information content provider."[78] As the relevant terms are defined, the government agency sponsoring an online consultation is deemed "a provider or user of an interactive computer service."[79] If a third-party information content provider posts defamatory material on the government's Web site, then the government does not qualify, legally, as the accountable publisher of that material.

Government officials may still be worried about potential liability for so-called constitutional torts under U.S. law. That is, even when no common law basis for a tort suit exists against a government official, there still may be liability where the official violates the constitutional rights of particular individuals. Given the complexity of the relevant constitutional doctrines described above, one can imagine officials worried that they may be liable in damages if they should inadvertently violate someone's First Amendment rights. For example, what would happen if an official mistakenly believed that the registration procedures created for an online forum were sufficiently protective of anonymity to pass constitutional muster but later discovered that the courts were of a different opinion?

In this context, the novelty of the situation works in favor of the government officials. The U.S. Supreme Court has held that government officials may not be sued personally in damages for violating anyone's constitutional rights unless their conduct violates "clearly established statutory or constitutional rights of which a reasonable person would have known."[80] An erroneous prediction of the exact contours of government's authority to shape the scope and conduct rules for an innovative online forum will all but certainly entail no prospect of individual liability for any official or employee involved. Unfortunately, it is difficult to offer such categorical assurances to executive officials in European states. In the European Union, Web site sponsors are not automatically exempt from responsibility for publishing third-party content they merely hosted. Member states are typically working out their rules in this respect, and it is at least possible to envision systems that would entail government take-down obligations that are enforceable in damages.

Conclusion

When governments contemplate the sponsorship of online public consultations, their initiatives are going to be shaped by law in at least two ways. First, the magnitude of legally imposed administrative burdens and potential liabilities will likely affect agencies' enthusiasm or lack of it for moving forward. The greater the apparent burden and potential risk, the less interest there is likely to be in making online consultation a routine feature of governance. On the other hand, if the design of law (and technology) permits the efficient conduct of online consultations and eliminates serious liability risk, then the position of agency staff who are eager to pursue online consultations will be significantly strengthened.

Second, the legal regime has implications for the actual design of the consultation. The terms of participation and the ways in which agencies use public information to frame the consultation must inevitably reflect the rules governing free speech rights and access to public documents.

As of mid-2011, postindustrial societies still appear to be at a stage where figuring out the details of relevant applicable law is difficult because the relevant laws and regulations were formulated largely in and for a predigital world. Much has to be inferred through analogy to the offline public sphere. Governments that are eager to promote online consultation would do well to consider the legal issues head on and adopt (or eliminate) legal rules after squarely considering their implications for online forums. When that happens, it may signal that online consultation is no longer conceptualized as the mere transfer online of what were historically offline processes but a new form of governance that requires its own distinctive legal framework.

Notes

1. U.S.C. tit. 44, sec. 3502(3).

2. Memorandum from Cass R. Sunstein, administrator, Office of Information and Regulatory Affairs, for the Heads of Executive Departments and Agencies, and Independent Agencies, re: Social Media, Web-Based Interactive Technologies, and the Paperwork Reduction Act, at 3–4 (April 7, 2010), available at http://www.whitehouse.gov/sites/default/files/omb/assets/inforeg/SocialMedia Guidance_04072010.pdf.

3. U.S.C. tit. 5, app. sec. 3(2).

4. Universal Declaration of Human Rights art. 21, G.A. Res. 217A, U.N. GAOR, 3d Sess., 1st plen. mtg., U.N. Doc. A/810 (December 12, 1948).

5. U.S. Constitution, amend. 1.

6. i2010 eGovernment Action Plan, COM (2006) 173. See also Plan-D for Democracy, Dialogue and Debate, COM (2005) 494.

7. The First Amendment provides: "Congress shall make no law respecting an establishment of religion, or prohibiting the free exercise thereof; or abridging the freedom of speech, or of the press; or the right of the people peaceably to assemble, and to petition the government for a redress of grievances." Although applicable through its own terms only to Congress, the U.S. Supreme Court has acknowledged its constraining force on all branches of the federal government and has held that, through the adoption of the Fourteenth Amendment, the First Amendment became binding on the states, as well. See Valley Forge Christian College v. Americans United for the Separation of Church and State, 454 U.S. 464, 511 (1982) (Brennan, J., dissenting) ("The First Amendment binds the Government as a whole, regardless of which branch is at work in a particular instance."); Joseph Burstyn, Inc. v. Wilson, 343 U.S. 495, 499 (1952) ("In a series of decisions beginning with *Gitlow v. People of State of New York*, 268 U.S. 652 (1925), this Court held that the liberty of speech and of the press which the

First Amendment guarantees against abridgment by the federal government is within the liberty safeguarded by the Due Process Clause of the Fourteenth Amendment from invasion by state action").

8. Universal Declaration of Human Rights, G.A. Res. 217A, U.N. GAOR, 3d sess., 1st plen. mtg., U.N. Doc. A/810 (December 12, 1948).

9. G.A. Res. 2200A (XXI), para. 21, U.N. GAOR, Supp. No. 16 at 52, U.N. Doc. A/6316 (1966), 999 U.N.T.S. 171, entered into force March 23, 1976.

10. Slovenian Constitution, art. 39, para. 1.

11. See, e.g., Police Department v. Mosley, 408 U.S. 92 (1972), R.A.V. v. City of St. Paul, 505 U.S. 377 (1992).

12. See, e.g., Simon & Schuster, Inc. v. Members of New York State Crime Victims Board, 502 U.S. 105 (1991).

13. Hungarian Constitution, art. 10, para. 1.

14. Ibid, art. 10, para. 4. The only exception pertains to cases where comments evidently lack rationale.

15. Convention on Access to Information, Public Participation in Decision-making and Access to Justice in Environmental Matters, June 25, 1998, 2161 U.N.T.S. 447, 38 I.L.M. 517, available at http://www.unece.org/env/pp/documents/cep43e.pdf (hereinafter Århus Convention).

16. Council Decision (EC) No. 2005/370 of February 17, 2005, on the Conclusion, on Behalf of the European Community, of the Convention on Access to Information, Public Participation in Decision-Making and Access to Justice in Environmental Matters, (2005) OJ L 124/1.

17. Århus Convention, art. 6, para. 8.

18. Odl. US: U-I-386/06, National Gazette of the Republic of Slovenia No. 32/2008.

19. U.S.C. tit. 5, sec. 553(c).

20. U.S.C. tit. 5, sec. 706.

21. National Tire Dealers and Retreaders Association v. Brinegar, 491 F.2d 31 (1974).

22. Roth v. United States, 354 U.S. 476 (1957).

23. Miller v. California, 413 U.S. 15, 24 (1973).

24. Brandenburg v. Ohio, 395 U.S. 444, 447 (1969).

25. La Ligue internationale contre le racisme et l'antisémitisme (Licra) and Union des étudiants juifs de France (UEJC) c. Yahoo!, Inc. et Societe Yahoo! France, Tribunal de grande instance, Ordonnance de référé, 22.5.2000.

26. Yahoo!, Inc. v. La Ligue contre le racisme et l'antisemitisme, 169 F. Supp. 2d 1181, 1194 (N.D. Cal. 2001), rev'd on procedural grounds, 433 F.3d 1199 (9th Cir. 2006).

27. See, e.g., Additional Protocol to the Convention on Cybercrime, Concerning the Criminalisation of Acts of a Racist or Xenophobic Nature Committed

Through Computer Systems (2003), available at http://conventions.coe.int/Treaty/EN/Treaties/Html/189.htm.

28. For example, the Slovenian Constitution prohibits "any incitement to national, racial, religious or other discrimination, and the inflaming of national, racial, religious or other hatred and intolerance" (art. 63). Similar provisions can also be found in France and Romania.

29. For example, under British freedom of speech legislation, denial of holocaust is allowed unless it incites racial hatred (Goldirova 2007).

30. Council of the European Union Joint Action on the Basis of Article K.3 of the Treaty on European Union, Concerning Action to Combat Racism and Xenophobia (96/443/JHA), 1995 OJ (C 327), available at http://eur-lex.europa.eu/LexUriServ/LexUriServ.do?uri=CELEX:31996F0443:EN:NOT.

31. Council framework decision 2008/913/JHA of November 28, 2008, on Combating Certain Forms and Expressions of Racism and Xenophobia by Means of Criminal Law, 2008 O.J. (L 328) 55.

32. United States v. Grace, 461 U.S. 171, 177 (1983).

33. Perry Educators Association v. Perry Local Educators' Association, 460 U.S. 37, 45 (1983).

34. Ibid., 46.

35. Ibid.

36. Cornelius v. NAACP Legal Defense and Educational Fund, 473 U.S. 788 (1985).

37. International Society for Krishna Consciousness v. Lee, 505 U.S. 672 (1992).

38. Between the categories of public forum and nonpublic forum, the U.S. Supreme Court has also recognized a category of limited public forum. It is not clear what difference it would make to how online consultations would be regulated if they were deemed limited public forums instead of nonpublic forums.

39. This is not hypothetical. In the opening months of the Obama administration, the Office of Science and Technology Policy created a blog through which it periodically solicits comments on a number of technology-related issues. In connection, for example, with an online Policy Forum on the Future of U.S. Advanced Manufacturing, the President's Council of Advisors on Science and Technology used an IdeaScale site with the following terms of participation (available at http://www.usa.gov/webcontent/open/terms/index.shtml):

Our Terms of Participation is intended to support open discussion while ensuring a respectful exchange of ideas. We reserve the option to review your ideas against these Terms before posting publicly, which could result in a delay. Ideas or comments will be removed from the site by staff if they include any of the following:

Threatening, slanderous or obscene language
Personal attacks
Discriminatory language (including hate speech) based on race, national origin, age, gender, sexual orientation, religion or disability

Sexually explicit material and other material that would violate the law if published here
Ideas or comments that promote services or products (non-commercial links that are relevant to this web site are OK)
Repetitive posts (for example, if you submit the same idea multiple times)
Embedded media, such as videos or photos (but hyperlinks to such media are OK)
Spam or undecipherable language (gratuitous links will be viewed as spam)
Copyright infringement
Personally identifiable information (e.g., social security numbers, postal and email addresses, phone numbers).

40. Steinburg v. Chesterfield County Planning Commission, 527 F.3d 377, 385 (4th Cir. 2008) ("[A] government entity such as the Commission is justified in limiting its meeting to discussion of specified agenda items and in imposing reasonable restrictions to preserve the civility and decorum necessary to further the forum's purpose of conducting public business. But any restriction must not discriminate on the basis of a speaker's viewpoint").

41. 460 U.S. 37 (1983).

42. Ibid., 52.

43. Cornelius v. NAACP Legal Defense and Education Fund, 473 U.S. 788 (1985).

44. Ibid., at 806.

45. 505 U.S. 672 (1992).

46. Ibid., 830.

47. Ibid., 831.

48. Collinson v. Gott, 895 F.2d 994 (4th Cir. 1990).

49. "A key issue to get rid of cheating [in online gaming] is to establish a stable online identity so you can identify a specific person online and enforce sanctions."

50. http://ec.europa.eu/yourvoice/index_en.htm.

51. Talley v. California, 362 U.S. 60 (1960); McIntyre v. Ohio Elections Commission, 514 U.S. 334 (1995).

52. New York Times Co. v. Sullivan, 376 U.S. 254 (1964).

53. Rosenblatt v. Baer, 383 U.S. 75, 85 (1966).

54. See, e.g., Dendrite International Inc. v. John Doe No. 3, 342 N.J. Super. 134, 775 A.2d 756 (2001).

55. California Code of Civil Procedure, sec. 425.16(b)(1) (West 2008).

56. Ibid., sec. 425.16(c).

57. Charter of Fundamental Rights of the European Union, art. 41, para. 3, December 7, 2000, 2000 O.J. (C 364) 1.

58. Slovenian Constitution, art. 62.

59. http://ec.europa.eu/yourvoice/index_en.htm.

60. Pirkko Kauppinen, Unit Transparency, Relations with Stakeholders and External Organisations, Secretariat General, personal interview.

61. A comprehensive review of the initiative appears in Committee on the Status and Future of Federal E-Rulemaking (2008).

62. U.S.C. tit. 5, sec. 553(c).

63. Portland Cement Association v. Ruckelshaus, 486 F.2d 375 (D.C. Cir. 1973); Association of Data Processing Service Organizations v. Board of Governors of the Federal Reserve System, 745 F.2d 677 (D.C. Cir. 1984).

64. For example, according to the Treaty of Amsterdam, "Any citizen of the Union, and any natural or legal person residing or having its registered office in a Member State, shall have a right of access to European Parliament, Council and Commission documents" (art. 255, para. 1). See also the Charter of Fundamental Rights of the European Union (note 58 above) and the Treaty Establishing a Constitution for Europe, October 29, 2004, 2004 O.J. (C310) 1.

65. U.S.C. tit. 5, sec. 552 (2006).

66. Ibid., sec. 552(a)(1).

67. Ibid., sec. 552(a)(1).

68. Ibid., sec. 552(a)(3), (b).

69. The University of Missouri Freedom of Information Center maintains links to all states' open records laws at http://www.nfoic.org/state-foi-laws.

70. U.S.C. tit. 5, sec. 552a (2006).

71. Ibid., sec. 552a(b)(3).

72. Ibid., sec. 552a(c).

73. Ibid., sec. 706.

74. Florida Prepaid Postsecondary Education Expense Board v. College Savings Bank, 527 U.S. 627 (1999); College Savings Bank v. Florida Prepaid Postsecondary Education Expense Board, 527 U.S. 666 (1999).

75. U.S.C. tit. 17, sec. 512 (c)(1)(C).

76. Barr v. Matteo, 360 U.S. 564 (1959).

77. U.S.C. tit. 28, sec. 2680(h).

78. U.S.C. tit. 80, sec. 230(c)(1).

79. "The term 'interactive computer service' means any information service, system, or access software provider that provides or enables computer access by multiple users to a computer server, including specifically a service or system that provides access to the Internet and such systems operated or services offered by libraries or educational institutions." U.S.C. tit. 47, sec. 230(f)(2). In running an online consultation, the government is enabling computer access by multiple users to a computer server.

80. Harlow v. Fitzgerald, 457 U.S. 800, 818 (1982).

References

Committee on the Status and Future of Federal E-Rulemaking. 2008. *Achieving the Potential: The Future of E-rulemaking—A Report to Congress and the President*. Washington, DC: ABA Section of Administrative Law and Regulatory Practice.

Daerr-Bannon, Kathleen L. 2008. "Cause of Action: Bringing and Defending Anti-SLAPP Motions to Strike or Dismiss." *Causes of Action*, 2nd, vol. 22, p. 317, II-B-8.

E-democracy.org. 2009. "Rules." Accessed December 7, 2010. http://pages .e-democracy.org/Rules.

Egenfeldt-Nielsen, Simon. 2006. "Mapping Online Gaming: Genres, Characteristics and Revenue Models." Accessed October 24, 2010. http://game-research. com/index.php/articles/mapping-online-gaming-genres-characteristics-and -revenue-models.

Froomkin, Michael. 2004. "Technologies for Democracy." *Democracy Online: The Prospects for Political Renewal through the Internet* 3:12–15.

Goldirova, Renata. 2007. "EU Agrees Breakthrough Hate-Crime Law." EUObserver.com, April 20. Accessed December 7, 2010. http://euobserver.com/9/ 23902/?rk.

Jesdanun, Anick. 2008. "Online Speech May Be Free But Is Subject to Delete." *Austin American-Statesman*, July 7. Accessed December 7, 2010. http://www .statesman.com/business/content/business/stories/technology/07/07/0707techfree speech.html.

Shane, Peter M. 2011. "Empowering the Collaborative Citizen in the Administrative State: A Case Study of the Federal Communications Commission." *University of Miami Law Review* 65, no. 2:483–505.

16

E-Democracy, Transnational Organizations, and the Challenge of New Techno-Intermediation

Oren Perez

One of the main dilemmas facing the global community today is the growing democratic deficit of the transnational legal system. The expanding power and reach of new transnational regimes—including the World Trade Organization (WTO), the International Criminal Court (ICC), and private, hybrid organizations like the International Organization for Standardization (ISO) and the Basel Committee—have made this dilemma more critical. The perception that this new transnational governance network is highly detached from the global citizenry it purports to serve, both in its democratic sensitivities and in its accountability, is generating a crisis of legitimacy (Castells 2005; Keohane 2003). Resolving this crisis and restoring the public faith in these global players are difficult tasks that require, among other things, the creation of institutional mechanisms that allow the global civil society to participate, in a meaningful way, in the creation and implementation of global norms and policies (Castells 2005, 16). Such mechanisms should offer the public direct access to processes of global norm production, which transcend national boundaries.

The Internet's capacity to transcend barriers of space and time seems to make it an ideal medium for transnational deliberation. As Manuel Castells notes, the "Internet as a global, horizontal means of communication provides a public space, both as an organizing tool, and as a means for debate, dialogue, and collective decision making. Wireless communication increases autonomy of networks of communication" (Castells 2005, 12). Whether the Internet can realize this potential and contribute to the development of inclusive and nonhierarchical decision making structures at the global level is still an open question. The Internet has played a major role in facilitating protests against various global regimes. Protestors have used the Internet extensively, both to publicize their critiques and to coordinate their actions.[1] Web sites such as Protest.Net, http://www.indymedia.org, and http://www.corpwatch.org[2] have turned into hubs of political communication. All of these Web sites include details of upcoming protests, action alerts, and links to other protest Web sites. Recent technological innovations such as Twitter and Atomkeep further expand the coordinating potential of the Net.[3]

Although the capacity of the Internet to transform traditional politics at both the local and global levels is widely acknowledged (Zysman and Weber 2001; Bach and Stark 2004; Riley 2003), its influence on the decision making structures of global organizations has been limited. The question remains, therefore, whether initial expectations regarding the Internet's capacity to foster inclusive structures of global law making are theoretically and practically sound. In addressing this question, I proceed in three steps. First, I examine whether the expectations regarding the Internet's transformative potential are based on a coherent vision of global democracy and on a sound theory of electronically mediated civic action. Second, I look at the practices of several international bodies, drawing on a typology of international organizations that distinguishes between treaty-based organizations such as the WTO and more hybrid institutions such as ISO and the Global Reporting Initiative (GRI). This brief empirical excursion can shed light on the question of the Internet's potential to reinvigorate the global democratic experience—covering both conceptual and pragmatic grounds. Finally, I discuss the role of new technological intermediaries in this evolving universe of electronic democracy. Electronic-mediated political action is not as free or sponta-neous as people imagine or expect. It is influenced and vulnerable to hierarchical and technical interventions, which tend to be highly nontransparent. As international organizations turn to the Web, this new form of intervention needs to be recognized and dealt with institutionally.

Democratic Intuitions at the Global Level

Global democracy is invoked increasingly—in both theory and prac-tice—as a source of normative legitimacy (Held 2003, 472; Fleming et al. 2003). However, the idea of global democracy raises various difficul-ties pertaining to both its theoretical underpinnings and its global appli-cability. From a theoretical perspective, the vision of global democratization includes several potentially conflicting commitments. The proponents of global democratization invoke commitments to inclusiveness and open decision making structures (which presupposes the possibility of true global polity); to a decision making process that is based on the possibility of reaching agreement through rational deliberation; to individual freedom and fundamental human rights; to the value of cultural pluralism; and to the inclusion of these core commitments in global governance institutions.[4]

These commitments conflict in various ways (which cannot be fully explored in this chapter). First, there are deep doubts whether the vision of a unitary global polity, which is presupposed by the call for global democratization, is realizable or even desirable (Keohane 2003). Second, the drive for democratic engagement at the global level is associated with the rise of strong global institutions—to the point that this phenomenon is perceived to be the reason for the democratization argument. However, an intrinsic tension seems to exist between the emergence of such institutions and the commitment to individual freedom and cultural pluralism. The democratic machinery has limits: as the distance between the global political center and the citizen body grows, so does the risk that the voices of the citizen and the local community will be ignored. Third, it is not clear whether the commitment to open deliberation and consensual decision making can be realized—even if one is optimistic about the new deliberative horizons opened by the Internet—given the vast cultural and ideological differences that characterize the contemporary global society and the ideological commitment to pluralism. The political institutions of majority voting and parliamentary representation offer a way to circumvent this normative divergence, but at the price of giving up the ideal of governing through deliberation.

E-democracy, despite the wide hopes associated with it (Castells 2005, 1516), cannot resolve the foregoing tensions. The contribution of the Internet to the development of global democracy should be conceived, I argue, in more modest terms. Through its rich portfolio of deliberative mechanisms—including social networks, chat rooms, instant messaging, and wikis—the Internet can expand the communicative horizon of the global society, facilitating the creation of a more complex global political arena. This discursive or communicative complexity—hosting and supporting diverse streams of thought—can be used to counter the rigidity and dogmatism of tyranny. Further, these new deliberative tools can be tailored to varied hierarchical configurations and institutional cultures. The use of e-democracy tools can therefore generate communicative complexity even in highly hierarchical institutional contexts.

The extensive global reach and rich repertoire of deliberation techniques of the Internet turn it into an essential tool in the effort to develop more democratic transnational governing structures. However, e-democracy is vulnerable to hierarchical and technical manipulation. The emergence of e-participation cannot be taken for granted and is highly dependent on the availability of central direction.[5] By emphasizing the enabling and anarchistic character of the Net, many writers have tended to overlook this dependency and its potential implications—in particular, the susceptibility of e-participation to hierarchical manipulation (Hammond and Lash 2000). Thus, one of the challenges facing those seeking to institutionalize mechanisms of e-participation is to find ways to promote coordinated activity yet keep the sponsors of such activity accountable. Recognizing that e-deliberation is not—and probably never has been—a completely spontaneous and free enterprise brings to the fore a new set of questions regarding the external intervention, manipulation, and choreography of the medium that provides the setting for the deliberation.

E-Democracy at the Transnational Level: Institutional Typology and Three Case Studies

A Typology of International Organizations

In discussing e-democracy initiatives at the global level, it is useful to distinguish between two general archetypes of international organizations. These dual institutional archetypes react differently to the challenge of democratization, generating distinct constellations of technologies, practices, and rules. The first archetype is the classical treaty-based intergovernmental organization (IGO). IGOs operate within the traditional boundaries of international public law. Their powers can be traced back to state consent, realized through interstate negotiations. The powers of some of these bodies—such as the WTO and the ICC—have evolved dramatically over the last two decades, creating a new type of IGO that has significantly more powers than its institutional ancestors (such as the International Labor Organization and the World Health Organization). Yet these global entities continue to operate within the conceptual boundaries of the Westphalian tradition (Perez 2007, 57). One of the repercussions of this conceptual canon is a limited recognition of the right of nonstate parties to take part in the creation and negotiation of new norms. As I demonstrate below in the context of the WTO, this conceptual background has limited the extent to which e-democracy initiatives can be incorporated in the WTO formal decision making structure.

The second archetype of international organizations is best catego-rized in a negative fashion as a residual category. It covers all those transnational bodies, initiatives, or networks that aspire to create, dis-seminate, and implement rules or standards with global reach but that have not been established through international treaties. I use the term *private international governance organization* (PIGO) to denote this institutional category. Because this is a residual category, it contains a wide variety of PIGOs that may be distinguished across multiple vectors. PIGOs may be distinguished, first, by the relative shares that firms, nongovernmental organizations (NGOs), and states exercise in their governance (Abbott and Snidal 2009, 512). Some PIGOs are dominated by firms (such as the International Chamber of Commerce), some are governed jointly by firms and state representatives (such as the ISO), and some are governed by a coalition of firms and NGOs (such as the GRI) (Abbott and Snidal 2009, 512–519). Further distinguishing vectors include the subject matter of these organizations' norm-production activity, the legal force of their normative output (that is, how hard or soft it is), and the extent to which they are engaged with enforcement or certification.[6] Generally, despite their institutional diversity, PIGOs have been more willing to experiment with novel decision making structures involving innovative e-democracy tools. The three case studies below provide an opportunity to develop provisional hypotheses about the ways in which PIGOs may differ in their approach to e-democracy.

Three Case Studies

The World Trade Organization: E-Democracy within a Modern Intergovernmental Organization

Classic IGOs have adopted a dual strategy in using the Internet to enhance their democratic sensitivities. First, the Internet was used as an instrument of transparency, hosting highly complex and cognitively rich databases. Second, it was used to support peripheral processes of con-sultation or deliberation. The WTO is a case in point.[7] The WTO is concerned primarily with the facilitation of transnational commerce and the abolition of trade barriers. The WTO differs from its predecessor, the General Agreement on Tariffs and Trade (GATT), in two key respects. First, unlike the weak dispute settlement system of the GATT, the WTO's dispute settlement system is highly autonomous and is much more immune to political pressures. Its establishment has marked the creation of a new and independent source of normative power in the global arena (Perez 2007). Second, the normative setting of the WTO is far more ambitious than that of the GATT. It is not limited to a single trade sector or to one type of regulatory barrier but reflects a broad attempt to integrate the global economy. This jurisdictional expansion has resulted in an increased incidence of conflicts between trade and other societal concerns such as environmental protection and labor rights and a growing public critique of its legitimacy and accountability (Perez 2004).

One way in which the WTO has sought to respond to the critique regarding its democratic deficit has been to increase the transparency of its operations, and to do so it has turned to the Web. Almost all WTO documents—including secretariat reports, committee protocols, and judicial decisions—are accessible online, which is an enormous improvement over the cloak of secrecy that characterized the GATT.[8] In addition, the WTO sought to promote wider public engagement in its affairs, and the Internet was seen as a crucial part of this strategy. A dedicated community forums section was created on the WTO Web site that was designed to serve the interests of the media, NGOs, and the general public—the goal being to provide an opportunity "for the public to comment on the WTO, its activities, and the trading system."[9] This section includes an open forum where participants can either join existing discussions (which can be initiated by users or by the WTO secretariat) or initiate their own WTO-related discussion. Among the topics discussed in the forum are the food crisis, international supply chains and greenhouse gas emissions, and ecology and the WTO.[10] In addition to the open e-forum, the WTO Web site includes an NGO Room[11] that includes documents from NGOs and notifications about NGO-related WTO activities. It also serves as a coordination hub before the biannual ministerial conferences. In addition to these online initiatives, the WTO has established an annual WTO Public Forum that provides an opportunity for "governments, non-governmental organizations, academics, businesses and students to come together to discuss issues regarding the multilateral trading system." The 2009 forum's theme was "Global Problems, Global Solutions: Towards Better Global Governance."[12]

These laudable initiatives do not appear to be leading to any great leaps forward in terms of public engagement. Although there seem to be a relatively wide interest in the WTO Forum,[13] the community forum has no formal standing within the WTO decision making structure. The site does not indicate how public feedback is (or has been) used by the organization. The opening paragraph to the NGO Room states that the WTO "recognizes the role NGOs can play to increase the awareness of the public in respect of WTO activities" but does not provide details about how NGOs can contribute more meaningfully to the substantive work of the WTO.[14] Overall, the use of new communication technologies by the WTO reflects an emerging recognition of the legitimate role of NGOs and civic society at large in the governance of the organization. However, for practical purposes, the influence of such groups on the decision making process is still highly limited and informal.

The International Organization for Standardization: E-Democracy within a Highly Institutionalized and Business-Oriented PIGO

The International Organization for Standardization (ISO) was established in 1947, continuing in effect the work of the International Federation of the National Standardization Associations that was established in 1926 but ceased to operate in 1942 due to World War II (Clapp 1998, 301; Kresse and Fadaie 2004, 910). The ISO comprises standard-setting organizations in 161 countries.[15] These national bodies differ in their structure: some are governmental bodies, some are private technical-industrial institutions, while others are of a hybrid private-public nature. Local firms have significant influence on the internal governance of these institutions (Abbott and Snidal 2009, 513). The global push toward standardization has increased the power and importance of international standard-setting organizations. Other influential organizations are the International Electromechanical Commission (IEC), which specializes in electronic engineering and telecommunication, and the Codex Alimentarius Commission, which specializes in food standards. The products of these organizations are to a large extent voluntary, but the globalization process and the new regime of the WTO have in effect upgraded their status, making it much more difficult for both private players and states to disregard them.[16]

Further, despite the apparently specialized and remote nature of their work, such bodies have substantial normative power that merits deeper public scrutiny. A good example is the work of the ISO in the areas of environmental management and, more recently, corporate social responsibility. The ISO 14000 series, which was developed by ISO in the mid-1990s, is a set of environmental standards covering a range of practices relating to management systems, auditing, performance evaluation, labeling, and life-cycle assessment . Unlike some of the ISO's other products, the ISO 14000 series is not technical in the sense that it does not comprise detailed technological or emissions protocols. The ISO 14000 series has a broader agenda, which is to teach organizations, in a general and abstract fashion, how to think about environmental problems. Furthermore, this normative agenda is not limited to the corporate realm. The ISO 14000 series seeks, in effect, to provide a comprehensive discourse—which would be used by society as a whole—for judging the environmental behavior of organizations.

The new ISO 26000, Guidance on Social Responsibility, which was published in 2010, represents a similarly ambitious and nontechnical vision. The standard seeks to provide guidance on the underlying principles of social responsibility and on ways to integrate socially responsible behaviour into existing organizational strategies, systems, practices and processes.[17] Unlike other ISO standards, this standard is not intended for certification purposes. Nonetheless, its definitions of the core subjects embraced by the notion of corporate social responsibility—human rights, labor practices, environment, fair operating practices, consumer protection, and community involvement—are likely to have substantial influence on the global market, given the ISO's dominant normative status. Indeed, the work of the ISO on this topic has generated wide controversy (Wood 2009).

Despite the broad normative implications of the ISO standards, its standard-setting process remains highly opaque (UNCTAD 1996). The standard-making process in the ISO provides few formal opportunities for public participation.[18] The main legislative work is carried out by ISO technical committees and subcommittees; only ISO members have the right to participate in the work of the various committees (that is, to receive drafts, make comments, and approve ISO standards).[19] The ISO online presence does little to break the closure of its norm-production process. The ISO Web site (www.iso.ch) does not offer real opportunities for public involvement. External observers cannot consult existing standards or drafts of future standards but are required to purchase them from the ISO, which retains intellectual property rights to them. The development of ISO 26000 has been exceptional in this regard. Because of the wide controversy this initiative has generated, ISO has decided to open the development process and in contrast to its common practice has made all its working documents available online.[20] It has also initiated a wide consultation process regarding the standard's content.[21] However, the dedicated ISO 26000 Web page does not provide mechanisms for online consultation (which takes place at offline meetings with various stakeholders) and remains strictly an information hub.

ISO's closed standard-setting structure casts considerable doubt over its claim that "ISO standards distill an international consensus from the broadest possible base of stakeholder groups."[22] The ISO, however, has introduced new communication technologies in an effort to improve its internal decision making processes. In 2001, a sophisticated system of electronic balloting was introduced that was designed to facilitate the collaborative development of standards and to speed up the process of voting and securing feedback on ISO draft standards (Weissinger 2001).[23] This system could provide interesting lessons on the potential advantages of an Internet forum in the development of global norms. The system remains closed, however, to nonmembers. To the extent that the ISO reaches out to civic society in its various activities (which are organized through technical committees), it does so mostly through dedicated offline meetings and not through its electronic system.

The Global Reporting Initiative, AccountAbility, and the Internet Corporation for Assigned Names and Numbers: E-Democracy within Newly Established PIGOs

Fascinating developments in the field of e-democracy have occurred in the context of new hybrid organizations that emerged over the last decade. These include organizations such as the Global Reporting Initiative (GRI), AccountAbility, and the Internet Corporation for Assigned Names and Numbers (ICANN). These organizations share an inclusive vision and a strong Web presence. Before examining the complex reasons underlying the relative openness of these hybrid bodies, I first consider their democratic initiatives. The GRI was founded in 1997 by the Coalition for Environmentally Responsible Economies in partnership with the United Nations Environment Program.[24] It is based on three (potentially conflicting) pillars—a commitment to multistakeholder decision making, an ideological commitment to the ethos of sustainable development, and a formal, hierarchical institutional structure.[25] The GRI commitment to consensual decision making is reflected, for example, in the text of the G3 Reporting Sustainability Guidelines (Global Reporting Initiative 2006, 2):

Transparency about the sustainability of organizational activities is of interest to a diverse range of stakeholders, including business, labor, non-governmental organizations, investors, accountancy, and others. This is why GRI has relied on the collaboration of a large network of experts from all of these stakeholder groups in consensus-seeking consultations. These consultations, together with practical experience, have continuously improved the Reporting Framework since GRI's founding in 1997. This multi-stakeholder approach to learning has given the Reporting Framework the widespread credibility it enjoys with a range of stakeholder groups.[26]

The GRI commitment to consensual decision making is fulfilled through multiple pathways—both online and offline.[27] It involves initial in-house rule development by a technical working group, a broad public consultation drawing both on Web-based consultation and offline meetings, and a further in-house refinement process by GRI's Technical Advisory Committee (which is responsible for incorporating the public input into the document) and the GRI's Stakeholder Council. Any document produced by the GRI must receive final approval from the GRI board of directors. The GRI also uses the Web to achieve maximum transparency of its various products. The GRI has produced two reporting guidelines over a period of four years—in both cases after an open consultation process.[28] The GRI's reflexive structure seems to have provided the organization with both innovative capacity and the legitimacy to carry out its mission. Further, it has produced highly influential normative products in a domain in which progress through the treaty-making route would have been difficult. To some extent, the success of the GRI may be attributed to the limited field—sustainability reporting—in which it operated. Despite the relative success of the GRI, the consultation procedures it established do not constitute a formal democratic structure. Although the GRI is committed to the idea of wide-ranging consultation, it kept final authority to itself.

A second ambitious example of an open deliberative process at the global level is the deliberative process initiated by AccountAbility in 2008, using a Wiki platform, with respect to the revision of the AA1000 Assurance Standard.[29] The AA1000 Assurance Standard is used to provide assurance on publicly available sustainability information, particularly sustainability reports.[30] AccountAbility is a global, not-for-profit self-managed partnership founded in 1995. Its governance structure is dominated by business and NGOs.[31] By drawing on a Wiki platform[32] to facilitate the collaborative drafting process, AccountAbility addressed two challenges—access and transparency. Thus, the introductory note to the wiki stated

The wiki makes it possible for thousands of individuals and organizations to provide their input without facing access barriers such as the cost of travel to meetings and the difficulty of cutting through dominant voices. It also keeps a transparent record of everyone who has participated as well as the nature of their input.[33]

The deliberation platform created by AccountAbility is not, however, completely anarchic. The final authority to approve the standard remains in the hands of the AccountAbility Standards Technical Committee. AccountAbility has committed to make any interventions of this committee transparent—that is, to publish them on the wiki.[34] The revised AA1000 Assurance Standard was published in October 2008.[35]

The more disappointing case of ICANN highlights the difficulties associated with the global democratic project. In 2000, the Internet Corporation for Assigned Names and Numbers attempted to develop a governance structure based on an electronically mediated model of representative democracy. ICANN tried to use the Internet to create legitimacy by opening its decision making process to the public (transparency) through ambitious, Web-based global elections for its central governing body, the At-Large Membership Program (Palfrey 2004, 412–414). ICANN's experiment was heavily criticized due to its failure to achieve true global representation and responsiveness to civic concerns, leading the organization to abandon its ambitious democratic aspirations.[36]

Toward a More General Analysis of Digital Openness at the Global Level

It is hard to draw decisive conclusions from these relatively narrow case studies, but it is possible make some initial observations. First, this brief empirical excursion demonstrates the deep malleability of the Internet and its capacity to fit into varied institutional configurations. Second, the approach of classic IGOs to the idea of Internet-mediated direct deliberation is still animated by their continuing commitment to the Westphalian narrative. This enduring commitment seems to bar any great leaps forward in incorporating e-democracy mechanisms into the decision making hierarchies of IGOs. Nonetheless, even a limited use of the Web—as a mechanism of transparency and a host of informal communications—could support and reinvigorate democratic sensitivities within the governing bureaucracies of IGOs.[37] Finally, with respect to PIGOs, the picture is different, reflecting a greater willingness to experiment with e-democracy. Two key factors emerge as predictors of digital openness. The first concerns the share of business and governments in the governance of the organization. The willingness of the organization to experiment with digital projects seems to be inversely correlated to the dominance of business and governments. This was reflected in the differences between ISO and GRI/AccountAbility. Another explanation for this increased willingness may be that PIGOs, because they are detached from the state-political infrastructure, have a greater need to achieve legitimization through Web-based public dialog. These preliminary observations need further and more comprehensive studies.

Global Administrative Law and the Challenge of the New Techno-Intermediaries

Digital democracy provides a promising mechanism for reinvigorating global democracy both as a mechanism of transparency (WTO) and as a mechanism of novel forms of consultation and deliberation (GRI, AccountAbility, and ICANN). Nonetheless, the Internet's capacity to facilitate meaningful democratic processes raises various questions. First, although the e-tools introduced by organizations such as GRI and AccountAbility seem promising in terms of democratic theory, their ultimate effect on the political process remains an open question. Particularly important in this context is the question of the effect of public input on the consequent legal product. Answering this question will require thorough empirical studies that explore in detail the norm-making dynamic within new global norm-making bodies such as the GRI or AccountAbility. These could focus[38] on the influence exerted by the hierarchical centers of these organizations on the norm-production process. In other words, was the final normative product determined by the center?[39] A second, related question concerns the extent to which these e-democracy initiatives have been able to support the emergence of lasting transnational communities.

A second question concerns the important role played by new techno-intermediaries in constructing the new e-tools. The various e-democracy technologies used by the institutions described above are the product of deeply opaque technical intermediation. The hidden work of the multiple technical intermediaries associated with these technologies can shape the way in which the political process unfolds. The multiple and nontrivial selections that underlie these various Web technologies may influence in various ways the deliberation or consultation process, possibly undermining their dialectical freedom.[40] Thus, for example, deliberation support technologies may hinder deliberation by restricting the forms of argument that can be invoked in the system or by intimidating certain type of users due to complex user interface (Rehg, McBurney, and Parsons 2005, 222–223). Visual aids, such as participatory mechanisms based on geographic information systems (GISs), are useful in enhancing understanding. However, the translation of raw data into maps, graphs, or charts involves various choices that often remain hidden from the user.[41] This new form of intermediation raises new types of agency problems and, with them, a question: "Who will monitor the work of these new techno-political intermediaries?"

One possible response to the new agency problems, which draws on Habermas's deliberative framework, would be to put these various technological schemes to some form of democratic test—that is—to make the various selections underlying them the subject of an open deliberative process.[42] It has been argued in the literature, for example, that the designers of the deliberative process should "foreground how information resources were produced," "demonstrate that information resources have multiple interpretations," "include multiple and conflicting information resources," and "encourage critical evaluation of information resources" (Ramsey and Wilson 2008). It is questionable, however, whether this solution could be implemented in practice. The costs of such second-level political deliberation may be prohibitive, and the technical nature of the questions involved may pose impossible cognitive challenges for the average citizen, discouraging any political contribution.

A more pragmatic solution is to facilitate and encourage reciprocal monitoring between various political intermediaries—including the new type of technopolitical mediators. This proposal does not reject the ideal of "informed citizenship," but it shifts the focus of the democratic gaze to the level of communication. The goal of democratic institutions becomes not achieving wide-ranging informed civic participation but attaining a communicatively complex political arena that hosts and supports diverse streams of thought. Achieving such a diverse discursive environment requires the creation of a network of competing political intermediaries.[43]

This proposal raises several challenges. First, a global society needs to encourage the emergence of political intermediaries with the capacity to criticize this new field of technopolitical intermediation. It is not clear to what extent some of the traditional observers of the political domain (such as journalists, political scientists, legal scholars, and NGOs) have the capacity to perform this new task. Second, and this is one of the new challenges of global (and national) administrative law, the law should create the conditions that will enable external observers to monitor the technical choices underlying the new Web technologies.

To enable such reciprocal monitoring, the field of global e-democracy—as part of the evolving field of global administrative law—will have to introduce several new principles. This question has not received sufficient attention in the global administrative law literature.[44] First, political intermediaries should have an option to voice their concerns at earlier stages of the development of new technological tools. It may be unrealistic to expect wide-ranging consultation on technical issues, but it seems reasonable to demand that international organizations initiate proactive consultation with relevant stakeholders. Second, external intermediaries, from academic scholars to NGOs, should have the right to access the raw data that allows them to scrutinize the process.[45] Third, in contemporary politics, many of the technopolitical choices that influence the way political data is presented and disseminated are made by private players—such as Google, Dow Jones Sustainability Indexes, AccountAbility, and others.[46] Given the significant effects of these "private" selections, modern global administrative law will have to develop ways to open up those private choices to public scrutiny.

These questions—the disclosure of hidden technical choices and the monitoring of technological intermediaries—need to be answered by a reconstructed doctrine of global administrative law. Whether the classical doctrines of administrative law can cope with this challenge will have to be explored as the use of digital consultation broadens. This problem certainly seems more challenging at the global domain than at the local because it lacks the rich system of administrative law existing at the domestic level.

Notes

1. The successful international campaign against the Organization for Economic Cooperation and Development's Multilateral Agreement on Investment is a case in point (Kurtz 2002; Warkentin and Mingst 2000).

2. For a list of International Human Rights Advocacy Groups, see http://www .hrweb.org/resource.html#International.

3. http://twitter.com/; http://www.atomkeep.com.

4. See, e.g., Held (2003), Walzer (2000), and Keohane (2003).

5. Shifting the participation process into the electronic domain does not resolve the basic collective-action dilemma that characterizes political action.

6. As a concrete example, the Equator Principles (http://www.equator-principles .com/principles.shtml), which provide guidelines for determining, assessing, and managing social and environmental risk in project financing, do not contain enforcement mechanisms. In contrast, ISO 14001—the most important global standard on environmental self-management—draws on an elaborated compli-

ance scheme and builds on the services of private verifiers (Potoski and Prakash 2006, 19).

7. For other examples, consider the Web sites of the ICC (http://www.icc-cpi. int/Menus/ICC?lan=en-GB) and the Climate Change Convention (http://unfccc .int).

8. See http://www.wto.org/english/docs_e/docs_e.htm. There have also been attempts by some WTO members to open the dispute settlement proceedings to the public, most recently in the case of United States—Measures Relating to Zeroing and Sunset Reviews—Recourse to Article 21.5 of the DSU by Japan (WT/DS322/RW) (hearing on June 29–30, 2009). See http://www.wto.org/ english/news_e/news09_e/hear_ds322_12jun09_e.htm, accessed June 21, 2009. This practice is still not part of the WTO rulebook (Lawrence 2007, 21–22).

9. See http://www.wto.org/english/forums_e/forums_c.htm, accessed June 21, 2009.

10. http://forums.prospero.com/wtoforum/start, accessed June 21, 2009.

11. http://www.wto.org/english/forums_e/ngo_e/ngo_e.htm, accessed June 21, 2009.

12. See WTO Public Forum 2009, http://www.wto.org/english/forums_e/ngo_e/ forum09_background_e.htm, accessed June 21, 2009.

13. I do not have complete historical data, but the forum seems to be highly active.

14. Ibid.

15. See also http://www.iso.org/iso/about.htm, accessed June 26, 2009.

16. Two agreements play a crucial role in this process—the Agreement on Technical Barriers to Trade and the Agreement on the Application of Sanitary and Phylo-sanitary Measures (Howse and Tuerk 2001).

17. See Committee Draft ISO/CD 26000, Guidance on Social Responsibility, ISO/TMB/WG SR N 157, December 15, 2008, introduction.

18. A thorough discussion of a ISO constitutional framework is beyond the scope of this chapter. For a more detailed discussion, see UNCTAD (1996, 21–40).

19. The details of the standard-setting process are set in *ISO/IEC Directive (part 1): Procedures for the Technical Work*, 5th ed. (a copy of which is available from the ISO Web site). A brief description can be found in the document *Stages of the Development of International Standards* (http://www.iso.org/iso/standards _development/processes_and_procedures/iso_iec_directives_and_iso_supple- ment.htm, accessed June 30, 2009). The ISO constitution distinguishes between three forms of membership. Full members have the right to participate as P- members in technical committees, which gives them the right and obligation to vote on all questions submitted for voting within the technical committee, includ- ing enquiry drafts and final draft international standards. Correspondent members can participate in the standard-setting work only as observing members (O-members), which allows them to attend meetings, receive documents, and

submit comments. A third category—subscriber membership, usually for countries with very small economies—establishes only a very limited contact with the ISO. See *Introduction to ISO* (available at www.iso.ch) and ISO/IEC Directive (part 1), paras. 1.7–1.7.5. Nongovernmental organizations can gain access to the ISO standard-setting process only as liaison organizations, a status that enables them to observe the standard-setting process but does not give them formal voting rights. Furthermore, to gain this limited access, NGOs have to get the approval of the ISO chief executive officer. See ISO/IEC Directive (part 1), paras. 1.15–1.15.5.

20. www.iso.org/sr, accessed December 1, 2010.

21. http://isotc.iso.org/livelink/livelink/fetch/2000/2122/830949/3934883/3935096/04_organization/org_str.html, accessed December 1, 2010.

22. ISO 2006, 3, http://www.iso.org/iso/iso_in_brief_2006.pdf, accessed December 1, 2010.

23. The new balloting scheme maintains the system of voting rights that was established by ISO/IEC Directive (part 1). See *Electronic Balloting: Systematic Review—User Guide Version 1, January 2007*, http://isotc.iso.org/livelink/livelink/fetch/2000/2122/5156198/5156199/Electronic_balloting_-_Systematic_Review_-_User_guide.pdf?nodeid=6093834&vernum=0, accessed November 21, 2007.

24. GRI, Who We Are, http://www.globalreporting.org/AboutGRI/WhoWeAre, accessed June 25, 2009.

25. Ibid.

26. It also finds resonance in the description of the GRI in its Web site: "The 'Global Reporting Initiative' is a large multi-stakeholder network of thousands of experts, in dozens of countries worldwide, who participate in GRI's working groups and governance bodies, use the GRI Guidelines to report, access information in GRI-based reports, or contribute to develop the Reporting Framework in other ways—both formally and informally." Ibid.

27. See Global Reporting Initiative, "Development Process," http://www.globalreporting.org/ReportingFramework/ReportingFrameworkOverview/DevelopmentProcess, accessed December 1, 2010.

28. Released in 2002 and 2006. GRI, G3 Online, http://www.globalreporting.org/ReportingFramework/G3Online , accessed October 6, 2007.

29. See http://www.accountabilityaa1000wiki.net/index.php/Structure, accessed June 28, 2009. The deliberation process took place in three phases of sixty to ninety days. The three periods ran from January 24 to April 4, 2008; April 30 to June 20; and July 7 to September 12. For two other examples of using wikis in the global arena see, the BioenergyWiki, http://www.bioenergywiki.net/index.php/Main_Page.

30. For an overview, see *Introduction to the Revised AA1000 Assurance Standard and the AA1000 AccountAbility Principles Standard 2008*, October 24, 2008, http://www.accountability21.net/uploadedFiles/publications/

Introduction%20to%20the%20revised%20AA1000AS%20and%20
AA1000APS%202008.pdf.

31. See http://www.accountability21.net/default2.aspx?id=54 and http://www
.accountability21.net/governance, accessed June 28, 2009.

32. A wiki is software that allows users to create and edit content in a collaborative manner. See http://en.wikipedia.org/wiki/Wikipedia:About.

33. Ibid.

34. Ibid., "The AccountAbility Standards Technical Committee."

35. http://www.accountability.org/standards/aa1000as/index.html. On September 2009, AccountAbility initiated another wiki-based consultation process on
another standard—the second edition AA1000 Stakeholder Engagement Standard (AA1000SES). See www.accountabilityaa1000wiki.net.

36. ICANN's experiment failed in the sense that ICANN has radically changed
its governance structure by adopting a much milder concept of democracy.
Nonetheless, ICANN's experiment constitutes an important milestone in the
attempt to transform the abstract idea of global democratization into a practical
model. For a detailed discussion and critique of ICANN's democratic experiment,
see Palfrey (2004).

37. One could foresee the WTO director general asking to receive a report of
the topics discussed at the WTO forum.

38. Such studies could examine the discursive features of the dialog and the
social profile of the participants.

39. See, e.g., Coglianese (2005) for a somewhat pessimistic observation on this
question (in the national context).

40. See also Rehg, McBurney, and Parsons (2005, 218–224).

41. For a global example, see the BP sustainability worldwide map (http://www.
bp.com: environment and society), which allows users to find out information
about BP actions by clicking on a global map (see also Ramsey and Wilson
2008).

42. Rehg, McBurney, and Parsons (2005, 224) note in that context that "AI
researcher cannot avoid being drawn into critical discussion as a participant on
a par with citizens-users."

43. In a similar fashion, Michael Walzer argued for the creation of a new global
governance structure (which he called a "the third degree of global pluralism")
that will be based on a "set of alternative centers and an increasingly dense web
of social ties that cross state boundaries" (Walzer 2000, 8).

44. See, for example, Kingsbury, Krisch, and Stewart (2005) and Kingsbury
(2009).

45. For an interesting example that illustrates the value of alternative interpretations of raw-data, see http://www.scorecard.org, which interprets the data
regarding toxic emissions disclosed in the EPA's Toxics Release Inventory (http://
www.epa.gov/tri).

46. As one example, the way in which Google ranks and orders politically relevant data has important consequences for the political process, given its monopoly status in the search field.

References

Abbott, Kenneth W., and Duncan Snidal. 2009. "Strengthening International Regulation through Transnational New Governance: Overcoming the Orchestration Deficit." *Vanderbilt Journal of Transnational Law* 42:502–578.

Bach, Jonathan, and David Stark. 2004. "Link, Search, Interact: The Co-Evolution of NGOs and Interactive Technology." *Theory, Culture and Society* 21, no. 3:101–117.

Castells, Manuel. 2005. "Global Governance and Global Politics." *Political Science and Politics* 38:9–16.

Clapp, Jennifer. 1998. "The Privatization of Global Environmental Governance: ISO 14000 and the Developing World." *Global Governance* 4:295–316.

Coglianese, Cary. 2005. "The Internet and Citizen Participation in Rulemaking." *I/S: A Journal of Law and Policy for the Information Society* 1, no. 1:33.

Fleming, Tony, Didier Jacobs, Heather Hamilton, Amelia Kuklewicz, James Riker, and Jan Aart Scholte. 2003. *The Challenge of Global Democracy: Report of an NGO Retreat Addressing the Democratic Deficits in International Decision Making*. Washington, DC: Oxfam America and Citizens for Global Solutions.

Global Reporting Initiative. 2006. *Sustainability Reporting Deadlines*. Amsterdam: Global Reporting Initiative. Accessed May 12, 2011. http://www.globalreporting.org/NR/rdonlyres/660631D6-2A39-4850-9C04-57436 E4768BD/0/G31GuidelinesinclTechnicalProtocolFinal.pdf.

Hammond, Allen, and Jonathan Lash. 2000. "Cyber-Activism: The Rise of Civil Accountability and Its Consequences for Governance." *iMP Magazine* (May).

Held, David. 2003. "Cosmopolitanism: Globalization Tamed?" *Review of International Studies* 29:465–480.

Howse, Robert, and Elisabeth Tuerk. 2001. "The WTO Impact on Internal Regulations: A Case Study of the Canada-EC Asbestos Dispute." In *The EU and the WTO: Legal and Constitutional Issues*, edited by G. D. Búrca and J. Scott, 283–328. Oxford: Hart.

Keohane, Robert O. 2003. "Global Governance and Democratic Accountability." In *Global Governance and Democratic Accountability*, edited by D. Held and M. Koening-Archibugi, 141. Cambridge: Polity Press.

Kingsbury, Benedict. 2009. "The Concept of 'Law' in Global Administrative Law." *European Journal of International Law* 20, no. 1:23–57.

Kingsbury, Benedict, Nico Krisch, and Richard B. Stewart. 2005. "The Emergence of Global Administrative Law." *Law and Contemporary Problems* 68, nos. 3–4:15–61.

Kresse, Wolfgang, and Kian Fadaie. 2004. *ISO Standards for Geographic Information.* Heidelberg: Springer.

Kurtz, Jurgn. 2002. "NGOs, the Internet and International Economic Policy Making: The Failure of the OECD Multilateral Agreement on Investment." *Melbourne Journal of International Law* 3:213–246.

Lawrence, Robert Z. 2007. *The United States and the WTO Dispute Settlement System.* CSR No. 25. New York: Council on Foreign Relations.

Murray, Paula C. 1999. "Inching toward Environmental Regulatory Reform: ISO 14000—Much Ado about Nothing or a Reinvention Tool?" *American Business Law Journal* 37:35–71.

Palfrey, John G. 2004. "The End of the Experiment: How ICANN's Foray into Global Internet Democracy Failed." *Harvard Journal of Law and Technology* 17:410–473.

Perez, Oren. 2004. *Ecological Sensitivity and Global Legal Pluralism: Rethinking the Trade and Environment Conflict.* Oxford: Hart.

Perez, Oren. 2007. "Purity Lost: The Paradoxical Face of the New Transnational Legal Body." *Brooklyn International Law Journal* 33:1–58.

Potoski, Matthew, and Aseem Prakash. 2006. "Institutional Design for EMS-Based Government Procurement Policies." *Global Environmental Politics* 6, no. 4:13–22.

Ramsey, Kevin S., and Matthew W. Wilson. 2008. "Rethinking the 'Informed' Participant: Precautions and Recommendations for the Design of Online Deliberation." In *Online Deliberation: Design, Research, and Practice*, edited by Todd Davies and Seeta Peña, 259–267. Chicago: CSLI Publications/University of Chicago Press. http://odbook.stanford.edu/static/filedocument/2009/11/10/ODBook.Full.11.3.09.pdf.

Rehg, William, Peter McBurney, and Simon Parsons. 2005. "Computer Decision-Support Systems for Public Argumentation: Assessing Deliberative Legitimacy." *AI and Society* 19:203–228.

Riley, C. G. 2003. *The Changing Role of the Citizen in the e-Governance and e-Democracy Equation.* Ottawa: Commonwealth Centre for e-Governance.

United Nations Conference on Trade and Development (UNCTAD). 1996. "ISO 14001: International Environmental Management Systems Standards—Five Key Questions for Developing Country Officials." Geneva: United Nations Conference on Trade and Development.

Walzer, Michael. 2000. "International Society: What Is the Best That We Can Do?" Occasional Paper 8, School of Social Science, Institute for Advanced Study, June.

Warkentin, C., and K. Mingst. 2000. "International Institutions, the State and Global Civil Society in the Age of the World Wide Web." *Global Governance* 6:237–257.

Weissinger, Reinhard. 2001. "Electronic Balloting: Get Ready—Vote Electronically!" *ISO Bulletin* 32 (April):3-6. www.iso.org/iso/livelinkgetfile?llNodeId=21156&llVolId=-2000.

Wood, Stepan. 2009. "Will ISO 26000 Corner the Market? Competition and Collaboration in Global Social Responsibility Standards Development." Paper presented at the Law and Society 2009 Annual Conference, Denver, May, 28–31.

Zysman, John, and Steven Weber. 2001. "Governance and Politics of the Internet Economy: Historical Transformation or Ordinary Politics with a New Vocabulary?" Paper BRIEWP141. Berkeley Roundtable on the International Economy, University of California, Berkeley.

IV

Conclusion

17

Making the E-Citizen: A Sociotechnical Approach to Democracy

Stephen Coleman

Rather than thinking of citizenship as a single set of norms and practices, it makes sense to understand it as comprising a diverse range of potential characteristics—from less to more democratic, participatory, deliberative, managed, autonomous, nationally rooted, and legally prescribed. Civic actors are in an open-ended, historically reflexive relationship to their political position in society. As Engin Isin (2008, 39) has put it: "Acts of citizenship are those acts through which citizens, strangers, outsiders and aliens emerge not as beings already defined but as beings acting and reacting with others."

Given this nonessentialist conception of citizenship, technologies cannot be inherently civicly enhancing. Determining which technologies appropriately support and enhance citizenship depends on a group's civic norms and practices. An authoritarian dictatorship might regard surveillant technologies (such as close-circuit cameras) as more important to civic cohesion than content-sharing media (such as YouTube). A populist democracy might regard efficient plebiscitary technologies (such as instant opinion polls) as more important than technologies that allow citizens to deliberate about their values and preferences. A more deliberative democracy is likely to be interested in technologies that facilitate, structure, and visualize mass argumentation but would distrust technologies that are owned or controlled by interested minorities that have the power to frame or skew public discussion. Saying that the Internet benefits civic expression and democratic policy making therefore jumps over two crucial questions: what sorts of civic expression and democratic policy making are being proposed, and which Internet features are available?

Most of the chapters in this volume implicitly answer those questions by supposing that we are talking about the norms of a liberal, representative democracy—a pluralistic public sphere of diverse interests and values in which citizens have the right to vote governments in and out, have freedom to speak and to publish views without fear of intimidation, have access to information from a range of unfettered sources, have opportunities to affect the government's decision making, and have the right to protest against unjust policies or laws. These norms—implied in Peter Shane's imagined nation of Agora (chapter 1 in this volume)—are frequently articulated as aspirations but have been incompletely realized, even in countries such as the United States and the mature democracies of the European Union. In addition to these fundamental constitutional ambitions, both defenders and critics of this broad conception of demo-cratic citizenship have demanded more than is currently available in the repertoire of civic action. As the technologies of communication have become more networked and accessible than ever before, normative civic prescriptions have increasingly emphasized participatory and delibera-tive forms of civic interaction both at the vertical path of citizens to political representatives and also at the lateral level of citizens to citizens (Shane 2004; Castells 2008; Coleman and Blumler 2009; Dahlgren 2009; Bang and Esmark 2009). This chapter explores three ways that particular constructions of citizenship might converge with specific affordances of the Internet to produce sociotechnical effects that shape the configura-tion of the democratic polity. The following analysis does not provide an exhaustive survey of various forms of e-citizenship but argues that normative constructions of citizenship always depend on technical real-ization and that the scope of technologies is always determined by nor-mative conceptions of what they may or may not be employed to make happen.

Info-Lite Citizenship

Although most democratic theorists characterize the role of the demo-cratic citizen in ambitious and demanding ways, political practitioners (politicians, party strategists, civil servants, journalists, and pollsters) tend to have lower expectations. In the name of realism and supported by a wealth of data showing how little interest the public seems to have in political affairs, a default position seems to be that the most that can be reasonably hoped for in a functioning democracy is for citizens to vote occasionally, trust elites to look after their interests, and protest when directly injured.

According to this standard conception, citizens acquire rudimentary information about the world around them. They do not involve themselves in detailed comparisons between sources of information and have little interest in analyzing degrees of truth. They are utilitarians who want to know just enough about the world around them to get by without having to devote long hours or deep thought to nuances of political messages. Schudson's (1998) notion that the media should be like fire alarms—arousing citizens in times of urgency and civic duty but otherwise leaving them to an info-lite existence—provides a foundation for one approach to using the Internet as a democratic medium. Following this model, journalists might establish online spaces for the fast transmission of bite-sized news headlines that busy people can pick up or leave at their leisure, and governments and political parties might go online to convey basic information about their positions. But these are unidirectional, informational services that are a far cry from attempts to engage citizens in policy formation or decision making. Politicians adhering to this model of citizenship would argue that after people vote for their chosen leaders, they do not want to be bothered with consultative and deliberative burdens.

This is a compelling notion of citizenship and its technological requisites and is undoubtedly accepted by many politicians and journalists. But from the perspective of democratic efficacy, it entails at least three risks. The first is that the information supplied by existing media and political sources may not provide citizens with an adequate picture of how their government is working and how decisions made at various levels of accountable and unaccountable governance will affect them. Media agendas are famously skewed by biased ownership, editorial priorities, and the unrepresentative backgrounds of journalistic elites. Political agendas are shaped by strategies of impression management that often involve secrecy, duplicity, and unsubstantiated claims. Even an info-lite citizenry that depends on headlines, sound bites, and pop analyses to inform its limited role as a voting demos could feel underserved by such a communication environment—or worse, might not have the means to understand why so much in the world around them seems not to go their way.

The second risk is that when faced with pressing political challenges—such as a fundamentally corrupt government, an illegal war to which most people are opposed, or an economic crisis resulting in unjust hardships—info-lite citizens will not have in place the experience, skills, or networks needed to respond. Inertia cannot be switched on and off. A system of political communication in which the overwhelming majority of people rarely say anything, leaving their thinking and speaking to elites, is acceptable only as long as elite actors and institutions are deemed to be wholly trustworthy. If one thinks of democracy as a vigilant means of insurance against potential betrayals of public trust, however, opportunities must exist for citizens to act in response to unacceptable leaders, institutions, and policies. In the absence of trusted channels of communication between citizens and government, there is a strong chance that collective action will bypass constitutional mechanisms, thereby widening the gap between official and vernacular politics. Because this gap is widely acknowledged to be a major cause of civic disengagement and disenchantment in many of the developed and developing democracies (Pharr and Putnam 2000; Crouch 2004; Hutcheson and Korosteleva 2006; Newton 2007), the absence of regular communications between representatives and those they claim to speak for could be seen as politically destabilizing.

The third risk entailed by info-lite citizenship is that the quality of policies and decisions produced by governments will not benefit from citizens' experiences and expertise. In fragmented, culturally diverse, postindustrial societies, one party, government, or elite cannot claim to have all the answers to complex and often unpredictable problems. The experiences and expertise of citizens are vital components of good policy making. But without an effective means of contributing knowledge, stories, and proposals to the governmental process, these lay assets are likely to be squandered. Top-down decisions, reflecting bureaucratic and oligarchic beliefs and interests, tend to fail when applied in the real world. If effective policy making and implementation calls for well-informed and robustly debated public input, then info-lite citizenship is unlikely to serve democracy well in the long run.

Governments subscribing to an info-lite conception of citizenship are likely to use the Internet in two ways. First, they might see online space as a place to disseminate the kind of information that they think citizens need to know. They welcome the opportunity to transmit messages without the interference of the media, which, they argue, generally undermine positive government news. They see the Web as a form of broadcasting that is characterized by audience receipt of one-way messages. Many governments still use the Internet in this fashion, ignoring its potential for interactive feedback or the cultural disdain that digitally literate citizens have for such practices (Ferber, Foltz, and Pugliesi 2005; Dawes 2008; West 2008).

A second government approach to info-lite citizenship might be to provide token opportunities for online communication between government departments, politicians, and citizens but to restrict these communications to little more than virtual postboxes leading nowhere. This can be done in a number of ways—encouraging citizens to submit ideas or petitions online without integrating such input into government planning, setting up online discussion forums or polls to gather public views on decisions that have already been taken, and inviting citizens to send messages to the president or prime minister and responding with standardized template messages. In short, the info-lite citizen is reduced to a state of disconnected spectatorship, enjoying the convenience of not having to think too much at the cost of permanent marginalization.

Push-Button Citizenship

Could the Internet transform democratic citizenship, transcending the need for elevated representatives to speak on behalf of remote constituents and allowing anyone to vote online on any issue confronting society at any moment of the day or night? Grossman (1995, 146), writing about the United States, has suggested that

In kitchens, living rooms, dens, bedrooms, and workplaces throughout the nation, citizens have begun to apply . . . electronic devices to political purposes, giving those who use them a degree of empowerment they never had before. . . . By pushing a button, typing on-line, or talking to a computer, they will be able to tell their president, senators, members of Congress, and local leaders what they want them to do and in what priority order.

As Dick Morris (2001, 1033), former strategic adviser to President Bill Clinton, has asserted:

The internet offers a potential for direct democracy so profound that it may well transform not only our system of politics but our very form of government. . . . Bypassing national representatives and speaking directly to one another, the people of the world will use the internet increasingly to form a political unit for the future.

In Estonia, the Today I Decide (TOM) project was established in 2001 by the then–prime minister, Matt Laar, to allow citizens to submit online proposals for legislation that, if supported by a sufficient number of site users, would have to be considered and responded to by civil servants. By June 2005, approximately sixteen hundred proposals had been submitted by over six thousand registered users, but most did not receive sufficient support to take them forward for consideration by government and hardly any have led to new laws (Pruulmann-Vengerfeldt 2007; Coleman and Kaposi 2009). Moreover, after a proposal has been submitted, TOM provides few opportunities for public debate about its merits or sensible amendment. As Pruulmann-Vengerfeldt (2007, 179) puts it:

Although users can post comments on the original ideas and give their support to these ideas by voting on them, the ideas remain fairly formatted and the system features do not allow the author of the ideas to react to the comments, and engage in a discussion about the proposed changes to their ideas. The author does have the time and opportunity to modify the proposal, but the lack of two-way communication nevertheless reduces the deliberative potential of TOM and makes it another channel for sending pre-prepared messages to the government.

A similar criticism has been leveled against the UK government's Number Ten e-petitions site, which allows citizens to seek support from other citizens for proposals to the British prime minister. Although the site was widely used initially, it resulted in many appeals to government with no opportunity for anyone to discuss their merits. Technopopulist gimmicks of this kind appear to be exploiting the Internet as a new space of political power. In fact, they reinforce a key weakness that has traditionally limited the force of public opinion—the lack of opportunities for citizens to compare and contrast their reasons for holding views; to debate and refine their collective positions within a fair, open, and constructive space; and to engage in such activities knowing that their elected representatives are similarly engaged.

Prior to the 2010 general election, the UK Conservative Party pledged to offer one million pounds to the developers of an online project that would help "to throw open the policy making process to the public, and harness the wisdom of the crowd so that the public can collaborate to improve government policy." The party claimed that a government led by them "would publish all government Green Papers on this platform, so that everyone can have their say on government policies, and feed in their ideas to make them better" (Conservatives.com 2009). Whether or not the Conservative Party intended that this new space would include, structure, and promote deliberation as well as preference counting remains unclear. No online development project has been initiated since they came to power as the leading party in the new coalition government. Without a deliberative dimension, such a plan amounts to little more than a new technique for aggregating raw, uninformed, and unrehearsed mass opinion rather than a means of cultivating the kind of civic debate that could result in more thoughtful policy making.

Indeed, the technocratic hyperbole in support of push-button citizenship builds on a failure to distinguish between democracy as a crude mechanism for majoritarian head counting and democracy as a culture of reflective public debate. Even without the Internet to make them possible, populist strategies have long been pursued by leaders offering "opportunistic policies with the aim of (quickly) pleasing the people/voters—and so 'buying' their support—rather than looking (rationally) for the 'best option'" (Mudde 2004). The mass media's sweeping addresses to an amorphous public have successfully propagated populist messages and created an illusory identity between leaders and led (Mazzoleni, Stewart, and Horsfield 2003). Little has been written about populist uses of the Internet, but they are implicit within the anarcho-consumerist rhetoric that ascribes "wisdom" to "crowds" (all and any crowds), as if the belief of many people in one thing justifies it. Consensus formed by groupthink and reached more rapidly by e-tools is not necessarily good for politics—which, in any nonutopian sense, must entail an agonistic engagement with competing interests, conflicting preferences, and discordant values.

The imagined push-button citizen is a teleological being who, given the right e-tools, will gravitate toward a general will founded on truth. The Internet, in this sense, is a mechanism for creating a citizenry that knows itself. I want to argue that there is no civic self to know—that the essential characteristics of democratic citizenship are reflexive uncertainty, agonistic contestation, and creative self-actualization.

Actualizing Citizenship

Despite the clear differences between these two conceptions of citizenship, both share a belief that citizens cannot be expected to engage in much reflection about the world beyond their immediate existences. The info-lite citizen is deemed to be too busy, lethargic, or incompetent to bother about influencing policy formation and decision making, and the push-button citizen is conceived as a creature of habit who is most comfortable in the homogeneity of the herd. In contrast to both of these definitions is the conception of the actualizing citizen—a social actor who is characterized by multiple connections, weak ties, a reflexive approach to identity and belonging, a postdeferential attitude toward authority, and a sense that political communication is a two-way street and not a flow of top-down messages from rulers to ruled. This is a Weberian ideal-type definition rather than an empirical description, but it captures ways in which citizenship is being practiced on new terms in late modernity. As Lance Bennett (2008, 13) has argued,

In the network society, individuals may belong to many loosely tied associational chains that connect them to their social and occupational worlds. A major consequence of the uprooting from the broad social influence of groups is that individuals have become more responsible for the production and management of their own social and political identities.(Bang and Esmark 2009) This transformation of the relationship between individual and society places increasing strains on parties and governments to appeal to highly personalized political preferences that are more difficult to address, much less satisfy, than the broad group or class interests of an earlier era. At the same time, individual citizens—particularly younger generations who have grown up in this new social and economic matrix—feel that their personalized expectations of politics are perfectly reasonable (reflecting who they are) and often find that politics and politicians either ignore them or are far off the mark in their communication appeals.

In this more fluid and unfettered conception of citizenship, the Internet is capable of shifting the emphasis of political communication away from simple message transmissions from A (usually a political elite) to B (usually a mass public) and toward interactions between B and A. The many who make up B can share ideas and experiences among themselves, and A can become more directly and authentically conversational with and responsive to B. Such a transformation in political communication would require a cultural shift in the way that societies think about and enact democracy. But some indications suggest that politicians recognize the need to engage with citizens—to tackle the complex and intractable social issues dominating late-modern politics and to address a prevalent public distrust of political elites and their exclusive modes of leadership. Some politicians also feel that the Internet—because of its inherent interactivity, low costs of entry, and networking propensities—could contribute vitally to a more democratized relationship between governments and governed. But for this to happen, the Internet needs to be seen as something more than a technology. As I have argued elsewhere, representation is not something that happens and is then mediated—as if communication were an historical after-event. One can only represent oneself or others through strategies and technologies of mediation. The moment of mediation is the moment of representation (Coleman 2010). The performance of citizenship is similar. Communication technologies are not a means of recording, circulating, or storing such performances. They are inherent to making them happen. How people actualize themselves as citizens is inseparable from the means of communicating that they have at hand. At the same time, technologies are shaped—and sometimes reshaped through creative or resistant practices—by the purposes that people have in mind for them.

In the context of policy making, a government wishing to actualize citizens would be likely to veer in the direction of coproduction, which has been defined by Ostrom (1999, 99) as the recognition "that the production of a service, as contrasted to a good, was difficult without the active participation of those supposedly receiving the service." Synergistic, dialogical, and flexible, a coproductive approach to governance is unlikely to appeal to politicians and bureaucrats (see chapter 11 in this volume) who doubt the capacity of citizens to contribute to wise and reflective policy making but might appeal to those who acknowledge (however reluctantly) that the changing terms of citizenship pose a stark choice between precipitous political disengagement and governance as partnership.

Both info-lite and push-button conceptions of citizenship tend to generate strategies for online communication that are designed to convey simple messages and gather simplistic responses, but governments that want to engage citizens in the coproduction of policy would likely focus on three principal uses of the Internet—to share experiences, to create opportunities for collaborative reflection, and to promote ways of exposing ideas to public reason.

Sharing Experience

Arendt (1958, 198) famously argued that citizenship

arises out of acting and speaking together, and its true space lies between people living together for this purpose, no matter where they happen to be. . . . It is the space of appearance in the widest sense of the word, namely, the space where I appear to others as others appear to me, where men exist not merely like other living or inanimate things, but make their appearance explicitly.

If we accept that being a citizen is more than being legally attached to a set of institutions or physically located within a national territory, then the means by which people appear to one another and gain social recognition are fundamental to their actualization as democratic actors.

The Internet allows people to make an appearance before others in a range of ways—from setting out formal political positions to spreading viral jokes, producing YouTube videos, or sharing stories about themselves. This range of communication, even more than the ease with which content can be produced and distributed, makes the Internet an exciting space for the expansion of public voice. In the past, there was limited media space for public comment, and becoming a political agenda setter tended to entail collusion with established political organizations. Today, however, new modes of public expression (such as digital storytelling and picture sharing) make it much more possible for institutional outsiders to initiate a public discussion. In authoritarian and highly managed regimes, this has opened civic spaces that flourish beyond the regulation of the state. But even in liberal democracies, new online spaces have raised the profile of traditionally marginalized groups and allowed new issues to enter the public sphere and affect the agendas of the mainstream media and political parties.

A government that wants to encourage actualizing citizenship would create online spaces in which people could post messages, stories, diaries, cartoons, and films to raise policy issues and perspectives that might not otherwise reach the political agenda. It would invite citizens to produce and circulate such content and would respond to it in ways that demonstrate a democratic sensitivity to public concerns, feelings, and values. Its responsive mode would amount to more than selective or moralizing official feedback but would reflect an appreciation that policy can make a lasting, positive difference only when it is rooted in a collective understanding of mundane experience.

Net-Working

A major challenge to all collective action is the cost of coordination. It is easier for well-resourced, organized, and confident people to find others like themselves than it is for those who have little money, time, or self-efficacy. Policy networks have been a major feature of contemporary governance, but they have tended to be dominated by actors and institutions that are capable of overcoming coordination barriers. According to some political scientists, the Internet could perform a key democratic role by lowering the costs of network formation and enabling dispersed social actors to work collaboratively on policy problems that affect them. Deibert (2000, 255–256) has argued that "one of the most dramatic" of the new opportunities facilitated by online communication "has been the flourishing of citizen networks":

Linked through the Internet across state borders, the tentacles of these citizen networks have begun to infiltrate nearly every major international political issue-area, from security to human rights to the governance of the global economy. Although many of the groups that make up these networks predate the advent of the Internet, there has been an explosive growth in their numbers in the past decade coinciding with its widespread popularity.

Most of these grassroots networks have been initiated by nonstate actors, however, and they often have opposed government policy agendas. Governments seeking to draw on the experiences and expertise of actualizing citizens would devise methods of social collaboration that can expand the range of people who shape the specific features of policy, while ensuring that the process does not become so diffuse that conclusions can never be reached. Mambrey and Doerr (2009) have shown how German city wikis have been used by citizens to reflect on their localities, and Poor (2005) has shown how the Slashdot Web site, in which messages from computer geeks are peer rated using a recommender system, meets key criteria of a public sphere: it is a space of discourse; it opens a space for a wide range of computer enthusiasts to come together and discuss many issues, including many political ones; and ideas are judged by their merit. Governments with a genuine interest in receiving citizen input to the policy process could promote and interact with networks of nurses, refuse collectors, firefighters, drug addicts, school students, and quantum physicists. These groups could be presented with policy problems that relate to them, urged to submit policy options, invited to think imaginatively about tradeoffs, and offered opportunities to move on to the deliberation of competing policies. This is all very different from the form of online public engagement that is most commonly initiated by contemporary governments in which citizens are invited to state their preferences, either in a short message or via a poll. In contrast to such tokenistic exercises, sustained policy networks that use creative methods of collaboration and shared vision could allow actualizing citizens to think through problems in ways that produce innovative and unexpected policy options.

Public Deliberation

When policy issues and options have been set out, they need to be opened up to the widest possible discussion. Public deliberation is the missing element of most contemporary democracies. Politicians often speak about the need for a public debate or an open national discussion, but this rarely amounts to more than a series of TV interviews, a few opinion polls, and the occasional online forum in which citizens are invited to have a say. Although most states take the electoral aspects of democracy seriously, they neglect the deliberative elements to the point that in most twenty-first-century polities, deliberative exercises generally take the form of social-scientific experiments (deliberative polls, citizens' juries, and consensus conferences) rather than institutional pillars of democracy. Exposing ideas to public reason tends to be regarded as a luxury supplement to the generally dull and uninvolving routines of political democracy.

The Internet's potential for enhancing many-to-many deliberation has generated much speculation and some interesting experimentation. Some positive reports have noted that online discussions widen participants' repertoire of arguments, introduce them to new perspectives, and lead to some shifts in preferences (Price and Cappella 2002; Barabas 2004; Shane 2004; Janssen and Kies 2005; Iyengar, Luskin and Fishkin 2005; Monnoyer-Smith 2007; Min 2007; Coleman and Blumler 2009). Online deliberation is an important way of sorting and ordering public preferences. The hope is that actualizing citizens will come out of a deliberative experience thinking more expansively than when they entered into it—not that they will change their minds but that they will know their minds better and know why they disagree with positions that they choose to reject.

As some of the chapters in this volume have indicated, online deliberation still faces several challenges. First, unless efforts are made to recruit a broad range of participants, online deliberation can exacerbate the exclusion of poorer, less educated, and less confident people and provide a further space in which higher-income, digitally connected people can make their views known (see chapters 6, 7, and 9 in this volume). Second, deliberative exercises too often focus on rationalism and neglect the importance of emotive expression and agonistic disagreement as ingredients of democratic discourse (see chapter 3 in this volume). Third, even when participation is inclusive and discursive modes of expression are unconstrained, online deliberation is often disconnected from the politicians and officials who formulate policy and make decisions. There is much constructive and lively public discussion of policy issues taking place online, but it tends to take place in parallel to—and remotely from—the official deliberations of councils, congresses, parliaments, and government departments.

Online or offline, public deliberation does not occur spontaneously. It amounts to more than spontaneous public talk. To develop a trusted online space for policy deliberation, a government needs to ensure that such debates are widely promoted, fairly moderated, honestly summarized, and formally responded to by relevant public bodies. Such a space cannot become a vehicle for partisan spin (and should therefore be supervised independently from government) and will lose credibility if it becomes a mere talking shop. To engage actualizing citizens in considering various competing policy options, a government must show that the conclusions emerging from public deliberation really do shape policy outcomes. In turn, citizens have to show that they can reflect as citizens who share social space with others rather than as socially unencumbered selves who are accountable only to their own interests and egos. To make both of these things happen, online deliberation needs to be structured, perhaps using tools for argument visualization and preference filtering. Some useful work has been done on ensuring that large-scale conversations across dispersed groups and locations are neither hijacked by the loudest voices nor reduced to a mass of indecipherable noise (Sack 2000; Donath 2002; Mancini and Buckingham-Shum 2006; Atkinson, Bench-Capon, and Modgil 2006; Renton and Macintosh 2007). Further work is needed to develop ways to generate public e-conversations that escape both excessive government control and unmanageable numbers of competing opinions.

Under Construction: The Incomplete Evolution of E-Citizenship

I have set out three arguments in this chapter. The first is that citizenship is a culturally constructed concept that is open to a number of competing interpretations, each of which is politically framed. The second is that citizenship is produced through strategies, techniques, and technologies. As Barry (2001, 9) has put it: "If we regard the public sphere as a set of spaces within which matters of truth and justice can be raised in public, then there is always a technical dimension to the specific forms that the public sphere can take and the connection and distinction between the realms of 'public' and 'private' politics." The third is that to engage with emerging forms of civic behavior—which I refer to as *actualizing citizenship*—governments need to adopt strategies and use technologies that respond to citizens' eagerness to define their relationship to society and its relationship to them. Rather than a technologically facilitated means of subsuming political subjects within the agenda, logic, and language of the state, e-citizenship can be seen as a democratic space where anyone can stake a claim to be heard and respected and all proposals have a chance of being acted on.

All the contributors to this volume are arguing that both citizenship and the Internet are incomplete construction projects that are open to public contention and endangered by dogmatic assumptions that they can be understood in only one way. We are arguing that the Internet can contribute to the invigoration of democratic citizenship but only if imaginative minds can generate creative policies to make this happen. We are arguing that—as with every previous communications revolution, including the alphabet, the printing press, and radio and television broadcasting—the regulation, patterns of use, and social ramifications of the Internet will be determined by the distribution of power shaping its evolution, meanings, and ambitions. And we are arguing that a key role of scholars is to both describe what is going on and engage critically with the flows and counterflows of latent and manifest potentiality that shape what will happen next.

References

Arendt, Hannah. 1958. *The Human Condition.* New York: Rowman and Littlefield.

Atkinson, K., T. Bench-Capon, and S. Modgil. 2006. "Argumentation for Decision Support." *Lecture Notes in Computer Science* 4080:822–831.

Bang, H., and A. Esmark. 2009. "Good Governance in Network Society: Reconfiguring the Political from Politics to Policy." *Administrative Theory and Praxis* 31, no. 1:7–37.

Barabas, Jason. 2004. "Virtual Deliberation: Knowledge from Online Interaction versus Ordinary Discussion." In *Democracy Online: The Prospects for Political Renewal through the Internet,* edited by Peter Shane, 239–252. New York: Routledge.

Barry, A. 2001. *Political Machines: Governing a Technological Society.* London: Athlone Press.

Bennett, W. L. 2008. "Changing Citizenship in the Digital Age." In *Civic Life Online: Learning How Digital Media Can Engage Youth,* edited by W. L. Bennett, 1–24. Cambridge: MIT Press.

Castells, M. 2008. *Communication Power.* Oxford: Oxford University Press.

Coleman, S. 2010. "Representation and Mediated Politics: Representing Representation in an Age of Irony." In *Political Communication in Postmodern Democracy: Challenging the Primacy of Politics,* edited by Kees Brants and Katrin Voltmer, 39–58. Basingstoke: Palgrave.

Coleman, S., and J. G. Blumler. 2009. *The Internet and Democratic Citizenship: Theory, Practice, Policy.* New York: Cambridge University Press.

Coleman, S., and I. Kaposi. 2009. "A Study of E-participation Projects in Third-Wave Democracies." *International Journal of Electronic Governance* 2, no. 4:302–327.

Crouch, C. 2004. *Post-Democracy.* New York: Wiley.

Dahlgren, P. 2009. *Media and Political Engagement: Citizens, Communication, and Democracy.* New York: Cambridge University Press.

Dawes, S. 2008. "The Evolution and Continuing Challenges of E-Governance." *Public Administration Review* 68:86–102.

Deibert, R. J. 2000. "International Plug 'n Play? Citizen Activism, the Internet, and Global Public Policy." *International Studies Perspectives* 1, no. 3:255–272.

Donath, J. 2002. "A Semantic Approach to Visualizing Conversations." *Communications of the ACM* 45, no. 4:45–49.

Ferber, P., F. Foltz, and R. Pugliese. 2005. "The Internet and Public Participation: State Legislature Web Sites and the Many Definitions of Interactivity." *Bulletin of Science, Technology and Society* 25, no. 1:85–93.

Grossman, Lawrence K. 1995. *The Electronic Republic: Reshaping Democracy in the Information Age.* New York: Viking.

Hutcheson, D., and E. Korosteleva. 2006. "Patterns of Participation in Post-Soviet Politics." *Comparative European Politics* 4, no. 1:23–46.

Isin, I. 2008. "Theorizing Acts of Citizenship." In *Acts of Citizenship*, edited by I. Isin and G. Nielsen, 15–43. New York: Zed Books.

Iyengar, S., R. Luskin, and J. Fishkin. 2005. "Facilitating Informed Public Opinion: Evidence from Face-to-face and Online Deliberative Polls." Accessed December 24, 2009. http://pcl.stanford.edu/common/docs/research/iyengar/2003/facilitating.pdf.

Janssen, J., and R. Kies. 2005. "Online Forums and Deliberative Democracy." *Acta Politica* 40, no. 3:317–335.

Mambrey, Peter, and Romy Doerr. 2009. "Local Encyclopedias beyond Mass Media and Government: City Wikis." Paper presented at the Eighth International EGOV Conference 2009, August 31 September 3.

Mancini, C., and S. Buckingham-Shum. 2006. "Modelling Discourse in Contested Domains: A Semiotic and Cognitive Framework." *International Journal of Human-Computer Studies* 64, no. 11:1154–1171.

Mazzoleni, G., J. Stewart, and B. Horsfield. 2003. *The Media and Neo-Populism: A Contemporary Comparative Analysis.* New York: Praeger.

Min, S.-J. 2007. "Online vs. Face-to-Face Deliberation: Effects on Civic Engagement." *Journal of Computer-Mediated Communication* 12, no. 4:11:1369–1387

Monnoyer-Smith, L. 2007. "The Public Debate Enacted: A French Learning Process." *Hermes* 47:21–28.

Morris, D. 2001. "Direct Democracy and the Internet." *Loyola of Los Angeles Law Review* 34, no. 3:1033–1053.

Mudde, C. 2004. "The Populist Zeitgeist." *Government and Opposition* 39, no. (4):542–563.

Newton, K. 2007. "Social and Political Trust." In *Oxford Handbook of Political Behavior*, edited by R. Dalton and Dieter Klingemann, 169–204. New York: Oxford University Press.

Ostrom, E. 1999. "Coping with Tragedies of the Commons." *Annual Review of Political Science* 2:493–535.

Pharr, Susan J., and Robert D. Putnam. 2000. *Disaffected Democracies: What's Troubling the Trilateral Countries?* Princeton, NJ: Princeton University Press.

Poor, N. 2005. "Mechanisms of an Online Public Sphere: The Website Slashdot." *Journal of Computer-Mediated Communication* 10, no. 2:article 4.

Price, V. and J. N. Cappella. 2002. "Online Deliberation and Its Influence: The Electronic Dialogue Project in Campaign 2000." *IT and Society* 1, no. 1: 303–329.

Pruulmann-Vengerfeldt, P. 2007. "Participating in a Representative Democracy: Three Case Studies of Estonian Participatory Online Initiative." In *Media Technologies and Democracy in an Enlarged Europe*, edited by N. Carpentier et al., 171–187. Tartu: Tartu University Press.

Renton, A., and A. Macintosh. 2007. "Computer Supported Argument Maps as a Policy Memory." *Information Society* 23, no. (2):125–133.

Sack, W. 2000. "Conversation Map: An Interface for Very-Large-Scale Conversations." *Journal of Management Information Systems* 17, no. 3:73–92.

Shane, Peter, ed. 2004. *Democracy Online: The Prospects for Political Renewal through the Internet*. New York: Routledge.

Schudson, M. 1998. *The Good Citizen: A History of American Civic Life*. New York: Free Press.

West, D. M. 2008. *Improving Technology Utilization in Electronic Government around the World 2008*. New York: Brookings Institute.

Contributors

Editors

Stephen Coleman is professor of political communication at the Institute of Communications Studies at the University of Leeds. His book *The Internet and Democratic Citizenship: Theory, Practice, Policy* (2009; written with Jay Blumler) won a Best Book Award from the Communication and Information Technologies Section of the American Political Science Association. His most recent book is *The Media and the Public: Them and Us in Media Discourse* (2010; written with Karen Ross).

Peter M. Shane is Jacob E. Davis and Jacob E. Davis II Chair in Law at The Ohio State University, Columbus. He has coauthored casebooks on administrative law and on separation of powers law. Other recent books include *Madison's Nightmare: Unchecked Executive Power and the Threat to American Democracy* (2009) and the edited volume *Democracy Online: The Prospects for Political Renewal through the Internet* (2004).

Other Contributors

Joachim Åström is associate professor in political science at Örebro University, Sweden. He is the coeditor (with Jan Olsson) of *Democratic eGovernance: Approaches and Research Directions* (2006).

Steven J. Balla is associate professor of political science, public policy and public administration, and international affairs at George Washington University, Washington, DC, where he is also a research affiliate at the George Washington Institute of Public Policy and a senior scholar at the Regulatory Studies Center. He is the coauthor (with William T. Gormley, Jr.) of *Bureaucracy and Democracy: Accountability and Performance.*

Andrew Chadwick is professor of political science and founding director of the New Political Communication Unit in the Department of Politics and International Relations at Royal Holloway, University of London. He is the coeditor (with Philip N. Howard) of the *Routledge Handbook of Internet Politics* (2009). His book *Internet Politics: States, Citizens, and New Communication*

Technologies (2006) won the best book award of the Communication and Information Technologies Section of the American Sociological Association. Andrew is founding editor of the Oxford University Press's Studies in Digital Politics book series.

Kevin Esterling is associate professor of political science at the University of California at Riverside. He is the author of *The Political Economy of Expertise: Information and Efficiency in American National Politics* (2004).

Rachel Gibson is professor of political science at the Institute for Social Change at the University of Manchester. She has published her work in many international journals and books and is currently working on a comparative study of the growth of citizen campaigning via new media.

Åke Grönlund is professor of informatics at Örebro University, Sweden. His research focuses on the coordination of human activities in organizations, virtual organizations, and social and professional networks using Internet communication technologies.

Sungsoo Hwang is assistant professor in the Department of Public Administration at Yeungnam University, Korea. He conducts research in the area of collaborative governance and citizen participation with an emphasis on information and communication technologies.

David Lazer is associate professor at Northeastern University, Boston, and director of the Program on Networked Governance (PNG) at Harvard University, Cambridge. He is the editor of the book *DNA and the Criminal Justice System: The Technology of Justice* (2004) and the coeditor (with Viktor Mayer-Schönberger) of *Governance and Information Technology: From Electronic Government to Information Government* (2007).

Jeffrey S. Lubbers is professor of practice in administrative law at Washington College of Law at American University, Washington, DC, and the former research director of the Administrative Conference of the United States. He is especially interested in the optimal design of electronic rulemaking processes, which are discussed in the fourth edition of his treatise *A Guide to Federal Agency Rulemaking* (2006).

Laurence Monnoyer-Smith is professor of communication sciences at the University of Technology, Compiègne, France. Her book *Communication and Deliberation: Technological Challenges and Transformation of Citizenship* (2010) examines the effects of technology on deliberation practices in Europe.

Michael Neblo is assistant professor of political science at The Ohio State University, Columbus. His book manuscript "Common Voices: Deliberative Politics in Theory and Practice" asks whether and how normative theories of deliberative democracy can be put into practice given the realities of modern politics.

Oren Perez is professor of law in the Faculty of Law at Bar-Ilan University, Ramat Gan, Israel. Perez is especially interested in the challenges of global governance, the transfer of powers from national levels to transnational levels, and the lack of democratic mechanisms at the international level. His work examines whether e-participation can be used to enhance democratic participation in governance, setting this exploration against the general problematic of collective action.

Vincent Price is provost and Steven H. Chaffee Professor of Communication and Political Science at the Annenberg School for Communication at the University of Pennsylvania, Philadelphia. His most recent research focuses on the role played by political conversation, particularly Web-based deliberation, in shaping public opinion.

Agnes I. Schneeberger is a PhD student at the Institute of Communications Studies at the University of Leeds. As part of the European Commission–funded project DEMO-Net: The eParticipation Network of Excellence, she is coauthor (with Ann Macintosh and Stephen Coleman) of "eParticipation: The Research Gaps" (2009).

Polona Pičman Štefančič is director of the Rea IT Research Centre, Slovenia. Her latest book is *e-Democracy* (2008).

Peter L. Strauss is the Betts Professor of Law at Columbia University, New York, and was the American academic coreporter for the *Rulemaking* volume of the American Bar Association's Section of Administrative Law and Regulatory Practice study of the administrative law of the European Union (2006). He is currently researching American and European rulemaking practice with particular attention to Internet consultation and to techniques for mediating the competing demands of politics and scientific analysis in policy making ostensibly grounded in "best science."

Scott Wright is lecturer in political communication at the University of East Anglia, Norwich. He has published widely in the field of e-consultations, with an emphasis on design and moderation issues.

Index